Contents

Appendices

Foreword

The primary purpose of the three volumes of the *International Aeronautical and Maritime Search and Rescue Manual* is to assist States in meeting their own search and rescue (SAR) needs, and the obligations they accepted under the Convention on International Civil Aviation, the International Convention on Maritime Search and Rescue, and the International Convention for the Safety of Life at Sea (SOLAS). These volumes provide guidelines for a common aviation and maritime approach to organizing and providing SAR services. States are encouraged to develop and improve their SAR services, co-operate with neighbouring States, and to consider their SAR services to be part of a global SAR system.

Each *IAMSAR Manual* volume is written with specific SAR system duties in mind, and can be used as a stand-alone document, or, in conjunction with the other two volumes, as a means to attain a full view of the SAR system. Depending on the duties assigned, it may be necessary to hold only one, or two or all three volumes.

The *Organization and Management* volume (volume I) discusses the global SAR system concept, establishment and improvement of national and regional SAR systems, and co-operation with neighbouring States to provide effective and economical SAR services;

The *Mission Co-ordination* volume (volume II) assists personnel who plan and co-ordinate SAR operations and exercises; and

The *Mobile Facilities* volume (volume III) is intended to be carried aboard rescue units, aircraft, and vessels to help with performance of a search, rescue, or on-scene co-ordinator functions, and with aspects of SAR that pertain to their own emergencies.

Mission Co-ordination

Chapter 1 presents an overview of the SAR system concept, including what is involved in providing SAR services, and why such services are required and beneficial. The SAR system is examined from a global, regional, and national perspective. Key components of the SAR system, such as rescue co-ordination centres (RCCs), operational and support facilities and the on-scene co-ordinator (OSC), are discussed.

Chapter 2 focuses primarily on SAR communications topics. These include distress communications, emergency beacons, communications for SAR operations and a variety of communications and safety systems related to or used by the SAR system.

Chapter 3 introduces the five stages through which responses to SAR incidents typically progress, describes the three emergency phases (uncertainty, alert and distress) and the first two stages (awareness and initial action) in detail, and provides additional valuable guidance for the early stages of a SAR incident.

Chapter 4 contains a detailed discussion of the theory and practice of search planning. It presents a complete yet practical application of search theory to the SAR search planning problem. It provides guidance for balancing the conflicting goals of covering large areas with limited facilities or using those facilities to achieve high probabilities of detection in small areas. The procedures outlined allow the search planner to determine the optimal area to search so that the chances of success are maximized.

Chapter 5 discusses search techniques and operations, including search facility selection, assessment of search conditions, search pattern selection for visual, electronic, night and land searches, search sub-area assignments, standard methods for designating and describing search sub-areas, planning of on-scene co-ordination, and finally compiling all this data into an attainable search action plan.

Chapter 6 describes aspects of rescue planning and operations such as logistics, modes of rescue, care and debriefing of survivors, handling of deceased persons, and certain special requirements involving aircraft crash sites.

Chapter 7 contains guidance for emergency assistance other than SAR in which the SAR system may become involved.

Chapter 8 discusses the orderly conclusion of SAR operations. The topics covered include closing of SAR cases, suspending search operations, reopening a suspended SAR case, completing final reports, conducting performance improvement reviews and case studies, and archiving SAR case files.

An extensive set of appendices is provided. These contain useful information, forms, checklists, step-by-step procedures, worksheets, and tables and graphs appropriate for daily use by RCC staff.

This Manual is published jointly by the International Civil Aviation Organization and the International Maritime Organization. It has been updated from earlier editions by including the amendments that were adopted by the seventy-fourth session of the IMO Maritime Safety Committee in June 2001 (which entered into force on 1 July 2002), by the seventy-fifth session in May 2002 (which entered into force on 1 July 2003), by the seventy-seventh session in June 2003 (which entered into force on 1 July 2004), by the seventy-eighth session in May 2004 (which entered into force on 1 July 2005), by the eightieth session in May 2005 (which entered into force on 1 June 2006), by the eighty-first session in May 2006 (which entered into force on 1 June 2007), by the eighty-third session in October 2007 (which entered into force on 1 June 2008), by the eighty-fifth session in December 2008 (which entered into force on 1 January 2009) and by the eighty-sixth session in June 2009 (which became applicable on 1 June 2010).

A new edition is published every three years. The 2013 edition includes the 2010 amendments (adopted by ICAO and approved by IMO's Maritime Safety Committee at its eighty-seventh session in May 2010 that became applicable on 1 June 2011) and the 2011 and 2012 amendments (adopted by ICAO and approved by IMO's Maritime Safety Committee at its ninetieth session in May 2012 that became applicable on 1 June 2013). The amendments were prepared by the ICAO/IMO Joint Working Group on Harmonization of Aeronautical and Maritime Search and Rescue at its sixteenth session in September 2009, seventeenth session in September 2010 and eighteenth session in October 2011, and were endorsed by the IMO Sub-Committee on Radiocommunications and Search and Rescue (COMSAR) at its fourteenth session in March 2010, fifteenth session in March 2011 and sixteenth session in March 2012.

The IAMSAR Manual is subject to copyright protection under ICAO and IMO. However, limited reproduction of forms, checklists, tables, graphs and similar content is allowed for operational use or training purposes.

Abbreviations and acronyms

A	search area
A/C	aircraft
ACC	area control centre
ACO	aircraft co-ordinator
AES	aeronautical earth station
AFN	aeronautical fixed network
AFTN	aeronautical fixed telecommunications network
AIP	aeronautical information publication
AIS	aeronautical information services
AIS	automatic identification system
AIS–SART	automatic identification system – search and rescue transmitter
AM	amplitude modulation
AMS	aeronautical mobile service
AMS(R)S	aeronautical mobile satellite (route) service
AMSS	aeronautical mobile satellite service
Amver	automated mutual-assistance vessel rescue
ARCC	aeronautical rescue co-ordination centre
ARSC	aeronautical rescue sub-centre
ASW	average surface wind
ASW$_e$	average surface wind error
ASWDV$_e$	drift velocity error due to ASW_e
ATC	air traffic control
ATN	aeronautical telecommunications network
ATS	air traffic services
C	coverage factor
C/C	cabin cruiser
CES	coast earth station
Cospas	Space System for Search of Vessels in Distress
CRS	coast radio station
C/S	call sign
CS	coast station
CS	creeping line search
CSC	creeping line search, co-ordinated
CSP	commence search point
CW	continuous wave
D	total drift

D_e	total drift error
DD	(leeway) divergence distance
DF	direction finding
DMB	datum marker buoy
DME	distance-measuring equipment
DRU	desert rescue unit
DSC	digital selective calling
DV_e	total drift velocity error
E	total probable error of position
EGC	enhanced group calling
ELR	extra-long-range aircraft
ELT	emergency locator transmitter
ENID	enhanced identity
EPIRB	emergency position-indicating radio beacon
ETA	estimated time of arrival
ETD	estimated time of departure
F/V	fishing vessel
FIC	flight information centre
FIR	flight information region
FLAR	forward-looking airborne radar
FLIR	forward-looking infrared
FM	frequency modulation
f_s	optimal search factor
f_v	#search facility velocity correction factor
f_w	weather correction factor
f_Z	effort factor
GES	ground earth station
GHz	gigahertz
GIS	geographic information system
GLONASS	Global Orbiting Navigation Satellite System
GMDSS	Global Maritime Distress and Safety System
GNSS	global navigation satellite system
GPS	global positioning system
GS	ground speed
gt	gross tonnage
HEL-H	heavy helicopter
HEL-L	light helicopter
HEL-M	medium helicopter
HF	high frequency
HQ	headquarters
I/B	inboard
IBRD	International 406 MHz Beacon Registration Database
ICAO	International Civil Aviation Organization

ICS	incident command system
IFR	instrument flight rules
ILS	instrument landing system
IMC	instrument meteorological conditions
IMO	International Maritime Organization
IMSO	International Mobile Satellite Organization
Inmarsat	satellite communication service provider for the GMDSS
INS	inertial navigation system
INTERCO	*International Code of Signals*
IP	initial position
ITU	International Telecommunication Union
JRCC	joint (aeronautical and maritime) rescue co-ordination centre
JRSC	joint rescue sub-centre
kHz	kilohertz
km	kilometres
kt	knot (nautical miles per hour)
l	search sub-area length
L	length
L_b	datum base line
LCB	line of constant bearing
LES	land earth station
LKP	last known position
LOP	line of position
Loran	long-range aid to navigation
LRG	long-range aircraft
LRIT	long-range identification and tracking
LSB	lower side band
LUT	local user terminal
LW	leeway
LW_e	leeway error
m	metres
M/V	merchant vessel
MAREC	Maritime Search and Rescue Recognition Code
MCC	mission control centre
MCW	modulated carrier wave
MEDEVAC	medical evacuation
MEDICO	medical advice, usually by radio
MF	medium frequency
MHz	megahertz
MMSI	maritime mobile service identity
MOB	man overboard
MRCC	maritime rescue co-ordination centre
MRG	medium-range aircraft

MRO ....mass rescue operation

MRSC .... maritime rescue sub-centre

MRU .... mountain rescue unit

MSI ....maritime safety information

n...number of required track spacings

N.. number of SAR facilities

NATO..North Atlantic Treaty Organization

NBDP...narrow-band direct printing

NM... nautical mile

NOTAM ....notice to airmen

NVG ....night vision goggles

O/B ....outboard

O/S..on-scene

OS... contour search

OSC ....on-scene co-ordinator

OSV .... offshore supply vessel

P/C .... pleasure craft

PIW ....person in water

PLB...personal locator beacon

POB .... persons on board

POC .... probability of containment

POD...probability of detection

POS..probability of success

POS$_c$ .... cumulative probability of success

PRU ....parachute rescue unit

PS..parallel sweep search

R ....search radius (actual)

R$_o$.. optimal search radius

R&D .... research and development

RANP .... regional air navigation plan

RB ....rescue boat

RC .... river current

RCC..rescue co-ordination centre

RF...radio frequency

RSC ....rescue sub-centre

RV ....rescue vessel

S/S...steam ship

S/V .... sailing vessel

S...track spacing

SAC ....short access code

SAR .... search and rescue

Sarsat .... Search and Rescue Satellite-Aided Tracking

SART ....search and rescue (radar) transponder

SC	search and rescue co-ordinator
SC	sea current
*SC*e	sea current error
SDP	search and rescue data provider
SES	ship earth station
SITREP	situation report
SMC	search and rescue mission co-ordinator
SMCP	(IMO) Standard Marine Communication Phrases
SOA	speed of advance
SOLAS	Safety of Life at Sea
SPOC	search and rescue point of contact
SR	separation ratio
SRG	short-range aircraft
SRR	search and rescue region
SRS	search and rescue sub-region
SRS	ship reporting system
SRU	search and rescue unit
SS	expanding square search
SSB	single side-band
SU	search unit
SUBSAR	submarine search and rescue
SURPIC	surface picture
T	search time available
T/V	tank vessel
TAS	true air speed
TC	tidal current
*TC*e	tidal current error
TCA	time of closest approach
TFR	temporary flight restriction
TLX	telex
TMAS	telemedical assistance service
TSN	track line search, non-return
TSR	track line search, return
TWC	total water current
*TWC*e.	total water current error
U	wind speed
UHF	ultra high frequency
UIR	upper flight information region
ULR	ultra-long-range aircraft
USAR	urban search and rescue
USB	upper side-band
UTC	co-ordinated universal time
UTM	universal transverse Mercator grid

v	speed of search object
V	SAR facility ground speed
VFR	visual flight rules
VHF	very high frequency
VLR	very-long-range aircraft
VMC	visual meteorological conditions
VMS	vessel monitoring system
VOR	VHF omnidirectional radio range
VS	sector search
VTS	vessel traffic services
w	search sub-area width
W	sweep width
WC	wind current
WC_e	wind current error
WMO	World Meteorological Organization
W_u	uncorrected sweep width
X	initial position error
Y	SAR facility position error
Z	search effort
Z_a	available datum effort
Z_r	relative effort
Z_{rc}	cumulative relative effort
Z_{ta}	total available search effort

Glossary

Aeronautical drift (D_a)	Drift caused by bailout trajectory or aircraft gliding distance.
Aeronautical information services (AIS)	A service established within the defined area of coverage responsible for the provision of aeronautical information/data necessary for the safety, regularity and efficiency of air navigation.
Aeronautical position	Initial position of a distressed aircraft at the time of re-entry, engine failure, aircrew ejection or bailout.
Aircraft co-ordinator (ACO)	A person or team who co-ordinates the involvement of multiple aircraft SAR operations in support of the SAR mission co-ordinator and on-scene co-ordinator.
Aircraft glide	Maximum ground distance an aircraft could cover during descent.
Alert phase	A situation wherein apprehension exists as to the safety of an aircraft or marine vessel, and of the persons on board.
Alerting post	Any facility intended to serve as an intermediary between a person reporting an emergency and a rescue co-ordination centre or rescue sub-centre.
Amver	A world-wide ship reporting system for search and rescue.
Area control centre (ACC)	An air traffic control facility primarily responsible for providing ATC services to IFR aircraft in controlled areas under its jurisdiction.
Automatic identification system (AIS)	A system used by ships and vessel traffic services (VTS), principally for identifying and locating vessels.
Automatic identification system – SAR transmitter (AIS–SART)	A survival craft transmitter that sends out an AIS position report based on a built-in GNSS receiver.
Available datum effort (Z_a)	The amount of effort available for assignment to a particular datum.
Awareness range	Distance at which a search scanner can first detect something different from its surroundings but not yet recognize it.
Awareness stage	A period during which the SAR system becomes aware of an actual or potential incident.
Captain	Master of a ship or pilot in command of an aircraft, commanding officer of a warship or an operator of any other vessel.
Checksum digit	A digit which is appended to a numeric data element and used to verify its accuracy. Checksum digits are computed by adding the digits of the data element.
Coast earth station (CES)	Maritime name for an Inmarsat shore-based station linking ship earth stations with terrestrial communications networks.

Commence search point (CSP)	Point normally specified by the SMC where a SAR facility is to begin its search pattern.
Conclusion stage	A period during a SAR incident when SAR facilities return to their regular location and prepare for another mission.
Co-ordinated search pattern	Multi-unit pattern using vessel(s) and aircraft.
Co-ordinated universal time (UTC)	International term for time at the prime meridian.
Cospas–Sarsat System	A satellite system designed to detect and locate activated distress beacons transmitting in the frequency band of 406.0–406.1 MHz.
Course	The intended horizontal direction of travel of a craft.
Coverage factor (C)	The ratio of the search effort (Z) to the area searched (A). $C = Z/A$. For parallel sweep searches, it may be computed as the ratio of sweep width (W) to track spacing (S). $C = W/S$.
Craft	Any air or sea-surface vehicle, or submersible of any kind or size.
Cumulative probability of success (POS_c)	The accumulated probability of finding the search object with all the search effort expended over all searches to date. POS_c is the sum of all individual search POS values.
Cumulative relative effort (Z_{rc})	The sum of all previous relative efforts plus the relative effort for the next planned search effort. This value determines the optimal search factor. $Z_{rc} = Z_{r\text{-}1} + Z_{r\text{-}2} + Z_{r\text{-}3} + ... + Z_{r\text{-next search}}$
Datum	A geographic point, line, or area used as a reference in search planning.
Datum area	Area in where it is estimated that the search object is most likely to be located.
Datum base line	That portion of a datum line that is drawn between two specific locations, such as way points on a distressed or missing craft's intended track line. May be extended to form a datum line that accounts for the probable error(s) of one or both locations.
Datum line	A line, such as the distressed craft's intended track line or a line of bearing, which defines the centre of the area where it is estimated that the search object is most likely to be located.
Datum marker buoy (DMB)	Droppable floating beacon used to determine actual total water current, or to serve as a location reference.
Datum point	A point, such as a reported or estimated position, at the centre of the area where it is estimated that the search object is most likely to be located.
Dead reckoning (DR)	Determination of position of a craft by adding to the last fix the craft's course and speed for a given time.
Digital selective calling (DSC)	A technique using digital codes which enables a radio station to establish contact with, and transfer information to, another station or group of stations.
Direction finding (DF)	Radiodetermination using the reception of radio waves for the purpose of determining the direction of a station or object.
Direction of current	Direction toward which a current is flowing. Also called "set".

Direction of waves, swell or seas	Direction from which the waves, swells, or seas are moving.
Direction of wind	Direction from which the wind is blowing.
Distress alert	The reporting of a distress incident to a unit which can provide or co-ordinate assistance.
Distress Phase	A situation wherein there is reasonable certainty that a vessel or other craft, including an aircraft or a person, is threatened by grave and imminent danger and requires immediate assistance.
Ditching	The forced landing of an aircraft on water.
Divergence distance	Distance between the left and right leeway divergence datums.
Drift	The movement of a search object caused by environmental forces.
Drift error (D_e)	See *Total probable drift error*.
Effort factor (f_Z)	(1) For point and leeway divergence datums, the effort factor is the square of the total probable error of position (E). $f_{Zp} = E^2$. (2) For line datums, the effort factor is the product of the total probable error of position (E) and the length of the line (L). $f_{Zl} = E \times L$.
Emergency locator transmitter (ELT)	A generic term (related to aircraft) describing equipment which broadcast distinctive signals on designated frequencies and, depending on application, may be automatically activated by impact or be manually activated.
Emergency phase	A generic term meaning, as the case may be, uncertainty phase, alert phase, or distress phase.
Emergency position-indicating radio beacon (EPIRB)	A device, usually carried on board maritime craft, that transmits a distress signal that alerts search and rescue authorities and enables rescue units to locate the scene of the distress.
False alarm	Distress alert initiated for other than an appropriate test, by communications equipment intended for alerting, when no distress situation actually exists.
False alert	Distress alert received from any source, including communications equipment intended for alerting, when no distress situation actually exists, and a notification of distress should not have resulted.
Fetch	The distance over which the wind blows in a constant direction, without obstruction.
First RCC	RCC affiliated with the shore station that first acknowledges a distress alert, and which should assume responsibility for all subsequent SAR co-ordination unless and until responsibility is accepted by another RCC better able to take action.
Fix	A geographical position determined by visual reference to the surface, referencing to one or more radio navigation aids, celestial plotting, or other navigation device.
Flight information centre (FIC)	A unit established to provide information and alerting services.

Forward-looking airborne radar (FLAR)	Any aircraft-mounted radar designed to detect targets on or near the ocean surface by scanning a sector typically centred in the direction of aircraft heading. FLAR may also perform weather avoidance/navigation in support of aircraft operations.
Forward-looking infrared (FLIR)	An imaging system, mounted on board surface vessels or aircraft, designed to detect thermal energy (heat) emitted by targets and convert it into a visual display.
General communications	Operational and public correspondence traffic other than distress, urgency and safety messages, transmitted or received by radio.
Geographic information system (GIS)	A system which captures, stores, analyses, manages and presents data that is linked to location.
Global Maritime Distress and Safety System (GMDSS)	A global communications service based upon automated systems, both satellite-based and terrestrial, to provide distress alerting and promulgation of maritime safety information for mariners.
Global Navigation Satellite System (GNSS)	World-wide position and time determination system that includes one or more satellite constellations and receivers.
Grid	Any set of intersecting perpendicular lines spaced at regular intervals.
Grid cell	A square or rectangular area formed by pairs of adjacent, perpendicular grid lines.
Ground speed (GS)	The speed an aircraft is making relative to the earth's surface.
Heading	The horizontal direction in which a craft is pointed.
Heave	The vertical rise and fall due to the entire ship being lifted by the force of the sea.
Homing	The procedure of using the direction-finding equipment of one radio station with the emission of another radio station, where at least one of the stations is mobile, and whereby the mobile station proceeds continuously towards the other station.
Hypothermia	Abnormal lowering of internal body temperature (heat loss) from exposure to cold air, wind, or water.
Indicated air speed (IAS)	The aircraft speed shown on the air speed indicator gauge. IAS corrected for instrument error and atmospheric density equals true air speed.
Initial action stage	A period during which preliminary action is taken to alert SAR facilities and obtain amplifying information.
Initial position error (X)	The estimated probable error of the initial position(s) at the beginning of a drift interval. For the first drift interval, this will be the probable error of the initially reported or estimated position of the SAR incident. For subsequent drift intervals, it will be the total probable error of the previous datum position(s).
Inmarsat	A system of geostationary satellites for world-wide mobile communications services, and which support the Global Maritime Distress and Safety System and other emergency communications systems.
Instrument flight rules (IFR)	Rules governing the procedures for conducting instrument flight. Also a term used by pilots and controllers to indicate type of flight plan.

Instrument meteorological conditions (IMC)	Meteorological conditions expressed in terms of visibility, distance from cloud, and ceiling less than the minima specified for visual meteorological conditions.
Joint rescue co-ordination centre (JRCC)	A rescue co-ordination centre responsible for both aeronautical and maritime search and rescue incidents.
Knot (kt)	A unit of speed equal to one nautical mile per hour.
Last known position (LKP)	Last witnessed, reported, or computed DR position of a distressed craft.
Leeway (LW)	The movement of a search object through water caused by winds blowing against exposed surfaces.
Leeway divergence angle	The average angle between an object's direction of leeway and the downwind direction. Leeway may diverge to either the right or the left of the downwind direction. Current evidence indicates that objects with significant leeway divergence angles rarely jibe or tack downwind.
Leeway error (LW_e)	The probable error of the leeway estimate.
Local user terminal (LUT)	An earth receiving station that receives beacon signals relayed by Cospas–Sarsat satellites, processes them to determine the location of the beacons, and forwards the signals.
Long-range identification and tracking (LRIT)	A system which requires certain vessels to automatically transmit their identity, position and date/time at six-hour intervals, in accordance with SOLAS regulation V/19-1.
Maritime domain awareness (MDA)	The effective understanding of any activity associated with the maritime environment that could impact upon the security, safety, economy or environment.
Mass Rescue Operation (MRO)	Search and rescue services characterized by the need for immediate response to large numbers of persons in distress, such that the capabilities normally available to search and rescue authorities are inadequate.
MAYDAY	The international radiotelephony distress signal.
MEDEVAC	Evacuation of a person for medical reasons.
MEDICO	Medical advice. Exchange of medical information and recommended treatment for sick or injured persons where treatment cannot be administered directly by prescribing medical personnel.
METAREA	A geographical sea area[*] established for the purpose of co-ordinating the broadcast of marine meteorological information. The term METAREA followed by a roman numeral may be used to identify a particular sea area. The delimitation of such areas is not related to and shall not prejudice the delimitation of any boundaries between States.
Meteorological visibility	The maximum range at which a large object, such as land masses or mountains, can be seen. Also referred to as Meteorological Range.
Mission control centre (MCC)	Part of the Cospas–Sarsat system that accepts alert messages from the local user terminal(s) and other mission control centres to distribute to the appropriate rescue co-ordination centres or other search and rescue points of contact.

---

[*] Which may include inland seas, lakes and waterways navigable by seagoing ships.

Narrow-band direct printing (NBDP)	Automated telegraphy, as used by the NAVTEX system and telex-over-radio.
NAVAREA	A geographical sea area* established for the purpose of co-ordinating the broadcast of navigational warnings. The term NAVAREA followed by a roman numeral may be used to identify a particular sea area. The delimitation of such areas is not related to and shall not prejudice the delimitation of any boundaries between States.
NAVTEX	The system for the broadcast and automatic reception of maritime safety information by means of narrow-band direct-printing telegraphy.
On-scene	The search area or the actual distress site.
On-scene co-ordinator (OSC)	A person designated to co-ordinate search and rescue operations within a specified area.
On-scene endurance	The amount of time a facility is capable of spending at the scene, engaged in search and rescue activities.
Operations stage	A period during a SAR incident when SAR facilities proceed to the scene, conduct search, rescue survivors, assist distressed craft, provide emergency care for survivors, and deliver survivors to a suitable facility.
Optimal search area	The search area which will produce the highest probability of success when searched uniformly with the search effort available.
Optimal search factor (f_s)	A value, based on the amount of relative effort available, which is used to estimate the optimal area to search so the chances of finding the search object are maximized. (see *Optimal search radius*).
Optimal search plan	A plan that maximizes the probability of success of finding the search object using the available search effort.
Optimal search radius	One-half the width of the optimal search area. Optimal search radius is computed as the product of the total probable error of position (E) and the optimal search factor (f_s). $R_o = E \times f_s$.
Overdue	A situation where a craft has failed to arrive at its intended destination when expected and remains missing.
PAN-PAN	The international radiotelephony urgency signal.
Personal locator beacon (PLB)	A portable device, manually activated, which transmits a distress signal on 406 MHz, and may have an additional homing signal on a separate frequency.
Pilot in command	The pilot responsible for the operation and safety of the aircraft during flight time.

---

* Which may include inland seas, lakes and waterways navigable by seagoing ships.

Place of safety	A location where rescue operations are considered to terminate; where the survivors' safety of life is no longer threatened and where their basic human needs (such as food, shelter and medical needs) can be met; and, a place from which transportation arrangements can be made for the survivors' next or final destination. A place of safety may be on land, or it may be on board a rescue unit or other suitable vessel or facility at sea that can serve as a place of safety until the survivors are disembarked at their next destination.
Planning stage	A period during a SAR incident when an effective plan of operations is developed.
Position	A geographical location normally expressed in degrees and minutes of latitude and longitude.
Positioning	Process of determining a position which can serve as a geographical reference for conducting a search.
Possibility area	(1) The smallest area containing all possible survivor or search object locations. (2) For a scenario, the possibility area is the smallest area containing all possible survivor or search object locations which are consistent with the facts and assumptions used to form the scenario.
Primary swell	The swell system having the greatest height from trough to crest.
Probability of containment (*POC*)	The probability that the search object is contained within the boundaries of an area, sub-area, or grid cell.
Probability of detection (*POD*)	The probability of the search object being detected, assuming it was in the areas that were searched. *POD* is a function of coverage factor, sensor, search conditions and the accuracy with which the search facility navigates its assigned search pattern. Measures sensor effectiveness under the prevailing search conditions.
Probability map	A set of grid cells covering a scenario's possibility area where each grid cell is labelled with the probability of the search object being in that grid cell. That is, each grid cell is labelled with its own *POC* value.
Probability of success (*POS*)	The probability of finding the search object with a particular search. For each sub-area searched, $POS = POC \times POD$. Measures search effectiveness.
Probable error (from statistics)	The range on either side of the average or expected value such that the probability of being within that range is 50%.
Relative effort (*Z_r*)	The amount of available search effort (Z) divided by the effort factor. The relative effort relates the size of the effort available for a particular search to the size of the search object's location probability distribution at the time of the search. $Z_r = Z/f_Z$.
Rescue	An operation to retrieve persons in distress, provide for their initial medical or other needs, and deliver them to a place of safety.
Rescue co-ordination centre (RCC)	A unit responsible for promoting efficient organization of search and rescue services and for co-ordinating the conduct of search and rescue operations within a search and rescue region. **Note:** The term RCC will be used within this Manual to apply to either aeronautical or maritime centres; ARCC or MRCC will be used as the context warrants.

Rescue sub-centre (RSC)	A unit subordinate to a rescue co-ordination centre, established to complement the latter according to particular provisions of the responsible authorities. **Note**: The term RSC will be used within this Manual except where it applies only to aeronautical or maritime; then ARSC or MRSC will be used.
Rhumb line	Straight line between two points on a Mercator projection chart.
SafetyNET	A service of Inmarsat enhanced group call (EGC) system specifically designed for promulgation of maritime safety information (MSI) as a part of the Global Maritime Distress and Safety System (GMDSS).
Scenario	A consistent set of known facts and assumptions describing what may have happened to the survivors.
Sea	Condition of the surface resulting from waves and swells.
Sea current (SC)	The residual current when currents caused by tides and local winds are subtracted from local current. It is the main, large-scale flow of ocean waters.
Sea current error (SC$_e$)	The probable error of the sea current estimate.
Search	An operation, normally co-ordinated by a rescue co-ordination centre or rescue sub-centre, using available personnel and facilities to locate persons in distress.
Search action plan	Message, normally developed by the SMC, for passing instructions to SAR facilities and agencies participating in a SAR mission.
Search and rescue airspace reservation	Temporary airspace reservation to prevent non-SAR aircraft from interfering with SAR operations.
Search and rescue briefing officer	An officer appointed, usually by the SMC, to brief departing SAR facilities and debrief returning SAR facilities.
Search and rescue case	Any potential or actual distress about which a facility opens a documentary file, whether or not SAR resources are dispatched.
Search and rescue co-ordinating communications	Communications necessary for the co-ordination of facilities participating in a search and rescue operation.
Search and rescue co-ordinator (SC)	One or more persons or agencies within an Administration with overall responsibility for establishing and providing SAR services, and ensuring that planning for those services is properly co-ordinated.
Search and rescue data provider (SDP)	A source for a rescue co-ordination centre to contact to obtain data to support search and rescue operations, including emergency information from communications equipment registration databases, ship reporting systems, and environmental data systems (e.g., weather or sea current).
Search and rescue facility	Any mobile resource, including designated search and rescue units, used to conduct search and rescue operations.
Search and rescue incident	Any situation requiring notification and alerting of the SAR system and which may require SAR operations.
Search and rescue liaison officer	An officer assigned to promote co-ordination during a SAR mission.
Search and rescue mission co-ordinator (SMC)	The official temporarily assigned to co-ordinate response to an actual or apparent distress situation.

Search and rescue plan	A general term used to describe documents which exist at all levels of the national and international search and rescue structure to describe goals, arrangements, and procedures which support the provision of search and rescue services.
Search and rescue point of contact (SPOC)	Rescue co-ordination centres and other established and recognized national points of contact which can accept responsibility to receive Cospas--Sarsat alert data to enable the rescue of persons in distress.
Search and rescue region (SRR)	An area of defined dimensions, associated with a rescue co-ordination centre, within which search and rescue services are provided.
Search and rescue service	The performance of distress monitoring, communication, co-ordination and search and rescue functions, including provision of medical advice, initial medical assistance, or medical evacuation, through the use of public and private resources, including co-operating aircraft, vessels and other craft and installations.
Search and rescue stage	Typical steps in the orderly progression of SAR missions. These are normally awareness, initial action, planning, operations, and mission conclusion.
Search and rescue sub-region (SRS)	A specified area within a search and rescue region associated with a rescue sub-centre.
Search and rescue unit (SRU)	A unit composed of trained personnel and provided with equipment suitable for the expeditious conduct of search and rescue operations.
Search area	The area, determined by the search planner, that is to be searched. This area may be sub-divided into search sub-areas for the purpose of assigning specific responsibilities to the available search facilities.
Search effort (Z)	A measure of the area a search facility can effectively search within the limits of search speed, endurance, and sweep width. Search effort is computed as the product of search speed (V), search endurance (T), and sweep width (W). $Z = V \times T \times W$.
Search endurance (T)	The amount of "productive" search time available at the scene. This figure is usually taken to be 85% of the on-scene endurance, leaving a 15% allowance for investigating sightings and navigating turns at the ends of search legs.
Search facility position error (Y)	Probable error in a search craft's position, based on its navigational capabilities.
Search object	A ship, aircraft, or other craft missing or in distress or survivors or related search objects or evidence for which a search is being conducted.
Search pattern	A track line or procedure assigned to an SRU for searching a specified area.
Search radius	The actual search radius used to plan the search and to assign search facilities. It is usually based on adjustments to the optimal search radius that are needed for operational reasons.
Search speed (V)	The speed (or velocity) with which a search facility moves over the ground when searching.
Search sub-area	A designated area to be searched by a specific assigned search facility or possibly two facilities working together in close co-ordination.

Secondary swells	Swell systems of less height than the primary swell.
Sensors	Human senses (sight, hearing, touch, etc.), those of specially trained animals (such as dogs), or electronic devices used to detect the object of a search.
Separation ratio (SR)	The ratio of the divergence distance (DD) between two leeway divergence datums to the total probable error of position (E). $SR = DD/E$.
Set	Direction towards which a current flows.
Ship reporting system (SRS)	Reporting system which contributes to safety of life at sea, safety and efficiency of navigation and/or protection of the marine environment. This is established under SOLAS regulation V/11 or, for SAR purposes, under chapter 5 of the International Convention on Maritime Search and Rescue, 1979.
Situation report (SITREP)	Reports, from the OSC to the SMC or the SMC to interested agencies, to keep them informed of on-scene conditions and mission progress.
Sortie	Individual movement of a resource in conducting a search or rendering assistance.
Surface drift	Vector sum of total water current and leeway. Sometimes called Total Drift.
Surface picture (SURPIC)	A list or graphic display from a ship reporting system of information about vessels in the vicinity of a distress situation that may be called upon to render assistance.
Surface position	The position of the search object on the earth's surface at the time of initial distress, or its first contact with the earth's surface.
Sweep width (W)	A measure of the effectiveness with which a particular sensor can detect a particular object under specific environmental conditions.
Swell	Condition of the surface caused by a distant wind system. The individual swell appears to be regular and smooth with considerable distance between rounded crests.
Swell direction	The direction from which a swell is moving. The direction toward which a swell is moving is called the down swell direction.
Swell face	The side of the swell toward the observer. The backside is the side away from the observer. These definitions apply regardless of the direction of swell movement.
Swell velocity	Velocity with which the swells advance with relation to a fixed reference point, measured in knots.
Telemedical assistance service (TMAS)	A medical service permanently staffed by doctors qualified in conducting remote consultations and well versed in the particular nature of treatment on board ship.
Tidal current (TC)	Near-shore currents caused by the rise and fall of the tides.
Tidal current error (TC_e)	The probable error of the tidal current estimate.
Time of closest approach (TCA)	Time during a satellite pass when the satellite is closest to a signal source.

Total available search effort (Z_{ta})
The total amount of search effort available at the scene; equal to the sum of the search efforts available from each of the search facilities at the scene.

Total drift error (D_e)
Also *total probable drift error*. The total probable error in the datum position that is contributed by the total drift velocity error (DV_e).
$D_e = DV_e \times t$, where t is the length of the drift interval in hours.

Total drift velocity error (DV_e)
Also *total probable drift velocity error*. The total probable error of the total drift velocity based on the probable errors contributed by the probable errors in the average surface wind, leeway, and total water current.

Total probable error (E)
The estimated error in the datum position. It is the square root of the sum of the squares of the total drift error, initial position error, and search facility position error.

Total water current (TWC)
The vector sum of currents affecting search objects.

Total water current error (TWC_e)
Also *total probable water current error*. The total probable error of the total water current based on either (a) the probable error of the measured total water current or (b) the probable errors of the wind current, tidal or sea current, and any other current that contributed to the total water current.

Track spacing (S)
The distance between adjacent parallel search tracks.

Triage
The process of sorting survivors according to medical condition and assigning them priorities for emergency care, treatment, and evacuation.

True air speed (TAS)
The speed an aircraft is travelling through the air mass. TAS corrected for wind equals ground speed.

Uncertainty phase
A situation wherein doubt exists as to the safety of an aircraft or a marine vessel, and of the persons on board.

Unnecessary SAR alert (UNSAR)
A message sent by an RCC to the appropriate authorities as a follow-up when the SAR system is unnecessarily activated by a false alert.

Unreported
A situation where a craft has failed to report its location or status when expected and remains missing.

Vector
A graphic representation of a physical quantity or measurement, such as wind velocity, having both magnitude and direction.

Vessel
A maritime craft.

Vessel monitoring system (VMS)
A tracking system which provides for environmental and fisheries regulatory organizations to monitor the position, time at a position, course and speed of commercial fishing vessels.

Vessel tracking
A generic term applied to all forms of vessel track data derived from multiple sources such as ship reporting systems, AIS, LRIT, SAR aircraft, VMS and VTS.

Vessel traffic services (VTS)
A marine traffic monitoring system established by harbour or port authorities to keep track of vessel movements and provide navigational safety in a limited geographical area.

Visual flight rules (VFR)	Rules governing procedures for conducting flight under visual meteorological conditions. In addition, used by pilots and controllers to indicate type of flight plan.
Visual meteorological conditions (VMC)	Meteorological conditions expressed in terms of visibility, distance from cloud, and ceiling equal to or better than specified minima.
Wave (or Chop)	The condition of the surface caused by local wind and characterized by irregularity, short distance between crests, whitecaps, and breaking motion.
Wind-corrected heading	The actual heading an aircraft is required to fly to make good an intended course.
Wind current (WC)	The water current generated by wind acting upon the surface of water over a period of time.
Wind current error (WC_e)	The probable error of the wind current estimate.

Chapter 1

The search and rescue system

1.1 System organization

Global SAR system organization

1.1.1 The International Civil Aviation Organization (ICAO) and the International Maritime Organization (IMO) co-ordinate, on a global basis, member States' efforts to provide search and rescue (SAR) services. Briefly, the goal of ICAO and IMO is to provide an effective world-wide system, so that wherever people may be in danger, in the air or at sea, SAR services will be available if needed. The overall approach a State takes in establishing, providing, and improving SAR services is affected by the fact that these efforts are an integral part of a global SAR system.

1.1.2 A basic, practical, and humanitarian effect of having a global SAR system is that it eliminates the need for each State to provide SAR services for its own citizens wherever they travel world-wide. Instead, the globe is divided into search and rescue regions (SRRs), each with a rescue co-ordination centre (RCC) and associated SAR services, which assist anyone in distress within the SRR without regard to nationality or circumstances.

National and regional SAR system organization

1.1.3 States, by being Party to the Safety of Life at Sea (SOLAS) Convention, the International Convention on Maritime Search and Rescue, and the Convention on International Civil Aviation, have accepted the obligation to provide aeronautical and maritime SAR co-ordination and services for their territories, territorial seas, and, where appropriate, the high seas. SAR services are to be available on a 24-hour basis.

1.1.4 To carry out these responsibilities, a State either should establish a national SAR organization, or join one or more other States to form a regional SAR organization. In some areas an effective and practical way to achieve this goal is to develop a regional system associated with a major ocean area and continent.

1.1.5 ICAO Regional Air Navigation Plans (RANPs) depict aeronautical SRRs for most of the world. Many States are given an area of responsibility which is usually composed of one aeronautical SRR. Maritime SRRs are published in the IMO SAR Plan, and are similar, but not necessarily identical, to aeronautical SRRs. The purpose of having SRRs is to clearly define who has primary responsibility for co-ordinating responses to distress situations in every area of the world, which is especially important for automatic routeing of distress alerts to responsible RCCs.

1.2 SAR co-ordination

1.2.1 The SAR system has three levels of co-ordination associated with SAR co-ordinators (SCs), SAR mission co-ordinators (SMCs), and on-scene co-ordinators (OSCs).

1.2.2 *SAR co-ordinators.* SCs have the overall responsibility for establishing, staffing, equipping, and managing the SAR system, including providing appropriate legal and funding support, establishing RCCs and rescue sub-centres (RSCs), providing or arranging for SAR facilities, co-ordinating SAR training, and developing SAR policies. SCs are the top level SAR managers; each State normally will have one or more persons or agencies for whom this designation may be appropriate. More information on SAR management responsibilities may be found in the *International Aeronautical and Maritime Search and Rescue Manual on Organization and Management*. SCs are not normally involved in the conduct of SAR operations.

1.2.3 SAR operations are normally carried out under the direction and supervision of an SMC, who is usually the supervisor of the RCC or RSC watch team. In multiple-incident situations this officer could be SMC for all incidents, or, for some of those incidents, the SMC role could be delegated to another suitably qualified member of the watch team. The SMC should in all cases be supported by RCC watch team members to undertake functions in the co-ordinating process such as communications, plotting, logging and search planning. For complex cases or those of long duration, the assisting team as well as the SMC must be replaced at regular intervals. The SMC must be able to competently gather information about emergencies, transform emergency incident information into accurate and workable plans and dispatch and co-ordinate the facilities which will carry out the SAR missions.

(a) The SMC is in charge of a SAR operation until a rescue has been effected or until it has become apparent that further efforts would be of no avail, or until responsibility is accepted by another RCC. The SMC should be able to use readily available facilities and to request additional ones during the operation. The SMC plans the search and co-ordinates the transit of SAR facilities to the scene.

(b) The SMC should be well trained in all SAR processes and be thoroughly familiar with the applicable SAR plans. The SMC must competently gather information about distress situations, develop accurate and workable action plans, and dispatch and co-ordinate the resources which will carry out SAR missions. The plans of operation maintained by the RCC provide information to assist in these efforts. Guidelines for SMC duties include:

– obtain and evaluate all data on the emergency;

– ascertain the type of emergency equipment carried by the missing or distressed craft;

– remain informed of prevailing environmental conditions;

– if necessary, ascertain movements and location of vessels and alert shipping in likely search areas for rescue, lookout (visual and electronic) and/or radio watch on appropriate frequencies to facilitate communications with SAR facilities;

– plot the area to be searched and decide on the methods and facilities to be used;

– develop the search action plan (and rescue action plan as appropriate), i.e., allocate search areas, designate the OSC, dispatch SAR facilities and designate on-scene communications frequencies;

– inform the RCC chief of the search action plan;

– co-ordinate the operation with adjacent RCCs when appropriate;

– arrange briefing and debriefing of SAR personnel;

– evaluate all reports from any source and modify the search action plan as necessary;

– arrange for the fuelling of aircraft and, if necessary, rescue vessels and, for prolonged search, make arrangements for the accommodation of SAR personnel;

– arrange for delivery of supplies to sustain survivors;

– maintain in chronological order an accurate and up-to-date record with a plot, where necessary, of all proceedings;

– issue progress reports;

– recommend to the RCC chief the abandoning or suspending of the search;

– release SAR facilities when assistance is no longer required;

– notify accident investigation authorities;

– notify police and other government authorities where relevant and necessary;

– if applicable, notify the State of registry of the aircraft or vessel in accordance with established arrangements; and

– prepare a final report on the results of the operation.

1.2.4 *On-scene co-ordinator.* When two or more SAR units are working together on the same mission, there is sometimes an advantage if one person is assigned to co-ordinate the activities of all participating units. The SMC designates this on-scene co-ordinator (OSC), who may be the person in charge of a search and rescue unit (SRU), ship or aircraft participating in a search, or someone at another nearby facility in a position to handle OSC duties. The person in charge of the first SAR facility to arrive at the scene will normally assume the function of OSC until the SMC directs that the person be relieved. Conceivably, the OSC may have to assume SMC duties and actually plan the search if the OSC becomes aware of a distress situation directly and communications cannot be established with an RCC. The OSC should be the most capable person available, taking into consideration SAR training, communications capabilities, and the length of time that the unit the OSC is aboard can stay in the search area. Frequent changes in the OSC should be avoided. Duties which the SMC *may* assign to the OSC, depending on needs and qualification, include any of the following:

– assume operational co-ordination of all SAR facilities on scene;

– receive the search action plan from the SMC;

– modify the search action plan based on prevailing environmental conditions and keeping the SMC advised of any changes to the plan (do in consultation with the SMC when practicable);

– provide relevant information to the other SAR facilities;

– implement the search action plan;

– monitor the performance of other units participating in the search;

– co-ordinate safety of flight issues for SAR aircraft;

– develop and implement the rescue action plan (when needed); and

– make consolidated reports (SITREPs) back to the SMC.

1.2.5 *Aircraft co-ordinator* The purpose of the aircraft co-ordinator (ACO) function is to maintain high flight safety and co-operate in the rescue action to make it more effective. The ACO function should be seen as a co-operating, supporting and advisory service. The ACO should normally be designated by the SMC, or if that is not practicable, by the OSC. The ACO function will normally be performed by the facility with the most suitable mix of communication means, radar, GNSS (Global Navigation Satellite System) combined with trained personnel to effectively co-ordinate the involvement of multiple aircraft in SAR operations while maintaining flight safety. Generally the ACO is responsible to the SMC; however, the ACO work on scene must be co-ordinated closely with the OSC, and if no SMC or OSC, as the case may be, the ACO would remain in overall charge of operations. Duties of the ACO can be carried out from a fixed-wing aircraft, helicopter, ship, a fixed structure such as an oil rig, or an appropriate land unit, such as an ATS unit or RCC. Depending on needs and qualifications, the ACO may be assigned duties that include the following:

– co-ordinate the airborne resources in a defined geographical area;

– assist in maintaining flight safety by issuing safety-related information;

– practise flow planning (example: point of entry and point of exit);

– prioritize and allocate tasks;

– co-ordinate the coverage of search areas;

– forward radio messages (can be the only duty);

– make consolidated situation reports (SITREPs) to the SMC and the OSC, as appropriate; and work closely with the OSC; and

– it is important that the ACO is aware of the fact that the participating airborne units, if possible, try to avoid disturbing other participating units with, for example, noise and rotor wind.

1.2.6   Airborne SRUs should make a standard joining entry report to the ACO when entering a search and rescue mission area, including:

–   call sign;

–   nationality;

–   type (specify fixed wing or helicopter and type);

–   position;

–   altitude (on pressure setting used);

–   ETA (at relevant point or search area);

–   endurance on scene; and

–   remarks (specific equipment or limitations).

1.3   SAR resources

1.3.1   The SAR organization includes all of those agencies which perform distress monitoring, communications, co-ordination, and response functions. This includes providing or arranging for medical advice, initial medical assistance, or medical evacuation, if necessary. SAR facilities consist of all of the public and private facilities, including co-operating aircraft, vessels, other craft and installations operating under co-ordination of an RCC. In establishing a SAR service, States should use existing facilities to the fullest extent possible. A successful SAR organization usually can be created without having designated, full-time SRUs.

1.3.2   A list of potential SAR resources is contained in the *International Aeronautical and Maritime Search and Rescue Manual on Organization and Management*.

1.3.3   *International resources.* Several resources exist internationally which can be used by RCCs while co-ordinating a specific SAR mission. Examples of such resources available for use by all RCCs are discussed in the following paragraphs.

Ship reporting systems and vessel tracking

1.3.4   Vessels at sea, although not always available to participate in extended search operations, are potential aeronautical and maritime SAR assets. Masters of vessels have a duty to assist others whenever it can be done without endangering the assisting vessel or crew. Various States have implemented ship reporting systems. A ship reporting system enables the SMC to quickly know the approximate positions, courses, and speeds of vessels in the vicinity of a distress situation by means of a surface picture (SURPIC), and other information about the vessels which may be valuable, e.g., whether a doctor is aboard. Masters of vessels should be encouraged to send regular reports to the authority operating a ship reporting system for SAR. Ships are a key SAR resource for RCCs, but requests for them to assist must be weighed against the considerable cost to shipping companies when they do divert to assist. Ship reporting systems enable RCCs to quickly identify the capable vessel which will be least harmed by a diversion, enabling other vessels in the vicinity to be unaffected.

1.3.5   The Amver system, the only world-wide system operated exclusively to support SAR, makes information available to all RCCs. Any United States RCC can be contacted for this type of SAR information. appendix O lists many of the ship reporting systems established for SAR, and will be updated as more information becomes available.

1.3.6   As well as ship reporting systems (SRS), RCCs can use vessel position data from various vessel tracking systems to support SAR operations. These may include the long-range identification and tracking (LRIT) system, the automatic identification system (AIS) system, fisheries and other vessel monitoring systems (VMS) and vessel traffic services (VTS) established to monitor port operations or to cover focal areas or sensitive areas. Data from each of these systems can be displayed by RCCs using geographic information systems (GIS) to produce a surface picture (SURPIC). SURPICs can be used to identify and locate potential rescue vessels as well as improve maritime domain awareness (MDA). In accordance with SOLAS regulation V/19-1, Contracting Governments should make provision to receive LRIT vessel position data for SAR. In accordance with IMO guidance material, RCCs can request LRIT data for SAR operations within their own SRR and for SAR co-ordination requirements outside it, as appropriate. Data on all vessels can be requested within a circular or rectangular area at no charge to the RCC.

Global Maritime Distress and Safety System

1.3.7 Ships subject to the SOLAS Convention should be outfitted with certain communications equipment, collectively referred to as the shipboard portion of the Global Maritime Distress and Safety System (GMDSS). Certain fishing vessels and other marine craft also may be obligated to carry GMDSS-compatible equipment, or may do so voluntarily. GMDSS is intended to provide automatic alerting and locating with minimal delay, a reliable network for SAR communications, integration of satellite and terrestrial communications, and adequate frequencies in all maritime bands.

1.3.8 RCC personnel should be familiar with the SOLAS GMDSS provisions, and associated IMO documents. The general goal of GMDSS is to take advantage of available technology to shift alerting emphasis from ship to ship (though this is still done), towards ship to shore, so that SAR professionals are rapidly alerted and can help arrange assistance. GMDSS capabilities of vessels not subject to SOLAS may range from full compliance to no GMDSS capabilities at all.

1.3.9 Introduction of GMDSS aboard only some vessels adds capabilities for those vessels, but also introduces incompatibility between those vessels and vessels not GMDSS equipped. It also introduces the need for some SAR authorities to support two maritime mobile and fixed systems. An initial goal of GMDSS was to eliminate the need for a continuous listening watch on VHF-FM channel 16. However, since most other vessels depend on channel 16 for distress, safety, and calling, IMO has decided that all GMDSS ships, while at sea, shall continue to maintain, when practicable, continuous listening watch on VHF-FM channel 16.

Aeronautical systems

1.3.10 Virtually all commercial aircraft on international routes are under positive control by air traffic services (ATS) units when they are airborne. ICAO has linked ATS units into a world-wide system. Consequently, there usually is little delay from the onset of an international commercial aircraft emergency until SAR agencies are notified, and there is often no need for an extended search if an aircraft should be forced down away from an airport. Aircraft may not be under positive control, which can result in delayed reporting of their emergencies. In some States, aircraft may not take off unless they have filed a flight plan and been granted clearance from the appropriate authorities.

1.3.11 Annex 10 to the Convention on International Civil Aviation allocates blocks of VHF band frequencies for aeronautical use; certain of these are allocated for specific purposes, while others are assignable. ICAO RANPs or other regional SAR plans or agreements may provide guidance on selection of appropriate aeronautical frequency bands for SAR.

1.3.12 121.5 MHz is the international aeronautical distress frequency. This frequency is monitored by ATS, some commercial airliners, and other aeronautical facilities, where needed, to ensure immediate reception of distress calls. Emergency locator transmitters (ELTs) are carried in most aircraft and operate on 406 MHz and 121.5 MHz for final homing.

SAR data providers

1.3.13 Several types of communications equipment transmit electronic identities and codes which must be used in conjunction with associated databases to decode emergency messages and obtain associated emergency information to support SAR. Maintainers of these databases are called SAR Data Providers (SDPs). Entities such as flag States, communication service providers, and the International Telecommunication Union (ITU) serve as SDPs, and it is important that RCCs know how to rapidly retrieve data from them when needed.

1.4 Medical assistance to vessels

1.4.1 The SMC should have procedures in place for responding to a request for medical advice at sea (MEDICO) and for medical evacuation.

1.4.2 MEDICO is an international term usually meaning the passing of medical information by radio. SAR agencies may provide medical advice either with their own doctors, or by arrangements with a telemedical assistance service (TMAS). (Such doctors should be trained, if possible, regarding the inherent risks associated with medical emergencies at sea and with medical evacuations, so that these factors can be considered in recommendations for treatment or evacuation.) There are organizations in some States which provide subscription and pay-per-use medical advice to vessels at sea. However, perhaps the best known TMAS is Centro Internazionale Radio-Medico (CIRM) in Rome, Italy. Section 2.27 provides some additional information. SMCs who hand off medical advice duties to another organization should monitor the situations, since they sometimes involve medical evacuations.

1.4.3 The ITU's *List of Radiodetermination and Special Service Stations* lists commercial and Government radio stations which provide free medical message service to ships. These incoming or outgoing messages should be prefixed with "DH MEDICO". Messages requesting medical advice are normally delivered to RCCs, hospitals or other facilities in accordance with prior arrangements.

1.4.4 Medical evacuation can be extremely hazardous to the patient and to the crews of the vessel and SRU, because of environmental conditions and dangers inherent in transferring a patient from a vessel to another vessel or helicopter. If the medical personnel consulted do not fully understand the risks, the SMC should explain the risks and ask for an opinion on the urgency of the medical situation and the necessity of and priority for evacuation. The SMC should obtain advice from medical personnel who understand these risks before deciding to carry out an evacuation. The final decision about whether it is safe to conduct an evacuation rests with the master or pilot in command of the rescue facility tasked with the evacuation. The risks of the evacuation must be measured against the risks to the patient and the SAR facility. Factors to consider include:

- medical capabilities of the SAR facility;

- weather, sea, and other environmental conditions;

- agreements between vessels and hospitals or commercial medical advisory services;

- the patient's clinical status; and

- the patient's probable clinical course if evacuation is delayed or not performed. A delayed evacuation, if the patient's condition permits, may:
  - provide for adequate planning by the SMC;
  - allow the SAR facility to remain within its range limits;
  - enable a daylight evacuation;
  - allow the vessel to enter port; or
  - allow the weather to improve.

1.5 Plans of operation

1.5.1 Each RCC should prepare comprehensive plans of operation for its SRR, and take into account agreements with providers of facilities or other support for SAR operations. The plans of operation should be brought up to date whenever a change in conditions or experience in actual operations and exercises makes this necessary or advisable.

1.5.2 The location of the RCC and the description of its area of responsibility should be published in a national document (e.g., the Aeronautical Information Publication (AIP) and annual Notices to Mariners). The plans of operation should include information on the following general categories:

- procedures for SAR co-ordination and types of SAR operations;

- responsibilities of personnel assigned to SAR operations;

- facilities;

> – communications;
>
> – operational information; and
>
> – training and discussion.

1.6   SAR operations stages

1.6.1   The success of a SAR mission often depends on the speed with which the operation is planned and carried out. The prompt receipt of all available information by the RCC is necessary for thorough evaluation of the situation, immediate decision on the best course of action, and a timely activation of SAR facilities. While no two SAR operations follow exactly the same pattern, SAR incidents do generally pass through defined stages, which can be used to help organize response activities. These stages are discussed in general terms below and expanded discussion is found in the remaining chapters of this volume. These stages should be interpreted with flexibility, as many of the actions described may be performed simultaneously or in a different order to suit specific circumstances.

Awareness stage

1.6.2   The SAR organization cannot respond to an incident until it becomes aware that people or craft need assistance. Therefore, the general public should be encouraged to report any abnormal occurrence which they have heard about or witnessed. SAR authorities must ensure that notification that an aircraft has crashed, or that an aircraft, ship, other craft or person(s) is overdue or in a state of emergency, can reach an RCC from any source, either directly or via an alerting post.

1.6.3   ATS units receive information on most commercial aircraft flights and are periodically in contact with the aircraft. An aircraft emergency therefore is likely to come to ATS attention first. An RCC will usually be notified by an ATS unit when an aircraft is, or may be, in a state of emergency. However, notification of a general aviation aircraft emergency may often come from a local airport, a concerned individual reporting it overdue or witnesses seeing an aircraft in difficulty or crash. When the nature of the emergency is such that local rescue facilities can handle the emergency, e.g., when an incident occurs at or near an aerodrome, the RCC will not always be informed.

1.6.4   In some areas, a coast radio station (CRS) provides the main link for ship-to-shore and shore-to-ship communications and, in this situation, it may be that the CRS usually receives the first information that a ship or other craft on the water is in distress. A CRS is required by international regulations to relay this information to SAR authorities. As a result, an RCC will often receive first notification that a ship or other craft is in distress from a CRS with which it is associated, or via its own communications facilities. Some RCCs may have radio or satellite communications capability that enables them to be alerted directly.

1.6.5   The RCC must keep a complete record of information it receives. Pre-printed forms often are used to ensure that full information about the SAR incident is obtained and remains available for review. Chapter 3 discusses these topics.

Initial action

1.6.6   Once an RCC receives an initial report about persons or craft in distress, some immediate action often is appropriate pending receipt and evaluation of more complete information. RCCs usually have in their plans of operation a checklist of steps to accomplish for each type of incident with which the RCC expects that it may become involved.

1.6.7   After evaluating all available information and taking into account the degree of emergency, the SMC should declare the appropriate emergency phase and immediately inform all appropriate centres, personnel and facilities. Three emergency phases have been established for classifying incidents and to help in determining the actions to be taken for each incident. These are:

> – uncertainty phase;
>
> – alert phase; and
>
> – distress phase.

1.6.8 Depending on how the situation develops, the incident may have to be reclassified. See chapter 3 for a complete discussion of initial action stage and emergency phases of a SAR incident. Emergency phases are only intended to be declared by RCC, an RSC, or an ATS unit.

1.6.9 Particularly for overdue craft, evaluation is a crucial function that the SMC performs during a SAR incident. All reports received before and during a SAR operation must be carefully evaluated to determine their validity, the urgency for action, and the extent of the response required. Chapter 4 discusses this process in detail. While evaluation of reports may be difficult and time-consuming, decisions must be made and action taken as quickly as possible. If uncertain information cannot be confirmed without undue delay, the SMC should act on a questionable message rather than wait for verification.

Planning stage

1.6.10 Comprehensive planning of SAR response tasks is essential, especially when the location of the distress situation is unknown and the survivors may move, for example, due to wind and water currents or by attempting to walk out of a remote land area. Proper and accurate planning is critical to SAR mission success; if the wrong area is searched, there is no hope that search personnel will find the survivors, regardless of the quality of their search techniques or the amount of their search effort. This requires proper training of the SMC and other RCC personnel. Computers can eliminate much of the detailed work in search planning, and can improve accuracy. Since not all States have access to computerized search planning, Chapter 4 of this volume contains the basic information on how to plan searches using manual methods.

Operations stage

1.6.11 The SAR operations stage encompasses all activities that involve searching for the distressed persons or craft, providing assistance, and delivering them to a place of safety. In this stage, the SMC assumes a monitoring and guidance role, ensuring that the search plan is received, understood, and followed by SAR facilities. They may also continue to gather or receive more information and assess this to see if it affects or changes any of the plans previously made. The RCC may also be the focal point for communications with other organizations. The RCC staff usually will spend most of this stage planning subsequent searches, based on updated information and the assumption that the present search will be unsuccessful. See chapter 5 for a discussion of search operations; see chapter 6 for guidance on rescue operations.

Conclusion stage

1.6.12 SAR operations enter the conclusion stage when:

- information is received that the aircraft, ship, other craft or persons who are the subject of the SAR incident are not in distress; or

- the aircraft, ship or persons for whom SAR facilities are searching have been located and the survivors rescued; or

- during the distress phase, the SMC determines that further search would be to no avail because additional effort cannot appreciably increase the probability of successfully finding any remaining survivors or because there is no longer any reasonable probability that the persons in distress have survived.

1.6.13 When SAR operations are terminated, all authorities, facilities, or services which have been activated must be immediately notified, as discussed in chapter 8.

1.7 Mission documentation

1.7.1 The RCC must record all information about each SAR incident as it is received, either in full or by reference to other permanent records such as separate reports, forms, folders, charts, telegrams, recorded radio frequencies and telephones, recorded radar data, etc. The form that this record keeping takes is not important so long as it is logically organized for easy retrieval. Sufficient information must be recorded and retained to completely re-create the case and show the rationale for all decisions taken.

Logs and diaries

1.7.2 The initial notification of an incident should be entered on a standard Incident Processing Form, supplies of which should be available at RCCs, RSCs, ATS units, and other alerting posts, as necessary. This form is needed to ensure that all available information on important details is obtained at first contact since it may be impossible or too time-consuming to obtain such information at a later stage. Use of an Incident Processing Form will ensure that all important details are elicited from the informant. This is particularly important if the informant is not experienced in maritime or aviation activities. The informant may be excited and under stress when making the report. The list is comprehensive and includes both the occupation and address of the informant as this information may help in assessment of the reliability of the report and permit additional information to be obtained later, if required.

1.7.3 As events unfold during a SAR incident, they should be recorded in a diary or log which will become part of the permanent case folder. The entries in the diary or log will be the primary record of the chronology of the case, which can be important for showing what information was available at each key decision point during the incident. Format is not important, though it is recommended that each page have the date and case name or case identifying number, all pages be consecutively numbered, and the time for every entry be recorded.

SAR forms

1.7.4 SAR forms serve many purposes and are in different formats. Their purposes include documenting information from the distressed craft, facilitating communications between RCCs and RSCs, briefing SAR crews, search planning, and facilitating communications among the SMC, OSC and SAR facilities. SAR forms are discussed throughout this volume and samples are provided in the appendices.

SAR charts and overlays

1.7.5 Sometimes the easiest way to organize geographic information during a SAR incident is to plot it on a chart. This is impractical if the RCC's case load is significant because no RCC has an inexhaustible supply of charts. The practical alternative is to plot all case-related information on flimsy paper or clear plastic laid over the top of the appropriate chart. If a separate flimsy overlay is used for basic case information and for laying out each search, it is much easier to evaluate what areas have been covered adequately and what areas will need further effort.

1.7.6 Electronic charting systems/geographic information systems (GIS) make it possible to create separate records of incident information plots regardless of the number of incidents being handled. The records are stored electronically and may also be printed for portable use, briefings, etc.

1.7.7 At the end of the case, these records should be marked with the date that each pertains to and with the case name or identifying case number. They then should be filed in the case incident folder.

SAR case files

1.7.8 All information pertaining to a specific SAR incident should be placed in an easily identified and labelled file folder and then stored. How long records are retained in storage is something each SC needs to decide. Some States retain all records for a few years and then place files dealing with significant, historically important, or sensitive incidents into permanent secure storage, discarding those dealing with routine matters. Establishing a policy on which types of cases belong in the "routine" category is a SAR management duty. Files pertaining to incidents that become the subject of legal proceedings should be retained until those proceedings are complete, including all appeals and legal reviews. Files that are to be permanently retained should be prominently marked so that they are not inadvertently discarded with the routine files.

SAR case analysis

1.7.9 To improve the overall SAR system effectiveness, RCC staff must help SAR managers review performance. SAR case analysis, discussed in chapter 8, can be a useful method for this review. In general, this analysis involves:

– reviewing specific cases to uncover lessons learned that can be applied in future operations; and

– analysing cumulative data to discover trends that may impact the allocation and location of SAR resources.

1.8 Training and exercises

1.8.1 The head of a SAR service is responsible for establishment of training programmes for SAR personnel to reach and maintain a high level of competence. The head of each facility is responsible for the training of personnel in the specialized techniques and procedures assigned to them, while each individual must assume responsibility to perform competently any assigned task.

1.8.2 Training of SAR service personnel can include the following:

– study of the application of SAR procedures, techniques and equipment through lectures, demonstrations, films, SAR manuals and journals;

– assisting in or observing actual operations; and

– exercises in which personnel are trained to co-ordinate individual procedures, practice skills and techniques in a simulated operation.

1.8.3 Training provides basic knowledge and skills. The head of the facility should have qualification and certification processes to ensure that personnel have sufficient experience, maturity, and judgement to perform assigned tasks.

(a) During a qualification process, the individual must, by demonstration of abilities, show mental and physical competence to perform as part of a team. Detailed qualification requirements vary with each type of workplace (a vessel, aircraft, or RCC). The trainee may be assigned to an associate who observes and can attest to the trainee's competence to perform each particular task. Thorough knowledge of the geographic area of operation should also be demonstrated.

(b) Certification is official recognition by the organization that it trusts the individual to use those abilities. Certain tasks may require periodic re-certification.

Note: The term "certification" is widely used by IMO, ICAO, and other organizations within the contexts of authorizing personnel or facilities to perform certain functions. In this chapter, certification is similarly used to authorize a properly trained and qualified person to perform assigned tasks.

Exercises

1.8.4 To reach a high degree of proficiency, all SAR facilities should periodically take part in co-ordinated SAR operations. Exercises may be used when the number of SAR operations is low, and especially with neighbouring States. Exercises test and improve operational plans and communications, provide learning experience, and improve liaison and co-ordination skills. Exercises should be conducted on three levels.

(a) The most simple type of exercise, a communications exercise, requires the least planning. It consists of periodic use of all means of communications between all potential users to ensure capability for actual emergencies.

(b) A co-ordination exercise involves simulated response to an emergency based on a series of scenarios. All levels of the SAR service are involved but do not deploy. This type of exercise can require considerable planning, especially where a number of other units or organizations are involved, and usually takes one to three days to execute. However, simulation exercises can be carried out more simply, for example, RCC personnel can conduct "internal" co-ordination exercises to simulate response to a scenario and practise their skills, techniques, procedures and processes. This may be as part of a programme of personnel competency maintenance training.

(c) The third type, a full-scale exercise or a field exercise, differs from the previous type in that actual SAR facilities are deployed. This increases the scope of SAR system testing and adds realistic constraints due to times involved in launching, transit, and activities of the SAR facilities.

1.8.5 Sample scenarios for a co-ordination exercise are provided below.

(a) A light aircraft that has not filed a flight plan is reported missing. Based on information received subsequently, the flight is reconstructed and all necessary actions are taken.

(b) A transport aircraft with a flight plan fails to make a position report or makes a distress call without giving a position. A simulated communication search is carried out and an air search is planned. A simulated search is then conducted with input from various simulated sources.

(c) A ship is reported 24 h overdue at its destination. A simulated search is carried out, using datum line search planning techniques. A simulated communication search is conducted involving relevant RCCs. Radio or satellite broadcasts are simulated.

1.8.6 The full-scale exercise requires detailed planning since actual SAR facilities are deployed, and it offers detailed, realistic experience and opportunities for testing and evaluating. The following may serve as a guide in developing a distress scenario.

(a) A search object resembling an aircraft is set up at an undisclosed location. A simulated flight plan is filed and one or two simulated position reports are received, but nothing more is heard until the aircraft is overdue at its destination. The appropriate emergency phase is declared and a simulated communication search is conducted. The SMC will assess all available information, plan a search (based on chapters 4 and 5 of this volume), and dispatch search facilities. Also, simulated reports from other reporting sources are received. Some of these reports will help in determining the correct search areas while others may be deliberately misleading. The text of all messages between participants in the exercise should begin with a prefix such as "EXERCISE" or "SAREX" to avoid any misunderstanding. The exercise ends when the search object is found.

(b) If the exercise concerns only the rescue of survivors, the SMC is given the exact location of the distress scene and the apparent condition of the survivors. The SMC must decide on the best method for rescue with available facilities and may send land vehicles, vessels and aircraft. A doctor, if available, could accompany the SAR facilities. On-scene SAR personnel may be required to transfer stretcher cases to the evacuation craft. Pararescue and medical teams could be sent and required to set up triage arrangements and support survivors using air-dropped survival stores.

1.8.7 The scale on which a combined multiple-agency exercise should be conducted and the number of facilities which should take part will depend upon the following:

– extent of the particular SAR service;

– anticipated demands upon the SAR service;

– extent to which private organizations and other agencies could be involved and on the SAR experience of their personnel;

– time interval since the last combined exercise; and

– general considerations of economy and value to and availability of participating facilities.

1.8.8 Planning involves: development of the concept (broad goals and objectives) of what is to be exercised; selection of participants (staff and facilities); detailed planning for how the exercise will be conducted; conduct of the exercise; and evaluation to determine lessons learned and to develop recommendations for future improvements. It is essential to have a clear understanding of which plans and procedures are being exercised. Scenarios can then be developed that pose specific situations to which personnel will react and respond. Response, or lack of response, in accordance with established policy and guidance, and need for additional policy guidance, is evaluated.

1.8.9 The evaluation process is crucial. Inputs should come from a team of evaluation experts who observe the exercise and from personnel who actually participated in the exercise scenarios. Those observing and evaluating the response must have expertise in the areas they are evaluating and clearly understand what is being evaluated. The evaluators should be familiar with how to properly handle the situations being posed and then record the participant's response to the objectives of the exercise. The final step is identification of weaknesses and development of recommendations for improvement. Subsequent exercises would emphasize these recommended changes and other concerns.

1.8.10 Adjacent RCCs should periodically carry out SAR exercises together to develop and maintain efficient co-operation and co-ordination between their services. These exercises need not always be on a large scale, but at least those SAR facilities which are likely to operate together should engage periodically in co-ordinating exercises. Much may be learned by exchanging information on training methods (e.g., programmes, literature, and films) and visits between staff of adjacent SRRs.

1.8.11 Additional information on planning and conducting exercises is provided in chapter 6 with regard to mass rescue operations.

Training of RCC and RSC personnel

1.8.12 The RCC and RSC have particularly important duties. Their personnel usually need formal SAR training. If unable to immediately attend formal training, they must receive a period of on-the-job training. Upon completion of training, the prospective RCC personnel should undergo qualification procedures. RCC staff should be fully qualified in SAR incident analysis, search planning, and SAR operations management.

1.8.13 One advantage of combining aeronautical and maritime RCCs into a joint RCC, and staffing the facility with both aviation and maritime specialists, is a synergistic approach to the solution of SAR incidents. RCC staff can share subject matter expertise and determine a more balanced and complete evaluation of each incident.

1.8.14 The formal training of RCC personnel should include:

- organization:
    - knowledge of the SAR organization and its relationship to the air traffic services;
    - knowledge of the SAR organization and its relationship to maritime safety and communication services;
    - knowledge of agreements made with facilities, neighbouring SAR services, etc.;
    - knowledge of capabilities and limitations of available facilities; and
    - knowledge of legal aspects, e.g., in a maritime incident, policies on towing and salvage;
- procedures:
    - how to obtain and evaluate information and reports;
    - alerting of facilities and commencement of SAR operations;
    - interpretation of different systems of position reporting;
    - determination of a search area;
    - search techniques and patterns for air, maritime and land facilities;
    - plotting of search information;
    - communications procedures;
    - rescue procedures;
    - supply-dropping procedures;
    - ditching assistance, interception and escort procedures; and
    - briefing and questioning of SAR personnel;
- administration:
    - routine administrative functions; and
- information:
    - visits to SAR facilities and supply depots, and participation in exercises, including packing and loading of survival stores; and
    - instruction through films, relevant journals, etc., on recent developments in the field of SAR.

1.8.15 RCC and RSC SAR training should also include many other topics. If search planning skills, knowledge and expertise gained from formal training are not used on a regular basis for operations or exercises, then periodic recurrent training must be implemented to ensure reliable and effective delivery of SAR services. Subject matter should include:

Aeronautical drift	MEDICO
AFN	Obtain and evaluate data
AFTN	On-scene co-ordinator duties
Bailout scenarios and planning	Parachute drift
Case studies	Plotting skills
Charts	Registration databases
Coastal SAR planning	Resource allocation
Computer applications	Risk assessment
Cospas–Sarsat	SAR agreements
Datum determination	SAR communications
Datum marker buoys	SAR mission co-ordination
Dealing with families	SAR operations conclusion
Dealing with public and news media	SAR phases, stages, and components
Documentation of incidents	SAR resource capabilities
Electronic sweep width	SAR system organization
Emergency care	SAR technology
Environmental factors	Search areas
Evaluation of flare sightings	Search patterns
Fatigue factors	Search planning
GMDSS	Ship reporting systems for SAR
International aspects	SRU selection
Interviewing techniques	Stress management
Leeway drift	Survival equipment
Legal concerns	Vessel tracking (AIS, LRIT, VMS and VTS)
Lookout skills and limitations	
Manoeuvring boards	Visual sweep width
Medical evacuations	Water currents
Medical advice	Weather

1.8.16 *Other SAR facilities.* Training for mobile facilities is discussed in the IAMSAR Manual, volume III, *Mobile Facilities*. This would include aspects of training for support facilities for mobile units, such as depots.

1.9 Improving professionalism

1.9.1 To increase the professionalism of their respective organizations, SAR personnel should:

– ensure that SAR procedures developed by IMO and ICAO are followed, and that supplemental plans of operation and procedures suitable to local SAR scenarios are developed and followed;

– ensure that SAR personnel have the maturity and competence to carry out assigned tasks;

– make arrangements to use all available resources for SAR, to the extent practicable;

– arrange to work with other States, especially as provided for in SAR agreements, and ensure that responsible personnel understand and follow such agreements;

– keep a complete and accurate log of operations;

– properly investigate and report any problems, and find ways to apply lessons learned to prevent future recurrences; and

–   ensure that once some specific step is taken (perhaps acknowledgement of a distress alert) which would lead those in distress to expect assistance, every effort is made to follow through, particularly since the survivors may forego other opportunities for help based on this understanding.

1.10 Public relations

1.10.1 The public should be informed during SAR operations, within the limits of confidentiality, of SAR system actions. The potential benefits of early release of information include:

–   additional information from the public, leading to more effective use of SAR resources;

–   fewer time-consuming requests from the news media; and

–   reduction in inaccurate public speculation about the SAR mission.

1.10.2 A SAR operation often creates great interest with the general public and with radio, television and newspapers. Contacts with media are normally the responsibility of managers or public affairs specialists, but may also be delegated to the RCC. It is important that a good relationship between the media and the RCC is established to ensure that information reaching the public is factual and complete. This relationship should be established prior to any major incident. The RCC should use the media to communicate its overall image, the services provided, and its impact on the community. The RCC can accomplish this by:

–   providing information to the local media about the RCC and the services it provides;

–   providing "good will" stories on an ongoing basis to build up the credibility with the media as a professional, concerned, and open organization; and

–   taking every opportunity to present news so that when a major SAR operation is being conducted, the media will be knowledgeable in reporting it.

1.10.3 Contact with the media can take many forms.

(a) In order to ensure the formulation of a consistent and controlled message to the public, media relations personnel should be designated as the focal point for the releases of information relating to SAR operations. In the conduct of major operations, the RCC should not normally be the contact point for the media because of the potential for negative impact on SAR operations if media interest becomes too extensive. All information released by the RCC should normally be approved by the SMC and appropriate authorities, and contain only factual information.

(b) Once initial media information has been released, the RCC should consider programming and advertising regular and frequent updates in order to address the needs of the media. These could take the form of further press releases or holding press conferences. A press conference gives the RCC the opportunity to initiate the following actions:

–   give information;

–   give interviews;

–   answer questions;

–   summarize what has happened and what the RCC is doing in order for the media to fully understand what has occurred;

–   give the RCC a "human face;" and

–   give the media controlled opportunities to obtain video footage, photographs, and audio for broadcast use.

(c) Interviews can be conducted. To avoid wrong information and misunderstandings, normally only a designated spokesperson should conduct interviews with the media. This will also allow the RCC to remain focused on its planning efforts. The spokesperson should be in direct contact with the RCC to ensure that complete and up-to-date information is obtained. In interviews with the media, the RCC spokesperson should exercise good judgement and avoid:

- personal judgements or demeaning information on the:
    - crew or missing persons; and
    - judgement, experience, behaviour or training of the master, pilot in command, or the crew;
- degrading opinions on the conduct of SAR operations (only factual information should be given);
- personal opinions or theories as to why the accident occurred or how it could have been avoided;
- being unduly pessimistic or optimistic on the chances of success;
- giving names of missing or distressed persons until every effort has been made to inform the relatives;
- giving the name of the operator or the owner of the aircraft, ship or other craft before they have been informed; and
- revealing names of persons who have given information related to the case.

(d) On the other hand, the type of information that the RCC spokesman could release, depending on the specific circumstances of the SAR operation, includes, but is not limited to:

- general reason for the SAR operation;
- type of aircraft or vessel involved;
- owner/operator of the aircraft or vessel (only after the owner/operator has been informed and given consent);
- name of vessel/flight number (only after the owner/operator has been informed and given consent);
- number of people on board;
- general area being searched;
- number and types of aircraft and vessels engaged in the search and the number of hours flown;
- arrangements for land or marine search (as applicable);
- details of other authorities participating in the search;
- contact number for use by the next of kin to obtain information;
- contact number for further information; and
- contact number for media enquiries.

1.10.4 Release of names can be a sensitive issue. Guidelines should be established in accordance with international and national laws and regulations.

(a) Names of civilian casualties should not be released until every effort has been made to contact family relatives. To accomplish notification, use whatever national and local public agencies are available. Until the relatives have been notified, normally only the number of deceased, survivors, and injured survivors should be released. Names of military casualties should be released only by the military service to which the casualties belong. When circumstances permit, queries on such casualties should be referred to the parent military service.

(b) Names of survivors should not be released until positive identification has been accomplished. Generally, survivor information should not be released prior to release of casualty information, although circumstances may permit exceptions. Survivors should be encouraged and assisted in contacting their families as soon as possible. However, SMCs should brief survivors on releasing information and possible reasons for withholding information.

1.10.5 When a major incident occurs, such as with a large aircraft or cruise ship, hundreds of persons may be at risk, involving many nationalities. Such an incident may result in the need for mass rescue operations (MROs), which are discussed in chapter 6. In this situation, the RCC could become the focus of world attention. Such events will undoubtedly require the involvement of other emergency service providers and a concerted effort will be required by the RCC if a consistent and controlled message to the public is to be maintained. Actions by the RCC may include the following:

– request representatives from involved emergency service providers to help staff a joint media relations team;

– select a spokesperson(s);

– issue a press release;

– make information available on the Internet;

– call a press conference;

– prepare a room for the media; and

– control media access.

1.10.6 Other considerations for public relations and management of a major incident include the following points:

(a) As soon as it is apparent to the RCC public relations staff that a major incident has occurred, informing the media will help establish the RCC as the primary source of information. Be clear, concise, and informative.

(b) Establishing the nationalities of those at risk will assist in anticipating where media enquiries will come from, and will assist in reducing media enquiries from States whose citizens are not involved.

(c) Due consideration should be given to the language used with the media. Local and international interest in the SAR operation may require use of a common language or availability of translators.

1.10.7 The SMC should be aware of the concerns of the relatives of missing persons. Waiting during searches and lack of information can be stressful to family members of those in distress, which could also affect RCC performance. During the search, the SMC or staff should maintain regular contact with the relatives to provide information and outline future plans; if possible, contact telephone numbers should be issued for relatives. Providing access to SMC headquarters, if appropriate, enables relatives to see the search effort. These steps assist the relatives in accepting the SMC's decision to conclude search operations even if the missing persons are not located.

1.10.8 Additional information on planning and public and media relations is provided in chapter 6 with regard to mass rescue operations.

1.11 Computer resources

1.11.1 Large amounts of computing and data storage capability can be obtained and maintained at a relatively low cost. Modern software makes development of helpful forms, computer aids, databases, and sometimes even some communications reasonably easy and inexpensive. Such aids can be developed by the user and do not require highly specialized expertise in the computing sciences. This is not true for software that directly addresses the search planning problem. Developing such software requires specialized expertise in computer modelling, the application of search theory and the application of environmental sciences such as meteorology and oceanography to SAR. Paragraph 1.11.9 lists some of the functional characteristics that should be considered for search planning software.

1.11.2 *Forms.* Word-processing software provides the capability to develop standard forms that best meet local, national, and regional needs. These forms may be printed on paper and completed by hand, or completed on the computer via the word processor. The functions of such forms include:

– ensuring critical data items are not forgotten;

– ensuring calculations are done in the correct order;

– saving time for the writer by having all standard information already on the form and requiring that only variable items need to be entered; and

– saving time for the reader by having all information presented in a standard, predictable format.

1.11.3 Examples of forms which may be useful include:

– search action plans;

– checklists;

– situation reports; and

– search planning worksheets.

1.11.4 *Computer aids.* The availability of electronic spreadsheets makes development of computer aids possible without doing computer programming in the traditional sense. Most of the work required by search planning worksheets, for example, could be done easily in spreadsheets. Having such spreadsheets helps in at least two respects.

(a) The search planner would have to enter only values needed as inputs. The spreadsheet software would do all the calculations required to produce the outputs (answers). This would relieve the search planner of most of the computational burden, reduce the potential for errors, and save valuable time.

(b) If an input value changed, the search planner would have to simply change the value of that item in the spreadsheet and all values based on it would be re-computed automatically, saving time and reducing the possibility of error.

1.11.5 A common use of spreadsheets is to track financial matters. The RCC and SAR managers can use this tool to prepare budgets, track expenditures, forecast fiscal requirements, and for other uses.

1.11.6 *Databases.* The primary purpose of most databases is to store detailed information. This information may then be accessed rapidly if detailed data is required, or consolidated and summarized into useful reports. Examples are shown below.

(a) *SAR system management data.* Number of alerts received by the system, number of responses, number of sorties, number of SRU hours expended while engaged in SAR activities, SAR incident locations, dates, times, numbers of lives saved, and value of property saved are some of the many types of information a SAR manager may find useful.

(b) *Search planning.* The RCC may develop its own databases as well as make use of existing database programs on a variety of information valuable to search planning. Examples include:

– an index to previous SAR incidents by distressed craft name or other identifier could lead to valuable information about that craft if it is involved in a later incident;

– a database of known debris locations from previous aircraft crashes or forced landings over land, or vessels recently sunk, may avoid wasting valuable search time investigating old SAR incident sites;

– in the maritime area, a database of past drift trajectories could improve estimates of survivor location in future incidents; and

– an environmental database, including sea currents, water temperatures, winds currents, etc.

(c) *Facilities and agencies*

– a database of SAR and medical facilities, such as hyperbaric chambers and hospitals and their capabilities, could aid rescue planners in determining the best place to take injured survivors; and

– lists of frequently-called agencies and telephone numbers can be kept in a database and rapidly accessed, when needed.

1.11.7 *Computer communications.* Many computers can communicate electronically. The communications medium is usually either a modem connected to ordinary telephone lines or a network card in the computer connecting it to a local area or wide area network (LAN or WAN). Before depending on this type of communication, however, SAR system managers, search planners, etc., need to confirm the availability and reliability of the communications path.

1.11.8 *SAR data providers.* There are basically two types of SAR data. First, there is data which might provide additional clues about the SAR incident, the survivors, or their craft which could help in finding the survivors. Second, there is data which is used directly in the search planning and rescue processes. Some data, such as weather, fall into both categories.

    (a) Data of the first type may already reside in existing databases. For example, if a State has a boat registration programme, information the search planner would find useful about a missing boat may be available in the database. Lloyds Registry of Shipping maintains an extensive database on commercial shipping, including specific data on the current status and history of virtually every vessel engaged in transoceanic trade. The Internet often provides a means to access this data as well as business and individual web sites which might provide pertinent information about the craft or persons in distress.

    (b) Data of the second type includes weather, wind, and sea current data which might be available from local weather bureaus. It could also include ship reporting systems such as Amver, which maintain a continuously updated plot of estimated locations for participating merchant vessels.

1.11.9 *Computer-based search planning.* The use of computers to support the search planning process is growing as it offers the SAR Co-ordinator greater flexibility to calculate a refined search area. Although there may be a tendency to computerise the manual method, computerising this overly simplified pencil-and-paper technique should be avoided. Computers make much more sophisticated techniques feasible, such as making the best use of increasingly available detailed environmental data for modelling and predicting drift, creating and testing various scenarios, integrating and evaluating the impact of late-arriving information, and simulating changes in the search object's status and type, etc. Perhaps most importantly, such models can produce optimal search plans that maximise the probability of success. SAR Co-ordinators are cautioned that they should be familiar with the basic theories of each Search Planning element to fully take advantage of the search planning software. SAR Co-ordinators are also reminded that computers are only devices that provide support; they cannot make important decisions and the quality of their outputs can only be as good as the quality of the inputs. Further information may be found in appendix P of this publication.

1.11.10 *Display of vessel tracking data.* A computer system with geographic information system (GIS) display capability is important for displaying vessel tracking data sourced from AIS, LRIT, VMS, VTS and other sources. The location of SAR units can also be tracked and displayed, as can search areas and other information.

1.12 Decision and management support

1.12.1 The Incident Command System (ICS) is a management tool growing in international use for managing any emergency event. It consists of procedures for organizing personnel, facilities, equipment, and communications at the scene of an emergency. ICS is intended to quickly blend numerous organizations into an effective response organization for any type and magnitude of emergency. ICS is a highly flexible concept for managing emergency events involving multiple jurisdictions and multiple agencies, such as major disasters or events involving hazardous materials. Similar systems should be used when ICS is not available.

    (a) ICS enables:

        – standardization of management systems among agencies and organizations;

        – management in both simple and complex emergency situations;

        – incoming resources to fit into the total emergency response system;

- a manageable span-of-control; and
- clear lines of authority.

(b) SAR is often a component of emergency response. Where ICS is implemented, SAR facilities may conduct simultaneous operations along with other types of responders under ICS management. ICS does not take control or authority away from the SAR service. Rather, the SMC, OSC or someone designated by the SMC serves as an "agency representative" to co-ordinate the SAR response with an "incident commander", who is recognized by an applicable emergency response plan as having overall responsibility for actions on scene.

(c) RCCs and RSCs should be aware of the general concepts of ICS where it is implemented. State emergency response, disaster response, or other similar agencies which use ICS are potential sources of guidance.

1.12.2 Additional information on incident management on ICS is provided in chapter 6 with regard to mass rescue operations.

Chapter 2

Communications

2.1 Distress communications

2.1.1 This chapter introduces distress alerting and SAR communications, and discusses mobile and land-based uses of communications equipment. The basic information on aeronautical and maritime communications, frequencies, equipment, and procedures provided here will need to be supplemented to gain adequate expertise. Specific information on how to use the systems and equipment must be obtained from communication service providers, equipment manufacturers, training institutions, and other available sources. Since the field of communications is vast, RCCs may find it useful to employ communications experts if they handle the majority of their communications needs directly.

2.1.2 Distress traffic includes all messages relating to immediate assistance required by persons, aircraft, or marine craft in distress, including medical assistance. Distress traffic may also include SAR communications and on-scene communications. Distress calls take absolute priority over all other transmissions; anyone receiving a distress call must immediately cease any transmissions which may interfere with the call and listen on the frequency used for the call.

2.1.3 Distress and safety communications require the highest possible integrity and protection from harmful interference. Any interference which puts at risk the operation of safety services or degrades, obstructs or interrupts any radio communications is harmful. Some frequencies are protected, in that they have no authorized uses other than for distress and safety. SAR personnel should be the last of all people to cause harmful interference, and should co-operate with law-enforcement authorities to report and stop incidents of interference.

2.1.4 Distress alerts may arrive at RCCs from a variety of equipment sources and via a variety of alerting posts. Alerting posts include, but are not limited to, coast radio stations (CRSs), Local User Terminals (LUTs) and Mission Control Centres (MCCs) of the Cospas–Sarsat System, Land Earth Stations (LESs) of the Inmarsat System, Air Traffic Services (ATS) units, commercially available emergency notification device service providers, public safety units such as police and fire departments, and vessels, aircraft, or other persons or facilities which may receive and relay such alerts. Alerting posts are any intermediary facilities which relay distress alerts between their source and the responsible RCC, and may even include other RCCs.

2.1.5 Aircraft or vessels in distress may use any means available to attract attention, make their positions known, and obtain help.

2.2 Aeronautical mobile service

2.2.1 When an RCC is involved with an aeronautical emergency, close co-ordination will be needed between the RCC, the aircraft in distress, and various aeronautical services directly involved with aircraft operations. Some functions described below which are important to RCC duties may be performed by other than RCC personnel, by staff which perform both RCC and other duties, etc., depending upon the circumstances of the RCC and the aircraft in distress.

2.2.2 Frequency bands allocated by ITU for the aeronautical mobile service include some in the high frequency (HF) spectrum (3,000 to 30,000 kHz), the very high frequency (VHF) spectrum (30 to 300 MHz), and the ultra-high frequency (UHF) spectrum (300 to 3,000 MHz).

2.2.3 Initial transmissions of aeronautical distress messages normally are on the frequency being used for en-route communications with the aeronautical stations. SAR facilities proceeding to assist aircraft should establish communications on that frequency. The frequency may be obtained from the controlling surface station; it will normally be used for initial communications and for ensuing communications among the distressed aircraft, assisting aircraft, and controlling surface radio station. Otherwise, when a SAR facility is within radio range of a distressed aircraft, the initial contact frequency would normally be 121.5 MHz for civil aircraft or 243 MHz for military aircraft of some States.

2.2.4 SAR procedures should be initiated if an aircraft or vessel becomes overdue or fails to make a report. For aircraft, this is usually accomplished through an ATS unit or the flight plan system. However, if radar or communications are unexpectedly lost with an instrument flight rules (IFR) or visual flight rules (VFR) aircraft, SAR procedures may be initiated.

2.2.5 Normally, a pilot should not be asked to change frequencies during an emergency without good reason. However, if the aircraft is in a remote location, air traffic facilities based at or near that location may be in a better position to assist. A decision to change a frequency should be based on the circumstances.

2.2.6 If necessary, and if weather and circumstances permit, RCCs may recommend that the aircraft maintains or increases altitude to improve communications, radar, or direction-finding (DF) reception.

2.2.7 ICAO Regional Air Navigation Plans (RANPs) or other regional SAR plans or agreements may provide guidance on selection of appropriate aeronautical frequency bands for SAR. (RANPs and other ICAO documents may be obtained from ICAO.)

VHF communications

2.2.8 The 121.5 MHz VHF AM aeronautical emergency frequency is normally only used for calling or for emergencies. In emergencies, the frequency may be used to provide:

– a clear channel between aircraft in distress and a ground station when normal channels are being used for other aircraft;

– a channel between aircraft and aerodromes not normally used by international air traffic;

– a common channel between aircraft, and between aircraft and surface facilities, involved in SAR operations;

– air-to-ground communications between aircraft and suitably equipped vessels and survival craft;

– air-to-ground communications with aircraft when airborne equipment failure prevents use of regular channels;

– a common channel between civil aircraft and intercepting aircraft or intercept control units, and between civil or intercepting aircraft and an ATS unit, if civil aircraft are intercepted; and

– a means for locating the signal source via land-based or mobile direction-finding.

2.2.9 Where a VHF frequency is needed for a common VHF channel between aircraft, and between aircraft and surface services involved in SAR operations, 123.1 MHz should be used when possible, and 121.5 MHz used if an additional frequency is needed. An ELT, EPIRB or PLB transmitting on 121.5 MHz may make the use of this frequency impractical for communications.

2.2.10 121.5 MHz services are normally available at any aeronautical facility where needed to ensure immediate reception of distress calls. Aerodromes should always monitor 121.5 MHz for voice emergency calls and ELT aural signals (which have a WOW WOW sound from the transmission of two alternating tones).

HF communications

2.2.11 Frequencies 3,023 kHz, 4,125 kHz, and 5,680 kHz may be used for on-scene and SAR co-ordination communications when range dictates need for high frequencies, when use of other frequencies or other factors make these the best frequencies available, or as a means for vessels and aircraft to communicate with each other.

2.3 Maritime radio service

2.3.1 Ships communicate with coast radio stations and with each other on maritime frequencies available in MF, HF and VHF bands. The GMDSS (Global Maritime Distress and Safety System) is mandatory for all SOLAS ships. Volume I, appendix G provides more information on carriage requirements for SOLAS ships.

MF communications

2.3.2 Medium frequencies (MF – 300 to 3,000 kHz), seldom used by aircraft, are commonly used for maritime services.

2.3.3 The frequency 2,182 kHz, an international maritime voice distress and safety frequency, is also available in designated SAR aircraft.

HF communications

2.3.4 A wide range of maritime HF frequencies are allocated, and subdivided for radiotelegraphy and radiotelephony. In certain areas of the world the radiotelephone frequencies 4,125 kHz and 6,215 kHz are designated to supplement the frequency 2,182 kHz for distress and safety purposes. HF radio can be useful in polar regions where geostationary satellite coverage may be limited. Also, HF email capability exists.

VHF communications

2.3.5 The frequency 156.8 MHz FM (channel 16) is the international VHF maritime voice distress, safety, and calling frequency. The frequency 156.3 MHz (channel 06) may be used on scene. AIS transmission from ships provides vessel identity, location and other information which can be useful for SAR purposes.

2.4 Modes of emission

2.4.1 Two radios which operate on a common frequency can usually communicate with each other within range; however, they must also use the same mode of emission. Emission modes are discussed in the ITU Radio Regulations. Different emission modes could prevent an aircraft and ship from communicating directly with each other even if they share a common frequency.

2.5 Global Maritime Distress and Safety System

2.5.1 Ships subject to the Safety of Life at Sea (SOLAS) Convention are obliged to be outfitted with certain communications equipment, collectively referred to as the shipboard portion of the Global Maritime Distress and Safety System (GMDSS). Certain fishing vessels and other marine craft may also carry GMDSS-compatible equipment.

2.5.2 Information on communications equipment which each SOLAS vessel carries should be available to RCCs via ITU publications and databases, if the vessel's flag State promptly informs ITU as required. Otherwise, RCCs may need to seek this data from the flag States, communications service providers, ship reporting system databases, or other sources. The information sources are called SAR data providers (SDPs); all GMDSS equipment should be registered with ITU or other suitable SDP which makes the data readily available to RCCs world-wide to support SAR.

2.5.3 RCC personnel should be familiar with the SOLAS GMDSS provisions, and associated IMO documents. GMDSS takes advantage of available technology to shift alerting emphasis from ship-to-ship (though this can still be done), and towards ship-to-shore, where SAR professionals can help arrange assistance. GMDSS capabilities of vessels not subject to SOLAS range from full compliance with SOLAS to no capabilities at all.

2.5.4 GMDSS-equipped ships can be expected to perform the following functions wherever they operate:

– transmit ship-to-shore distress alerts by two independent means;

– receive shore-to-ship alerts (usually relayed by RCCs); and

- transmit and receive:
  - ship-to-ship alerts;
  - SAR co-ordinating communications;
  - on-scene communications;
  - locating signals;
  - maritime safety information;
  - general radio communications to and from shore; and
  - bridge-to-bridge communications.

2.5.5 Most SOLAS ships can be expected to have at least the following equipment (consult the SOLAS Convention and paragraphs 2.5.6 through 2.5.14 for requirements):

- VHF radiotelephone (channels 6, 13 and 16);
- VHF DSC (channel 70) transmitter and watch receiver;
- SART (radar) and/or AIS–SART;
- NAVTEX receiver;
- EGC if operating outside NAVTEX range; and
- EPIRB, as appropriate.

2.5.6 Channel 6 may be used for communications with vessels for SAR operations. Channel 13 is used for safety of navigation ship-to-ship. Channel 16 is used for distress and safety traffic, and also may be used by aircraft for safety purposes. Channel 70 is used as a digital selective calling (DSC) channel in the maritime mobile service for distress, safety, calling, and reply.

2.5.7 DSC is used for calling and replying, and for transmitting, acknowledging and relaying distress alerts. It allows a specific station to be contacted and made aware that the calling station wishes to communicate with it, and to indicate how to reply, or what station to listen to for subsequent distress traffic. It also can make "all ships" calls. Follow-up communications are made on an appropriate non-DSC frequency. DSC radio users need to understand the basic operation of the radio, how DSC acts as an automated watch, and the importance of registering the radio and keeping it on and tuned to the DSC channel.

2.5.8 SOLAS ships sailing beyond range of a VHF DSC coast radio station must also have an MF DSC (2,187.5 kHz) transmitter and watch receiver. If sailing beyond range of an MF DSC coast radio station, they must have an Inmarsat Ship Earth Station (SES) or an MF/HF DSC transmitter and watch receiver including narrow-band direct printing (NBDP). If operating outside Inmarsat coverage (i.e., in the polar areas), they must have the MF/HF DSC capability.

2.5.9 Narrow-band direct printing (NBDP) is a radio telex system.

2.5.10 A search and rescue radar transponder (SART) interacts with vessel or aircraft radars (9 GHz) for locating survival craft. SART responses show up as a distinctive line of 12 equally spaced blips on compatible radar displays, providing a bearing and range to the SART. A SART is a portable device which should be taken into a lifeboat or liferaft when abandoning ship.

2.5.11 AIS search and rescue transmitter (AIS–SART) is a portable manual deployment survivor-locating device intended for use on liferafts or survival craft and is an alternative to a radar SART. The device sends updated position reports using a standard AIS class A position report. It has a built-in GNSS receiver.

2.5.12 NAVTEX is an NBDP telex system for promulgating safety information which is automatically printed by an on-board NAVTEX receiver. NAVTEX range is generally less than 300 nautical miles from the broadcasting station. NAVTEX receivers are designed to ignore repeated broadcasts they have already received, and to sound an alarm upon receipt of urgent or distress traffic. Users can programme the equipment to receive only the types of information they want to be automatically printed out. All properly formatted NAVTEX messages contain a content indicator in their heading. The printing of certain categories of messages cannot be suppressed regardless of the number of times it is received. NAVTEX receivers are relatively inexpensive; boaters and other seafarers should be encouraged to use them and to leave them turned on when under way.

2.5.13   Enhanced group call (EGC) is part of the Inmarsat system that complements the NAVTEX system to supply SafetyNET and similar services (Inmarsat and SafetyNET are further discussed later in this chapter). SafetyNET is used by SAR, meteorological, and navigation authorities for promulgation of maritime safety information (MSI). Some Inmarsat coast earth stations (CESs) also offer EGC FleetNET services used for fleet management and general information to particular groups of ships; RCCs may find such services useful for certain applications, such as sending messages to a standard list of other RCCs.

2.5.14   GMDSS introduces better communications for certain vessels, but leaves the existing terrestrial system for others; some effects are that SAR authorities must support two maritime mobile systems, and some vessels cannot call each other. For example, if SOLAS ships discontinue watchkeeping on channel 16 in favour of automated technologies, most vessels will still depend on channel 16 for distress, safety, and calling.

2.6   406 MHz distress beacons, EPIRBs and PLBs

2.6.1   Maritime emergency position-indicating radio beacons (EPIRBs) have been accepted into the GMDSS. These beacons operate on 406 MHz and may have a 121.5 MHz final homing signal. The signals are relayed via Cospas–Sarsat satellites, local user terminals (LUTs) and mission control centres (MCCs) to SAR points of contact (SPOCs) which include RCCs.

2.6.2   LUTs are Cospas–Sarsat earth stations. MCCs collect, store, and sort data from LUTs and other MCCs, exchange data within the system, and provide alert messages to the SPOCs, which include points outside the SAR system where no RCC is available.

2.6.3   Cospas–Sarsat also relays alerts from aviation 406 MHz emergency locator transmitters (ELTs), and from 406 MHz personal locator beacons (PLBs). Signals from 121.5 MHz and 243.0 MHz ELTs and EPIRBs may also be relayed by aircraft in flight via an ATS unit, but signals from these beacons are not processed by satellites and are not part of GMDSS. Some national regulations may allow for the 121.5 MHz ELT on domestic flights. This old style ELT depends on other aircraft or airport facilities to detect its aural signal. All 406 MHz distress beacons are electronically similar, the main differences being construction, activating mechanisms and slight differences in coding protocols. While ELTs, EPIRBs and PLBs each have intended user communities, unintended users may activate the devices in an emergency.

2.6.4   Most 406 MHz distress beacons provide a homing capability on 121.5/243/406 MHz; some EPIRBs may also integrate AIS–SARTs into their designs.

2.6.5   Most ELTs, EPIRBs and PLBs provide homing signals on 121.5 MHz; some also use 243 MHz and some EPIRBs may also integrate SARTs into their designs.

2.6.6   Most 406 MHz distress beacons are designed to activate automatically when a vessel sinks or an aircraft crashes (EPIRB alerts tell whether the beacon was activated automatically or manually). PLBs are manually activated. Some PLB users may carry the devices for use aboard aircraft or vessels, though they are not designed to be equivalent to, nor suitable for use as, EPIRBs or ELTs.

2.6.7   Cospas–Sarsat position information is determined using a Doppler plot resulting from relative motion between the ELT or EPIRB signal source and the orbiting satellites. Alert messages provide two positions an equal distance on each side of the satellite track, and a confidence level to help in assessing which one is the correct one. Some initial 406 MHz distress beacon alerts may also have integral Global Navigation Satellite System (GNSS) capabilities. RCCs should consult the appropriate Cospas–Sarsat documentation for more information.

2.6.8 RCCs use the message country codes to direct them to the appropriate States where information can be obtained about the distressed craft from emergency databases (if owners of coded 406 MHz distress beacons properly register the ELTs); 121.5 and 243 MHz beacons are not coded and registered. (The country codes directly correspond to the ITU maritime identity digits (MIDs) used to identify flag States.)

2.6.9 Signals from 406 MHz distress beacons can be stored aboard a satellite and relayed to ground later if no LUT receiver is immediately within view of the satellite, enabling the system to operate in a global mode with fewer LUTs required.

Note: For more information on equipment, performance standards, alert messages, distribution procedures, users instructions, and other Cospas–Sarsat related matters, Cospas–Sarsat Secretariat should be contacted.

2.6.10 Users of 406 MHz distress beacons need to be informed about how to properly install, register, and use this equipment, and what happens when these devices are activated. They should be made to understand that these are the alerting means of last resort, which should not be depended upon to replace two-way communications as the primary means of alerting.

2.7 Satellite communications

2.7.1 Other satellite systems are available which can be used for distress alerting with various degrees of effectiveness, but the primary ones used for SOLAS compliance are Cospas–Sarsat and Inmarsat.

2.7.2 Inmarsat uses satellites in each of the areas listed below. Together the satellites provide coverage along the entire equator between 70° latitude north and south, and serve aeronautical, land, and maritime users.

–   Atlantic Ocean Region – East (AOR-E)

–   Pacific Ocean Region (POR)

–   Indian Ocean Region (IOR)

–   Atlantic Ocean Region – West (AOR-W)

2.7.3 Ocean area access codes for contacting vessels via satellite vary. RCCs must be aware of the telephone and telex access codes (similar in use to international telephone access numbers) appropriate for their service providers.

2.7.4 Inmarsat type-approved ship earth stations (SESs) and aeronautical earth stations (AESs) transmit via the satellites to land earth stations (LESs), also known as coast earth stations (CESs) for maritime functions and ground earth stations (GESs) for aeronautical functions. Each ocean area has at least one Network Co-ordinating Station (NCS) which manages multiple system uses and users.

2.7.5 A variety of Inmarsat equipment may be used by vessels to send distress alerts, each with its own capabilities. Some have a distress button which can send basic pre-formatted automatic data alerts. Most Inmarsat alerts provide position data which has been automatically updated, but some equipment alternatively offers manual updating, which experience has shown to be unreliable.

2.7.6 Inmarsat-B and Fleet 77 SESs can handle distress communications, telephone calls, telex calls (Inmarsat-B only), facsimile, data, and other general services. The Inmarsat-C SES is a message-only transfer terminal; it does not handle voice communications, but it is important because of its EGC capability, relatively low cost to obtain and operate, versatility when coupled with a personal computer, and widespread use. Various types of Inmarsat-C terminals are also used on land by trucks and other mobile units. Other common maritime terminals carry Inmarsat designations such as M, Mini-C, F77, F55 and F33. In addition to its GMDSS-compliant services, Inmarsat provides a distress and urgency voice-calling service via its series of FleetBroadband terminals. These ship earth stations can connect a mobile user directly with a designated RCC depending on the vessel's geographic position. These terminals also provide urgency communication for medical advice, medical assistance and maritime assistance through the use of two-digit SACs.

2.7.7 New satellite systems are emerging which can relay distress alerts. Many vessels are equipped with systems that provide comprehensive online connections to Internet, voice, facsimile and data communications for such functions as online email, short message system (SMS), video conferencing and medical examination and reporting. These commercial satellite systems are not primarily designed for alerting, but may be used for subsequent SAR communications between ships or aircraft and RCCs or RSCs, or as a link to the on-scene co-ordinator.

2.7.8 Portable satellite handsets are available which provide voice and text messaging capabilities. Some of these handsets use GNSS to provide position information, which may be made available to the RCC. These handsets are not normally designed for use in the maritime environment, for example, they may not be waterproof. They are also not GMDSS-compliant.

2.8 Vessel–aircraft communications

2.8.1 Civil vessels and aircraft may need to communicate with each other if either is in an emergency situation or performing SAR services. Since these occasions are infrequent, civil aircraft may be reluctant to carry additional equipment for these purposes; incompatible equipment makes communications difficult.

2.8.2 The aeronautical mobile service uses amplitude modulation (AM) for VHF telephony while the maritime mobile service uses frequency modulation (FM). Except for SRUs, most small vessels normally cannot communicate on 3,023 and 5,680 kHz, or on 121.5 and 123.1 MHz.

2.8.3 The following frequencies may be used between vessels and aircraft when compatible equipment is available.

 (a) *2,182 kHz*. Many vessels, especially fishing vessels, and nearly all ships, are equipped to use 2,182 kHz. Some transport aircraft can transmit on 2,182 kHz, and aircraft designated for maritime SAR operations are required to carry this frequency. Aircraft may have difficulty calling up vessels on 2,182 kHz, as vessels normally guard this frequency through automatic means and are alerted when the MF DSC alarm signal is transmitted.

 (b) *4,125 kHz*. This frequency may be used by aircraft to communicate with ships for distress and safety purposes. All ships may not carry this frequency (most SOLAS ships and many other vessels do). If an aircraft needs help from a ship, SAR authorities can notify ships in the vicinity of the situation and ask them, if practicable, to set up watch on frequency 4,125 kHz.

 (c) *3,023 and 5,680 kHz*. These are HF on-scene radiotelephony frequencies for SAR. Designated SAR aircraft and most civil aircraft carrying HF equipment can operate on these frequencies; they may also be used by vessels (nearly all SOLAS ships) and coast radio stations engaged in co-ordinated SAR operations.

 (d) *121.5 MHz AM*. This is the international aeronautical distress frequency. All designated SAR aircraft and civil aircraft carry equipment operating on 121.5 MHz; it may also be used by maritime craft. Passenger ships must be able to communicate for SAR purposes on this frequency. All aircraft are required to guard this frequency, flight-deck duties and equipment limitations permitting.

 (e) *123.1 MHz AM*. This aeronautical on-scene frequency may be jointly used by aircraft and vessels engaged in SAR operations. Passenger ships must be able to communicate for SAR purposes on this frequency.

 (f) *156.8 MHz FM*. This is the VHF maritime distress and calling frequency (channel 16) carried by most ships; civil aircraft do not normally carry radios that can use this frequency, but some aircraft that regularly fly over water do, usually in portable equipment. Designated SAR aircraft should be able to use this frequency to communicate with vessels in distress and assisting vessels.

2.8.4 Once alerted, RCCs can often help aircraft make arrangements for direct communications with vessels, or provide a message relay. An aircraft in distress over an ocean area can be expected to contact an ATS unit about the situation on the frequency being used for air traffic control purposes. If ditching at sea is likely, the ATS unit will immediately advise the responsible RCC, which can alert ships in a position to assist and arrange an escort aircraft or other appropriate measures.

2.8.5 Regardless of whether the ship or the aircraft needs help, RCCs can sometimes enable communications between them by asking the ship(s) to establish a listening watch on 4,125 kHz if possible, or on 3,023 kHz otherwise. The aircraft will attempt to establish communications on 4,125 kHz, and if unsuccessful will try on 3,023 kHz.

2.8.6 If the threat of ditching subsides, or the vessel no longer needs aid, all alerts must be cancelled immediately.

2.9 Survival and emergency radio equipment

2.9.1 Aeronautical and maritime survival radio equipment also operates on 121.5 MHz, a frequency which can be used for alerting, homing, and on-scene communications, depending on equipment design.

2.9.2 The ultra-high frequency (UHF) 406 MHz is reserved solely as an alerting frequency for ELTs, EPIRBs and PLBs.

2.9.3 2,182 kHz, 121.5 MHz, and 156.8 MHz may be available for use in vessel and aircraft survival craft.

2.9.4 Many civil aircraft world-wide, especially operating on international flights and over ocean areas, carry an ELT which operates on 406 MHz for alerting and 121.5 MHz for final homing. SAR aircraft should be able to home on this frequency to help locate survivors. Many ELTs also provide homing signals on 243 MHz to take advantage of military aircraft capabilities. An increasing number of ELTs use 406 MHz alerting signals with one or both of the other two frequencies used for homing. 406 MHz satellite ELTs offer coded identities and other advantages which can reduce SAR response time by up to several hours over what would be possible with non-coded ELTs.

2.9.5 Passenger ships, regardless of size, and cargo ships of 300 gross tons and over must carry radar transponders operating in the 9 GHz band and have to be outfitted with a radar capable of operating on the 9 GHz band. Ships may carry either a radar transponder(s) and/ or an AIS–SART.

2.9.6 Passenger ships, regardless of size, and cargo ships of 300 gross tons and over must carry at least two portable survival craft VHF transceivers, and cargo ships of 500 gross tons and over must carry at least three. If they operate in the 156–174 MHz band, they will use channel 16 and at least one other channel in this band. Portable DSC equipment can transmit on at least one of the following frequencies: 2,187.5 kHz, 8,414.5 kHz, or channel 70 VHF.

2.9.7 When carried aboard vessels or other craft, EPIRBs can send signals on 406 MHz for alerting and 121.5 and 243 MHz for final homing. EPIRB signals indicate that a distress exists and facilitate location of survivors during SAR operations. For this to be effective, searching craft should be able to home on the signals intended for this purpose, or on the alerting frequency itself (which will be non-continuous if it is 406 MHz).

2.10 Mobile telephones – satellite and cellular

2.10.1 A mobile telephone can be a satellite or cellular telephone. The satellite telephone connects to orbiting satellites and can provide regional or global coverage. Cellular telephones connect to a local terrestrial network of radiocommunications base stations known as cell sites. Many aspects of the guidance below regarding cellular telephones can also apply to the satellite telephone. Cellular telephones work well for point-to-point conversations within range of supporting cellular networks, and some cellular telephones can shift to satellite communications when they are moved outside terrestrial cells. However, these popular, inexpensive, and multi-purpose devices have limitations in emergencies involving SAR in the maritime environment, and, therefore, the advantages of dedicated marine communications systems should continue to be stressed by national administrations. Here are some limitations about which SAR authorities should make cellular telephone users in the aviation and maritime communities aware, so they are less likely to abandon use of radios:

- use of a VHF radio in a distress situation for a MAYDAY call not only alerts SAR personnel, but other vessels, aircraft or stations within range, often enabling faster assistance from a variety of closer potential rescuers;

- the user must know or look up any needed telephone number if they want to use a cellular telephone for that purpose;

- radio signals can be used effectively to help locate survivors using either land or mobile DF equipment, but cellular telephones require close time-consuming co-ordination with service providers to identify the cell from which a call was placed (usually a 10–15 mile radius);

- VHF radios allow receipt of safety advisories, while cellular telephones do not;

- battery-powered cellular telephones are good for only a limited amount of talk time before batteries need to be changed or recharged;

- cellular telephone service providers can deny service to selected cellular telephones without advance notice (e.g., for late payment of fees);

- in disaster areas, cellular systems quickly become saturated with callers, making calls to others in the same area nearly impossible; and

- where installed, cellular phone coverage in the maritime environment can be limited, intermittent, or non-existent, based on several factors to include cellular tower accessibility and orientation in relationship to a cellular telephone call initiated from an offshore or coastal area.

2.10.2 When receiving an alert via cellular telephone, SAR personnel should obtain the following information:

- caller's complete cellular telephone number;
- caller's cellular service provider;
- roam number if needed to recall the user;
- other means of available communications; and
- an alternative point of contact.

2.10.3 The caller might be advised to ensure the phone is left on to receive further communications, or agree on a communications schedule. The caller might also be advised that the cellular number may need to be broadcast if an assistance broadcast is made. (Caution should be used in actually broadcasting the number, since this would enable anyone for any reason to call and tie up communications.)

2.10.4 Cellular service providers may be able to provide some of the following help in finding the position of callers in an emergency:

- call trace to the receiving cell while the call is connected, and an estimate of maximum range from the tower;

- approximate position based on the assessment of signal strength or time difference of arrival to several tower sites or from the cell phone's GNSS-derived positioning obtained either through direct means, in which a call is placed by the cellular user or by dialling the cellular number of the individual in distress (if known), or through indirect means via the phone's standby connectivity to the cellular network (provided the phone is powered on), which can be of particular use in instances where an individual may not be able to place or answer a call;

- cell tower location(s) of the last series of calls placed by the caller (useful for proximity searches), its associated traffic data, if available; and

- notification when a call is made from the user's number (useful in overdue cases).

2.10.5   SAR authorities should make all appropriate arrangements (i.e., legal, logistic, etc.) with cellular service providers in their SRR to obtain the critical information in 2.10.4 in as quick a manner as possible and to establish regulations that require wireless providers to provide this information either through network-based or handset-based (e.g., built-in GNSS receiver) capabilities. Similar arrangements and protocols should also be made with emergency or public safety service agencies so that SAR-related emergencies may be directed to the appropriate SAR authority along with the caller's name, location, and other pertinent information when and where available.

2.10.6   National administrations should consider establishing free of charge, abbreviated telephone numbers to connect callers with emergency or public safety service agencies (e.g., "1-1-2", "9-1-1", "9-9-9") or direct cellular call connection numbers to SAR authorities (e.g., "1-6-1-6" in France and "1-5-3-0" in Italy) in order to provide emergency services and SAR authorities with an expedient means of notification from cell phone users in an emergency, and to publicize this information widely.

2.11   Special circumstances

2.11.1   It helps to have more than one means of communication to account for special circumstances.

2.11.2   Sometimes rescuers on scene must communicate with each other and survivors by unaided voice or portable radios, especially if survivors are entrapped, other emergencies like a fire or oil spill are also being responded to on scene, or large numbers of survivors are being rescued or triaged. For these cases, it may be important to:

–   plan ahead for how responders from different organizations on scene will be able to communicate with each other; and

–   when practicable, keep noisy helicopters and non-essential aircraft away from the immediate site until they are actually needed.

2.11.3   Emergency plans for aerodromes should include guidance on how multi-agency, multi-jurisdictional communications will be managed and carried out when authorities besides those at the airport must respond to an emergency. One suitable all-risk methodology used in some States is called the Incident Command System (section 1.12).

2.12   Communications for SAR operations

2.12.1   RCCs should refer to additional sources of information about the types of equipment and systems used aboard aircraft, vessels, and survival craft, e.g., IMO and ICAO publications, government communication authorities, service providers, equipment manufacturers, and appropriate training institutions.

2.12.2   If they have the capabilities, vessels normally monitor any DSC distress frequency available, as well as MSI (NAVTEX, SafetyNET, etc.) and Inmarsat broadcasts. Most vessels monitor channel 16; when practicable, some ships may discontinue aural radio watches and depend more on alarms to make them aware of incoming distress traffic.

2.12.3   Distress traffic, including critical SAR communications, should be sent using distress priority when possible to help ensure it is noticed and acted upon.

2.13   Communication equipment identities

2.13.1   A mobile station is normally identified by vessel or aircraft radio call sign; a maritime mobile service identity (MMSI) number; or a seven or nine digit identity for Inmarsat terminals. Survival craft radios use the parent craft's call sign followed by two digits (other than 0 or 1 if they immediately follow a letter). Satellite ELTs and EPIRBs are identified by a three–digit MID or country code followed by either a six-digit MMSI number (for EPIRBs), a serial number, or a radio call sign. Country codes should indicate the State where the associated registration data to support SAR operations may be obtained, but may just indicate the flag State if the beacon is not properly registered or coded.

2.13.2 MMSIs are usually assigned by flag State Administrations, and all are supposed to be reported to and published by ITU. MMSI numbers consist of three digits representing the MID, followed by digits indicating the particular vessel. A list of MIDs is available in the ITU Radio Regulations, and a more updated list may be obtained from ITU via the Internet. This can be a useful database when following up a DSC distress alert. MMSIs are also used in the AIS for vessels, base stations, aids to navigation, SAR aircraft and AIS–SARTs. The various platforms can be differentiated by reference to the MMSI format and from databases.

2.14 False alerts

2.14.1 False alerts are any alerts received by the SAR system which indicate an actual or potential distress situation, when no such situation actually exists. The term "false alarm" is sometimes used to distinguish a false alert known to have originated from an equipment source intended to be used for distress alerting. Causes of false alerts include equipment malfunctions, interference, testing, and inadvertent human error. A false alert transmitted deliberately is called a hoax.

2.14.2 It is essential that SAR personnel treat every distress alert as genuine until they know differently.

2.14.3 SAR personnel are often in a unique position to be aware of false alerts and investigate their causes; so it is important that records be kept on the numbers of such alerts and their causes, and that these data be provided to authorities who can use regulation enforcement, improved training or equipment standards, etc., to improve alerting integrity. An unnecessary SAR alert (UNSAR) message sent to appropriate authorities for follow-up can be used to prevent further false alerts.

2.15 SAR data providers

2.15.1 Although some voice and data distress alerts fail to do so, all distress alerts should arrive with suitable identities and position information. Automatic pre-formatted messages should comply with formatting standards and be registered with an appropriate SAR data provider (SDP). Comprehensive, accurate registration databases available on a 24-hour basis can be critical to successful handling of SAR cases, and for identifying vessels using electronic radio identities without having to dispatch a SAR facility.

2.15.2 Perhaps the most important elements of the above information are the emergency contacts on land representing the craft owner or operator. The value of this information is independent of the type of communications involved.

2.15.3 Inmarsat data are available to SAR organizations on a 24-hour basis unless owners have requested an unlisted registration. RCCs must request the data directly from Inmarsat, or from its LESs if the data have been downloaded to them.

2.15.4 406 MHz distress beacon serial identities should only be used by States willing to maintain a comprehensive database accessible to all RCCs on a 24-hour basis, or to make equivalent registration provisions. Cospas–Sarsat databases normally include the types of information discussed above. Cospas–Sarsat provides its International 406 MHz Beacon Registration Database (IBRD) online and free of charge. Each SAR service has access to the IBRD to obtain beacon registration data by means of arrangements made by its Administration's National Point of Contact with Cospas–Sarsat. More details can be found in chapter 4 of the IAMSAR Manual, volume I, *Organization and Management*.

2.15.5 ITU maintains a list of call signs, MMSIs, selective call numbers, owner and operator information, and craft communications capabilities, in its electronically accessible Telecom Information Exchange Services (TIES) database and in published documents. ITU Radio Regulations require States to register MMSI assignments with ITU. ITU information is available by computer using the Internet file transfer protocol (ftp).

2.15.6 The IMO SAR Plan or the GMDSS Master Plan may provide information about how to acquire registration data for various systems, along with the information these documents and ICAO RANPs contain on RCCs and SPOCs. If no other information is available about national databases and SDPs of other nations, RCCs should consult with an RCC in the State concerned to see whether and how the data are available.

2.15.7 Users subject to IMO/ICAO regulation carry, as a minimum, a 406 MHz distress beacon that is compatible with established international Cospas–Sarsat systems and compliant with ICAO and IMO. Non-regulated users may, as a matter of choice, carry other commercially available emergency notification devices.

2.16   RCC and RSC communications

2.16.1 National plans should provide for operational matters to be handled promptly at the RCC level or below in the SAR system, including making and responding to requests for assistance. Advance provisions should be made for rapid co-ordination with other agencies for SAR-related territorial entry if necessary.

2.16.2 Telephone and facsimile capabilities are essential for RCCs and RSCs, but other valuable systems for RCCs and Cospas–Sarsat MCCs are ICAO's Aeronautical Fixed Telecommunications Network (AFTN) and its more modern Aeronautical Telecommunications Network (ATN). These systems can handle message priorities, are among the most reliable links in some areas, and comprise an extensive world-wide network with terminal connections at aviation facilities near most RCCs and RSCs. ICAO has authorized their use for maritime SAR where more suitable resources are unavailable.

2.16.3 Communication links to ARCCs can usually be satisfied by capabilities available to the nearest Flight Information Centre (FIC) or Area Control Centre (ACC). If the ARCC is not co-located with such facilities, additional circuits may be needed to interconnect with them.

2.17   Maritime radio telex

2.17.1 Telex messages may be sent via satellite or terrestrial radio. Radio telex is sometimes called radio teletype (RTT) or narrow-band direct printing (NBDP).

2.17.2 RCCs and RSCs may use radio telex for shore-to-ship distress traffic. Such services should be established and indicated in the ITU *List of Coast Stations*.

2.17.3 Each station having radio telex capabilities is assigned a selective call number in addition to its regular station identity, but MMSI numbers may also be used for radio telex. Selective call numbers for coast stations are four digits, and are listed in the ITU *List of Coast Stations*; selective call numbers for vessels (which normally need to send radio telex via a coast station, due to the equipment required) are listed in the ITU *List of Ship Stations* and have five digits.

2.17.4 NAVTEX is used to promulgate navigation and meteorological warnings and other safety-related information to vessels and may be used by SAR personnel for SAR-related broadcasts.

2.17.5 The World Wide Navigational Warning System (WWNWS) is for long-range NAVAREA warnings and coastal NAVTEX warnings. It provides for globally co-ordinated transmissions by giving NAVAREA Co-ordinator duties to a State for each of 21 NAVAREAs as shown in figure 2-1.

2.17.6 While all WWNWS broadcasts must be in English, additional broadcasts may be made in a second language.

2.17.7 The types of warnings which SAR personnel may send over WWNWS include distress alerts and information about overdue or missing aircraft or vessels. Collectively, these types of alerts, combined with navigation and meteorological warnings, are called maritime safety information (MSI).

2.18   Inmarsat SafetyNET

2.18.1 Inmarsat also can and should be used to broadcast MSI. Every RCC should make arrangements with an associated NAVAREA Co-ordinator or other authority recognized by Inmarsat to make such broadcasts on its behalf over Inmarsat's SafetyNET system. SafetyNET provides an automatic, global method of broadcasting SAR messages to vessels in both fixed and variable geographic areas. SafetyNET broadcasts can be received by vessels equipped either with SafetyNET receivers or Inmarsat-C SESs configured to perform EGC receiver functions.

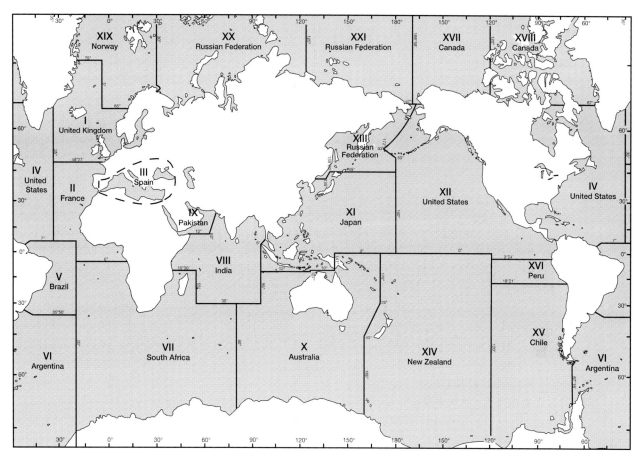

Figure 2-1 – *NAVAREAs*

2.18.2 A SafetyNET Users Manual should be obtained from Inmarsat. This Manual prescribes procedures and exact coding which must be followed for preparing SafetyNET broadcasts, including SAR broadcasts.

2.18.3 It is appropriate and advisable to promulgate distress alerts over both NAVTEX and SafetyNET. All SOLAS ships and many fishing and other vessels sailing within NAVTEX coverage areas can be expected to carry 518 kHz NAVTEX receivers. However, some may carry equipment to receive MSI over SafetyNET in addition to NAVTEX.

2.18.4 Normally, the most practical way to handle SAR broadcasts over SafetyNET is to send them to all vessels within a desired radius of a specified position.

2.18.5 Using an all-ships broadcast to identify a vessel to divert for SAR operations requires time to obtain responses from available vessels, and to select an appropriate one for the task, and may affect quite a few vessels. As a first step it may be prudent to determine whether an appropriate ship can be identified via Amver or another ship reporting system, and contacted. Other factors should be considered, such as the high cost of ship diversions, the likelihood of the alert being false, and the potential proliferation of distress and urgency traffic which sounds bridge alarms. SafetyNET is a reliable, economical and important SAR tool, but it must be used wisely.

2.19 Radio telegraph

2.19.1 Radio telegraph (WT) is a Morse Code service. The basic Morse signals are displayed in appendix A.

2.19.2 WT has been a core part of the maritime mobile service since the early 20th century, and will continue to be voluntarily used into the next century; however, SOLAS vessels are not required to continue use of the service. A key value of this service is that it overcomes language barriers, but it depends upon trained radio operators.

2.20 Phonetic alphabet and figure code

2.20.1 An example of phonetic alphabet and figure code which may be used when speaking or spelling out call signs, names, search area designations, abbreviations, etc., is found in the *International Code of Signals*. There are other versions of the phonetic alphabet which may be used just as effectively.

2.21 Spoken emergency signals and procedural words

2.21.1 There are three spoken emergency signals used by aircraft and vessels:

(a) Distress signal: MAYDAY is used to indicate that a mobile craft is in distress and requires immediate assistance, and has priority over all other communications, for example, when a vessel has a man overboard, the distress signal precedes the distress message.

(b) Urgency signal: PAN-PAN is used when the safety of a mobile craft is in jeopardy or an unsafe situation exists that may eventually involve a need for assistance, and has priority over all but distress traffic.

(c) Safety signal: SÉCURITÉ (pronounced SE-CURE-E-TAY) is used for messages concerning safety of navigation or giving important meteorological warnings.

2.21.2 Any message beginning with one of these signals has precedence over routine messages. The signal is repeated three times at the beginning of the message. The hearer should listen, not transmit during these messages, and assist if possible.

2.21.3 An aircraft commander or vessel captain experiencing a distress situation should declare a distress condition using the MAYDAY signal. However, if these words are not used, and there is any doubt about whether an emergency exists, the hearer should assume it is an actual or potential emergency and obtain enough information to handle the emergency intelligently.

2.21.4 Basic spoken radio procedural words which SAR personnel should understand and use are found in appendix A.

2.22 On-scene communications

2.22.1 Besides equipping SAR aircraft to communicate on the frequencies 2,182 kHz, 3,023 kHz, 4,125 kHz, 5,680 kHz, 121.5 MHz, and 123.1 MHz, some SAR authorities have provided for other communication equipment on scene, such as:

– AIS to detect the AIS search and rescue transmitter (SART) and/or SART-compatible 9 GHz radars for SAR facilities;

– disposable droppable radios operating on 123.1 MHz VHF/AM which can be dropped for survivors to use in communicating with SAR aircraft or SAR vessels on scene; and

– radio installation aboard SRUs which will activate DSC alerts aboard vessels in the vicinity to help establish communications with them more directly.

2.22.2 The means of communication between SAR facilities and the RCC or RSC depends upon local plans and arrangements, and on whether the RCC or RSC is communicating directly or via an alerting post.

2.23 Electronic positioning

2.23.1 While information is often received about the position of a distressed craft when the SAR system is alerted, many alerts are received without positions or with inaccurate ones. Positioning is the determination of the general location or co-ordinates of the scene of the distress, while direction finding or homing is used to help pinpoint the position.

2.23.2 Distress position data are crucial to SAR personnel. Vessels and aircraft use various navigation equipment to determine their own positions, and sometimes this equipment is connected to or integrated with communications equipment to include positions in alert messages automatically. Electronic positioning means include radio beacons used in conjunction with radar, Decca, Loran A, and Loran C.

2.23.3 Bearings from shore can be obtained by shore facilities within range of radio or other electronic signals compatible with DF equipment. Two or more bearings plotted as lines of position (LOPs) can fix the position of an aircraft or vessel by triangulation. Some maritime SAR authorities operate DF services to obtain bearings to channel 16 transmissions. DF equipment can be effectively used whether it is fixed on land or installed aboard SAR facilities.

2.23.4 There are also a variety of satellite systems used for positioning. These systems, Global Navigation Satellite Systems (GNSS), e.g., GLONASS and the Global Positioning System (GPS), are based on a constellation of satellites. They are available for a wide variety of three-dimensional position fixes for military and civilian uses world-wide. Three-dimensional capability and accuracy to within 10 m makes it attractive for aeronautical applications. However, many GNSS-equipped devices are capable of determining positions only to within 100 m accuracy.

2.23.5 Having a very precise GNSS search target position is valuable, but does not alleviate the need for homing capabilities, especially if the SAR facility is not also GNSS-equipped, or if operations take place at night or in other low-visibility conditions.

2.24 Codes, signals and standard phrases

2.24.1 Publications which can be used to assist in overcoming language barriers and communication difficulties between vessel and aircraft crews, survivors, and SAR personnel include the *International Code of Signals,*[*] *International Regulations for Preventing Collisions at Sea*, the *IMO Standard Marine Communication Phrases* (SMCP) (Assembly resolution A.918(22)), Annex 10 to the Convention on International Civil Aviation and PANS-ATM (ICAO Document 4444). These documents should be included in RCC libraries and be understood by the staff, who should be able to comprehend and transmit messages using these phrases. Ships should carry these documents. SRUs should carry the *International Code of Signals*.

2.24.2 These references are all available from IMO and certain speciality bookstores world-wide. Only a few provisions of the references are duplicated in this Manual.

2.24.3 Most ship masters, aircraft pilots, air traffic controllers, SAR personnel, etc., have a working knowledge of the English language. However, they must sometimes communicate with those who cannot speak or understand English, or when voice communications are not possible under the circumstances. In these situations, the Code and the IMO SMCP can be essential.

2.24.4 Signalling means covered in the Code include flags (it contains a colour plate of the international flags and pennants), flashing lights, sound, voice, radio, hand signals, and visual signals. It includes: signalling instructions; general and medical signal codes; distress and lifesaving signals; radiotelephone procedures; national identity signals for vessels and aircraft; and visual signals with which persons in distress can seek assistance and help those responding. Aviation air-to-surface and surface-to-air signals, and ground-to-air visual codes for use by SAR facilities are also included.

2.24.5 The IMO SMCP is intended to improve safety by standardizing phrases. The phrases of the IMO SMCP should be used routinely in preference to words of similar meaning to help their use become common and accepted. The IMO SMCP is based on the English language.

2.24.6 With the decreasing use of Morse Code, the *International Code of Signals* and the IMO SMCP (Assembly resolution A.918(22)) will become increasingly important. It may be of assistance to refer to these documents in international SAR agreements as provisions for use during operations, training, and exercises when SAR facilities of more than one country are co-operating in response to a distress incident.

---

[*] The first draft of the Code of Signals was prepared in 1855. Responsibility for it passed to several organizations until its sponsorship was assumed in 1959 by what is now IMO. ICAO and other Organizations assisted in its development. The Code can be used for almost any means of communication and can overcome language barriers for safety of navigation and during emergencies.

2.24.7   While tools like the Code and IMO SMCP exist, they should not be necessary for verbal communications among SAR personnel and others who should be able to speak English due to the nature of their duties. RCCs should plan to have staff with a working knowledge of English to enable timely and effective communications with aircraft, vessels, and other RCCs.

2.24.8   Where neighbouring States use languages other than English, it is useful to have someone at the RCC or on call capable in those languages too. Advantage can also be taken of the increasing trend of communication service providers to offer translation services on the telephone or even by text translation on the Internet. Confirmation of verbal conversations with facsimile or other written means can reduce misunderstandings, and expedite co-ordination processes.

2.24.9   A few distress signals are provided in appendix A for emphasis or for discussion of visual detectability (RCCs should still be familiar with the references cited above).

2.24.10   IMO–ICAO surface-to-air visual signals and additional visual signals are found in appendix A.

2.25   First RCC

2.25.1   The concept of "first RCC" has been developed to show how an MRCC that receives a distress alert has responsibility to do what it can to acknowledge the alert, and arrange assistance, until it can identify another RCC willing and better able to respond. Section 3.6 provides additional discussion.

2.25.2   This same philosophy is applied when an MRCC receives an HF alert which may have been received by other MRCCs as well, or when other RCCs may have also received an alert from the distressed craft from a different alerting device. Until it is known that another RCC better able to respond has accepted SAR co-ordination duties, any RCC receiving an alert should consider itself to be the "first RCC".

2.26   SAR operations communications

2.26.1   The SAR plan should publish the frequencies available for assignment as control, on-scene, monitor, homing, and public relations channels. Use should be made of any existing communications facilities where practicable and all facilities should be regularly used or tested.

2.26.2   The SMC should select SAR-dedicated frequencies, inform the OSC, ACO or SAR facilities, and establish communications with adjacent RCCs and SAR facility parent agencies as appropriate. If multiple assets are assigned, the OSC should maintain communications with all maritime SAR facilities and the ACO with all aeronautical SAR facilities and both with the SMC; the OSC and ACO would communicate with each other as specified by the SMC. A primary and secondary frequency should be assigned for on-scene communications.

2.26.3   The OSC should be authorized to control communications on scene and ensure that reliable communications are maintained. SAR facilities normally report to the OSC and/or ACO on an assigned frequency. If a frequency shift is carried out, instructions should be provided about what to do if intended communications cannot be re-established on the new frequency. All SRUs should carry a copy of the *International Code of Signals*, which contains communications information internationally recognized by aircraft, vessels, and survivors.

2.27   SAR operations messages

2.27.1   SAR operations messages include situation reports (SITREPs), search action messages, rescue action messages, "all ships" broadcasts, aircraft alerting messages, and other SAR messages. These messages should be unclassified, in plain language, and require no key to interpret. RCCs should establish a standard sample message file, or computer templates and programs, to aid in quickly drafting and releasing the types of messages used regularly.

RCC–RCC distress alert information formats

2.27.2   When an RCC must pass distress alert information to another RCC, there is need for consistency of formats and styles, for all essential information to be provided, and for the information to be easily and clearly understandable. Model formats provided in appendix B have been developed for relay of Inmarsat-C, and DSC distress alerts between RCCs.

RCC Cospas–Sarsat message formats

2.27.3   Standard formats have been developed for RCCs to use in communicating with any MCC of the Cospas–Sarsat system when necessary, and for the transfer of information from the MCC to the RCC. Appendix B contains sample formats for these messages. All Cospas–Sarsat message samples are also available in Cospas–Sarsat document G.007 *Handbook on distress alert messages for RCCs*.

2.27.4   Whenever new communications systems are being developed, or the alert messages of existing systems are being modified, the closer the messages can be made to conform to this standard, the better they will serve the SAR system.

Situation report

2.27.5   The OSC and/or ACO uses a situation report (SITREP) to keep the SMC informed of on-scene mission progress and conditions, and normally addresses SITREPs only to the SMC unless otherwise directed. The SMC uses SITREPs to keep superiors, other RCCs and RSCs, and any other interested agencies informed of mission progress. For cases where pollution or threat of pollution exists as the result of the casualty, the appropriate agency tasked with environmental protection should be an information addressee on all SITREPs.

2.27.6   Often a short SITREP is used to provide the earliest notice of a casualty or to pass urgent details when using the SITREP to request assistance. A full SITREP is used to pass amplifying information during SAR operations, or to inform SAR authorities of the home State of the craft in distress.

2.27.7   Initial SITREPs should be transmitted as soon as details of an incident become clear enough to indicate SAR system involvement, and should not be delayed unnecessarily for confirmation of all details. Further SITREPs should be issued as soon as other relevant information is obtained. Information already passed should not be repeated. During prolonged operations, "no change" SITREPs should be issued at intervals of about three hours to reassure recipients that nothing has been missed. When the incident is concluded, a final SITREP should be issued as confirmation.

2.27.8   While SITREP format is usually established by agency directives, the standard format shown in appendix I should be used for international communications between RCCs. Each SITREP concerning the same casualty should be numbered sequentially.

2.27.9   Regardless of format, SITREPs usually provide the following information:

(a)   *Identification:* usually in the subject line, the SITREP number, identification of the craft, and a one- or two-word description of the emergency. The perceived phase of the emergency should be indicated. SITREPs should be numbered sequentially throughout the case. When an OSC and/or ACO is relieved on scene, the new OSC and/or ACO should continue the SITREP numbering sequence.

(b)   *Situation:* a description of the case, the conditions that affect the case, and any amplifying information that will clarify the problem. After the first SITREP, only changes to the original reported situation need be included.

(c)   *Action taken:* a report of all action taken since the last report, including results of such action. When an unsuccessful search has been conducted, the report includes the areas searched, a measure of effort such as sorties flown or hours searched, and the coverage factor.

(d)   *Future plans:* a description of actions planned for future execution, including any recommendations and, if necessary, a request for additional assistance.

(e)   *Status of case:* this is used only on the final SITREP to indicate that the case is closed or that search is suspended pending further developments.

2.27.10 The SMC should develop a search action plan and a rescue action plan as appropriate. In some situations these plans may be combined into one message.

Search action message

2.27.11 After a search action plan is developed as discussed in section 5.13, it is provided to the OSC and/ or ACO and SAR facilities on scene in a search action message. Potential parts of the message are given below. Appendix L contains an example.

2.27.12 The message should include a summary of the on-scene situation, including the nature of the emergency, the last known position, search target description, types of detection aids and survival equipment which survivors may have, present and forecast weather, and SAR facilities on scene.

2.27.13 The message should include a listing of the search area(s) and sub-areas that can be searched by the SAR facilities in the allotted time.

2.27.14 The message should assign primary and secondary control channels, on-scene, monitor and press channels, and special radio procedures, schedules, or relevant communication factors.

2.27.15 It is better to release the message early. If a "first light" search is being planned, parent agencies providing SAR facilities should typically receive the message at least six hours before departure time. The message can always be expanded or amended later.

2.27.16 The message normally includes six parts:

    (a) *Situation:* includes a brief description of the incident, position, and time; number of persons on board (POBs); primary and secondary search targets, including the amount and types of survival equipment; weather forecast and period of forecast; and SAR facilities on scene.

    (b) *Search area(s):* presented in column format with headings for area, size, corner points, other essential data.

    (c) *Execution:* presented in column format with headings for area, SAR facility, parent agency, pattern, creep direction, commence search points, and altitude.

    (d) *Co-ordination:* designates the SMC, OSC and ACO; SAR facilities on-scene times; track spacings and coverage factors desired; OSC instructions, e.g., on use of datum marker buoys; airspace reservations; temporary sea exclusion zones; aircraft safety instructions; SAR facility change of operational control information if pertinent; parent agency relief instructions; and authorizations for non-SAR aircraft in the area.

    (e) *Communications:* prescribes control channels; on-scene channels; monitor channels; SAR vessel electronic identification; and press channels.

    (f) *Reports:* requirements for OSC reports of on-scene weather, progress and other SITREP information; and for parent agencies to provide at the end of daily operations, e.g., sorties, hours flown, area(s) searched, and coverage factor(s).

Rescue action message

2.27.17 In conjunction with the search action plan, the SMC may then develop a rescue action plan. It is provided to the OSC, ACO and SAR facilities on scene in a rescue action message. Potential parts of the message, similar to those for a search action message, are noted below.

    (a) *Situation:* includes a brief description of the incident; number of persons requiring rescue; extent of injuries; amount and type of survival equipment; weather forecast and period for forecast; and SAR facilities on scene.

    (b) *Rescue area:* describes the position of the incident by proper name of the area and latitude and longitude, or by bearing from a known geographical point; and access routes to be followed by SAR facilities.

(c) *Execution:* gives SAR facilities assigned, including facility call sign and parent agencies providing the SAR facilities; rescue method to be attempted; aerial delivery of supplies or other supporting equipment to SAR facilities and SMC supportive arrangements.

(d) *Co-ordination:* designates the SMC, OSC and ACO; on-scene rendezvous time for SAR facilities; SAR facility change of operational control instructions; parent agency relief instructions; temporary flight restrictions; and authorization for non-SAR aircraft in the area.

(e) *Communications:* prescribes control and on-scene channels; call signs of aircraft assigned high-altitude communications relay duties; and any other relevant communications information.

(f) *Reports:* discusses required OSC reports to the SMC and parent activity reports.

2.27.18 The example search action message in appendix L also generally shows how the rescue action message should be formatted for the information just discussed.

Communication searches

2.27.19 SMCs conduct communication searches when facts are needed to supplement initially reported information. Efforts are continued to contact the craft, to find out more about a possible distress situation, and to prepare for or to avoid a search effort. Section 3.5 has more information on communication searches.

MEDICO Communications

2.27.20 The ITU *List of Radiodetermination and Special Service Stations* lists commercial and Government radio stations that provide free medical message service to ships. These messages should be prefixed with "DH MEDICO." These messages are normally delivered to RCCs, hospitals or other facilities with which the communications facility has made prior arrangements.

2.27.21 Since SAR services include provision of medical advice and medical evacuations, and since relayed requests for medical advice is an indicator of potential need for a medical evacuation, SAR services and communications facilities used for SAR should support and monitor such communications and offer these services free of charge.

2.27.22 SAR services may provide medical advice either with its own doctors or via a TMAS. (Such doctors should be trained regarding the inherent risks associated with medical emergencies at sea and with medical evacuations, so that these factors can be taken into account in recommendations for treatment or evacuation. However, the final decision about whether it is safe to conduct an evacuation rests with the person in command of the rescue facility tasked with conducting the evacuation.)

2.27.23 There are several enterprises in some States which provide subscription and pay-per-use medical advice to vessels at sea. However, perhaps the best known TMAS is Centro Internazionale Radio-Medico (CIRM) in Rome, Italy.

2.27.24 Good communications are essential for an effective telemedical assistance service. Telemedical communications are considered to be safety or urgency communications and as such should have priority over routine traffic and normally be free of charge to the mariner.

2.27.25 The ship's captain, who is responsible for treatment on board, must be able to access the TMAS of his choice. Choice may be based on his nationality, the ship's flag and, especially, the language spoken.

2.27.26 Recording of the date and time of all TMAS communications and archiving of secure tape will enable essential data to be preserved should they be required in the event of legal proceedings. All recorded information is subject to medical privacy in the same way as the content of a medical file.

2.27.27 Voice communication is the basis of telemedical advice. It allows free dialogue and contributes to the human relationship, which is crucial to any medical consultation. Text messages are a useful complement to the voice telemedical advice and add the reliability of writing. Facsimile allows the exchange of pictures or diagrams, which help to identify a symptom, describe a lesion or the method of treatment. Digital data transmissions (photographs or electrocardiogram) provide an objective and potentially crucial addition to descriptive and subjective clinical data.

2.27.28   Given the international dimension of maritime navigation, a medical problem may occur on board a ship far from its country of origin. In such a case, the master will normally call his national TMAS, which can perform a telemedical consultation in his language. Should there be a need, following the consultation, for an evacuation to the nearest shore, the master will normally contact the MRCC responsible for the search and rescue region involved.

2.27.29   In order to facilitate and enhance planning of the medical aspects of the evacuation, all available medical information collected by the first-contacted TMAS should be transferred to the TMAS attached to the responsible MRCC. This is to avoid any additional teleconsultation by the second TMAS. A "Medical Assistance at Sea, TMAS – TMAS Medical Information Exchange Form" can be used for this purpose. See appendix R.

2.27.30   Communication between the ship and TMAS can be established via coast radio stations using VHF, MF or HF radio. Inmarsat satellite communications can be accessed by use of special access codes (SAC) 32 for medical advice and 38 for medical assistance or MEDEVAC. Inmarsat Land Earth Stations (LES) normally route SAC 32 direct to a TMAS and SAC 38 to the associated RCC. Inmarsat can support voice and telex (telex only for Inmarsat-C).

Commercial device notification (non-Cospas–Sarsat) messages

2.27.31   When a commercial locating, tracking and emergency notification service provider (non-Cospas–Sarsat) must pass distress alert information to an RCC, there is need for consistency of formats and styles, for all essential information to be provided, and for the information to be easily and clearly understandable. Model formats provided in appendix B have been developed for relay of alerts between commercial providers and RCCs.

2.28   GMDSS Master Plan

2.28.1   Regulation 5 of chapter IV of the 1988 Amendments to the SOLAS Convention requires that every Contracting Government provide to IMO information on its shore-based facilities to support ships carrying GMDSS communications equipment off its coasts. IMO collects and publishes this information in an indispensable reference for RCCs; its short name is the GMDSS Master Plan.

2.28.2   An up-to-date copy of this Plan should be acquired as a reference for all aeronautical and maritime RCCs, communications facilities, ships, and maritime training institutes.

2.28.3   The GMDSS Master Plan shows for every country: the status of its VHF, MF, and HF DSC installations; its Inmarsat, SafetyNET, NAVTEX, and HF NBDP services; its satellite EPIRB registration information, MCCs, and LUTs; and which RCCs are using SESs. This information is given in list form and on maps, and distinguishes between operational and planned facilities.

2.29   Supplemental capabilities

2.29.1   Instant-replay recording equipment to record aeronautical or maritime voice communications can help document and verify information, and make it readily available for future reference and for other RCC or RSC watchstanders to hear. This is especially valuable for radio communications.

2.29.2   Telephone equipment like answering machines, voice mail, call forwarding, automatic speed dialling and re-dialling, and caller identification can perform tasks which include the following: record announcements, invite the caller to leave a message, improve the chances that an incoming call will be successfully received, save time, and reduce errors. These labour-saving devices are a convenience to the caller if the RCC staff cannot answer the call immediately due to other calls or duties, but are no substitute for 24-hour watchstanding.

2.29.3   Caller identification is an especially valuable feature for any emergency organization to have on the receiving telephone, though it is not yet available world-wide.

2.30 Difficulties in contacting vessels

2.30.1 Even with modern communications, SAR authorities sometimes have difficulty contacting vessels to verify a distress situation or seek assistance. Reliable shore-to-ship communications is of great importance in providing timely assistance.

2.30.2 Under long-standing traditions of the sea and various provision of international law, ship masters are obligated to assist others in distress at sea whenever they can safely do so.

2.30.3 Whenever problems exist which may contribute to difficulties in contacting vessels, they must be identified and resolved if possible. When SAR authorities experience such a difficulty, some constructive steps they may directly or indirectly take to address the matter include:

– contact vessel owners or operators for an explanation if a vessel which is fitted with GMDSS equipment does not respond to calls from SAR authorities ashore;

– if an explanation for failure to respond to calls from SAR authorities seems insufficient or suggestive of other problems, arrange a compliance inspection, or notify the vessel's owner and Administration of registry for corrective actions;

– use regulations to require all vessels which carry GMDSS equipment to maintain appropriate GMDSS watches, and ensure that appropriate regulatory authorities attempt to enforce the regulations;

– develop a national maritime education, information, and follow-up programme to ensure that responsible authorities, manufacturers, training institutes, shipping officials, and GMDSS service providers know, understand, and properly implement requirements for distress and safety communications and assisting persons in distress;

– provide guidance to vessels on the importance of equipment registration, of proper watch-standing, of avoiding false alerts, and of following up to cancel any inadvertent alerts;

– review broadcast practices to minimize excessive use of messages which cause audible alarms to sound on ship bridges, of message categories which cannot be suppressed by the ship, of unnecessary duplication of MSI to the same ocean areas, or of transmission to an unnecessarily large area or number of vessels; and

– ensure that SAR personnel have ready access to suitable GMDSS databases to support SAR, and access to use of DSC shore stations domestically or through co-operative arrangements with neighbouring States or assisting vessels.

2.31 Unbarring of Inmarsat SESs by RCCs

2.31.1 Inmarsat sometimes finds it necessary to bar a vessel's SES from transmitting and receiving communications. In such cases, the SES can still be used by vessels to send distress alerts or make distress calls. In the case of an emergency, an RCC will initially attempt to contact the vessel to ascertain whether the distress alert is real or inadvertent. If the RCC is unable to communicate with the vessel, they will then check its status in the MRCC Database. Mandatory or discretionary barring will prevent communications with the vessel. The RCC may then call its associated LES, to confirm the barring status of the terminal. The LES will verify the status by referring to the appropriate tables (barring/authorization, etc.). If the terminal status is confirmed as barred, the RCC will then request the LES to unbar the terminal so that communications with the vessel can be established. If the RCC is unable to communicate with the LES, or requires the terminal to be unbarred by more than one LES, it should contact Inmarsat Customer Services or Inmarsat Network Operations Centre (NOC), or both.

2.31.2 Any RCC that is not associated with an Inmarsat LES may not know through which LES it is attempting to communicate with a vessel. There can be a number of reasons why a non-associated RCC is unable to communicate with the vessel, including barring of the vessel or local/national telecommunication issues. If local/national telecommunication issues are not relevant and barring is suspected, the RCC should first try to contact the vessel via an Inmarsat associated RCC, who will be able to arrange for the barring to be lifted. Alternatively, the non-associated RCC may contact either Inmarsat Customer Services or Inmarsat NOC (or both) which operate on a 24-hour basis. Inmarsat will check its Electronic Service Activation System (ESAS) for the correct status of the terminal, i.e., active, barred, etc. If the terminal is found to be active and not barred, Inmarsat will assist the RCC by providing any other information or advice as requested.

2.31.3 Additionally, vessels equipped with Voice Distress-enabled FleetBroadband terminals may be similarly barred. However, LESs will be unable to assist in these cases and the RCC should contact either the Inmarsat Customer Services which operates on a 24-hour basis or the Network Operations Centre (NOC), which also operates on a 24-hour basis, who will be able to arrange the necessary unbarring.

2.31.4 When the distress situation is resolved, the RCC should inform the LES(s) and either the Inmarsat Customer Services or the NOC, at the earliest opportunity, to reinstate the barring on the terminal.

2.32 Radio call signs for aircraft involved in a search and rescue operation

2.32.1 A prefix call sign makes the task/function of a specific aircraft easier to be understood by other aircraft and participating units in the same area.

2.32.2 The prefix call sign can also give the aircraft priority in some situations.

2.32.3 State authority responsible for air regulation shall arrange that use of prefix call sign will coincide with other national air regulations.

2.32.4 During search and rescue missions and exercises it is recommended that the following prefix call signs be used before the ordinary radio call sign or as a specific mission call sign.

"RESCUE"	for all airborne units involved in a rescue mission
"AIR CO-ORDINATOR"	for the aircraft co-ordinator (ACO)
"SAREX"	for all airborne units involved in international/national exercises

2.33 Vessel tracking communications

2.33.1 Various forms of communication can be used for vessel tracking. Ship reporting systems can use voice reporting over VHF and HF, DSC and Inmarsat. Many ship reporting systems use Inmarsat-C polling or Inmarsat automated position reporting (APR). AIS uses a time-division multiple access (TDMA) scheme to share the VHF frequency, also known as the VHF Data Link (VDL). There are two dedicated frequencies used for AIS: AIS 1 (161.975 MHz) and AIS 2 (162.025 MHz). LRIT can employ any form of communication which meets the required functional specification, but most vessels use Inmarsat equipment to report every six hours to their data centre via a communications provider and application service provider. Vessel monitoring systems (VMS) can use various systems for tracking, including Inmarsat, Iridium and Argos.

Chapter 3

Awareness and initial action

3.1 General

3.1.1 When the SAR system first becomes aware of an actual or potential emergency, the information collected and the initial action taken are often critical to successful SAR operations. It must be assumed that in each incident there are survivors who will need assistance and whose chances of survival are reduced by the passage of time. The success of a SAR operation depends on the speed with which the operation is planned and carried out. Information must be gathered and evaluated to determine the nature of the distress, the appropriate emergency phase, and what action should be taken. Prompt receipt of all available information by the RCC or RSC is necessary for thorough evaluation, immediate decision on the best course of action, and a timely activation of SAR facilities to make it possible to:

– locate, support and rescue persons in distress in the shortest possible time; and

– use any contribution survivors may still be able to make towards their own rescue while they are still capable of doing so.

3.1.2 Experience has shown that the chances for survival of injured persons decrease by as much as 80% during the first 24 h, and that those for uninjured persons diminish rapidly after the first three days. Following an accident, even uninjured persons who are apparently able-bodied and capable of rational thought are often unable to accomplish simple tasks, and are known to have hindered, delayed or even prevented their own rescue.

3.1.3 This chapter introduces the five stages of a SAR response, describes in detail the three emergency phases of a SAR incident, discusses the first two SAR stages in detail (the remaining three stages are covered later in this volume), describes designation of the RCC or RSC responsible for initiating SAR action, and provides some general SMC considerations.

3.2 SAR stages

3.2.1 The response to a SAR incident usually proceeds through a sequence of five stages. These stages are groups of activities typically performed by the SAR system in responding to a SAR incident from the time the system becomes aware of the incident until its response to the incident is concluded. The response to a particular SAR incident may not require the performance of every stage. For some incidents, the activities of one stage may overlap the activities of another stage such that portions of two or more stages are being performed simultaneously. The five SAR stages are described below.

(a) *Awareness.* Knowledge by any person or agency in the SAR system that an emergency situation exists or may exist.

(b) *Initial action.* Preliminary action taken to alert SAR facilities and obtain more information. This stage may include evaluation and classification of the information, alerting of SAR facilities, communication checks, and, in urgent situations, immediate performance of appropriate activities from other stages.

(c) *Planning.* The development of operational plans, including plans for search, rescue, and final delivery of survivors to medical facilities or other places of safety as appropriate.

(d) *Operations.* Dispatching SAR facilities to the scene, conducting searches, rescuing survivors, assisting distressed craft, providing necessary emergency care for survivors, and delivering casualties to medical facilities.

(e) *Conclusion.* Return of SRUs to a location where they are debriefed, refuelled, replenished, and prepared for other missions, return of other SAR facilities to their normal activities, and completion of all required documentation.

3.2.2 This chapter discusses the first two stages, awareness and initial action. These stages can be associated with any or all three of the emergency phases of uncertainty, alert and distress which are discussed below.

3.3 Emergency phases

3.3.1 Emergency phases are based on the level of concern for the safety of persons or craft which may be in danger. Upon initial notification, a SAR incident is classified by the notified RCC, RSC, or air traffic services (ATS) unit as being in one of three emergency phases: uncertainty, alert or distress. The emergency phase may be reclassified by the SMC as the situation develops. The current emergency phase should be used in all communications about the SAR incident as a means of informing all interested parties of the current level of concern for the safety of persons or craft which may be in need of assistance.

Uncertainty phase

3.3.2 An uncertainty phase is said to exist when there is knowledge of a situation that may need to be monitored, or to have more information gathered, but that does not require dispatching of resources. When there is doubt about the safety of an aircraft, ship, or other craft or persons on board, or it is overdue, the situation should be investigated and information gathered. A communications search may begin during this phase. An uncertainty phase is declared when there is doubt regarding the safety of an aircraft, ship, or other craft, or persons on board. For aircraft, an uncertainty phase is declared when:

(a) no communication has been received from an aircraft within a period of thirty minutes after the time a communication should have been received, or from the time an unsuccessful attempt to establish communication with such aircraft was first made, whichever is the earlier; or,

(b) an aircraft fails to arrive within thirty minutes of the last estimated time of arrival (ETA) last notified to or estimated by air traffic services (ATS) units, whichever is the later, except when no doubt exists as to the safety of the aircraft and its occupants.

For ships or other craft, an uncertainty phase is declared when it has:

(a) been reported overdue at its intended destination; or

(b) failed to make an expected position safety report.

Alert phase

3.3.3 An alert phase exists when an aircraft, ship, or other craft or persons on board are having some difficulty and may need assistance, but are not in immediate danger. Apprehension is usually associated with the alert phase, but there is no known threat requiring immediate action. SRUs may be dispatched or other SAR facilities diverted to provide assistance if it is believed that conditions might worsen or that SAR facilities might not be available or able to provide assistance if conditions did worsen at a later time. For overdue craft, the alert phase is considered when there is a continued lack of information concerning the progress or position of a craft. SAR resources should begin or continue communications searches, and the dispatch of SRUs to investigate high-probability locations or overfly the craft's intended route should be considered. Vessels and aircraft passing through areas where the concerned craft might be located should be asked to maintain a sharp lookout, report all sightings and render assistance if needed. An alert phase is declared when:

(a) following the uncertainty phase, subsequent attempts to establish communication with the aircraft, ship, or other craft have failed, or inquiries to other relevant sources have failed, to reveal any news of that craft;

(b) an aircraft has been cleared to land and fails to land within five minutes of the estimated time of landing and communication has not been re-established with the aircraft;

(c) information has been received which indicates that the operating efficiency of the aircraft, ship or other craft has been impaired, but not to the extent that a forced landing or distress situation is likely, except when evidence exists that would allay apprehension as to the safety of that craft and its occupants;

(d) an aircraft is known or believed to be the subject of unlawful interference; or

(e) a ship is under attack or threat of attack from pirates or armed robbers.

Distress phase

3.3.4 The distress phase exists when there is reasonable certainty that an aircraft, ship, or other craft or persons on board is in danger and requires immediate assistance. For overdue craft, a distress exists when communications searches and other forms of investigation have not succeeded in locating the craft or revising its ETA so that it is no longer considered overdue. If there is sufficient concern for the safety of a craft and the persons aboard to justify search operations, the incident should be classified as being in the distress phase. For aircraft, a distress phase is declared when:

(a) following the alert phase, the further unsuccessful attempts to establish communication with the aircraft and more widespread unsuccessful inquiries point to the probability that the aircraft is in distress;

(b) the fuel on board is considered to be exhausted, or to be insufficient to enable the aircraft to reach safety;

(c) information is received which indicates that the operating efficiency of the aircraft has been impaired to the extent that a forced landing is likely;

(d) information is received or it is reasonably certain that the aircraft is about to make or has made a forced landing, except when there is reasonable certainty that the aircraft and its occupants do not require immediate assistance; or

(e) a downed aircraft is inadvertently located as the result of a sighting or of homing on an ELT transmission.

3.3.5 For ships or other craft, a distress phase is declared when:

(a) positive information is received that a ship or other craft or a person on board is in danger and needs immediate assistance;

(b) following the alert phase, further unsuccessful attempts to establish contact with the ship or other craft and more widespread unsuccessful inquiries point to the probability that the ship or craft is in distress; or

(c) information is received which indicates that the operating efficiency of the ship or other craft has been impaired to the extent that a distress situation is likely.

3.3.6 Checklists are helpful in gathering information and listing the actions to be taken by the RCC or RSC. The Uncertainty phase checklist can be found in appendix D, the Alert phase checklist in appendix E, and the Distress phase checklist in appendix F.

3.4 Awareness stage

3.4.1 The SAR system's first notification of an actual or potential SAR incident initiates the awareness stage. Persons or craft in difficulty may report a problem, alerting posts may receive information, nearby personnel may observe an incident, or an uncertainty may exist due to lack of communication or to non-arrival. Anyone who becomes aware of an actual or potential SAR incident should report it immediately to the appropriate RCC or RSC if known, or to the nearest RCC or RSC otherwise. If an SRU receives the information, it should also respond to the incident as appropriate.

3.4.2 All reports concerning an incident which are received before and during a SAR operation must be carefully evaluated to determine their validity, the urgency for action, and the extent of the operation required. The evaluation must be thorough, decisions must be made, and action taken as quickly as possible. If confirmation of uncertain information cannot be obtained without undue delay, the RCC should act on a doubtful message rather than wait for verification. Reports of overdue craft present particular evaluation challenges.

(a) *Communication delays.* In some areas of the world, communication delays may prevent timely reports of positions and arrivals. Trends in delays should be kept in mind by the RCC or RSC when estimating the significance of a report to prevent unnecessary alerts of the SAR services.

(b) *Weather conditions.* Adverse weather may contribute to communication delays or deviations from flight or voyage plans.

(c) *Habits of the pilot or captain (if known).* Some pilots in command or masters of vessels are known to react in a certain manner in certain circumstances. Knowledge of their habits, including preferred routeings, may provide guidance in the evaluation of an incident and the subsequent planning and execution of search operations.

3.4.3 *Air Traffic Services Units.* ATS units receive information on most aircraft flights and are periodically in contact with them. Most of this information will come from aircraft reporting directly to ATS units. An aircraft emergency and its development is therefore likely to come to their notice first. It is for these reasons that each ATS unit:

– provides alerting services to all aircraft flights known to it; and

– area control centres and flight information centres serve as a collecting point for all information concerning an aircraft emergency within its flight information region (FIR).

3.4.4 An ATS unit will usually notify its associated RCC when an aircraft is actually or likely in a state of emergency. However, when the nature of the emergency is such that local rescue facilities can deal with it, such as when an incident occurs at or near an aerodrome, the RCC may not be informed. The notification from an ATS unit to an RCC will contain information, if available, in the order listed below.

– UNCERTAINTY, ALERT or DISTRESS as appropriate to the phase of emergency

– Agency and person calling;

– Nature of the emergency;

– Significant information from the flight plan:

– A/C call sign and type;

– point of departure and departure time;

– route of flight;

– destination and ETA;

– number of persons on board;

– endurance;

– colour and distinctive markings;

– survival equipment carried;

- dangerous goods;
- telephone number of pilot in command;

- Unit which made last contact, time, and frequency used;
- Last position report and how the position was determined (course, speed, altitude);
- Any action taken by the reporting office;
- Any direction finder equipment available; and
- Other information.

An MRCC may also request an ATS unit to provide the above information in the case of an aeronautical incident at sea. The MRCC should communicate first with a local ATS unit, such as an aerodrome tower. An ARCC, a Flight Information Centre (FIC) or an area control centre (ACC) may also have relevant information, or may be able to assist with investigations using aeronautical communications and resources.

3.4.5 *Coast Radio Stations (CRS).* When a CRS receives the first information that a maritime craft is in distress, it is required by international regulations to relay this information to the SAR authorities. An RCC or RSC will often receive first notification that a ship or other craft is in distress from a CRS with which it is associated. The notification from a CRS to an RCC or RSC will contain, if available, the following information.

- Name and call sign (or ship station identity) of the ship or craft;
- Nature of the emergency;
- Type of assistance needed;
- Time of communication with the ship or craft;
- Position or last known position of the ship or craft;
- Description of the ship or craft;
- Intentions of the captain;
- Number of POB if known; and
- Other information.

3.4.6 *Notification by other sources.* All persons are encouraged to report any abnormal occurrence they have witnessed or heard about. Notification that an aircraft has crashed, or an aircraft, ship, or other craft is overdue or in a state of emergency, may therefore reach an RCC from any source, either directly or relayed through an alerting post.

3.4.7 A record of events should be maintained by the RCC.

(a) The RCC should open a log for each incident to record all information as it is received, either in full or by reference to other permanent records such as separate reports, forms, folders, charts, telegrams, recorded radio frequencies and telephones, and recorded radar data.

(b) The initial notification should be entered on a standard Incident Processing Form. This form should be available at RCCs, RSCs, ATS units, and other alerting posts as necessary. It is used to obtain the important information at first contact since it may be impossible or too time-consuming to obtain such information later. Its use will prevent the loss of details. The form lists the occupation and address of the reporting source to help assess the reliability of the report and for obtaining additional information.

3.4.8 After evaluating all available information and if an emergency phase is declared, the RCC or RSC should immediately inform all appropriate authorities, centres, services, or facilities. When more than one RCC may have received the distress alert, the RCCs should quickly co-ordinate and each should advise the other of the action it has taken on the alert. This can be done by any practical means, including Inmarsat FleetNET and Inmarsat–C service, or ICAO's AFTN. This especially applies to an initial Cospas–Sarsat alert where the A and B positions can be in different SRRs.

3.5 Initial action stage

3.5.1 The initial action stage is when the SAR system begins response, although some activities, such as evaluation, may begin during the preceding awareness stage and continue through all stages. Initial action may include SMC designation, incident evaluation, emergency phase classification, SAR resources alert, and communication searches. Since no two SAR operations follow exactly the same pattern, it is not possible to develop comprehensive procedures that apply at all times. Basic procedures, as outlined below, may be adopted for each phase of emergency. These procedures should be interpreted with flexibility as many of the actions described may be performed simultaneously or in a different order to suit specific circumstances.

Uncertainty phase initial actions

3.5.2 When an uncertainty phase has been declared by the RCC, RSC, or ATS unit, the RCC or RSC should:

(a) Immediately appoint a SAR mission co-ordinator (SMC) and inform appropriate SAR authorities, centres, services, and facilities of this action. The identity of the RCC or RSC where SMC functions are being performed for an incident should never be in doubt. One RCC or RSC may request another to assume the role of SMC whenever such a change will aid the response effort. (See also the discussions of "First RCC" in section 3.6 and SMC considerations in section 3.8.)

(b) Verify the information received, if necessary and if it does not cause undue delay.

(c) When no flight plan has been filed or, in the case of ships or other craft, no information is available on the intentions of the captain, attempt to obtain information from which the route and times of departures and arrivals of the aircraft, ship, or other craft may be reconstructed.

(d) Maintain close liaison with the appropriate ATS or CRS facility, so that:

– new information (such as that obtained through a communication search, verification of flight plan, or review of weather information passed to the pilot before and during the flight) will be available immediately for evaluation, plotting, decision-making, etc.; and

– duplication of action will be avoided.

(e) Plot the actual track of the craft involved, as far as it is known, and the intended or estimated track beyond that point, making use of all relevant information.

(f) Conduct a communication search.

(g) For ships or other craft, send an Urgency broadcast via NAVTEX and SafetyNET requesting ships to keep a lookout by all means available for missing or overdue ships or other craft.

3.5.3 The communication search can be conducted by two primary methods.

(a) Attempt to communicate with the aircraft, ship, or other craft by all available means.

(b) Determine its most probable location by:

– making inquiries at aerodromes (including the aerodrome of departure) and other locations where an aircraft might have landed or at locations where a ship or other craft might have stopped or called (including the point or port of departure); and

– contacting other appropriate sources, e.g., aircraft known or believed to be on the same route or within communication range, vessels at sea which may have sighted the ship or craft, ship reporting and vessel tracking systems that may provide SURPICs, and other persons who have knowledge of the intentions of the pilot in command or ship's captain, such as the craft's operating authority.

3.5.4   When the communication search or other information received indicates that the aircraft, ship, or other craft is not in distress, the RCC will close the incident and immediately inform the operating agency, the reporting source, and any alerted authorities, centres, services, or facilities. However, if apprehension regarding the safety of the aircraft and its occupants continues, the uncertainty phase should progress to the alert phase.

Alert phase initial actions

3.5.5   An alert phase may be declared by an RCC, RSC, or ATS unit. Aircraft can pose added difficulties, so if an aircraft SAR operation is probable, the RCC may need to give an earlier alert to SAR resources, or advise RCCs along its intended route, or dispatch an escort aircraft (see section 7.2 on escort). For aircraft, ships, other craft, or persons, recommended RCC or RSC actions are described below.

3.5.6   Upon the declaration of an alert phase, the RCC or RSC should:

(a)   Initiate or continue any appropriate or incomplete actions normally performed during the uncertainty phase. In particular, ensure an SMC has been appointed and that all interested parties have been informed of this action.

(b)   Enter in a log all incoming information and progress reports, details of action as described below, and subsequent developments.

(c)   Verify the information received.

(d)   Obtain information about the aircraft, ship or other craft from sources not previously contacted, such as:

   –   communication stations associated with radio navigation aids, radar facilities, direction-finding stations and any other communication stations which might have received transmissions from the aircraft, ship or other craft. (These facilities should also be requested to guard specified radio frequencies.); and

   –   all possible landing or stopping points along the intended route, and other agencies and facilities included in the flight or voyage plan, which may be capable of providing additional information or verifying information on hand.

(e)   Maintain close liaison with associated ATS units, CRS, and similar alerting posts so that any new information obtained from other aircraft and ships will be made available immediately for evaluation, plotting, and decision-making and so that duplication of effort can be avoided.

(f)   Plot relevant details obtained through the actions described above on an appropriate map or chart to determine the probable position of the aircraft, ship or craft and its maximum range of action from its last known position and plot the positions of any ship or craft known to be operating in the vicinity.

(g)   As appropriate, initiate search planning and report any action taken to the associated ATS unit or CRS.

(h)   Whenever possible, communicate to the craft's operating agency, owner, or agent all information received and action taken.

(i)   Thoroughly evaluate the craft's intended route, weather, terrain, possible communication delays, last known position, last radio communication and operator's qualification.

(j)   For aviation incidents, estimate fuel exhaustion time and note the aircraft's performance under adverse conditions.

(k)   Request assistance from ATS or CRS facilities who may assist by:

   –   passing instructions and information to the distressed craft, or to the craft reporting the distress;

   –   informing craft operating in the vicinity of the distress of the nature of the emergency; and

   –   monitoring and keeping the RCC and RSC informed on the progress of any craft of which the operating efficiency has been impaired to the extent that a distress is likely.

3.5.7   When information received indicates that the aircraft, ship or other craft is not in distress, the RCC will close the incident and immediately inform the operating agency, the reporting source and any alerted authorities, centres, services, or facilities. If the craft has not been located when all efforts have been completed, or if the time of an aircraft's estimated fuel exhaustion has been reached, whichever occurs first, the craft and its occupants should be considered to be in grave and imminent danger. The alert phase should then progress to the distress phase. The decision to declare the distress phase should be taken without undue delay and on the basis of past experience with similar situations.

Distress phase initial actions

3.5.8   A distress phase may be declared by an ATS unit, an RCC or an RSC. The SAR system may be able to respond quickly by dispatching SAR facilities and effecting the rescue. If a search is required, the search planning guidance in chapter 4 should be used.

3.5.9   Upon the declaration of a distress phase, the RCC or RSC should:

(a)   Initiate or continue any appropriate or incomplete actions normally performed during the uncertainty and alert phases. In particular, ensure an SMC has been appointed and that all interested parties have been informed of this action.

(b)   Examine the detailed plans of operation for the conduct of SAR operations in the area.

(c)   Determine the availability of SAR facilities to conduct SAR operations and attempt to obtain more facilities if a need for them is anticipated. Check vessel tracking systems (e.g., AIS, LRIT, VMS and VTS) for vessels which may be able to assist.

(d)   Estimate the position of the distressed craft, estimate the degree of uncertainty of this position and determine the extent of the area to be searched. If a significant search effort is anticipated, use the search planning techniques described in chapter 4 to maximize the chances of finding the survivors with the available search facilities. Chapter 5 contains information on the conduct of search operations.

(e)   Develop a search action plan (chapters 4 and 5) or rescue planning (chapter 6), as appropriate, for the conduct of the SAR operation and communicate the plan to the appropriate authorities.

(f)   Initiate the action and pass relevant details of the plan on to:

   –   the ATS unit, or CRS, for transmission to the distressed craft or to the craft reporting the distress or to the SAR resources; and

   –   all RCCs and RSCs along the intended route of the distressed craft as well as those whose SRRs are within the maximum radius of action as determined from the last known position (the possibility area).

   Note: The ATS units, CRSs, and RCCs so informed should pass any information they receive about the incident to the responsible RCC.

(g)   Amend the plan as the operation develops.

(h)   Notify the State of Registry of the aircraft, or the owner or agent of a ship or other craft.

(i)   Notify the appropriate accident investigation authorities.

(j)   Request at an early stage such aircraft, vessels, CRSs, or other services not specifically included among SRUs, as are in a position to do so, to:

   –   maintain a listening watch for transmission from the distressed craft, from survival radio equipment, or from an ELT or EPIRB;

   –   assist the distressed craft as far as practicable; and

   –   inform the RCC or RSC of any developments.

(k)   Notify the distressed craft's operating agency and keep it informed of developments.

3.5.10 When the distressed craft has been located and the survivors rescued, the RCC or RSC will terminate the SAR operation, close the case and immediately advise the operating agency, the reporting source, and any alerted authorities, centres, services, or facilities. To ensure that search facilities remain under some type of flight or vessel following system, SMC activities should not be terminated until all SAR facilities have established alternate following plans, where they apply. Guidance on conclusion of SAR operations is found in chapter 8.

3.6 Designation of the RCC or RSC responsible for initiating SAR action

3.6.1 Typically, an RCC will receive a distress alert and assume responsibility for SAR operations for that incident. However, there may be times when the first RCC to receive the distress alert will not be the responsible RCC, such as when the distress is in another SRR. When an RCC or RSC receives information indicating a distress outside of its SRR, it should immediately notify the appropriate RCC or RSC and take all necessary action to co-ordinate the response until the appropriate RCC or RSC has assumed responsibility. Figure 3-1 depicts the recommended actions of the "First RCC" that receives the distress alert. The following text provides guidance on the responsibilities of that RCC. There should be no undue delay in initiating action while determining the responsible RCC.

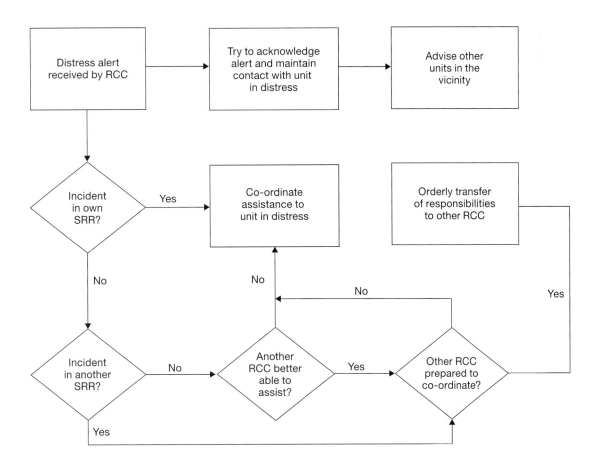

Figure 3-1 – *Actions of the "First RCC"*

Position of aircraft, ship or craft is known

3.6.2 When it is likely that other RCCs have also received alerts from the distressed craft, any RCC receiving an alert should assume responsibility until co-ordination with the other RCCs can take place and the appropriate RCC assumes responsibility.

3.6.3 When the position of the distressed craft is known, the responsibility for initiation of a SAR operation will be that of the RCC or RSC in whose area the craft is located.

3.6.4 When the RCC or RSC recognizes that the distressed craft is continuing its flight or voyage and may leave the SRR for which it is responsible, it should take the following actions.

(a) Alert the RCCs associated with the planned or intended route of the distressed craft, and pass on all information.

(b) Continue co-ordination of the SAR operation until it has been notified by an adjacent RCC or RSC that the distressed craft has entered its SRR and that it is assuming responsibility. When transferring the SAR operation to another RCC or RSC, the transfer should be documented in the RCC or RSC log.

(c) Remain ready to assist until informed that this is no longer required.

Position of aircraft, ship or other craft is not known

3.6.5 When the position of the distressed craft is unknown, the RCC or RSC should assume responsibility for the SAR operation and consult adjacent RCCs along the route of the craft concerning which centre will assume primary responsibility and designate an SMC.

3.6.6 Unless otherwise agreed among the RCCs or RSCs concerned, the RCC or RSC assuming responsibility should be determined as follows:

(a) If the last reported position of the distressed craft falls within an SRR, the RCC or RSC responsible for that SRR should assume responsibility for co-ordinating the response.

(b) If the last reported position falls on the line separating two adjacent SRRs, the RCC or RSC responsible for the SRR toward which the distressed craft was proceeding should assume co-ordination responsibilities.

(c) If the craft was not equipped with suitable two-way radio communication or not under obligation to maintain radio communication, the RCC or RSC responsible for the SRR containing the distressed craft's intended destination should assume co-ordination responsibilities.

Transferring responsibilities between RCCs and RSCs

3.6.7 When transferring the co-ordination of a SAR operation to another RCC or RSC, the transfer should be documented in the RCC or RSC log. The initiating RCC may invite the other RCC to take over responsibility or the other RCC may offer to take over responsibility. The responsibility is retained by the initiating RCC until the other RCC formally accepts responsibility. All participating SAR units are to be advised of the transfer. Procedures to transfer SMC responsibility to another RCC should include:

– Personal discussion between the SMCs of both RCCs concerned; and

– Exchange of data using SITREP form including full details of action taken.

– Details to be included in the process of transfer between RCCs should be as follows:

    – Date and time of transfer:

    – From (RCC):

    – To (RCC):

        (1) Identity of casualty

        (2) Position

        (3) Number of persons in distress

        (4) Description of casualty

        (5) Weather on scene

        (6) Initial actions taken

        (7) Areas already searched (including POD)

(8)   Alerted units

(9)   Current/present search in sub-areas

(10)   Endurance of existing SAR units on scene

(11)   Availability of SAR units on scene (hours/days)

(12)   Communication plan

(13)   Confirmation that all participating SAR units have been advised of the transfer of the responsibility.

3.7   RCC procedures for requesting SAR facilities

3.7.1   When an RCC, at the request of another RCC, provides facilities to assist in SAR operations, the RCCs should agree upon position, start time on scene, expected time on scene, communications, operational limitations, and time of assumption of co-ordination responsibility by the requesting RCC. The RCCs should also agree upon how the SAR facilities will be briefed and tasked. The RCC providing the facilities will advise them of these procedures. Once the SMC has assumed co-ordination of the SAR facilities, it will keep the RCC which provided the facilities informed of progress.

3.8   General considerations for the SMC

3.8.1   SMC duties can be demanding. The gathering of information, evaluation of this information, and initiation of action all require concentrated effort on many details. The SMC will find the various forms, checklists, worksheets, tables and graphs provided in the Appendices to be very helpful. The following paragraphs provide some general guidance for the early stages of a SAR operation, including information gathering and preparation for the possible need to plan searches.

Information gathering and analysis

3.8.2   *Information gathering.* To co-ordinate a response to a SAR incident most effectively, the SMC should have accurate, timely, and complete information about the incident and the subsequent status of survivors. Usually, not all the needed information is provided to the SMC. In fact, the fate of the distressed craft and any survivors is often a mystery in the early stages of the incident. For this reason, the SMC should initiate and actively pursue an investigation of the incident and related circumstances so the needed information can be obtained. Such investigative efforts are often similar in outline to scientific or police investigations. The SMC should interview, or have other qualified persons interview, anyone who might have some knowledge of the distress incident, distressed craft, or the persons aboard the distressed craft. These interviews may lead to additional persons, agencies, or other sources of information. The SMC should try to determine the most likely cause of the distress, if not already known, by consulting weather bureaus, ships, and aircraft, and by locating any known hazards to the distressed craft on an appropriate map or chart. There is almost no limit to the number of possible sources of information or the number of possible scenarios for what might have happened to the distressed craft. This means that the SMC should perform two apparently opposite activities:

–   think of additional possibilities which should be investigated, and

–   try to eliminate the maximum number of possibilities from further consideration through the investigative process.

3.8.3   *Information evaluation and analysis.* As information is gathered, it should be verified to the extent possible and then evaluated and analysed with respect to all the information previously gathered. It is possible, even likely, that some of the information gathered will be unrelated to the SAR incident, or misleading, or even false. The SMC should always be alert for such situations and should assign each item a level of relevance and reliability. Like most investigative efforts, the basic method of analysis is the process of elimination. For example, if the only known fact is that a distress has occurred, then the distress position could be anywhere on the globe. Add the fact that the distress alert was transmitted by the distressed craft using a line-of-sight communications device, and all of the earth's surface except that which is within a certain range of the receiving antenna is eliminated.

3.8.4   *Assumptions.* In the early stages of a SAR incident, it is almost certain that the SMC will need to make some assumptions about the cause, nature, time, or place of the SAR incident. It is very important that such assumptions be kept separated from the known facts. It is always important to distinguish conclusions based strictly on known facts from those based partially on assumptions. It is also important to re-evaluate all assumptions regularly and as new information becomes available. Re-evaluating assumptions is especially critical. Any assumption which is allowed to go unquestioned for too long a period begins to falsely assume the appearance of fact. If this is allowed to happen, an otherwise excellent SAR effort may not succeed because the search planner's judgement was clouded by a false assumption being used as factual information.

Urgency of response

3.8.5   The nature of the incident and the rate at which the situation may worsen usually determine the urgency of response. The SAR system should provide prompt and effective assistance to all incidents, particularly those involving grave or imminent danger. The time to begin searching may depend on the amount of daylight remaining. Since the chances of survival diminish with time, a few hours of searching during remaining daylight may be more productive than waiting until the next day for a full-scale search effort. Influencing factors are the number of SAR facilities available and the seriousness of the incident. For a known distress, a SAR facility, preferably the craft closest to the scene or the quickest response SRU, should be immediately dispatched to confirm the distress position. SAR incidents are almost always time-critical.

(a)   Survival times vary with local conditions, such as terrain, climate, ability and endurance of survivors, and emergency survival equipment and SRUs available.

(b)   It should be assumed that all survivors are incapacitated, capable of surviving only a short time, under great stress, experiencing shock, and requiring emergency medical care. Survivors may be uninjured but still unable to assist in their own rescue. Some may be calm and rational, some hysterical, and others temporarily stunned and bewildered.

(c)   The probability of the search object remaining close to the position of the distress incident decreases with time. Floating search objects drift, and survivors on land may be walking. If the search object is mobile, the size of the search area must increase with time. Delay may dramatically increase search area size, possibly beyond what the available search facilities can cover. For survivors adrift in rapid water currents, the best chance of locating them is soon after they have gone adrift, while the search area is still small.

3.8.6   Environment-related factors may severely limit available rescue time. Survivor life expectancy varies with the use of life jackets, immersion suits, the type of clothing worn, the clothing's wetness, survivor activity, initial body temperature, physical and psychological condition, thirst, exhaustion, hunger and will to live. Many individuals exceed typical life expectancies or tolerance times. Individuals can exceed common life expectancies or tolerance times. (Regarding survival in cold water, the IMO provides more information in its *Pocket Guide for Cold Water Survival.*)[*]

(a)   Exposure to the chilling effects of cold air, wind, or water can result in hypothermia, the abnormal lowering of internal body temperature. The rate of body heat loss increases as air and water temperatures decrease. Death from hypothermia occurs over four times more often in water than on land.

(b)   The term "cold" can be applied to water as warm as 25°C (77°F); long periods of immersion in water as high as this temperature can result in a fall in deep body temperature. It follows that most of the planet is covered in "cold" water.

(c)   Wind is a factor for exposed survivors, as body heat loss accelerates with increasing wind velocity. Figure N-13 in appendix N shows the effects of various wind speed and air temperature combinations, and indicates the equivalent temperature on dry skin in still air. This emphasizes the need to shelter survivors who would otherwise be exposed to severe cold.

---

[*] Refer to IMO publication, sales number IB946E.

(d) The warmest ocean water that can be expected at any time of year is 29°C (84°F). About one third of the earth's ocean surface has water temperatures above 19°C (66°F). Figure N-14 in appendix N shows the realistic upper limit of survival time for people wearing normal clothing in water at various temperatures. The graph is based on the analysis of known survival cases and laboratory experimentation, and shows a reasonable upper limit for search duration. The search planner must remember that this graph can only be indicative and that a number of uncertainty factors can improve or reduce survival time.

(e) Guidelines based on analysis of accidents, together with laboratory-based experimental evidence, show a clear correlation between water temperature, body cooling and survival times. However, it is also apparent that, because of the vast array of personal factors that can influence survival time in cold water, this time can vary from seconds to days. Factors that slow the loss of body heat are:

–   high body fat;

–   heavy clothing;

–   survival clothing; and

–   the use of a protective behaviour.

Factors that make a person lose body heat faster are:

–   gender (females are more prone to hypothermia);

–   age (children and the elderly are more prone to hypothermia);

–   low body fat;

–   light clothing;

–   exercising (such as situations where persons without lifejackets have to swim); and

–   seasickness.

Thus, in water at 5°C (41°F), the 50% survival time for a normally-clothed individual is estimated to be about one hour, with a recommended search time of six hours. The corresponding times for 10°C (50°F) are two hours and 12 h. While in water at 15°C (59°F) the 50% survival time is about six hours, with the recommended search time of 18 h. Between 20°C (68°F) and 30°C (86°F) search times exceeding 24 h should be considered and searching for several days should be considered for water temperatures at the upper end of this temperature scale.

As there are many factors to consider, this model cannot be used for all situations. SOLAS survival suits are meant to keep a person alive for 24 h in extremely cold water and a person may be able to keep himself out of the water by climbing onto wreckage, for example. It should be kept in mind that factors working positively on survival times are often unknown to the SMC. Some of these factors include, but are not limited to, the following:

–   Near-naked swimmers would be at the lower ranges of these times. In calm water there may be an exceptional individual (someone who is very fat and fit, for example) who will exceed expectations. If it is known that the victim is such an individual, consideration should, exceptionally, be given to extending the search times from 3–6 to 10 times the predicted 50% survival time.

–   For inshore incidents, survival times may be less because of breaking water and adverse currents. However, consideration must be given to the possibility that the inshore survivor managed to get ashore. Consequently, the limiting effects of cold water cooling will no longer be the only consideration and the search must be continued until the shore has been thoroughly searched.

–   For offshore incidents, it is reasonable to expect that individuals may be better equipped to survive and have access to appropriate protective clothing, such as lifejackets and possibly liferafts. Consequently, search times for them should be at the upper limits of those expected (10 times predicted 50% survival time), unless obviously adverse conditions prevail, and should exceed them if it is possible that survivors may have been able to get out of the water.

    – Survival time is shortened by physical activity (such as swimming) and increased by wearing heavy clothing and, if wearing a lifejacket, adopting protective behaviour (such as huddling with other survivors or adopting a foetal position in the water). Specialized insulated protective clothing (such as immersion suits or wet suits) is capable of increasing survival time from two to 10 times. The SMC should bear in mind that ingress of as little as half a litre of water into an immersion/survival suit can reduce its insulation value by 30% and that wave height of one metre can reduce it by an additional 15%.

    Predicting survival times for immersion victims is not a precise science; there is no formula to determine exactly how long someone will survive or how long a search should continue. The SMC must make some difficult decisions based on the best information available and a number of assumptions and should extend the search time beyond that which they can reasonably expect anyone to survive.

(f) The presence of certain animals may increase hazards and reduce expected survival time. The SMC should be aware of what animals or marine life may be in the search area and where to acquire specialized medical help quickly.

(g) Heat stress and dehydration are dangers in hot climates, particularly desert areas. The most severe form of heat stress is heatstroke, when body temperature rises. If the body temperature rises above 42°C (107°F) for sustained periods, death usually occurs. Dehydration is a critical factor both in hot climates and survival at sea; a person without water will die in a few days. A combination of high temperatures and lack of water will quickly aggravate heat stress and dehydration. In high-humidity areas, the water needs of the body are about one half those in deserts at equal temperatures.

3.8.7 The terrain may determine the type of search pattern needed and the SAR facility selected. Manoeuvrable aircraft effective at high altitudes may be required in rugged mountain areas. Helicopters may not be able to operate in the thin air and turbulence associated with mountain contour searches. The survival kit carried by the distressed craft and the hoist devices on the SAR facility also influence decision-making. Dense foliage may hamper visual and electronic searches and require a greater number of aircraft and ground SAR facilities, and closer search track spacing. The presence of electrical power lines, towers and bridges should be considered when planning search altitudes and areas. Prominent landmarks can be used as boundaries and checkpoints for laying out overland air and ground search areas. Aircraft with poor navigation equipment and inexperienced ground SAR facilities may be more effective when using easily recognized boundaries. The type of rescue team used after the distress site has been located is also dependent on the terrain. Local law-enforcement authorities, forest service personnel, mountain rescue clubs, ski clubs, or pararescue teams may be required.

3.8.8 Weather may limit SAR operations. Not only are search objects more difficult to detect, but facilities operate less efficiently in turbulence or rough seas. Knowledge of weather conditions and prudent judgement will increase the likelihood of success and SAR facility safety.

(a) If existing weather will not allow a search without unduly endangering additional lives, the search should be delayed. If weather is good but forecast to deteriorate, rapid action is necessary, possibly in lieu of detailed planning.

(b) Wind, visibility, and cloud cover influence search sweep width.

(c) Safety of the SAR personnel involved must be of concern to the SMC. Low ceilings and restricted visibility are particularly hazardous to aircraft. If the search is to be conducted where there are few navigation aids and poor visibility exists, the SMC may suspend search operations or limit the number of SAR facilities. OSCs may suspend the search to ensure the safety of the SAR personnel.

3.8.9 *Flares.* Red flares, orange smoke, and pyrotechnics are recognized as maritime and aeronautical emergency signals. Reports of flare sightings may be one of the most common distress alerts sent to the RCC. When evaluating reports of flare sightings, the SMC should determine the location of the flare by carefully questioning the informant and analysing the data. The following steps may be used.

(a) Plot the location of each informant at the time of the sighting.

(b) Obtain the characteristics of the flare, such as colour, intensity, duration, and trajectory.

(c) Plot the position of the flare, preferably with cross bearings from more than one sighting. To obtain a line of position (LOP) from an informant, the angle of the sighting relative to a known bearing should be requested. If the informant does not have a compass, the angle could be determined by relation to a geographic feature such as the shoreline, a ridge line, or a straight road.

(d) If only one sighting is available, obtain an LOP from the informant as described in the previous paragraph and estimate distance to the search object. This estimate should be based on a description of the flare, its observed height, the height of the eye of the informant, and the visibility. If the information is limited, determine the maximum distance the flare could be seen and extend the search area appropriately.

(e) Check with the military services to see if they had any training or operations in the area.

3.8.10 *SAR operations risks.* Safe and effective SAR operations depend on co-ordinated teamwork and sound judgement relating to risk assessment. Saving distressed persons and the safety of SAR personnel should be of equal concern to the SMC. Once SAR personnel are proficient in their duties, the team leader, e.g., pilot in command, captain, SMC, or OSC, must ensure that the personnel perform properly as a team with a common mission. Mishaps often follow a chain of errors that can start with mistakes made during SAR planning and lead to poor decisions during operations. Team safety is supported by keeping everyone informed, matching resource capabilities to tasks, detecting and avoiding errors early, following standard procedures, and adjusting to non-standard activities.

(a) All reasonable action should be taken to locate distressed persons, determine their status, and effect their rescue. However, the risks inherent in any SAR response must be considered against the chances for success and the safety of SAR personnel.

(b) The search or rescue action plan provided by the SMC is guidance for the OSC and SAR facilities on scene. The OSC may adjust the action plan based on the situation on scene; however, when practicable, the OSC should only vary facility tasking after consultation with the SMC. SAR facilities should keep the OSC advised of any difficulties encountered.

3.8.11 *Available facilities.* SMCs must be constantly aware of the status of all available facilities. Lack of SAR resources can be caused by crew fatigue, need for SRU maintenance, or involvement in another operation. A system for monitoring the status of all SRUs should be available to each SMC.

3.8.12 *Re-evaluation of initial incident data.* The SMC should remain constantly alert to new developments affecting conclusions and assumptions. When time is critical, SRUs may be immediately dispatched with incomplete information. Therefore, SMCs should seek additional data to verify the information used to establish the distress location. Since trauma and shock can distort factual observation and memory, accounts by on-scene witnesses should be verified. Independent witness reports, SAR facility observations, current charts and tables, and radio logs are also helpful. The SMC should use the new information to review and revise, as necessary, the current assumptions.

Chapter 4

Search planning and evaluation concepts

4.1 Overview

4.1.1 The objective of this chapter is to describe some basic concepts of search theory in understandable terms. This knowledge will make the detailed search planning worksheets and procedures in appendices K and L and the graphs and tables in Appendix N more meaningful. All of the basic search theory concepts are described in this chapter. Practical examples are provided for each concept, showing how it may be applied to the search planning problem. These examples require only basic arithmetic skills and an understanding of the basic probability concepts encountered in everyday life. Although search planning is sometimes perceived to be complex, each step is relatively simple. Practice and perseverance in proceeding through all the steps will enable the search planner to make the most effective use of the available search facilities. The worksheets and instructions in appendices K and L summarize the search planning procedures without all of the accompanying explanations provided in this chapter. Examples provided later in this chapter will help the reader to understand how the theory is applied.

4.1.2 Search planning involves the following steps:

– evaluating the situation, including the results of any previous searching;

– estimating the distress incident location and probable error of that location;

– estimating the survivors' post-distress movements and probable error of that estimate;

– using these results to estimate the most probable location (datum[*]) of survivors and the uncertainty (probable error of position) about that location;

– determining the best way to use the available search facilities so the chances of finding the survivors are maximized (optimal search effort allocation);

– defining search sub-areas and search patterns for assignment to specific search facilities;

– providing a search action plan that includes a current description of the situation, search object description(s), specific search responsibilities to search facilities, on-scene co-ordination instructions, and search facility reporting requirements.

These steps are repeated until either the survivors are located or evaluation of the situation shows that further searching would be futile.

4.1.3 This chapter describes the basic concepts underlying the first five steps listed above. Chapter 5, where detailed planning for the conduct and co-ordination of search operations is discussed, covers the last two steps.

4.1.4 The methods given in this chapter and in chapter 5 have been simplified for manual use. A computer program can be developed based on this manual solution which could save time and reduce the chance of mathematical errors but the search plans would not be any better than the results produced by hand. Computers, including typical personal computers and laptops, have large computing and

---

[*] The term *datum* is used extensively in this chapter to mean a geographic point (or set of points), line, or area used as a reference in search planning. This term, with a similar definition, is also used in surveying, mapping, and geology.

data storage capability and can be programmed to use advanced simulation techniques. Search plans produced by simulation techniques can be significantly better than those produced by the correct application of the methods contained within this Manual. Appendix P describes some of the functions a computer-based search planning aid should provide.

4.2   Evaluating the situation

4.2.1   Searching is the most expensive, risky, and complex aspect of the SAR system. Often, it is also the only way survivors may be located and assisted. Before a search is undertaken and at frequent intervals during its progress, all information received must be carefully analysed and evaluated. The primary concerns are ensuring all clues about the survivors' probable status and location are properly evaluated, and ensuring the safety of the search facilities and their crews. Some of the clues which may indicate the survivors' location or situation include:

(a)   *Intentions.* The intended route of the distressed craft is always an important clue to the probable location of the distress incident. Even when the distressed craft is able to transmit its position, comparison with the intended route can be an important indicator. If the position is close to where the craft intended to be at that time, the search planner should place a high level of confidence in it. However, if the position does not agree with the craft's intentions, then other possibilities need to be investigated. For example, the distress position may have been garbled in transmission, or digits may have been transposed when it was copied or transcribed for relay to the RCC. In another possible scenario, the craft may have changed its intended route in an attempt to avoid a hazard or get to a place of safety.

(b)   *Last known position (LKP).* The craft's last known position and its associated time is an important clue because it eliminates all the possibilities associated with earlier times. It is also an indicator of how well the craft was following its intended route and its true rate of progress up to that point. If the time of the distress is known, but not the position, this information allows the search planner to make a better estimate of the distress location.

(c)   *Hazards.* Another clue to the distress location and time is any available information about hazards along the craft's intended route. One of the most common hazards is adverse weather conditions. Careful estimates of the craft's pre-distress motion coupled with information about the movements and intensity of weather fronts, storms, etc., may allow the search planner to estimate the probable location and time of the distress incident.

(d)   *Condition and capability.* The airworthiness or seaworthiness of the craft may be an indicator of whether the craft is likely to have suffered a casualty that would slow its progress or cause a change in plans. It is also an indicator of how well the craft may be able to handle adverse weather conditions. The type and condition of navigation aids is an indicator of how well the craft could maintain its intended track and whether it was likely to get lost or encounter a known hazard unexpectedly. The availability, type, and condition of survival craft (such as liferafts) provides a clue about post-distress survivor movements.

(e)   *Crew behaviour.* The experience, training, habits, medical condition, and probable actions of the craft's crew provide clues about both pre- and post-distress behaviour, which, when analysed with other clues, may provide better estimates of the time and location of the distress incident and any subsequent voluntary survivor movements.

(f)   *On-scene environmental conditions.* Conditions at the scene provide clues about the continued survival of the distressed persons. Such things as temperature extremes, availability of potable water, or presence of dangerous animals should be considered. On-scene conditions can also affect post-distress movements. Survivors on land may move away from the distress scene to seek shelter, water, avoid or escape local dangers, etc. Survivors at sea will drift away from the distress scene under the influence of local winds and currents.

(g)   *Results of previous searching.* When search results are negative, that is, when searching was done but the survivors were not located, the impact on the search planning process is not obvious. However, as discussed in sections 4.6 and 4.7 below, negative search results do provide important clues which may help locate the survivors in later searches.

4.2.2   The many diverse criteria involved in estimating the likely location(s) and condition(s) of the survivors make it impossible to give detailed, step-by-step instructions on how to make such estimates. Sound judgement and careful analysis of all available clues are therefore required to produce a valid assessment on which to base a search.

4.3   Estimating the distress incident location

4.3.1   The first step in either marine or land search planning is to determine the limits of the area containing all possible survivor locations. This is usually done by determining the maximum distance the survivors could have travelled between the time of their LKP and the known or assumed time of the distress incident, and drawing a circle of that radius around the LKP. Knowing the extreme limits of possible locations allows the search planner to determine where to seek further information related to the missing craft or persons and whether an incoming report might apply to the incident. However, systematic search of such a large area is normally not practical. Therefore, the next step is to develop one or more scenarios, or sets of known facts plus some carefully considered assumptions, describing what may have happened to the survivors since they were last known to be safe. Each scenario must be consistent with the known facts of the case, have a high likelihood of being true, and allow the search planner to establish a corresponding geographic reference, or datum, for the survivors' most probable location.

> **Note:** It is important throughout the case to distinguish conclusions based strictly on known facts from those based partially on assumptions. It is also important to re-evaluate all scenarios and assumptions regularly and as new information becomes available. Re-evaluating assumptions is especially critical. Any assumption which is allowed to go unquestioned for too long a period begins to falsely assume the appearance of fact. If this is allowed to happen, an otherwise excellent search effort may not succeed because the search planner's judgement was clouded by a false assumption being used as factual information.

4.3.2   A datum may be a point (or set of points), line, or area. The datum for the initial distress incident is first estimated from the known facts of the case, and possibly some assumptions which have a high likelihood of being true. Appendix K contains guidance for estimating the distress incident time and location. This datum for the distress incident is then adjusted to account for estimates of post-distress survivor motion and a new datum on which to base a search is computed. Finally, the level of uncertainty about the new datum is evaluated and limits are estimated for the smallest area containing all possible locations consistent with the scenario on which the new datum is based. This area is called the "possibility area" for that scenario.

Distribution of possible search object locations

4.3.3   The distribution of search object location probabilities within the possibility area is an important consideration in search planning because it affects how the available search facilities should be deployed. Possibility areas may be centred upon a single datum point, centred along a datum line, or defined by a geometric figure or figures covering some portion of the earth's surface.

(a)   The location probabilities may be evenly distributed throughout the possibility area, or there may be some sub-areas which are more likely to contain the search object than others. When the available clues do not provide a clear indication of which sub-areas are more probable and which are less probable, then distress incident, search object, and survivor location probability distributions[*] may be estimated by assuming a standard distribution.

---

[*] The terms *probability distribution*, *probability density*, and *density* are often used interchangeably in the literature of applied statistics. Definitions of these terms for seach planning purposes are provided in the Glossary, but no formal training in probability theory or statistics is required for using the procedures described in this volume.

(b) The two types of standard distributions most frequently used are those based on the standard normal distribution[*] (bell curve) and those based on the uniform distribution. For datum points and lines, appropriate variations on the standard normal distribution are usually used. For datum areas, a uniform distribution is most often used. However, when enough information is available, the search planner's analysis and judgement will often produce a better, and in some ways a less complicated, generalized distribution. Use of these distributions is discussed further in sections 4.6 and 4.7.

Initial distress incident location probability distributions

4.3.4 Several types of probability distribution are described and illustrated below. In the graphic representations, peaks represent locations where the probability density (amount of probability per unit area) is highest. There are basically three types of information which may be available about the location of a distress incident.

(a) *Point.* This is the simplest and most specific type. It may be specified by latitude and longitude, range and bearing from a known point, or other method for specifying a geographic position. It is usually obtained from either the distressed craft itself or from external position-fixing equipment (such as two or more lines of bearing from independent direction-finding stations or positions provided by satellites such as Cospas–Sarsat). If the time of the incident is known but not the datum, the incident position may be estimated based on the LKP and the craft's intentions. The distribution of incident location probabilities is generally assumed to be that given by a circular normal probability density function. Under this assumption, the probability density is highest near datum and decreases as the distance from datum increases. The incident's probable position error (X) (discussed in paragraph 4.3.5) is defined to be the radius of the circle having a 50% chance of containing the actual location of the incident. A circle with three times this radius would contain virtually all possible incident locations. Figure 4-1 illustrates the graphs of a circular normal distribution in a three-dimensional view where the vertical axis represents probability density, and also as a contour graph (similar to a topographic map of mountainous terrain).

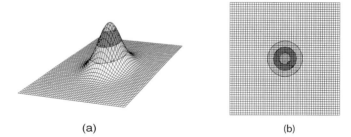

(a)   (b)

Figure 4-1 – *Probability density distribution for a point datum with top view*

(b) *Line.* This can be either an intended or assumed track line or a line of bearing (such as that obtained from direction-finding equipment). The distribution of possible incident locations is generally assumed to be more concentrated near the line and less concentrated farther away. Specifically, the distribution of possible incident locations on either side of the line is assumed to follow a normal distribution. The distribution along the line is generally assumed to be uniform unless there is specific information favouring one part of the line over another. Figure 4-2 illustrates the graphs of a typical line-centred normal distribution. Figure 4-3 shows how a line datum of equal length connecting two point datums would look. In the centre it is essentially identical to the line-centred datum of figure 4-2. Usually, the distribution depicted by figure 4-2 will be used for a line datum regardless of whether it connects datum points. Doing this makes the computations simpler but still provides a near-optimal result.

---

[*] The standard normal distribution (also called the "bell curve" because of its shape or the "gaussian distribution" after the German mathematician Karl Friedrich Gauss) is defined by a specific mathematical function. It has been found through experience that most errors of measurement and a large variety of physical observations have approximately normal distributions. In fact, its frequent appearance in nature is the reason this particular distribution is called "normal".

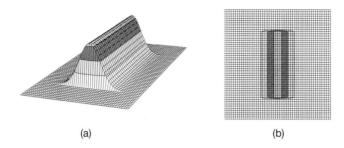

(a)   (b)

Figure 4-2 – *Probability density distribution for a line datum with top view*

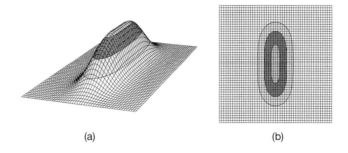

(a)   (b)

Figure 4-3 – *Probability density distribution for a line datum
connecting two point datums with top view*

(c)   *Area.* This can be a fishing area or other area of operation. Generally, possible incident locations within such an area are assumed to be evenly distributed (uniform distribution) unless there is specific information which favours some parts of the area over others (generalized distribution). Figure 4-4 illustrates a uniform distribution over an area. Figure 4-5 illustrates a generalized distribution.

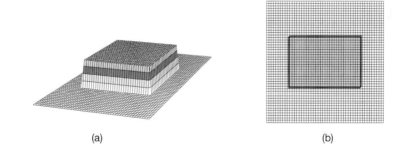

(a)   (b)

Figure 4-4 – *Uniform probability density distribution with top view*

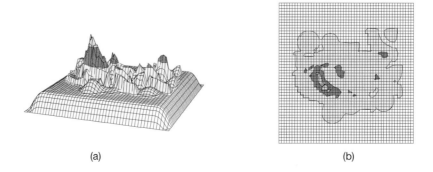

(a)   (b)

Figure 4-5 – *Generalized probability density distribution with top view*

Incident position error (X)

4.3.5   Even when a specific position is reported, some allowance for position error must be made, based upon the navigational capabilities of the reporting source and the distance travelled since the last navigational fix. The probable error of position is the radius of a circle having a 50% chance of containing the actual incident position. Guidance is provided in tables N-1 through N-3 for estimating the size of probable position error for different types of craft and navigation equipment.

4.4   Survivor motion after the distress incident

4.4.1   Survivors of a distress incident may move away from the location where the incident occurred before assistance arrives. Aircraft can glide a considerable distance following an engine failure. A pilot may bail out and parachute to the ground, drifting some distance during the descent. Movement of survivors on land will be largely affected by their condition, their knowledge of survival skills, the terrain, and possibly the weather conditions. They may move away from the scene in search of water, shelter, food, or human habitation. For aircraft incidents over land, it is usually best to first locate the site of the forced landing or crash and then search for survivors in the surrounding area. Survivors on the ocean usually cannot remain at the scene unless their survival craft has an anchor and the water is shallow enough to use it. Without an anchor or in deep water, the survivors drift with the winds and water currents, although they may affect their motion with a drogue or sail on their survival craft. Drift in the marine environment is discussed below. Procedures and worksheets for estimating a new maritime datum position from an old one based on survival craft drift are provided in appendix K of this volume.

Aeronautical drift

4.4.2   When an aircraft experiences a casualty, such as an engine failure, which makes further flight unsafe or impossible, the pilot will normally attempt to descend in the safest possible manner by either gliding, using a parachute, or using a combination of these two methods. Appendix K contains worksheets for computing aeronautical drift in these situations and appendix N contains graphs and parachute drift tables for use with these worksheets.

    (a)   *Gliding.* The safest descent may involve gliding or flying at greatly reduced power toward the most suitable available site for a forced, off-aerodrome landing. Aircraft can glide a considerable distance. The key factors are power-off rate of descent, glide airspeed, and height above the surface. Since glide ratios vary widely, the manufacturer of the distressed aircraft or pilots experienced with that type of aircraft should be consulted regarding glide and forced landing characteristics.

    (b)   *Parachute drift.* If parachutes are available, the pilot in command may elect to use this method of descent. This situation is rare in civil aviation but more common in military aviation. If the survivors leave the aircraft while it is still airborne, their landing site and the crash site of the aircraft may be widely separated from each other and from the bail-out position. Drift characteristics for modern civilian parachutes can vary widely. For civilian cases, the manufacturer of the parachute or another knowledgeable source should be consulted for the information needed to determine how far the survivor(s) may have drifted during descent.

Maritime drift

4.4.3   Two types of forces cause survival craft on the ocean to move or drift: wind and current. To compute the area where the survivors may be located, it is necessary to estimate the rate and direction of drift. This requires estimates of the winds and currents in and around the area containing the possible distress locations. The two components of drift are leeway and total water current (TWC).

    (a)   *Leeway (LW).* The force of the wind against the exposed surfaces of the craft causes it to move through the water in a generally downwind direction. This is called leeway. A drogue (sea anchor) may be deployed to decrease the rate of leeway. The shapes of the exposed and underwater surfaces can affect the rate of leeway and cause the leeway direction to diverge to the left or the right of the downwind direction. (The average angle between the search object's leeway direction and the downwind direction is known as the *leeway divergence angle*). Whether the craft's leeway will diverge to the left or the right is unknown. This uncertainty requires that both possibilities be considered. Estimates of wind direction and speed may be obtained from direct observation at the scene, output from computer models used for weather prediction, local weather bureaus and, as a last resort, wind roses on pilot charts. Leeway rates and leeway directions may be computed from leeway graphs provided in appendix N using the procedures provided with the Leeway worksheet in appendix K.

(b) *Total water current (TWC)* can have several components. Some or all of the following may be included:

    (1) *Sea current (SC)*. This is the main large-scale flow of ocean waters. Sea currents near the surface are of principal interest to search planners. Near shore or in shallow waters, sea current is usually less important than the tidal current or the local wind current. Sea currents are not always steady, so averages should be used with caution. Sea current estimates may be obtained from direct observation at the scene (such as ship set and drift, trajectories of drifting objects having zero leeway), output from computer models of ocean circulation, and hydrographic tables and charts.

    (2) *Tidal or rotary currents*. In coastal waters, currents change in direction and speed as the tides change. They may be estimated from tidal current tables, current charts, and pilot charts. However, local knowledge often will be of the greatest value.

    (3) *River current*. This should be considered only if the survivors may be in, or near, the mouth of a large river (such as the Amazon).

    (4) *Local wind current (WC)*. Local wind current is due to the effect of sustained local winds on the water's surface. The exact effect of wind in creating local wind currents is not clear, but it is generally assumed that after 6 to 12 h with the wind in a constant direction, a local surface current is generated. The estimated average wind velocity and direction for the previous 24 to 48 hours should be verified by contacting ships which have been in the vicinity of the distress scene. The direction and velocity of local wind current can be estimated using the Local Wind Current Graph in figure N-1.

Vector (direction and speed) values must be obtained for each of these which is present and added, vector fashion, to obtain the total water current (TWC). Figure 4-6 shows how to compute TWC offshore in the open ocean.

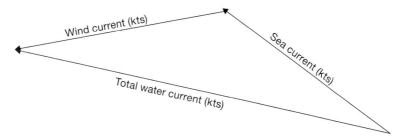

Figure 4-6 – *Computing total water current from sea current and wind current*

Wind and current observations

4.4.4 The best way to obtain wind and TWC information is through direct observation. One way to get such observations is from ships passing through the area. Such vessels should be asked to report set and drift as well as wind and other weather observations. If they are available, the observed movements of drifting buoys designed to have zero leeway and move with the surface currents can be used to determine TWC. Some States maintain inventories of datum marker buoys (DMBs) which may be deployed by SRUs and either relocated by means of a radio beacon or tracked by satellite to measure surface currents. Many other satellite-tracked buoys are adrift in the world's oceans in conjunction with various oceanographic studies. Unfortunately, there is no centralized database for identifying the principal investigator for a study and no mechanism for obtaining near-real-time observations for search planning purposes. However, it may be worthwhile to contact nearby universities or Government agencies engaged in oceanographic studies and determine whether they have, or can obtain, more accurate TWC information than that already available to the search planner. *Caution: Many drifting buoys used in oceanographic studies are drogued to move with sub-surface currents. Those that move with the upper one or two metres of the ocean measure total water current while those that are designed to move with deeper currents tend to measure only sea current.* Advance planning and an exchange of visits between search planners and nearby oceanographers would help in establishing ways to obtain near-real-time sea current data suitable for use in search planning.

Other sources of wind and current data

4.4.5   While direct observations provide the best data for the place and time of the observation, such data are not always available when and where they are needed for search planning. The next best source of data is the output of computer models used for predicting weather and sea conditions. Output from such models, especially weather models, is widely distributed around the globe and is often used by local weather bureaus, which modify it to account for local observations and effects. Each RCC should work closely with weather bureaus in its area of responsibility to ensure this source of environmental data is available when needed. *Caution: Output from some sea current prediction models includes local wind effects based on wind predictions. The search planner should NOT add local wind current to such sea current predictions.* Finally, pilot charts, hydrographic atlases, tidal current tables, etc., may be used to obtain estimates for current. *Sea currents taken from pilot charts or hydrographic atlases for areas having persistent winds, that is, nearly constant wind speed and direction almost all the time, should not have wind current added to them. This typically applies to areas of the world affected by trade winds, such as the north-east trade winds between southern Europe and the Caribbean basin.*

Estimating survivor drift

4.4.6   Once the directions and speeds of the leeway and TWC vectors are estimated, the directions and rates of drift are computed by adding the leeway and TWC vectors as shown in figure 4-7. Normally, all velocities are computed in nautical miles per hour (knots).

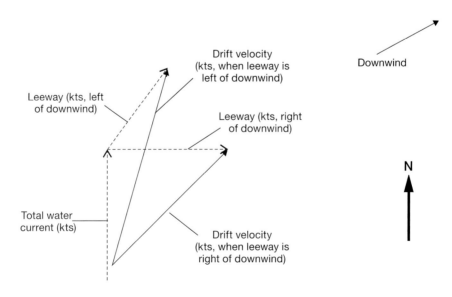

Figure 4-7 – *Computing drift speeds and directions from total water current and leeway*

Establishing a new datum

4.4.7 The estimated distance an object has drifted is computed as the number of hours since the last computed datum multiplied by the drift speed, using the familiar formula:

distance = speed × time.

(a) *Single point and leeway divergence datums.* Updating a previous point datum to account for drift motion and to produce a new point datum is done by moving from the previous datum in the direction of the drift vector for a distance equal to the estimated drift distance, as shown in figure 4-8. In a drift involving leeway, the first drift interval will produce two new datum points, one for each of the leeway vectors. Thereafter, it is assumed that the "left" datum will always use the leeway vector that is to the left of the downwind direction and the "right" datum will always use the leeway vector that is to the right of the downwind direction.

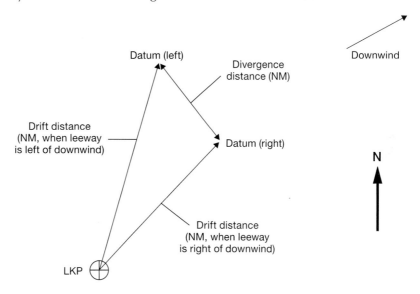

Figure 4-8 – *Determining new datums and divergence distance*
(drift distance = drift speed × time adrift)

(b) *Line and area datums.* If the drift forces (wind and current) are nearly the same everywhere in the search and surrounding areas, the new line or area datum location is found by moving it in the same fashion as point datums are moved using the average of the winds and currents. However, if the drift forces at some points on the line or in some sub-areas of the scenario's possibility area are significantly different from those in others, it becomes necessary to carefully choose a representative set of points to treat as datum points. These datum points should be chosen so that all significant variations in winds and currents are represented. Estimates for drift direction and distance must then be computed separately for each chosen point and a new datum point estimated. Finally, a new datum line or area based on the new datum points must be estimated. Figure 4-9 shows a situation where a craft's intended track line crossed a strong sea current. Note the difference in the shapes of the intended track and the new datum.

Drift error (D_e)

4.4.8 The computed drift velocities and the resulting drift distances are uncertain figures.

(a) While the leeway characteristics of many types of craft have been approximately determined by experiment, those of the remaining craft are only rough estimates. Furthermore, few leeway studies have data for high wind speeds. Therefore, estimates for high wind speeds are likely to be inaccurate. Often it is not known whether a drogue or sea anchor has been deployed. Most craft show a tendency to have leeway off the downwind direction, creating even more leeway uncertainty. Techniques for estimating local wind current also produce uncertain results. Neither wind nor sea current data typically exist on a scale precise enough to make accurate computation of an object's actual drift trajectory possible.

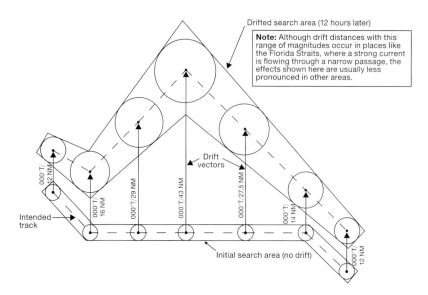

Figure 4-9 *– Effects of a strong current, such as the Gulf Stream,*
on probable survivor locations

(b) The search planner is faced with computing the trajectory of a small solid object suspended at the turbulent interface between two huge fluid masses – the ocean and the atmosphere – with only sparse and uncertain data. The search object's motion cannot be predicted with absolute certainty under these conditions.

(c) The combined effects of the uncertainties in both environmental data and drift characteristics of the search object are taken into account by calculating the probable drift error rate (total probable drift velocity error) in knots. Multiplying the length of the drift interval in hours by this value gives the total probable drift position error (D_e). If uncertainty values are unavailable, a probable error rate of 0.3 knots is usually assumed for each component of the drift velocity. The greater the uncertainty about the object's drift characteristics of the winds and currents driving it, the greater the probable drift error rate estimate will be.

4.5 Total probable error of position

4.5.1 Datum estimates are subject to a number of errors. Knowing the total effect of these errors is important because it determines how much of the surrounding area should be searched with the available search effort to maximize the chances of finding the search object. For point datums, the total probable error of position (*E*) defines the circular area having a 50% chance of containing the survivors, taking into account the probable error in the incident position (*X*, see paragraph 4.3.5), the probable error in the drift estimate (D_e, see paragraph 4.4.8) if drift is a factor, and the probable error in the search craft's position (*Y*, see paragraph 4.5.2). Sections 4.6 and 4.7 describe how the total probable error of position is used to determine the best area to search with the available search facilities.

4.5.2 *Search facility position error (Y).* The search facility's ability to accurately locate the search area has an impact on the size of the area which needs to be covered in order to avoid missing important portions. The probable error in search facility position may be estimated using the guidance provided in tables N-1 through N-3 for estimating the size of probable position error for different types of craft and navigation equipment. The search planner may use other, more accurate, estimates if they are available.

4.5.3 *Total probable error of position (E).* The total probable error in an estimated datum position is a function of the probable error in the estimated distress incident position (*X*), the probable error in estimated post-distress survivor movement (D_e), and the probable position error of the search facility (*Y*). The formula for computing total probable error of position is:

$$E = \sqrt{D_e^2 + X^2 + Y^2}$$

When post-distress survivor movement may be disregarded, this formula becomes:

$$E = \sqrt{X^2 + Y^2}$$

4.6 Search planning and evaluation factors

4.6.1 To get the maximum benefit from the remainder of this chapter, the search planner needs to be familiar with the following definitions. The terms marked with an asterisk (*) are discussed more fully in the subparagraphs following the list.

*Scenario** – A consistent set of known facts and assumptions describing what may have happened to the survivors. It usually consists of a sequence of actual and assumed events starting sometime prior to the distress incident and continuing to the present time. The most likely scenario(s) are used as a basis for planning searches.

*Possibility area** – (1) The smallest area containing *all* possible survivor or search object locations. (2) For a scenario, the possibility area is the smallest area containing *all* possible survivor or search object locations which are consistent with the facts and assumptions used to form the scenario.

*Search object** – A ship, aircraft, or other craft missing or in distress, or survivors or related search objects or evidence for which a search is being conducted. That is, any object or signal from the survivors or their craft which may lead search facilities to the survivors or provide additional clues about the survivors' status or location.

*Probability of containment (POC)** – The probability that the search object is contained within the boundaries of an area, sub-area, or grid cell.

*Probability map** – A set of grid cells covering a scenario's possibility area where each grid cell is labelled with the probability of the search object being in that grid cell. That is, each grid cell is labelled with its own *POC* value.

*Sweep width (W)** – A measure of the effectiveness with which a particular sensor can detect a particular object under specific environmental conditions. Sweep width values for combinations of sensor, search object and environmental conditions are computed from the sweep width tables provided in appendix N.

*Search effort (Z)** – The area effectively swept by a search facility within its assigned search sub-area. Search effort is computed as the product of search speed (V), search endurance (T), and sweep width (W). $Z = V \times T \times W$.

*Effort factor (f_Z)** – (1) For single point and leeway divergence datums, the effort factor is the square of the total probable error of position (E). $f_{Zp} = E^2$. (2) For line datums, the effort factor is the product of the total probable error of position (E) and the length of the datum line (L). $f_{Zl} = E \times L$.

*Relative effort (Z_r)** – The amount of available search effort (Z) divided by the effort factor. The relative effort relates the size of the effort available for a particular search to the size of the search object's location probability distribution for that search. $Z_r = Z/f_Z$.

*Cumulative relative effort (Z_{rc})** – The sum of all previous relative efforts plus the relative effort for the next planned search effort. This value determines the optimal search factor. $Z_{rc} = Z_{r-1} + Z_{r-2} + Z_{r-3} + ... + Z_{r-\text{next search}}$.

*Optimal search factor (f_s)** – A value which, when multiplied by the total probable error of position (E), produces the optimal search radius. $R_o = E \times f_s$. The width of the optimal search square (point datums) or rectangle (leeway divergence and line datums) is always twice the optimal search radius. Width $= 2 \times R_o$.

*Coverage factor (C)** – The ratio of the search effort (Z) to the area searched (A). $C = Z/A$. For parallel sweep searches, it may be computed as the ratio of sweep width (W) to track spacing (S). $C = W/S$.

Probability of detection (POD)* – The probability of the search object being detected, assuming it was in the areas that were searched. *POD* is a function of coverage factor, sensor, search conditions and the accuracy with which the search facility navigates its assigned search pattern.

Probability of success (POS)* – The probability of finding the search object with a particular search. For each sub-area searched, *POS = POC × POD*. For several simultaneous searches or several searches within a specific period of time (for example, on a particular day) for the same search object, the total *POS* is the sum of all the individual search sub-area *POS* values.

Cumulative probability of success (POS$_c$)* – The accumulated probability of finding the search object with all the search effort expended over all searches to date. *POS$_c$* is the sum of all individual search *POS* values.

Grid – Any set of intersecting perpendicular lines spaced at regular intervals.

Grid cell – A square or rectangular area formed by pairs of adjacent, perpendicular grid lines.

On-scene endurance – The amount of time a facility may spend at the scene engaged in search and rescue activities.

Optimal search plan – A plan that maximizes the probability of success attained using the available search effort.

Search area – The area, determined by the search planner, that is to be searched. This area may be sub-divided into search sub-areas for the purpose of assigning specific responsibilities to the available search facilities.

Search endurance (T) – The amount of "productive" search time available at the scene. This figure is usually taken to be 85% of the on-scene endurance, leaving a 15% allowance for investigating sightings and navigating turns at the ends of search legs.

Search speed (V) – The speed (or velocity) with which a search facility moves over the ground when searching.

Search sub-area – A designated area to be searched by a specific assigned search facility or possibly two facilities working together in close co-ordination.

Sensors – Human senses (sight, hearing, touch, etc.), those of specially trained animals (such as dogs), or electronic devices used to detect the object of a search.

Possibility sub-area – Any sub-division of the possibility area. Possibility areas are usually divided into sub-areas to develop a probability map or description of the distribution of probable search object locations within the range of all possible locations. When used in this way, each possibility sub-area is assigned a Probability of Containment (*POC*) value based on the likelihood of the search object being in that sub-area. Possibility sub-areas are usually cells in a grid but use of grids is not required. Possibility sub-areas may or may not correspond to designated search sub-areas.

Track spacing (S) – For searches using equally spaced parallel sweeps, track spacing is the distance between the centres of adjacent sweeps, or, in other words, the spacing between adjacent search facility tracks or search legs.

4.6.2   *Scenario.* As discussed in chapter 3, the available information about a SAR incident is often incomplete, may contain errors, and may be misleading. To make up for these deficiencies, the search planner must create one or more accounts of what probably happened to the survivors from the time they were last known to be safe up to the current time. These accounts, part fact and part assumption, are called scenarios. Scenarios are the basis for planning a search. To be valid, a scenario must be consistent with the known facts of the situation. To justify using it as a basis for searching, a scenario should have a high probability of being true. If several possible scenarios exist, the search planner must decide which are the most likely to be true and pursue them accordingly. As new information becomes available, search planners should modify, discard or create new scenarios as needed to ensure all those under consideration are consistent with all the available data. Creating, re-evaluating, modifying, and discarding scenarios requires sound, mature judgement, experience, knowledge, skill, and self-discipline. Scenario analysis and development, along with related investigative efforts to obtain more information, often determine a successful outcome to the distress incident. The search planner must think like a detective who is trying to solve an important case or a scientist who is trying to answer an important question. Lines of evidence must be followed to see where they lead. The available facts must be viewed from different perspectives. Missing information must be filled in with different, but plausible, assumptions to create plausible scenarios. At times, several scenarios can be developed that are consistent with all or most of the known facts. These scenarios must be carefully evaluated and weighted according to the search planner's judgement about which scenarios are more likely and which are less likely to represent the actual situation. These efforts can be difficult, demanding tasks and require dedication by the search planner to attain the best chance for success.

4.6.3 *Possibility area.* This term is used in two ways. The first usage describes every possible location regardless of how likely or unlikely the chances are for finding survivors there. The second usage defines a (usually) much smaller area containing all possible locations which are consistent with a particular scenario the search planner has developed.

> **(a)** The first meaning of possibility area is the smallest area that includes every physically possible location, however unlikely it may be. For example, the possibility area for a missing aircraft is an approximately circular area centred on the aircraft's last known position and extending in all directions as far as its remaining fuel would carry it, accounting for wind effects at all possible altitudes the aircraft might have used. Knowing the extent of this area is useful for deciding which aerodromes and other facilities (police and fire departments, etc.) to query for possible additional information about the aircraft. It is also useful for distinguishing incoming reports which might be related to the missing aircraft from those that are not. However, this type of possibility area is usually not very useful for planning searches because it is normally much too large to search effectively with the available search effort. Frequently search planners deal with this problem by creating scenarios from the known facts and some logical assumptions about what most likely happened.

> **(b)** The second meaning of possibility area is the smallest area that includes every possible location which is consistent with a particular scenario. This is called the scenario's possibility area. Usually this area is much smaller than that described in paragraph 4.6.3 (a) and is very useful for planning searches. In fact, the primary function of scenario development is to focus the search effort so the most likely locations may be searched effectively. For the remainder of this chapter, this more restrictive second meaning will be used unless otherwise noted.

4.6.4 *Search objects.* While the ultimate goal of searching is to locate and assist distressed persons, searchers need to be alert for objects or signals which may provide clues about their location. Search objects include such things as:

– boats, rafts and other survival craft;

– debris or other evidence of the distress incident; and

– signals, such as those discussed in chapter 2, from the survivors or their equipment. Such signals may be visual, aural or electronic.

All search objects have characteristics that determine how well they can be detected by various sensors under various environmental conditions. Some search objects, particularly in the marine environment, also have motion characteristics which determine the possible range of their post-distress movements.

4.6.5 *Probability of containment (POC).* Once a datum for a search has been established, the search planner must decide exactly where and how to search the surrounding area. The possibility area is defined as the smallest area which contains all possible survivor locations (POC = 100%) consistent with the facts and assumptions (scenario) under consideration. Even a single scenario's possibility area can be too large to search effectively with the available search facilities. Often, some sub-areas are more likely to contain survivors than others. In this case, the search planner should divide the possibility area into sub-areas and estimate the POC for each sub-area. One simple technique is to place a grid over the possibility area, dividing it into a number of cells. A POC value then needs to be assigned to each cell to produce a probability map. These values may be subjective estimates based on the search planner's best judgement, or they may be taken from a standard assumed probability distribution. In either case, it is important to ensure that the total of all cell probabilities initially adds up to 100%. As the search progresses, POCs of areas that have been searched need to be updated as described in paragraph 4.6.11.

4.6.6 *Probability map.* Figure 4-10 shows the specific numeric probabilities, expressed as percentages, associated with each cell of a grid laid over the standard assumed initial distribution around a datum point. That distribution is of the circular normal type. The probability of the search object being contained in the dashed circle whose radius is the total probable error of position (*E*) is 50%. The remaining area in the corners of the centre cell have a 7.91% probability of containing the search object, making the total POC for the cell 57.91%.

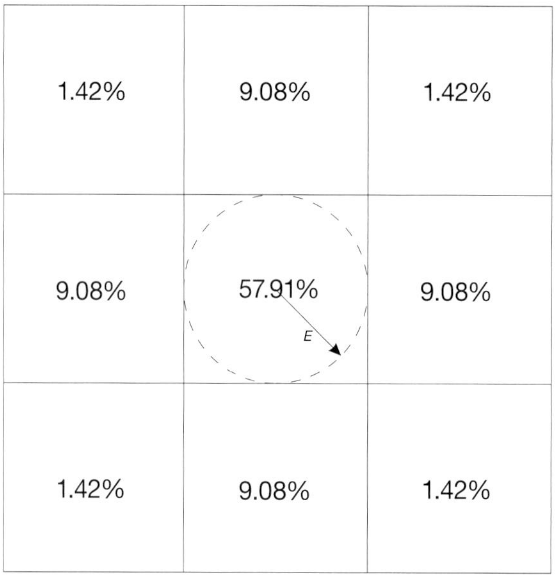

1.42%	9.08%	1.42%
9.08%	57.91% *E*	9.08%
1.42%	9.08%	1.42%

Figure 4-10 – *Probability map for a point datum*

Figure 4-11 shows the initial cell probabilities as they might appear for a line datum. The instructions and standard probability values needed for preparing initial point and line datum probability maps are provided in appendix M. Before any searching is done, the total of all cells should theoretically equal 100%. In practice, the initial total may vary slightly due to rounding errors for individual cell probabilities. Similar probability maps are used later to show how the probability of success for a search is computed.

0.2%	0.2%	0.2%	0.2%	0.2%	0.2%	0.2%	0.2%	0.2%	0.2%
2.2%	2.2%	2.2%	2.2%	2.2%	2.2%	2.2%	2.2%	2.2%	2.2%
5.2%	5.2%	5.2%	5.2%	5.2%	5.2%	5.2%	5.2%	5.2%	5.2%
2.2%	2.2%	2.2%	2.2%	2.2%	2.2%	2.2%	2.2%	2.2%	2.2%
0.2%	0.2%	0.2%	0.2%	0.2%	0.2%	0.2%	0.2%	0.2%	0.2%

Datum line →

Figure 4-11 – *Example of a completed probability map for a line datum*

4.6.7   *Sweep width (W).* Sweeping an area visually or with electronic sensors is analogous to sweeping a floor with a broom. Usually the most efficient way to sweep a floor is with a series of parallel strokes spaced at equal intervals. For a broom, the sweep width is equal to the width of the broom. The same principle applies to searching, although the effect of a single sweep is not quite as sharply defined as it is for a broom. Sweep width is a measure of the ability to detect a search object. Large objects are easier to see on clear days than small objects and therefore have larger visual sweep widths. All objects are easier to see when the air is clear than when it is hazy, which makes an object's visual sweep width higher on a clear day than on a hazy day. Objects made of metal are usually easier to detect by radar than those of a similar size and shape made of fibreglass, which means that metal objects usually have larger radar sweep widths than fibreglass ones. For each combination of sensor, search object, and set of environmental conditions, a sweep width can be estimated using tables of values (described below) based on many years of experience and testing. Not all search objects within one-half of the sweep width either side of the search facility will be detected and there will be times when search objects are detected at greater distances. In fact, the probability of a search object being detected if it is more than one-half sweep width from the search facility's track is equal to the probability it will be missed if it is inside that distance. This property results from the mathematical definition of sweep width used in search theory. Figure 4-12 illustrates the detection profile (also called a *lateral range curve*) and sweep width for visual search under ideal conditions.[*]

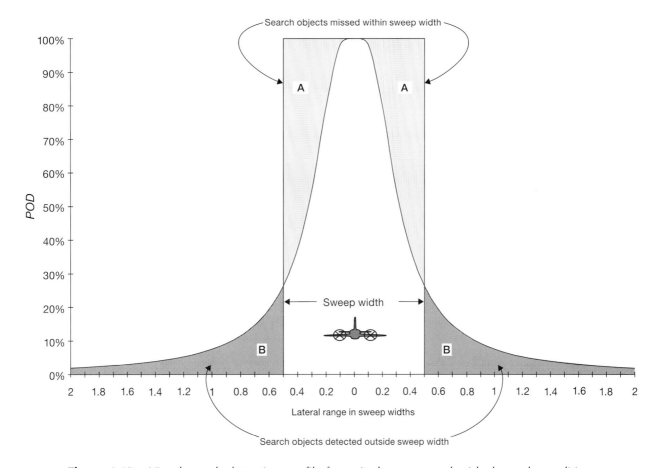

Figure 4-12 – *Visual search detection profile for a single sweep under ideal search conditions*

---

[*] This profile is based on the *inverse cube law* of visual detection first proposed by B.O. Koopman circa 1946 and described again in his book, *Search and Screening*, Pergamon Press, 1980.

(a) *Computing sweep width.* Actual values for sweep widths depend on the sensor, the search object, and the on-scene environmental conditions. Tables of uncorrected sweep width values and correction factors are provided in appendix N to aid the search planner in estimating sweep width values for a given set of circumstances. The sweep width used in planning and evaluating the search is computed as the product of the uncorrected sweep width and all the correction factors.

(b) *Example.* If the search facility is a merchant vessel, the primary "sensor" is the eyes of the crew (visual search), the search object is a 6-person liferaft, meteorological visibility is 28 km (15 NM), and the wind is 30 km/h (16 kts), the sweep width is computed as follows:

Uncorrected sweep width (W_u) = 11.5 km or 6.2 NM

Weather correction factor (f_w) = 0.9

W = 11.5 km × 0.9 = 10.4 km, or

W = 6.2 NM × 0.9 = 5.6 NM

where the uncorrected sweep width and weather correction factor values were taken from tables N-4 and N-7.

4.6.8 *Search effort (Z).* The number of available search facilities and their capabilities determine the available search effort. Factors to be considered include search speeds, search endurances, sensors, weather conditions, search altitudes, visibility, terrain, size of the search object, etc. These factors determine the sweep width and how much distance a search facility can cover in the search area. The search speed, endurance and sweep width determine the search effort available from each facility.

(a) *Search effort computation.* A search facility's available search effort is the product of its search speed (V), search endurance (T), and sweep width (W):

$Z = V \times T \times W$

The total available search effort (Z_{ta}) available from several facilities is the sum of the efforts available from each facility:

$Z_{ta} = Z_{f-1} + Z_{f-2} + Z_{f-3} + ...$

(b) *Example.* If an aircraft search facility's assigned search sub-area will be approximately 100 nautical miles from its base of operations, its transit speed to and from its assigned search sub-area is 200 knots, its search speed is 160 knots, and its total endurance is six hours, then a total of one hour will be spent in transit, leaving five hours for on-scene activities. To allow time for investigating sightings and navigating turns at the ends of the search legs, the on-scene endurance is reduced by 15% to give the search endurance. The search endurance is then 85% of the on-scene endurance which is computed as 0.85 × 5 or 4.25 h. If the sweep width is three nautical miles, then the available search effort (Z) for that facility is computed as follows:

Z = 160 × 4.25 × 3 = 2,040 square nautical miles

Note: The masters of vessels and pilots in command of aircraft are the best sources for estimates of available on scene endurance times and search speeds for their craft. These individuals should be consulted before a search plan involving them is finalized.

4.6.9 *Effort factor (f_Z).* In order to determine the optimal area to be searched around a point datum or along a line datum with a given amount of search effort, it is necessary to compare the size of the available effort with the size of the search object location probability distribution. The basis for such a comparison is the effort factor, which is proportional to the area covered by the distribution.

(a) *Point datums.* For point datums, the effort factor is the square of the total probable error of position (E):

$f_{Zp} = E^2$

(b) *Line datums.* For line datums, the effort factor is the product of the total probable error of position (E) and the length of the datum line (L):

$$f_{Zl} = E \times L$$

(c) *Point datums connected by a line datum.* The probability distribution centred on a "pure" datum line is assumed to be uniform along the line and normally distributed on either side of the line. The probability of the search object being beyond either end of the line is assumed to be zero. When two point datums are connected by a line datum, this is a reasonable approximation if the distance between the datums is large compared to the average of their respective total probable errors of position. The procedures described in the example of paragraph 4.7.5 will produce a near-optimal search factor for small to moderate levels of relative effort when L is computed as the distance between the datum points.

Note: For larger relative efforts (Z_r greater than 10) or short distances between datum points (L less than $5 \times E$), one alternative is to increase the value of L so the datum line extends beyond the datum points. Another alternative is to evaluate search areas based on both the point datum effort factor (f_{Zp}) and the line datum effort factor (f_{Zl}) and choose an optimal search factor somewhere between the one recommended for a point datum and the one recommended for a line datum. The closer the points are to one another, the more the distribution will resemble that of a single point datum. No matter how small L becomes, the effort factor should never be less than E^2. That is, if L is less than E, use f_{Zp}, not f_{Zl}. The length and width of the search area may be adjusted by the search planner as needed to accommodate the shape of the distribution.

4.6.10 *Relative effort (Z_r).* To determine the optimal area to be searched around a point datum or along a line datum with a given amount of search effort, it is necessary to compare the size of the available effort with the size of the search object location probability distribution to be searched. This is done by computing the ratio of the available effort to the effort factor as follows:

$$Z_r = Z_{ta}/f_Z$$

4.6.11 *Cumulative relative effort (Z_{rc}).* It is also necessary to account for all previous effort when determining the next optimal area to search with the present or projected available effort. This is done by computing the sum of all previous relative efforts and the one computed for the next search. Thus:

$$Z_{rc} = Z_{r-1} + Z_{r-2} + Z_{r-3} + \dots + Z_{r-\text{next search}}$$

The cumulative relative effort is used with the optimal search factor graphs in appendix N to determine the optimal search factor to use in planning the next search. Cumulative *relative* effort is used rather than cumulative effort to ensure that any changes in the total probable error of position from one search to the next are automatically taken into account when computing the optimal search factor. Examples are given in section 4.7.

Note: Relative effort and cumulative relative effort are used only for planning optimal searches for single point, leeway divergence and line datums. For area datums, another technique, described in paragraph 4.7.6, is used.

4.6.12 *Optimal search factor (f_s).* The optimal search factor is used together with the total probable error of position (E) to compute the optimum size of the next search area. The optimal search radius is:

$$R_o = f_s \times E$$

As discussed further in section 4.7, the width of the optimal search square (for point datums) or rectangle (for leeway divergence and line datums) is always twice the optimal search radius.

4.6.13 *Coverage factor (C).* The coverage factor compares the amount of searching done in an area to the size of that area. For accurately navigated search patterns that fill the area, it is a measure of how well the area was covered.

    (a) *Universal definition.* The coverage factor is the ratio of the search effort (Z) expended in a search sub-area to the size of that area (A):

$$C = Z/A$$

    (b) *Example 1.* If the available search effort is 1,000 square nautical miles and the area to be searched is 2,000 square nautical miles, then searching the entire area would result in a coverage factor of 1,000/2,000 or 0.5. Searching only half the area would result in a coverage factor of 1,000/1,000 or 1.0 for the half that was searched and zero for the other half.

    (c) *Parallel Sweep Definition.* For parallel sweep search patterns, an equivalent way to compute coverage factor is to take the ratio of sweep width (W) to track spacing (S):

$$C = W/S$$

    (d) *Example 2.* If a search sub-area is completely covered with a parallel sweep search pattern having a track spacing of 5 nautical miles and the sweep width for the search object is 3 nautical miles, then the coverage factor is $\frac{3}{5}$ or 0.6.

4.6.14 *Probability of detection (POD).* The probability of detection is a measure of how well an area has been searched. Therefore, POD is closely related to coverage factor. In fact, POD is a function of the amount of searching done in an area, the sensor's detection profile, and the method of moving the sensor through the area. Search patterns with equally spaced parallel sweeps tend to maximize POD if they are perfectly navigated. As conditions deteriorate, due to weather, search facility navigation error or both, the POD is adversely affected. Not only can the effective sweep width decrease as conditions deteriorate, the detection profile can change in a way that reduces the detection advantage obtained by using parallel sweeps. Figure 4-13 shows typical visual detection profiles for both ideal and normal search conditions. The POD graph in figure N-10 shows the corresponding curves for average POD in an area covered by equally spaced parallel sweeps as a function of the coverage factor[*]. When search conditions are ideal, the upper POD curve may be used. In normal conditions, the lower POD curve should be used. Intermediate values may be used if conditions are between ideal and normal. It should be noted that "normal conditions" include any situation significantly less than ideal. Anytime the corrected sweep width for a search object is less than the maximum uncorrected sweep width for that object, conditions are less than ideal. By the time the corrected sweep width for a search object is down to one half the maximum possible value for that object, the lower curve should be in use.

    (a) *Example 1.* The sweep width for a downed aircraft (less than 5700 kg) from an altitude of 300 m in hilly terrain with a visibility of 6 km is about 2.3 km. The maximum uncorrected sweep width for the same object from the same altitude is 5.6 km when the visibility is 37 km or greater. Since 2.3 is less than half of 5.6, search conditions are normal and the lower POD curve should be used.

    (b) *Example 2.* Search conditions are also considered normal when the probable search facility navigation error is as large as, or larger than, the sweep width. This means search facility navigation error need not be large in absolute terms to make use of the lower POD curve appropriate. Search objects are often small with correspondingly small sweep widths. By the time the probable search facility navigation error is as large as the sweep width, the lower curve should be in use. If the sweep width is two miles, then a probable search facility navigation error of only two miles would be needed to drop POD estimates to the lower curve.

    Note: POD is *not* a measure of the search effort's chances for success (probability of success or POS), although there is a relationship between POD, POS, and the probability of the search object being contained in the area searched (POC). POD is only a conditional probability which measures the chances of finding the search object if it happens to be in the area searched. POS and the relationship among POD, POC, and POS are discussed in paragraph 4.6.15.

---

[*] The "ideal'" POD curve in figure N-10 is based on Koopman's inverse cube law of visual detection while the "normal" curve is based on the so-called *random search curve*, also covered in *Search and Screening* (see note 4).

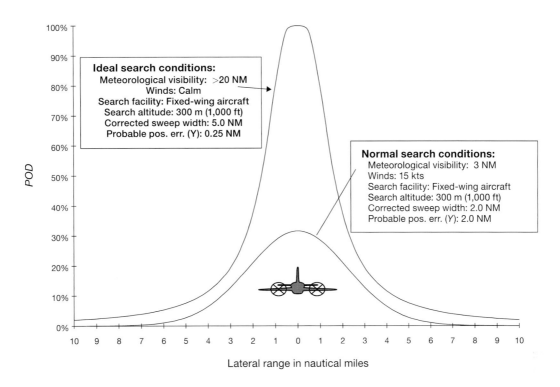

Figure 4-13 *–An example of visual search direction profiles for a single sweep [search object: boat 7 m (23 ft)]*

4.6.15 *Probability of success (POS).* The probability of success is the probability of finding the search object. *POS is the true measure of search effectiveness.* Finding the search object depends on two things: having sensors capable of detecting it, and placing those sensors close enough to the search object to make detection likely. POD measures the chances of detecting the search object *if* it is actually in the area searched. POC measures the likelihood of the search object actually being in the area searched. A thorough search of an area (*POD* ≈ 100%) which has almost no chance of containing the search object (*POC* ≈ 0%) has almost no chance of succeeding (*POS* ≈ 0%). Likewise, a very normal search of an area (*POD* ≈ 0%) that almost certainly contains the search object (POC ≈ 100%) also has almost no chance of succeeding (*POS* ≈ 0%). If either *POD* or *POC* is zero, so is the *POS* for that particular effort. In other words, if the search object is not in the search area, no amount of search effort can find it; and failing to search the area which does contain the search object will never produce a successful result. Only if both *POD* and *POC* equal 100% is success guaranteed. The actual *POS* usually lies between these extremes. All intermediate POS values are possible from different combinations of values for *POC* and *POD*.

(a) The equation describing the relationship of *POS* to *POC* and *POD* is:

$$POS = POC \times POD$$

(b) *Example.* If the *POC* for a search sub-area is 65% (0.65) and the search effort expended in that sub-area produces a coverage factor of 1.0, the *POD* under ideal conditions is estimated to be 79% (0.79). The *POS* for that sub-area is then computed as:

$$POS = 0.65 \times 0.79 = 0.51 \text{ or } 51\%$$

For normal search conditions, the *POS* would be:

$$POS = 0.65 \times 0.63 = 0.41 \text{ or } 41\%$$

4.6.16 *Updating POCs to account for previous searching.* Even when it is unsuccessful, searching a sub-area provides information about the survivors' probable location; it provides new evidence which now makes it less likely they were in the searched area. In the example of paragraph 4.6.15 above, the initial *POC* for the sub-area searched was 65%. Searching that area without finding the survivors means the search planner should revise the estimate of their likelihood of being in that area downward by an appropriate amount. This is done using the following equation:

$$POC_{new} = (1 - POD) \times POC_{old}$$

For areas *not* searched, *POC* does not change. That is, $POC_{new} = POC_{old}$.

(a) *Example 1.* Using the *POC* and *POD* values from 4.6.15, the new *POC* for ideal search conditions is computed as:

$$POC_{new} = (1.0 - 0.79) \times 0.65 = 0.21 \times 0.65 = 0.14 \text{ or } 14\%$$

(b) *Example 2.* For normal search conditions, the new *POC* is computed as:

$$POC_{new} = (1.0 - 0.63) \times 0.65 = 0.37 \times 0.65 = 0.24 \text{ or } 24\%$$

(c) *Example 3.* Another way of looking at this process is to note the *POS* of the search done under ideal conditions, which was 51%. That is, searching extracted 51% of the probability from the distribution and all of it came from the one sub-area that was searched, which only had 65% of the probability to begin with. Hence, 65% − 51% = 14%, which is the same result as before. Similarly, for the search done under normal conditions, 65% − 41% = 24%.

4.6.17 *Cumulative probability of success (POS_c).* Cumulative *POS* measures the effectiveness of all searching done to date. It is the sum of all the *POS* values for each search. For example, if the *POS* for the first search was 40% and that for the second search was 35%, then the total *POS* for the two searches would be 75%. This in turn means the remaining probability of the search object being in the possibility area is now only 25%. In fact the cumulative POS after completion of the nth search is:

$$POS_c = POS_1 + POS_2 + POS_3 + ... + POS_n$$

and also:

$$POS_c = 1 - \text{(The total of all } POC_{new} \text{ cell values in the possibility area after the } n^{th} \text{ search)}$$

Searching may be thought of as a means for subtracting probability from a scenario's possibility area and putting it into *POS* and POS_c. As POS_c rises toward 100%, the total *POC* in the scenario's possibility area decreases toward 0%. A high POS_c value is an indicator that further efforts in that scenario's possibility area are likely to be futile. Things to consider when POS_c reaches a high value are discussed in paragraph 4.7.9. For optimal square searches around a point datum, cumulative *POS* may be obtained directly from figure N-11 by entering the point datum POS graph with the cumulative relative effort. For optimal rectangular searches along a line datum, cumulative *POS* may be obtained from figure N-12 by entering the line datum POS graph with the cumulative relative effort.

4.7 Optimal search effort allocation

4.7.1 The search planner's problem, in simple terms, is one of determining how to make the most effective use of the available search facilities. Survivors need to be located quickly if lives are to be saved. Searching is expensive and sometimes puts the search facilities at increased risk. Both of these facts make achieving the maximum search effectiveness an important consideration. In the following paragraphs, a strategy for the deployment of search facilities is described which maximizes search effectiveness. This is accomplished by:

- dividing the scenario's possibility area into sub-areas;
- estimating a *POC* for each sub-area;
- developing a search plan that maximizes *POS*;
- conducting the search plan;
- updating all *POC* values to reflect the search results; and
- using the updated *POC* values to maximize *POS* for the next search.

This strategy is also self-correcting. Even if the choice of initial *POCs* does not place the search object in a sub-area having a high *POC* value, following this strategy will tend to move the focus of the search toward the survivors' actual location.

4.7.2 *Effort allocation.* Most of the time, the search planner does not have enough search facilities to attain a high coverage factor over all possible survivor locations or even all those associated with a particular scenario. The problem then becomes one of deciding where to place the search effort and how much to concentrate it to maximize the chances for success. The search planner must decide whether to search a small area with a high coverage factor or a larger area with a lower coverage factor. The best choice is usually the one which maximizes POS. Maximizing POS depends on:

– how much search effort is available; and

– how the search object location probabilities are distributed.

Paragraphs 4.7.3 through 4.7.6 provide guidance on how to optimally allocate effort for three standard types of search object location probability distributions and a generalized distribution.

4.7.3 *Uniform distributions.* According to search theory, the best way to search evenly distributed search object location probabilities is to spread the available effort uniformly over the scenario's entire possibility area. This will always produce the maximum *POS*, even though *POD* values may be low. In practice, however, coverage factors of less than 0.5 are not recommended. Initial probability maps for uniform distributions are usually made by laying a regular grid of equally sized cells over the possibility area and placing an equal amount of probability in each cell. The amount of probability in each cell would be equal to 1.0 (or 100%) divided by the number of cells. In a 10 × 10 grid (100 cells), each cell would be assigned a *POC* of 1%.

4.7.4 *Distributions concentrated around a datum point.* When a single position is used as the datum for planning a search, the distribution of search object location probabilities is assumed to be circular normal. When graphed in three dimensions (*X*, *Y*, and Probability Density), it looks like the graph in figure 4-1(a). Corresponding probability maps, using grids with different cell sizes but covering the same relative area, are provided in appendix M.

    (a) The optimal search area for the next search around a datum point is found by:

        (1) Computing the relative effort available for the next search (Z_r);

        (2) Computing the cumulative relative effort (Z_{rc}) as the sum of all previous relative efforts plus the relative effort available for the next search;

        (3) Using Z_{rc} and the appropriate graphs in figures N-5 and N-6 to find the optimal search factor (f_s);

        (4) Multiplying the total probable error of position (*E*) by the optimal search factor (f_s) to get the optimal search radius (R_o), and drawing a circle of that radius with its centre at the datum position; and

        (5) Drawing (circumscribing) a square around the circle (figure 4-14) with the length of one side equal to $2 \times R_o$ and computing its area as $4 \times R_o^2$.

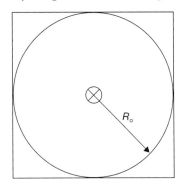

Figure 4-14 – *The optimal search square for a point datum*

Once the optimal search area has been found, the search planner can determine the optimal coverage factor (C), the corresponding probability of detection (POD), and the expected cumulative probability of success (POS_c) as shown in examples that follow. The search planner can then proceed to divide the search area into search sub-areas and select search patterns as needed for assignment to specific search facilities, as discussed in chapter 5.

(b) *Examples.*

(1) *First search.* Suppose search conditions are ideal, the computed total probable error of position (E_1) is 15 NM and the effort available (Z_1) is 1,850 NM^2. Computing the relative effort (Z_{r-1}) for the first search:

$$Z_{r-1} = Z_1/E_1{}^2 = 1,850/225 = 8.2$$

Because this is the first search:

$$Z_{rc} = Z_{r-1} = 8.2$$

From the graphs for point datum optimal search factors in figure N-5, the optimal search factor (f_s) is 1.3. Using this optimal search factor, the optimal radius (R_{o1}) for this search is:

$$R_{o1} = f_{s-1} \times E_1 = 1.3 \times 15 = 19.5 \text{ NM}$$

The optimal first search area (A_1) is then computed as:

$$A_1 = 4 \times R_{o1}{}^2 = 4 \times 19.5^2 = 4 \times 380.25 = 1,521 \text{ NM}^2$$

The optimal coverage factor (C_1) for this search is computed by:

$$C_1 = Z_1/A_1 = 1,850/1,521 = 1.2$$

From the POD graph, figure N-10, the *POD* for this search is about 87%. From the point datum POS graph, figure N-11, the cumulative *POS* (POS_c) will be about 68% following the search.

(2) *Second search.* Suppose the first search was performed using the optimal area and coverage computed in example (1). Assume conditions for the second search are ideal, the effort available for the second search (Z_2) is 3,267 NM^2, and the total probable error of position (E_2) is now 18NM. The relative effort for this search (Z_{r-2}) is:

$$Z_{r-2} = Z_2/E_2{}^2 = 3,267/324 = 10.1$$

The cumulative relative effort (Z_{rc}) is computed as:

$$Z_{rc} = Z_{r-1} + Z_{r-2} = 8.2 + 10.1 = 18.3$$

From the graphs for point datum optimal search factors in figure N-6, the optimal search factor (f_{s-2}) is 1.7. The optimal radius for the second search (R_{o2}) is:

$$R_{o2} = f_{s-2} \times E_2 = 1.7 \times 18 = 30.6 \text{ NM}$$

The optimal search area for the second search (A_2) is then computed as:

$$A_2 = 4 \times R_{o2}{}^2 = 4 \times 30.6^2 = 4 \; 936.4 = 3,745 \text{ NM}^2$$

The optimal coverage factor (C_2) for this search is computed by:

$$C_2 = Z_2/A_2 = 3,267/3,745 = 0.9$$

From the POD graph, figure N-10, the *POD* for this search is about 74%. From the point datum POS graph, figure N-11, the cumulative probability of success (POS_c) following the second search is about 87%.

(c) *Probability maps.* Initial probability maps for datum points are provided in appendix M. The POC values contained in each grid are based on the same circular normal probability distribution. Each grid covers the same amount of the distribution – only the cell size and the number of cells changes. The number of cells ranges from 9 (3 × 3) to 144 (12 × 12). These grids may be used to update *POC* values and also compute *POS* and *POS_c*. Probability maps are very useful when searching for stationary search objects even when the map probabilities must be updated by hand. Their use is always highly recommended for this type of search. However, when searching for moving objects, such as a boat or raft adrift on the ocean, maintaining probability maps by hand can prove to be very difficult. Updating of probability maps to account for *both* unsuccessful prior searching *and* increasingly uncertain search object drift is such a complex task that it is better left to computers programmed for the purpose.

4.7.5 *Distributions concentrated along a datum line.* When a line is used as the datum for planning a search, the distribution of search object location probabilities is assumed to be uniform along the line and normal on either side. When graphed in three dimensions (X, Y, and Probability Density), it looks like the graph in figure 4-2 (a). Instructions for creating probability maps for line datums, using grids with different cell sizes, are provided in appendix M.

    (a) The optimal search area for a line datum is found using the same general procedure as that just described for point datums. However, the effort factor is computed slightly differently (see paragraph 4.6.9 and the examples below), a separate set of graphs, provided in appendix N, are used for finding the optimal search factor and cumulative *POS*, and the recommended search area is a rectangle and not a square.

    (b) *Examples.*

        (1) *First search.* Suppose search conditions are normal, the computed total probable error of position (E_1) is 10 NM, the length (L) of the datum line is 100 NM, and the effort available (Z_1) is 2,100 NM^2. Computing the relative effort (Z_{r-1}) for the first search:

$$Z_{r-1} = Z_1/E_1^2 = 2{,}100/1{,}000 = 2.1$$

Because this is the first search:

$$Z_{rc} = Z_{r-1} = 2.1$$

From the graphs for line datum optimal search factors, figure N-7, the optimal search factor (f_s) is 1.05. Using this optimal search factor, the optimal radius (R_{o1}) for this search is:

$$R_{o1} = f_{s-1} \times E_1 = 1.05 \times 10 = 10.5 \text{ NM}$$

The optimal first search area (A_1) is then computed as:

$$A_1 = 2 \times R_{o1} \times L = 2 \times 10.5 \times 100 = 2{,}100 \text{ NM}^2$$

which is a 21 NM by 100 NM rectangle with its major axis centred on the datum line. The optimal coverage factor (C_1) for this search is computed by:

$$C_1 = Z_1/A_1 = 2{,}100/2100 = 1.0$$

From the POD graph, figure N-10, the *POD* for this search is about 63%. From the line datum POS graph, figure N-12, the cumulative *POS* (POS_c) will be about 50% following the search.

        (2) *Second search.* Suppose the first search was conducted using the optimal area and coverage computed in Example (1). Assume conditions for the second search are normal, the effort available for the second search (Z_2) is 4,000 NM^2, the total probable error of position (E_2) is unchanged at 10 NM, and the length (L) remains 100 NM. The relative effort for this search (Z_{r-2}) is:

$$Z_{r-2} = Z_2/E_2^2 = 4{,}000/1{,}000 = 4.0$$

The cumulative relative effort (Z_{rc}) is computed as:

$$Z_{rc} = Z_{r-1} + Z_{r-2} = 2.1 + 4.0 = 6.1$$

From the graphs for line datum optimal search factors in figure N-8, the optimal search factor (f_{s-2}) is 1.5. The optimal radius for the second search (R_{o2}) is:

$$R_{o2} = f_{s-2} \times E_2 = 1.5 \times 10 = 15 \text{ NM}$$

The optimal search area for the second search (A_2) is then computed as:

$$A_2 = 2 \times R_{o2} \times L = 2 \times 15 \times 100 = 3,000 \text{ NM}^2$$

which is a 30 NM by 100 NM rectangle with its major axis centred on the datum line. The optimal coverage factor (C_2) for this search is computed by:

$$C_2 = Z_2/A_2 = 4,000/3,000 = 1.33$$

From the POD graph, figure N-10, the *POD* for this search is about 74%. From the line datum POS graph, figure N-12, the cumulative probability of success (POS_c) following the second search is about 80%.

(c) *Probability maps.* Initial probability cross-section values for datum lines are provided in appendix M and instructions for using them to create initial probability maps for line datums are contained in appendix M. The *POC* values contained in each strip are based on the same standard normal probability distribution. Each strip covers the same amount of the distribution – only the cell size and the number of cells change. The number of cells ranges from 3 to 12. Probability maps made by means of these strips may be used to update *POC* values and also compute *POS* and POS_c.

4.7.6 *Generalized distributions.* The technique described below may be applied to any probability map. However, it is usually applied to probability maps where the search object location probability distribution is not centred on a point or line or differs from one of the standard distributions in some other respect. Sub-paragraphs (a) and (b) below provide a general description of a multiple-trial method for determining the best way to use the available search effort. The remaining subparagraphs explain the necessary preparations in more detail and provide examples of this technique's use in a sample search planning problem.

(a) *Multiple-trial method.* The only way to determine the optimal allocation of search effort for non-standard distributions is to perform multiple trials where the available effort is applied to different amounts of area on the probability map. The length, width and position of each trial area should be adjusted so it contains as much probability as possible. The *POS* for each trial area is computed and the one which has the highest *POS* is the one that should be searched. Three trials are recommended in which searches with coverage factors of 1.0, 0.5, and 1.5 are tested to see which produces the highest *POS*. To compute the area (A) which can be searched with a given amount of search effort (Z) at the different coverages (C), the equation from section 4.6 relating these three quantities:

$$C = Z/A$$

is solved for A. The resulting formula for A as a function of effort and coverage factor is:

$$A = Z/C$$

(b) *Performing the trials.* In the first trial, the amount of area that can be searched exactly equals the available search effort. To perform the first test, a probability map is prepared and one or more rectangles are formed which have a total area equal to the available search effort. Multiple rectangles may be needed in situations where multiple high-probability cells exist but are separated by enough distance that it is not convenient (maybe not even possible) to include them in a single rectangle while maintaining a reasonable coverage factor. The length(s) and width(s) of the rectangle(s) are chosen so that when they are plotted on the probability map, the maximum amount of probability is contained in the proposed search area(s). The POS for the coverage 1.0 search is then computed. A similar test is performed for each of the other trial coverage factors. In the second trial, the search area is twice the available effort and in the third trial the search area is $\frac{2}{3}$ of the available search effort. The trial which produces the highest POS is then used to plan the search. If time and computing facilities allow, further trials may be computed in an attempt to generate a higher POS value. In general, it is usually best to search the areas with the highest probability densities first and leave the lower density areas for later. If the cells of the probability map are of equal size, the POC values may be used directly. If they are of different sizes, then dividing the POCs by the areas of their respective cells may be necessary to determine where probability densities are the highest.

(c) *Detailed preparation.* After determining the possibility area for a scenario, the search planner must divide it into grid cells and assign a POC to each cell to create the initial probability map. The sum of all POCs on the initial probability map should equal 100%. Next, the search planner needs to estimate the available search effort and compute the amount of area which can be covered in each trial. If the probability map consists of cells of equal size, the search planner may find it convenient to note how many cells can be covered for each of the three coverage factors. For example, if the probability map consists of cells measuring 10 NM on a side, so each cell covers 100 NM^2, and the available search effort is 1,600 NM^2, then 16 cells may be covered with a coverage factor of 1.0, 32 cells may be covered with a coverage factor of 0.5, and 10.667 cells may be covered with a coverage factor of 1.5. For convenience, the search planner may wish to adjust the trial area and coverage so a whole number of cells forming a rectangle is used for the trial. In the last example above, it would probably be easier to test the top 10 cells at a coverage of 1.6, the top 11 cells at a coverage of 1.4, or the top 12 cells at a coverage of 1.3, especially if their locations on the probability map naturally form a rectangle. (The only rectangle 11 cells will form is one that is one cell wide and eleven cells long. This may be appropriate for a datum line but in other situations, odd numbers of cells are usually inconvenient for search planning purposes.) Sometimes, it may be helpful to form a convenient rectangle by including a few low-probability cells adjacent to the high-probability cells. These types of adjustments will still produce valid results while often eliminating the need to deal with fractions of cells or non-rectangular shapes.

(d) *Sample search planning problem.* The pilot of a small executive jet reported its position at 1300Z. Next reporting position was 50 NM further along the intended track. The pilot expected to reach that point at 1315Z. The next point after that was the destination airport, a further 50 NM along the course. No further transmissions were received from the aircraft; visual flight conditions covered the entire area. At 1345Z the responsible ATS unit reported the foregoing facts to the RCC and stated that the plane had not landed at the destination (which was the closest airport to the 1300Z position) nor was it in radar contact. From this information, the search planner computed the aircraft's ground speed as 200 knots (50 NM in 15 min = 200 knots). A forced landing or crash is assumed and the search planning process is begun. The probable error of the aircraft's reported position is estimated to be 10 NM. Based on this and other information, the search planner developed a scenario, determined a corresponding possibility area, divided it into rectangular cells, and assigned POC values as shown in figure 4-15. Within each cell, the distribution of search object location probabilities is assumed to be uniform. Search conditions are ideal and a sweep width of 2.0 nautical miles is computed.

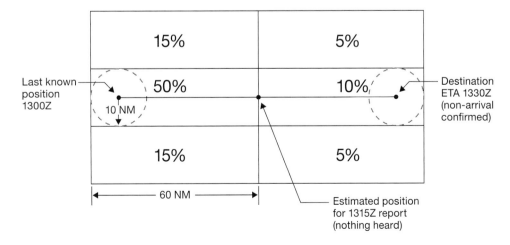

Figure 4-15 *–Search planner's scenario with POC values*

(e) *First search.* In the examples that follow, the multiple-trial technique for determining the optimal search area is demonstrated for three different levels of available search effort.

(1) *Example 1.* Assume the available search facility has a search endurance of four hours at a search speed of 150 knots. The available search effort is computed to be $150 \times 4 \times 2$ or 1,200 square miles. The available effort (1,200 NM^2) is just enough to cover the 50% cell (1,200 NM^2) with a coverage factor of 1.0 as shown in figure 4-16 (a). Multiplying *POC* by *POD* (0.5 × 0.79), a POS of 39.5% is computed. If the area searched is doubled (to 2,400 NM^2) as shown in figure 4-16 (b), a *POC* of 65% can be attained but the coverage factor drops to 0.5. Again multiplying *POC* by *POD* (0.65 0.47), a *POS* of 31% is obtained. Decreasing the area searched to two-thirds of the original (or 800NM^2) as in figure 4-16 (c), the *POC* is estimated to be two-thirds of 50% or 33%. For this trial the coverage factor is 1.5 and the corresponding *POD* is 0.94. The *POS* for this trial is 0.33 × 0.94 or 31%. In this example, the first alternative produces the highest *POS* and is the one on which the search plan should be based.

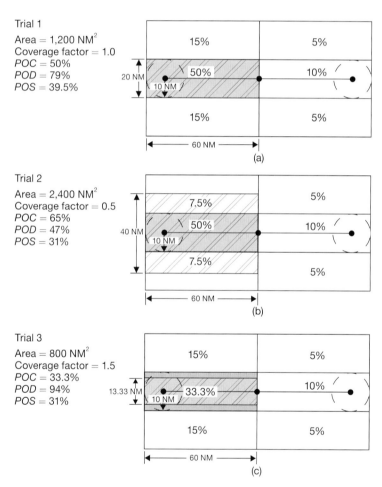

Figure 4-16 – *Available effort = 1,200 NM²*

(2)   *Example 2.* For this example, assume that only 600 square miles of search effort are available. Again starting with a trial coverage factor of 1.0, only half of the 50% cell can be covered. This produces a *POS* of 0.25 × 0.79 or 19.75%. Doubling the area covered so the entire 50% cell is covered at a coverage factor of 0.5, the *POS* is 0.50 × 0.47 or 23.5%. Reducing the area covered to two-thirds of that used in the first trial produces a *POC* of $\frac{2}{3}$ × 0.25 or 17% and a POS of 0.17 × 0.94 or 16%. The second trial produces the highest POS this time and is the one which should be used to plan the search. Figure 4-17 illustrates these three trials.

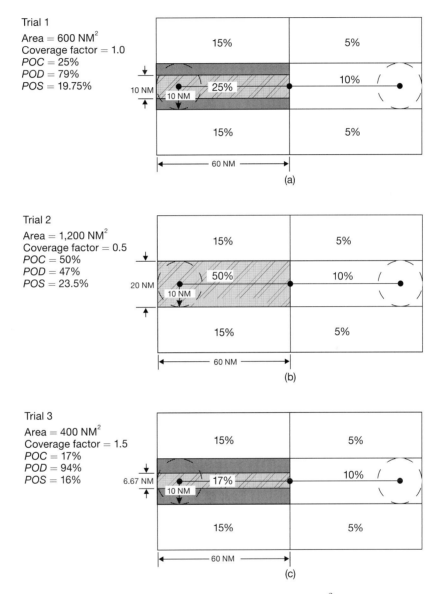

Figure 4-17 *– Available effort = 600 NM²*

(3) *Example 3.* For this example, assume that 1,800 square miles of search effort are available. This is enough to cover the 50% cell and one-quarter of each 15% cell at coverage 1.0. The total *POC* is then 57.5% and the *POS* is 0.575 × 0.79 or 45.43%. Doubling the area searched would allow coverage of the 50% cell and both of the 15% cells for a total *POC* of 80%. However, the coverage factor would only be 0.5 and the resulting *POS* would be 0.8 × 0.47 or 37.6%. Reducing the search area to two-thirds of that used in the first trial allows coverage of just the 50% cell but with a coverage factor of 1.5. The resulting *POS* is 0.5 × 0.94 or 47%. The third trial produces the highest *POS* and should be the one used to plan the search. Figure 4-18 illustrates these three trials.

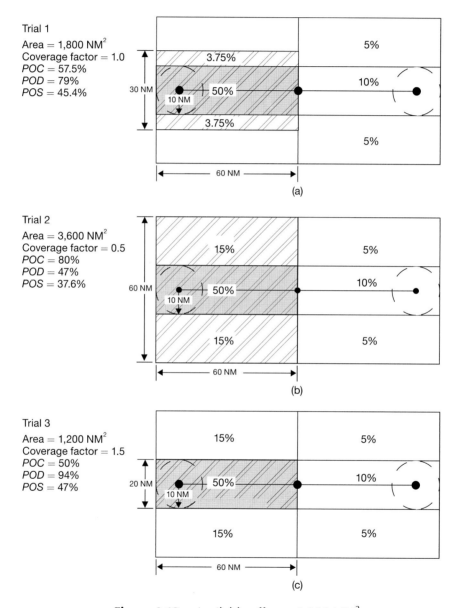

Figure 4-18 – *Available effort = 1,800 NM²*

(f) *Analysis of the trials.* In these three examples, the recommended search sub-area was always the same – namely the cell with 50% *POC*. Only the recommended coverage changed, based on the amount of available search effort. This was due mainly to the choice of *POC* values for the cells. The fact that one half of the probability is contained in only one-sixth of the scenario's possibility area gives that cell a much higher probability density than any other cell. This makes it the best place to put the entire search effort most, but not all, of the time. If the available search effort is increased to 2,400 square miles, then covering all of the 50% cell and half of each 15% cell at coverage 1.0 will produce a *POS* of 51%. The next trial will produce a *POS* value of 42% for twice the area at coverage 0.5 and the last trial will produce a *POS* value of 52% for two-thirds the area at a coverage of 1.5. This last trial would cover the 50% cell plus one-sixth of each 15% cell. However, putting *all* the search effort into the 50% cell at a coverage of 2.0 produces only a 49% *POS*. Even in a distribution with a high concentration of probability in one cell, it eventually becomes optimal to increase the area searched rather than just increase the coverage of the cell with the highest probability density. If the distribution of probabilities among the cells had been more nearly uniform, increasing the area searched rather than the coverage factor would have become optimal sooner. This principle is illustrated in the examples of paragraph 4.7.6.

(g) *Updating the probability map.* After each search, the *POC* values in each grid cell that was searched need to be updated according to the formula given in paragraph 4.6.11. The examples below continue with the missing aircraft scenario used in example 1 of paragraph 4.7.6 (e) above. In that example, the 50% cell was to be searched with a coverage of 1.0. The examples below assume this search has been completed. The new POC for the cell searched is now $(1 - 0.79) \times 0.5$ or 11%. The updated *POCs* are shown in figure 4-19.

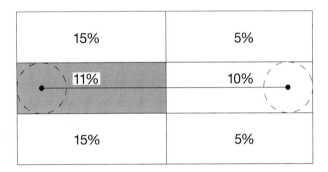

Figure 4-19 – *POC values after the first search*
(POS$_c$ = 39%)

(h) *Second search.* Conditions for the second search are assumed to be ideal. In the examples below, the multiple-trial technique is again used to find the best search area.

    (1) *Example 1.* If the available search effort is again 1,200 square miles, then the highest *POS* (14.1%) will be attained by searching the two 15% cells with a coverage factor of 0.5. This result was found by using the multiple-trial technique for coverage factors of 1.0, 0.5, and 1.5 as described above in the examples for the first search.

(2) *Example 2.* Suppose the available search effort is increased to 2,400 square miles for the second search. Now, both 15% cells can be searched, as shown in figure 4-20 (a), with a coverage of 1.0, producing a *POS* of 23.70%. At a coverage of 0.5, the four highest cells can be searched, as shown in figure 4-20 (b). The total *POC* for these cells is 51%, giving a *POS* of 0.51 × 0.47 or 23.97%. Increasing the coverage to 1.5 allows covering only two-thirds of each 15% cell, as shown in figure 4-20 (c). This produces a *POS* of only 18.80%. In looking at these numbers, it seems likely that the optimal coverage lies somewhere between 0.5 and 1.0 and probably closer to 0.5. The available effort will allow searching the three highest cells with a coverage of 0.67, as shown in Figure 4-20 (d).

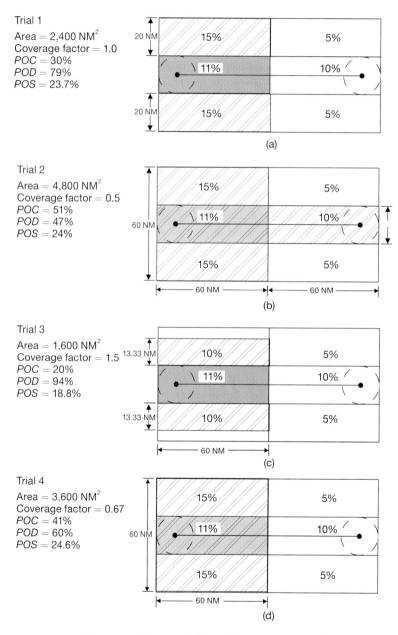

Figure 4-20 – *Available effort = 2,400 NM²*

The resulting *POS* is 0.41 0.6 or 24.6%. In this instance, the additional trial has shown that searching the three cells having the highest *POCs* with a coverage factor of 0.67 is a more nearly optimal allocation of the available search effort than any of the previous trials. The new *POCs* resulting from this search are shown in figure 4-21. The probability map is now ready for use in planning the third search, if it is needed.

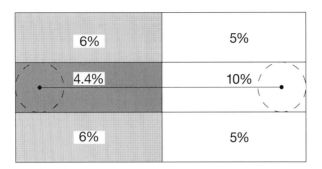

Figure 4-21 *– POC values after the second search*
(POS$_c$ = 63.6%)

4.7.7   *Other Factors.* The preceding paragraphs describe how to optimally allocate search effort based on theoretical considerations. There are also many practical, and sometimes conflicting, considerations which may influence the final search plan. Some things the search planner should evaluate are:

(a)   *Anticipated increases in survivor location uncertainty.* If the survivors are, or may be, moving, the uncertainty in their location will increase with every passing hour. In some instances, however, the increase will be sudden and large. For example, the possible distress incident locations may be limited to a canyon or valley (on land) or a bay, estuary, or strait (at sea). If the survivors are in motion and not located quickly, the distribution of possible locations may spread beyond the limited area, becoming quite large and dispersed. This will greatly complicate the search planning problem. Therefore, the search planner may wish to deploy the available search facilities in a way that prevents probability from "escaping" the initial, more confined, area and becoming dispersed over a much larger and less well-defined area. Such a strategy may well reduce the POS on earlier searches in exchange for increasing it on later searches and keeping the search planning problem manageable.

(b)   *Forecast search conditions.* Weather forecasts are always an important consideration when planning searches. If search conditions are very poor, it may be wise to wait and apply the search effort after conditions have improved. Similarly, if search conditions are now good or excellent, but poor conditions are predicted for later searches, the search planner should seek to obtain and deploy as much search effort as possible before conditions deteriorate.

(c)   *Survival times.* The chances for continued survival following a distress incident usually decrease rapidly with the passage of time, especially for injured persons, persons in the water, or persons exposed to temperature extremes. This fact, together with the theoretical considerations discussed earlier in this chapter, means a substantial first search effort should be given very serious consideration despite the logistical and co-ordination problems associated with mounting a large search effort on short notice.

(d)   *Search object motion during the search.* Search objects, especially maritime ones, are often in motion while search facilities are looking for them. Despite their slow speed as compared with the search facilities', this motion can be an important factor. If the effects of search object motion are ignored, they can, in some situations, destroy search effectiveness. To prevent this from happening, search legs should always be oriented in the same direction in which the search object is expected to move during the search. The search area should be extended in the direction of search object motion far enough to ensure that search objects in the original search area at the beginning of the search will still be in the extended area at the end of the search. This is discussed further in chapter 5.

(e) *Late clues.* Sometimes, the assumptions upon which previous search plans were based are shown to be incorrect in some way by the arrival of new information not available earlier. If the most probable scenario based upon the new information is significantly different from the previous one, it may be necessary to recompute all previous results, accounting for the impact of the new information. It may even be necessary, in extreme cases, to discard all previous results and start over.

(f) *Practical considerations.* There are, of course, many other practical considerations used in deciding exactly which sub-areas to search and what coverages to use. Maintaining safe separations among the search facilities, search facility sensor and navigational capabilities, and choices of search patterns are just some of the things which affect the final search plan. Search planners should modify the recommended search sub-areas and coverages as needed to account for all the practical considerations. *POS* values tend to be very stable near the point of perfectly optimal effort allocation. This allows the search planner the freedom needed to adapt the theoretically optimal allocation of effort to the realities imposed by the environment and the capabilities of the search facilities. Normally, the small changes from optimal values required for the purpose of developing a practical search plan will not have a large impact on search effectiveness (POS). Therefore, the search planner may make such changes with confidence. However, after each search cycle (for example, at the end of each search day), search planners should also be sure to re-compute all relative effort and cumulative relative effort values based on actual effort expended in the search sub-areas. They should also re-compute all coverage factors, *POD*, *POC*$_{new}$, *POS* and *POS*$_c$ values based on the actual sub-areas searched and actual effort expended in them. This information will be needed to plan subsequent searches.

4.7.8 *Updating distributions to account for search object motion.* The examples in sections 4.6 and 4.7 assumed the effects of search object motion, if any, on the probability distribution were not significant. In fact, the only indication of search object motion was the change in total probable error of position from the first search to the second in paragraph 4.7.4 (b). (The situation there would correspond to subparagraph (a) below.) For moving search objects, adjusting the grid cells to reflect the search object's motion between searches and the increasing uncertainty in its location is a necessary, but sometimes difficult, task if probability maps are to be used effectively in this situation. The generation and maintenance of probability maps for searches involving moving objects is best left to computers programmed for the purpose. To manually update a probability map for a drifting object, the first step is to ensure all the *POC* values for the existing grid have been updated. In the marine environment the next step depends on the environmental situation as it affects drift.

(a) *Similar drift forces everywhere.* If the drift forces are about the same everywhere in the vicinity of the scenario's possibility area, then creating a new probability map simply involves moving the existing grid to the new location and expanding it to account for any increase in the total probable error of position. The *POC* values within grid cells would not change. Figure 4-22 illustrates this principle, although the distance between datums and the increase in area has been exaggerated for clarity.

(b) *Significant differences in drift forces.* If the drift forces in one part of the scenario's possibility and surrounding area are significantly different from those elsewhere, simply moving and expanding will not be sufficient. The grid will also have to be distorted to fit the shape of the new possibility area. One way to do this would be to use the corner points, or centre points, or both, of the grid cells as datum points when updating the datum for drift. If the drift forces in a sub-area are sufficiently similar, cells could be grouped and moved together, reducing the number of drift computations required. Again, *POC* values would not change but would simply move with their respective cells. If the distortion is too great, the search planner may wish to consider developing a new regular grid, laying it over the distorted one and estimating new *POC* values from the distorted probability map. Figure 4-23 illustrates a distorted probability map.

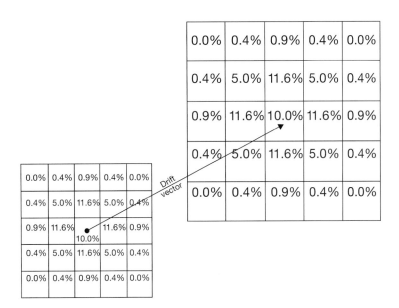

Figure 4-22 *– Adjusting a probability map for drift motion when drift forces are about the same throughout the possibility area (drift distance and area expansion exaggerated for clarity)*

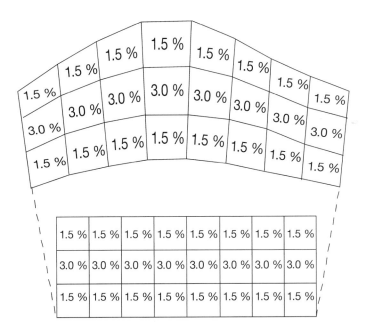

Figure 4-23 *– Adjusting a probability map for drift motion when drift forces vary from one place to another in the possibility area (drift distance and area expansion exaggerated for clarity)*

4.7.9 *Using POSc.* The value of POS_c provides one indicator of when further searching in the current scenario's possibility area will no longer produce a reasonable likelihood of locating the survivors. A POS_c value of 99% means that no matter how much effort is put into the scenario's possibility area on the next search, the POS for that search can be no better than 1%. A high POS_c value can mean one of the following things about the scenario being used as a basis for planning the search:

(a) The search object never existed or has ceased to exist and cannot be found. For example, persons and liferafts that go down with the ship cannot be located by searching the ocean's surface.

(b) The search object exists but is not in the scenario's possibility area. In this case, the analysis of the available information and clues may have been flawed, or some critical item may have been in error, causing search facilities to be sent to the wrong place. As POS_c values continue to rise without the search object being located, the possibility of an incorrect assessment of the available data or the presence of an erroneous data item must be taken more and more seriously. Assumptions are particularly susceptible to error. Their status as assumptions, and not facts, is easily forgotten if care is not taken to keep them separate from the known facts throughout the search planning process. Regular and frequent review and re-analysis of all available information and clues will go a long way toward detecting false data items, preventing misinterpretation of correct data items, and improving the accuracy of the scenario(s) under consideration.

4.7.10 *Summary.* The strategy of maximizing the POS for each search provides important guidance to the search planner in determining where and how to apply the available search effort. Over time, it tends to move the search effort toward the survivors even if they are not initially in the cells having the largest estimated POCs. Even if the probability maps and POC values are only approximate, using this strategy will produce much better results than not using it at all. When search object motion is not a consideration, developing and updating probability maps is relatively easy. When search object motion is involved, updating probability maps can become very complex. Section 4.8 discusses computer aids which may be available to assist the search planner with this and other complexities in the search planning process. In the absence of such aids, the search planner should carefully make the simplifications needed to keep the problem manageable.

4.8   Computer-based search planning aids

4.8.1 As shown by sections 4.6 and 4.7 above, determining the best way to allocate the available search effort can involve a considerable amount of computation. The same is true for determining probability maps for new datum lines or areas when there are significant variations in winds and currents. The number and accuracy of the computations which can be done by the search planner without a computer are necessarily quite limited. Computer programs can be used to great advantage in relieving the search planner of much of the computational burden, allowing more computations of greater complexity to be done in less time with greater accuracy. These programs can be made relatively small, simple, and narrow in scope by limiting them to specific search planning functions. On the other hand, they can be quite large and sophisticated, addressing the entire search planning problem, including the optimization of search effort allocation over several search cycles. Such sophisticated software requires specialized expertise to develop and maintain. However, with a well designed user interface, it can be used by search planners with relatively little training.

4.8.2 *Uses of computers in search planning.* Computers may be used to perform computations in support of the following search planning functions:

– calculate drift estimates, including leeway, local wind current, tidal currents, etc.;

– calculate total probable errors of position, sweep widths, search endurances, search efforts, search areas, coverage factors, etc.;

– create or record probability maps, update them and compute probability of success estimates (POS and POS_c);

– compute optimal allocation of available search effort;

– calculate search sub-area parameters, including commence search point, track spacing, turn points for each leg in the search pattern, corner points, centre point, length, width, orientation, area, time to complete at various search speeds, etc.;

– display, compare, and combine clues and probability maps associated with different scenarios;

- account for each variable in the search planning process and its particular uncertainty, including wind and wind uncertainty, current and current uncertainty, incident position and its uncertainty, incident time and its uncertainty, search object type, drift characteristics, and detection characteristics and their respective uncertainties, etc.;

- with appropriate geographic display software and databases, display probability maps, search sub-areas, search patterns, etc., on appropriate chart images;

- with appropriate geographic display software and databases, allow much of the search planning process to be done quickly and interactively on the computer screen;

- maintain and provide easy, rapid access to a variety of useful databases such as locations of known crash sites from previous SAR incidents, location, status, and characteristics of SRUs and other facilities, etc.; and

- with modems or network connections, provide another communications path for obtaining environmental data, delivering search action plans, etc.

4.8.3 Computers and appropriate software can provide a great deal of assistance to the search planner. Even relatively inexpensive computer systems can support most of the activities listed above. However, computers and computer-based aids do have their limitations, as discussed below.

- Computers are tools which can enhance and aid, but cannot replace, the human search planner's judgement or analytical and co-ordination skills;

- computer systems (hardware and software) must be properly maintained and replaced every few years, at some level of expense;

- at least some training is required to master the operation of the computer and search planning software;

- it is easy to become dependent on the computer and allow manual search planning skills to lapse; and

- redundant computer systems, preferably at different sites to reduce the impact of a catastrophe at a single site, are required, especially if dependence on the computer is heavy.

Chapter 5

Search techniques and operations

5.1 Overview

5.1.1 The previous chapter described how to determine the optimal area where the available search effort should be deployed. Once the optimal search area has been determined, a systematic search for the search object should be planned. Before a search operation takes place, the search planner should provide a detailed search action plan to all involved facilities, specifying when, where and how individual search facilities are to conduct their search operations. Co-ordination instructions, communications frequency assignments, reporting requirements, and any other details required for the safe, efficient and effective conduct of the search must also be included in the search action plan.

5.1.2 As a minimum, developing a search action plan consists of the following steps:

- selecting search facilities and equipment to be used;

- assessing the search conditions;

- selecting search patterns to cover the optimal search area as nearly as may be practical;

- dividing the search area into appropriate sub-areas for assignment to individual search facilities; and,

- planning on-scene co-ordination.

5.2 Selection of search facilities

5.2.1 The types and numbers of available search facilities, along with the sweep width(s), determine how much search effort will be available at the scene. Small search efforts will result in correspondingly small probabilities of success, even when the effort is deployed in the most optimal fashion, and it will probably take longer to locate survivors. Since survival times may be limited and locating survivors almost always becomes more difficult as time passes, it may be necessary to seek additional search facilities early in the search planning process. It is usually preferable to use larger rather than smaller numbers of search facilities for the first few searches. By doing this, survivors are often located sooner rather than later, and the need for a much larger, prolonged search effort is avoided. No matter how many search facilities the search planner tries to obtain, it is unlikely that so many will be made available that they cannot be used effectively.

5.2.2 Detailed factors for the SAR planner to consider in selecting search facilities are discussed in appendix G. Search procedures and scanner techniques are presented in the *International Aeronautical and Maritime SAR Manual for Mobile Facilities*.

5.3 Assessing search conditions

5.3.1 The graphs in appendix N used for determining the optimal search factor for a given amount of available effort, the probability of detection and the cumulative probability of success (POS_c) all contain two curves. One curve is used for searches performed under ideal search conditions and the other is used when search conditions are poor. The differences in the search plan and the attainable POS between ideal and poor conditions are usually significant. Therefore, it is important to accurately assess the search conditions. The two primary factors in determining search conditions are:

– the sweep width, which in turn depends on a number of factors related to the search object, sensor(s) used, and environmental conditions; and,

– the ability of the search craft to accurately navigate its assigned search pattern.

Sweep width

5.3.2 One of the primary indicators of whether search conditions are ideal or normal is the sweep width. Experiments have shown that sweep width decreases as search conditions deteriorate. Experiments have also shown that detection profiles under normal search conditions are generally lower and flatter than they are under ideal search conditions. These results are also supported by search theory. In addition, search theory goes on to predict that probabilities of detection for the same coverage factors will be lower for searches performed under normal conditions than for searches performed under ideal conditions. Therefore, the corrected sweep width is important for two reasons. First, it is one of the three factors which determine how much search effort is available (see paragraph 4.6.8). Second, when it is compared to the uncorrected sweep width for ideal search conditions, it may be used to determine how ideal or normal the actual search conditions are. The following list describes factors which separately, or in combination, may affect sweep width.

(a) The type of search object affects sweep width. Search objects are easier to detect when they contrast significantly with their background. In daylight visual searches, the type, size, colour, and shape of the search object are important factors, while for night-time visual searches, search object illumination and reflectivity are important. In radar searches, line of sight, radar cross-section, and signal strength are key factors. All search objects should be sought from a direction in which they receive the best illumination, colour brightness, or contrast.

(b) Meteorological visibility is an important factor in determining sweep widths for visual searches. Meteorological conditions may reduce visibility in the search area or interrupt or prevent the start of search operations.

    (1) In poor visibility, fog will make visual search ineffective if not impossible. Electronic search is normally the only appropriate means of detecting search objects from an aircraft, although aural search can also be effective for boats and ground parties in small search areas. For example, survivors can sometimes be located by their cries for help in conditions of restricted visibility. For an aural search to be effective, searchers must remain silent for periods of time and remove all possible distracting noise by shutting engines down, turning off radios, etc. Dogs which rely on their sense of smell to locate survivors may also be used effectively when visibility is low.

    (2) Smog and haze may reduce the effectiveness of daylight search, while night signals are less affected.

    (3) Low clouds may render search ineffective. For example, a ceiling of 150 m (500 feet) will not make search impossible but will normally reduce the sweep width and, consequently, the available search effort. However, low clouds normally do not significantly affect searches conducted by surface facilities except where a thick overcast layer reduces light levels at the surface.

    (4) Precipitation will reduce visibility and may prevent the search facility from completing its assigned search area. Snow or heavy rain will also make scanning from side stations and use of searchlights and electro-optical systems limited or ineffective. Precipitation adversely affects both visual and radar searches.

(c) The type of terrain or conditions of the sea can affect sweep widths in almost all situations. On a flat area with little or no vegetation, a search object can be seen easily, while it may be very difficult to detect the search object in a forested area or in mountainous terrain. On a smooth sea, any object or disturbance of reasonable size may be seen fairly easily, but whitecaps, foam streaks, breaking seas, salt spray, and the reflection of the sun tend to obscure a search object or reduce the chances of seeing it or its signals. Patches of seaweed, oil slicks, cloud shadows, marine life, or other distractions may be mistaken for a small search object such as a liferaft.

(d)   The height of the look-out or other sensor above the surface can also have an impact on sweep width. It is not possible to prescribe a search height suitable for all situations. For vessels, the height of the bridge is usually the most suitable for look-outs. For aircraft, the highest reasonable search altitude above the surface is usually considered to be 450 m (1,500 ft) for daylight visual search. A search height of 150 m (500 ft) may be suitable for a helicopter or a slow fixed-wing aircraft while impracticable for most jet aircraft. Table N-5 may serve as a guide in planning searches with helicopters and table N-6 may be used to estimate sweep widths for fixed-wing aircraft. Note that it is usually impractical to search for persons in the water from aircraft flying at altitudes greater than 150 m (500 ft).

(e)   The time of day is another important consideration. The best time for visual searching during daylight is from mid-morning to mid-afternoon, when the sun is at a relatively high elevation. Visual search at night will be futile unless it is known that the survivors have night signalling devices such as flares or lights, or can generate light in some other way such as by building a fire. However, where it is safe for search units to continue and active aids, such as searchlights, radar, infrared devices, low-light television, or night vision devices are available and usable, then searches could continue.

(f)   For daylight searches, the position of the sun is important. The searcher will see objects more easily and from greater distances when looking away from the sun. The effect of haze is much greater when looking towards the sun, so that objects on sea and land lose their distinctive colours and may be lost in a pattern of glaring light and shadows. Looking away from the sun, the land and the sea are much darker, there is no glare, the haze is more transparent, white-caps are highly visible, and all coloured objects tend to contrast more with their backgrounds. Therefore, search patterns should be oriented so that look-outs spend as little time as possible looking towards the sun. In any event, look-outs should be provided with sunglasses.

(g)   Look-out effectiveness is crucial to visual searches. The effectiveness of look-outs depends on their training, alertness and motivation, the suitability of their positions, the duration of the search, the roughness of the terrain for searchers on the ground, of the sea for vessel look-outs, and of air turbulence for aircraft look-outs. An adequate number of look-outs should be carried to ensure all quadrants about the search facility are scanned. On long searches, extra look-outs should be carried so rest periods may be provided to combat the effects of fatigue. For aircraft, the search speed is important to look-out effectiveness because it affects the rate of angular (relative bearing) change as the aircraft passes by the search object. When the angular change reaches 30° per second, the ability to see a search object is reduced. By the time it reaches 40° per second, the ability to see a search object is reduced to half the value associated with the same range and no angular change. When angular change increases, look-outs also tend to look farther away from the aircraft in order to reduce the angular change. At a height of 60 m (200 ft) the highest search speed should be 110 km/h (60 knots), and at a height of 150 m (500 ft), the maximum search speed should be 280 km/h (150 knots) to ensure an effective search. (See the *International Aeronautical and Maritime SAR Manual for Mobile Facilities* for scanning techniques and for training of look-outs).

5.3.3   Sweep width estimates for the marine environment are provided in tables N-4, N-5, and N-6, depending on whether the search facility is a merchant vessel, helicopter, or fixed-wing aircraft. Table N-7 gives weather-based sweep width correction factors applicable to all types of search facilities. Table N-8 gives additional sweep width correction factors for aircraft search facilities operating under conditions of reduced meteorological visibility. Sweep width estimates for searches over flat, open terrain are provided in table N-9. Search objects are more difficult to find in mountainous terrain or terrain heavily covered with vegetation such as forests. Table N-10 gives sweep width correction factors to use when the terrain is not flat and open.

Accuracy of navigation by search facilities

5.3.4   In addition to expanding the size of a search area, the navigational accuracy with which search facilities are able to complete their assigned search patterns has an important bearing on the coverage of the area and the probability of detection. With one possible exception (boats searching for persons in the water, discussed further in the note following paragraph 5.5.5), dead-reckoning navigation alone generally produces poor results, particularly for search aircraft. Map-reading can be effective over land in visual meteorological conditions. In areas where navigation aids are limited, search patterns should be selected so that greatest possible use is made of the aids that are available. Aircraft with area navigation capabilities can be used for all search patterns in all areas. Alternatively, patterns providing a reference point or a visual navigation aid, such as a vessel or a smoke float, should be considered. Co-ordinated air–surface searches with the vessel providing a navigation reference for the aircraft may increase search pattern accuracy, particularly in areas far from shore.

5.3.5   To be effective, search patterns must be accurately navigated. The size of the search facility's probable position error relative to the size of the sweep width determines how much the probability of detection will be affected by the search facility's navigational limitations. A position error of two miles is not usually significant if the sweep width for that search is 20 miles. However, if the sweep width is only two miles, the effect of a two-mile position error on probability of detection will be substantial.

Evaluating search conditions

5.3.6   Search conditions should be considered normal:

(a)   whenever the corrected sweep width is less than or equal to one-half of the uncorrected value for a given search object and sensor under ideal environmental conditions; and,

(b)   whenever the search facility's probable error of position (Y) is equal to or greater than the sweep width.

For example, the conditions for a visual search from a merchant vessel for a 12 m (40 ft) boat when the visibility is 9 km (5 NM) or less should be considered normal because the sweep width is less than one-half the value for visibilities of 37 km (20 NM). Table N-4 shows a sweep width of 8.3 km (4.5 NM) for a visibility of 9 km (5 NM), which is less than half the sweep width value of 21.5 km (11.6 NM) for visibilities of 37 km (20 NM) or more. If a fixed-wing aircraft is being used to search for a 4-person liferaft from an altitude of 300 m (1,000 ft) on a clear, calm day and the aircraft's probable error of position is 5.6 km (3.0 NM), search conditions should be considered normal since the sweep width for such a search is only 4.3 km (2.3 NM).

Note: Search conditions should be considered ideal only when the sweep width is at or near its maximum value and the navigational error of the search facility is small in comparison to the sweep width. Search conditions are normal more often than they are ideal.

5.3.7   Procedures for computing sweep width from the sweep width tables in appendix N are included with the Effort allocation worksheet in appendix L.

5.4   Selecting search patterns

5.4.1   The basic technique for searching an area is to move look-outs and/or electronic sensors through the area, using one of a few standard patterns. This technique has several benefits.

(a)   A regular, organized pattern of search ensures the entire assigned area is covered more or less uniformly.

(b)   Regular patterns improve the probability of detection (POD) as compared to random, disorganized searching, especially when search conditions are ideal.

(c)   Standard patterns are easier to communicate accurately and compactly with less chance of error or misunderstanding.

(d)   Standard patterns make multiple-facility search efforts easier to co-ordinate.

(e)   Standard patterns are safer to perform, especially in multiple-facility efforts.

5.4.2 The selection and orientation of a search pattern are very important and all pertinent factors should be considered before a selection is made. Search pattern(s) and their directional orientation(s) should meet the criteria listed below.

   (a)   They should be appropriate for the:

   –   degree of uncertainty in the search object's position;

   –   navigational capabilities of each search facility;

   –   type of sensor(s) being employed;

   –   primary type of search object or signal the search facility is attempting to detect and locate;

   –   environmental conditions;

   –   direction and rate of the search object's predicted movement during the search; and,

   –   time limits imposed by the survivors' expected survival time, search facility endurance, availability of daylight, etc.

   (b)   It should be within the operational capability of each available search facility to accurately and safely complete its assigned pattern.

   (c)   The expected result should be worth the estimated time and effort (see the discussion on using POS_c in paragraph 4.7.9).

   (d)   The selected search patterns should minimize the risk of collision with other search facilities, allow adequate fuel reserves, and avoid, where practicable, navigation hazards.

5.4.3 Close attention should be paid to air traffic in the area of the search. Normally more than one aircraft should not be assigned to the same search sub-area at the same time. Multiple aircraft operating together in the same search sub-area distracts aircrew attention from the search and decreases the flexibility to respond to sightings or drop markers, flares, rafts, etc. This does not preclude an electronic search from taking place at high altitude while a visual search is done at a lower level. In fact, the pilot in command of an aircraft doing a high-level electronic search may be an excellent choice for on-scene co-ordinator, or may be assigned as aircraft co-ordinator when multiple aircraft are involved.

5.4.4 When it is known or likely that a survival beacon may be available in the distressed craft or survival craft or be carried on the person of a survivor, an electronic search using an appropriate pattern should be carried out by a fast aircraft flying at a high level while a visual search is carried out at a lower level or on the surface.

5.4.5 Search patterns co-ordinated between air and surface facilities offer a number of advantages. For example, the surface facility:

   –   can act as an excellent navigational and reference datum for the search aircraft, particularly during maritime searches far offshore;

   –   can be directed toward survivors as soon as they are located;

   –   can keep the aircraft informed of weather and other conditions at the scene;

   –   may relay progress reports for the aircraft; and,

   –   can assist the crew of the search aircraft should a forced landing be necessary.

5.4.6 The search patterns described below are arranged in the following four general categories:

   –   visual search patterns;

   –   electronic search patterns;

   –   night search patterns; and,

   –   land search patterns.

The most commonly used search patterns are also included in the *International Aeronautical and Maritime Search and Rescue Manual for Mobile Facilities* carried aboard all merchant vessels.

Search area coverage records

5.4.7 It is imperative that a record be kept of the areas searched. The crews of search facilities should plot actual search coverage as tracks are flown. One method of doing this is to shade or cross-hatch the areas searched and to outline the areas not searched on a map or chart of the appropriate scale. This information must be reported back to the SMC so the search may be evaluated, probability maps and probabilities of success updated, and the next search planned. It is important that the SMC also receives information on how effective the search facilities considered their search to have been, given the search conditions at the time.

5.5   Visual search patterns

Sector search (VS)

5.5.1 Sector searches are most effective when the position of the search object is accurately known and the search area is small. Examples of this situation include a crew member seeing another crew member fall overboard from a ship or a reported distress from a craft which provides a very accurate position. Sector searches are used to search a circular area centred on a datum point, as shown in figure 5-1. They are easy to navigate and provide intensive coverage of the area near the centre, where the search object is most likely to be found. Due to the small area involved, this procedure must not be used simultaneously by multiple aircraft at the same or similar altitudes or by multiple vessels. Instead, an aircraft and a vessel may be used together to perform independent sector searches of the same area.

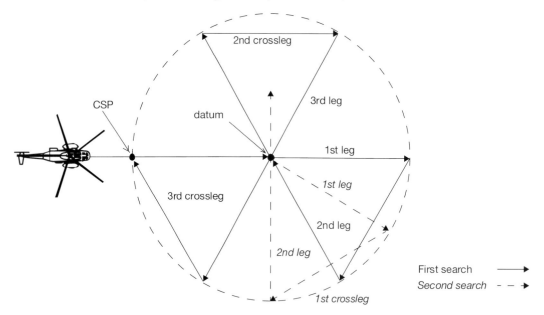

Figure 5-1 *– Sector pattern: single-unit*

5.5.2 A suitable marker (for example, a smoke float or a radio beacon) may be dropped at the datum position and used as a reference or navigational aid marking the centre of the pattern. Each search leg should then pass the marker at close range or directly overhead. When the sector search is used over a marker at sea, adjustment for the effects of total water current on the search object's motion during the search is easier. The first leg should usually be down-drift. For aircraft, the search pattern radius usually lies between 5 NM and 20 NM. The angle between successive search legs will depend on the radius used and the maximum track spacing at the ends of the search legs. For vessels, the search pattern radius is usually between 2 NM and 5 NM, and each turn is 120°. Normally, all turns in a sector search are made to starboard.

5.5.3 If the search object is not located by the time the sector search pattern has been completed one time, it should be rotated and repeated with the second set of search legs falling half-way between the search legs followed during the first search, as indicated by the dashed search legs in figure 5-1.

Expanding square search (SS)

5.5.4 The expanding square search pattern is also most effective when the location of the search object is known with relatively good accuracy. The commence search point (CSP) for this pattern is always the datum position. The pattern then expands outward in concentric squares as shown in figure 5-2, providing nearly uniform coverage of the area around the datum. If the datum is a short line instead of a point, the pattern may be changed to an expanding rectangle. Due to the small area involved, the same cautions about the use of multiple search facilities as previously mentioned for the sector search also apply to the expanding square pattern.

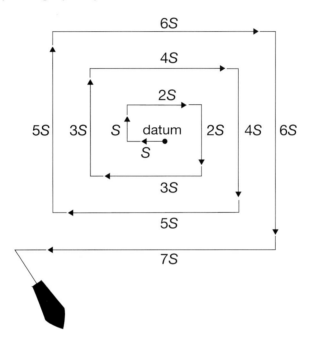

Figure 5-2 – *Expanding square search (SS)*

5.5.5 The expanding square pattern is a precise pattern and requires accurate navigation. To minimize navigational errors, the first leg is usually oriented directly into the wind. The lengths of the first two legs are equal to the track spacing and the lengths every succeeding pair of legs are increased by another track spacing. For successive searches in the same area, the direction of the search legs should be changed by 45° as shown in figure 5-3.

Note: Expanding square patterns are often appropriate for vessels, small boats or helicopters, but not necessarily fixed-wing aircraft, to use when searching for persons in the water or other search objects with little or no leeway as compared to the magnitude of the total water current. In such cases, it may be appropriate for the vessel or small boat to navigate the pattern by careful dead reckoning rather than by precise electronic or visual navigation. Just as a sector search pattern automatically compensates for total water current when using a floating marker as a navigational reference, a vessel's DR naviga-tion of an expanding square also automatically compensates for the effects of total water current.

Track line search (TS)

5.5.6 The track line search pattern is normally employed when an aircraft or vessel has disappeared without a trace while *en route* from one point to another. It is based on the assumption that the distressed craft has crashed, made a forced landing or foundered on or near the intended route and concentrates the search effort near this datum line. It is usually assumed that the survivors are capable of attracting the search facility's attention at a considerable range by some means such as a signalling mirror or coloured smoke (daylight), flares, flashing light or signal fire (night), or electronic beacon (day or night). The track line search consists of a rapid and reasonably thorough search along the intended route of the distressed craft. The search facility may search along one side of the track line and return in the opposite direction (TSR), as shown in figure 5-4, or it may search along the intended track and once on either side, then continue on its way and not return (TSN), as shown in figure 5-5. Due to their high speed, aircraft are frequently employed for track line searches, normally at a height of 300 m to 600 m (1,000 ft to 2,000 ft) above the surface during daylight or at 600 m to 900 m (2,000 ft to 3,000 ft) at night. This pattern is often used as an initial search effort because it requires relatively little planning and can be quickly implemented. If the track line search fails to locate the survivors, then a more intensive search over a wider area should be undertaken.

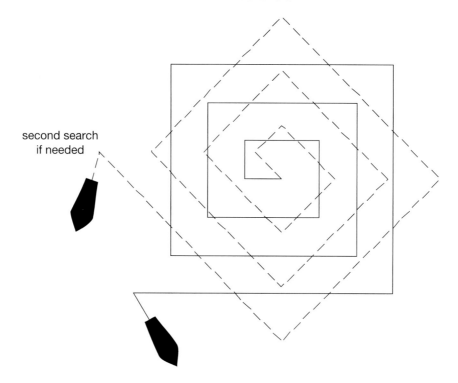

Figure 5-3 – *Second expanding square search*

5.5.7   Aircraft and ships of opportunity following the same or a similar route as that of the missing craft should be asked to divert to assist in the search. This will mean diverting to follow the distressed craft's most probable route or a nearby parallel course. When multiple facilities are requested to assist in this manner, and especially if they are moving in opposite directions, the search planner must ensure all facilities are aware of the presence of the others and avoid requesting facilities moving in opposite directions to follow exactly the same track on opposite headings. For aircraft of opportunity, track line searches should be regarded as additional to searches by SAR facilities with trained crews as an *en-route* aircraft may:

–   not carry sufficient or competent look-outs;

–   have to fly at normal operating levels and speeds rather than at optimum search heights and speeds; and,

–   have to fly above clouds.

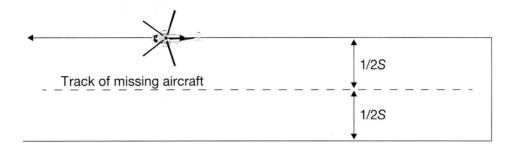

Figure 5-4 – *Track line search, return (TSR)*

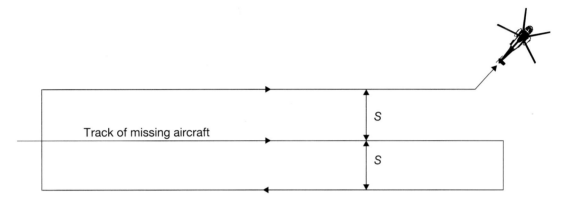

Figure 5-5 – *Track line search, non-return (TSN)*

Parallel sweep search (PS)

5.5.8 The parallel sweep search pattern is normally used when the uncertainty in the survivor's location is large, requiring a large area to be searched with a uniform coverage. It is most effective when used over water or reasonably flat terrain. A parallel sweep search pattern covers a rectangular area. It is almost always used when a large search area must be divided into sub-areas for assignment to individual search facilities which will be on scene at the same time.

5.5.9 To perform a parallel search pattern, the search facility proceeds to the commence search point (CSP) in one corner of its assigned sub-area. The CSP is always one-half track space inside the rectangle from each of the two sides forming the corner. The search legs are parallel to the long sides of the rectangle. The first leg is set at a distance equal to one-half the track spacing from the long side nearest the CSP. Successive legs are maintained parallel to each other and one track spacing apart. Figure 5-6 illustrates a PS search pattern. Figure 5-7 shows how a PS search pattern can be navigated using a hyperbolic navigation system such as LORAN. Figure 5-8 shows how to use distance-measuring equipment (DME) to navigate a PS pattern.

5.5.10 A parallel sweep search covering a single sub-area is normally performed by a single facility. As discussed in paragraph 5.4.3, the use of multiple aircraft working together in the same search sub-area at similar altitudes is discouraged. However, there are cases where multiple facilities may be used to great advantage. Ships, fishing vessels, etc., which may be passing through or near the search area may be asked to divert along specific parallel tracks passing through the search area, as shown in figure 5-9, while maintaining a sharp lookout for the survivors. This type of search can be both effective and efficient. Similarly, *en-route* aircraft may be asked, via the appropriate ATS unit, to divert through the search area along parallel tracks while listening for signals from an emergency beacon. However, for safety reasons, use of *en-route* light aircraft on VFR flight plans for visual search in the manner of vessels is not recommended.

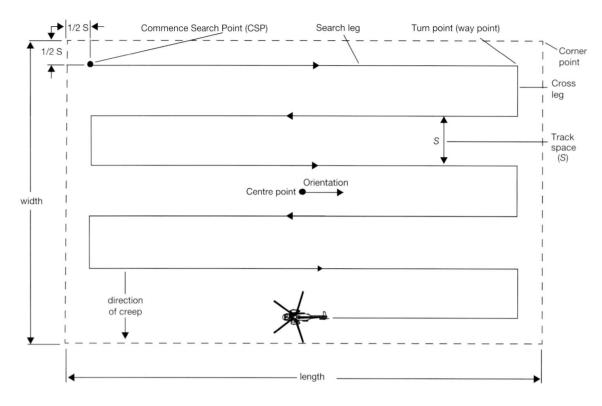

Figure 5-6 – *Parallel sweep search (PS)*

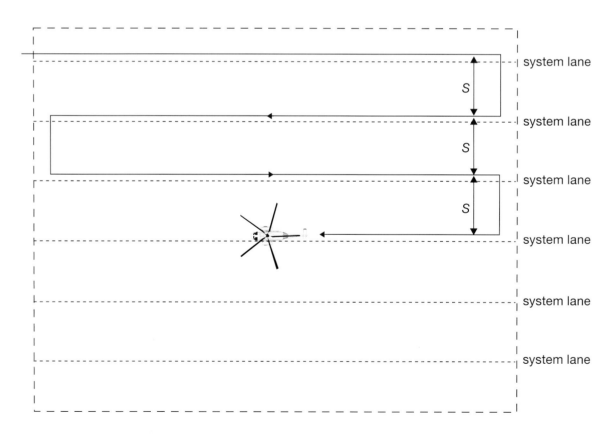

Figure 5-7 – *Parallel sweep search – based on hyperbolic navigation system*

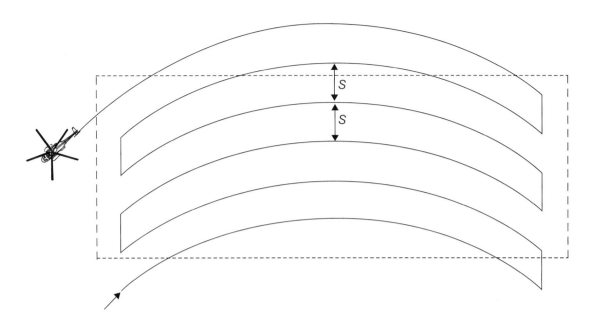

Figure 5-8 –*Parallel sweep search – based on distance-measuring equipment*

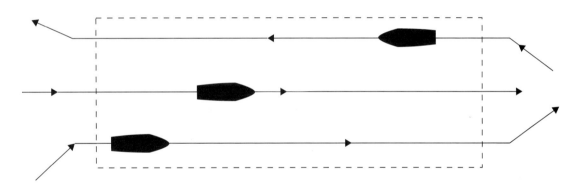

Figure 5-9 – *Diverting merchant vessels to follow parallel tracks through a search area*

Creeping line search (CS)

5.5.11 The creeping line search pattern is basically the same as a parallel sweep search except that the search legs are parallel to the short sides of the rectangle instead of the long sides. Because the CS pattern requires many more turns to cover the same area, it is usually not as efficient as the PS pattern unless it is used by an aircraft working in co-ordination with a vessel (see 5.5.12). Figure 5-10 shows a CS pattern.

Creeping line search, co-ordinated (CSC)

5.5.12 A co-ordinated air–maritime search is usually accomplished by co-ordinating the movements of an aircraft flying a creeping line search with those of a vessel moving along the major axis of the search area in the direction of the aircraft's creep. The aircraft's search legs are flown at right angles to the vessel's track. The vessel's speed, the aircraft's speed, the length of the aircraft's search legs and the track spacing are all planned so that the aircraft's advance in the direction of creep equals the speed of the surface facility. When correctly performed, the aircraft should pass directly over the vessel at the centre of each search leg, as shown in figure 5-11.

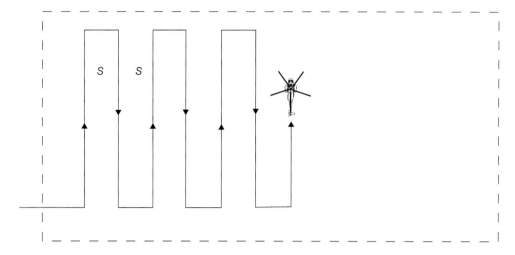

Figure 5-10 *– Creeping line search (CS)*

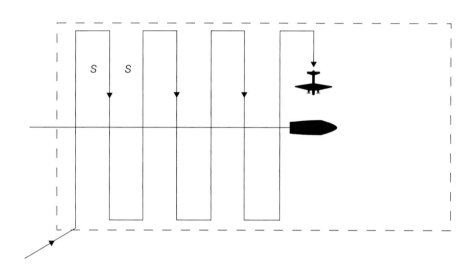

Figure 5-11 *– Creeping line search, co-ordinated (CSC)*

5.5.13 The relationship among the speed of the surface facility, the aircraft's speed, the track spacing and the length of the search legs is defined by the following equation:

$$V_s = (S \times V_a)/(L + S),$$

where V_s is the speed of the surface facility in knots, S is the track spacing in nautical miles, V_a is the aircraft's true air speed (TAS) in knots, and L is the length of the aircraft's search leg in nautical miles.

Contour search (OS)

5.5.14 The contour search is used around mountains and in valleys when sharp changes in elevation make other patterns impracticable. The mountain is searched from top to bottom, never from bottom to top. The search is started above the highest peak with the search aircraft completely circling the mountain at that level. To permit the aircraft to descend smoothly and safely to the next contour search altitude, which may be 150 m to 300 m (500 ft to 1,000 ft) lower, the aircraft may make a descending orbit away from the mountain before resuming the contour search at the lower altitude. When there is not enough room to make a circuit opposite to the direction of the search, the aircraft may spiral downwards around the mountain at a low but approximately constant rate of descent. If, for any reason, the mountain cannot be circled, successive sweeps at the same altitude intervals as listed above should be flown along its side. Valleys are searched in circles, moving the centre of the circuit one track spacing after each completed circuit. Figure 5-12 illustrates a contour search pattern.

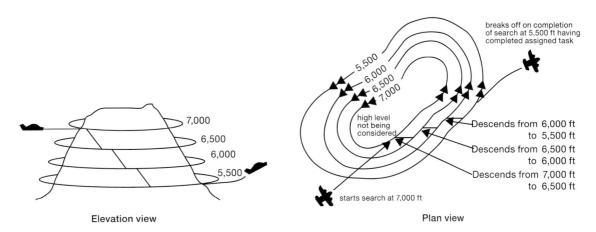

Figure 5-12 *–Contour search (OS)*

5.5.15 A contour search may be very dangerous. Therefore, extreme caution should be used when searching mountains, canyons, and valleys. The safety matters that should be considered are listed below.

(a) The crew must be very experienced, well briefed and have accurate large scale maps (1:100,000 scale maps are recommended)..

(b) Mountainous search areas should be assigned to multi-engine aircraft whenever possible.

(c) During the search, all the pilot's attention will be devoted to flying the aircraft. The pilot must evaluate forward terrain to avoid any hazard (such as power lines, cables, etc.) and anticipate the possibility of terrain-induced visual illusions which may jeopardize aircraft safety. When searching valleys, the pilot must plan ahead to ensure that the aircraft can either climb out of difficulty or turn around, knowing at all times which way to turn in case of an emergency.

(d) Weather conditions in the search area must be good. Both visibility and turbulence must be constantly monitored. Flights should be avoided in mountainous areas when winds exceed 56 km/h (30 knots) because downdraughts can exceed 10 m/s (2000 ft/min).

(e) Before take-off, the crew should study large-scale contour maps indicating terrain elevations and contour lines. Areas of possible severe turbulence should be identified. Pilots should determine turbulence and downdraughts before descending to search altitude and flying close to a mountainside (see paragraph 5.5.16). Wind direction and air current in mountainous areas may vary greatly. If turbulence is encountered, the pilot should take immediate steps to keep from exceeding the structural limits of the aircraft;

(f) Aircraft should not enter any valley which is too narrow to permit a 180° turn at the altitude flown, unless a safe exit route is available ahead of the aircraft. Searches should be flown close to one side of a canyon or valley so that the entire width may be used if a 180° turn becomes necessary. A similar method should be applied when making a contour search of a mountain.

(g) The aircraft should be highly manoeuvrable, have a high rate of climb, and a small turning radius.

(h) Only one aircraft should be assigned to each contour search area to avoid possible collision with other search aircraft.

Turbulence considerations for contour searches

5.5.16 Orographic turbulence may be found as updraughts on the upwind side of slopes and ridges and on the downwind side as downdraughts. The extent of the turbulence on the downwind side depends on the wind speed and the steepness of the slope. Orographic turbulence will be more intense when climbing a rough surface. The safest crossing of mountain peaks and ridges at low relative altitudes under windy or turbulent conditions is downwind, where any downdraughts will be met after the high point in the terrain is crossed. If this is not practical, altitude should be increased before crossing these areas. The procedure to transit a mountain pass is to fly close to that side of the pass where there is an updraught. This will provide additional lift and maximum turning space in case of an emergency, and a turn into the wind will be a turn to lower terrain. Flying through the middle of a pass may be dangerous as this allows the least turning space and, in addition, often is the area of greatest turbulence.

Shoreline search

5.5.17 The marine equivalent to the contour search is the shoreline search. Small vessels, or aircraft capable of safely flying at low altitudes and speeds, are normally used in order to pass close enough to the shoreline to permit careful inspection. Vessels engaged in shoreline searches must be aware of navigational constraints and any limitations imposed by sea conditions. Search planners should consider the possibility of survivors clinging to navigational aids such as buoys, or to rocks offshore. Survivors may make their way to any dry land they may drift close enough to see. Survivors may also anchor their boat or raft or tie it to an offshore navigational aid if they drift into shallow water but still cannot see land or believe they cannot make it to shore unaided. Search facilities should pay special attention to any such possible places in their sub-areas where the survivors may have succeeded in arresting their drift.

5.6   Electronic search patterns

Survival beacon search

5.6.1 When it is known or believed that an aircraft, vessel, or persons in distress are equipped with a survival beacon, an electronic search at high level should be initiated immediately whether or not any message has been received via the Cospas–Sarsat system (see section 2.6). In addition to EPIRBs and PLBs operated by survivors, many aircraft carry ELTs that start operating when the G-forces reach a certain level, such as in a crash. The electronic search should not preclude the initiation of a visual search at lower levels since the success of an electronic search depends on the ability of the survival beacon to transmit a signal.

5.6.2 The sweep width in an electronic search should be estimated based on horizon range for the level chosen for the search, since most emergency beacons operate on frequencies that may be received only by line-of-sight. However, if the probable detection range is known and is less than the horizon range, it should be used instead. When the probable detection range of a survival beacon is not known, the estimated sweep width over the sea or over flat terrain with little or no tree coverage should be about one-half of the horizon range shown in table N-12. Over jungle areas and in mountainous terrain, the sweep width estimate may have to be reduced to as little as one-tenth of the horizon range. In mountainous terrain or areas covered with dense vegetation, the range of the signal will be reduced considerably as compared to the range over water or flat land.

5.6.3 Normally, a parallel sweep or creeping line pattern should be employed for survival beacon searches. Although the detection profiles for electronic searches are likely to be different from those of visual search, the optimal search effort allocation techniques described in chapter 4 may be applied and should give results that are reasonably close to optimal. If the initial search of an area does not locate the beacon, the area should be searched again with the search legs of the second pattern oriented at right angles to those of the first pattern. If the beacon remains unlocated but confidence is high that it is in the area and working, a third search with search legs parallel to those of the first search but offset by one-half of a track space may be considered. In mountainous areas, the first search should be arranged so the search legs cross the predominant ridge lines at right angles if at all possible.

5.6.4 One of the following procedures may be used to locate a survival beacon once it has been detected.

   (a)   For search facilities with homing capability, the search facility homes on the survival beacon as soon as the signal is detected. The survival beacon signal may be picked up quickly if the search facility proceeds towards the datum point where the search object location probability density is the highest. If this is unsuccessful, a systematic search of the area will have to be made, using the sector, expanding square, parallel sweep, or creeping line search pattern with a track spacing based on the optimal value for the available search effort.

(b) When reports are received of detections of a 121.5 MHz or 243 MHz signal from overflying aircraft (these signals are not processed by the Cospas–Sarsat system), a search area will need to be established so that an electronic search can be conducted for the beacon. Appendix S can be used for guidance on determining a search area and how that area should be searched.

(c) For aural electronic search by a facility without homing capability, a radio-frequency signal from a survival beacon is detected and converted electronically to an audible sound which at least one member of the search facility crew can hear via a speaker or earphones. The following procedures are normally used only by aircraft. (The procedures could be used by vessels but the lack of equipment for detecting the signal as well as the low height of the vessel make this a less practical search technique.)

(1) In a map-assisted aural electronic search, the aircraft flies a "boxing in" pattern on the assumption that the area of equal radio signal strength is circular. The position of the aircraft is plotted on an appropriate map or chart as soon as the signal is heard for the first time. The pilot continues on the same heading for a short distance, then turns 90° left or right and proceeds until the signal fades. This position is noted. The aircraft now turns 180° and once again the positions of where the signal is heard and where it fades are plotted. The approximate position of the survival beacon can now be found by drawing lines (chords) between each set of "signal heard" and "signal faded" positions, then drawing the perpendicular bisectors of each line and noting the position where they intersect. The aircraft can then proceed to that position and descend to a suitable altitude for visual search. The construction of such a plot is shown in figure 5-13.

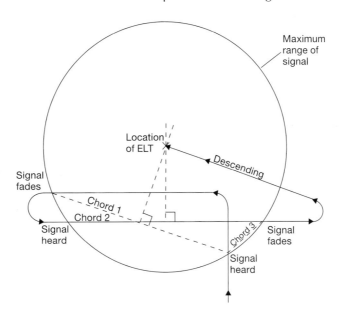

Figure 5-13 – *Map-assisted aural electronic search*

(2) With the time-assisted aural electronic search, the time when the signal is first heard is noted, but the aircraft continues on the same heading until the signal fades, when the time is noted again and the length of time during which the signal was heard is computed as the difference between the two. The aircraft then performs a 180° procedure turn and returns along its original track in the opposite direction for half the amount of time just computed. At that point, the aircraft turns 90° right or left and continues until the signal fades. The aircraft then makes another 180° procedure turn and the time when the signal is heard again is noted. The aircraft continues on that heading until the signal again fades, noting the time and computing the signal's duration as the difference between the two times. The aircraft then performs a third 180° procedure turn and proceeds in that direction for one half of the last computed signal duration. It then descends to an appropriate altitude for visual search. Figure 5-14 illustrates the geometry of this procedure.

Note: En-route aircraft may be very helpful and should be requested to listen on the survival beacon's 121.5 MHz alerting or homing frequency and report the positions where the signal is first heard and where it fades.

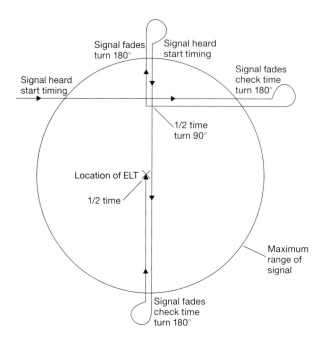

Figure 5-14 – *Time-assisted aural electronic search*

Radar searches

5.6.5   Radar is primarily used in maritime search. Most available airborne radars would be unlikely to detect typical search objects on land except for metal wreckage in open areas such as desert or tundra.

5.6.6   The sweep width to employ in computing the optimal search area will depend on the type of radar, height of the antenna, amount of environmental clutter and "noise", radar cross-section of the search object, radar beam refraction due to atmospherics, and operator ability. It should be noted that when the wave height increases to above one to two metres (three to six feet), the probability of detecting a small search object rapidly decreases for most radars and, consequently, so does the sweep width. For aircraft, the search altitude used should normally range between 800 m and 1,200 m (2,400 ft and 4,000 ft) for small search objects. The altitude used for large search objects should not exceed 2,400 m (8,000 ft). It is advisable to consult with the pilot in command when estimating the aircraft radar's sweep width and establishing a suitable track spacing for the existing search conditions.

5.7   Night search patterns

Parachute flare searches

5.7.1   Detection of survivors at night is unlikely if they have no night signalling devices such as flares or lights. The use of aircraft parachute flares does not appreciably increase the chance of detection. This type of illumination has very limited potential in searches for anything other than large objects located in well-defined search areas on flat land or at sea. It should also be noted that over land, a look-out will be confused by silhouettes or reflections from objects other than the search object.

5.7.2   Parachute flares should not be dropped over inhabited areas unless exceptional circumstances warrant their use. Flares should not be used over any land area unless there is no risk that a ground fire may be started. Flare usage over land is always subject to the prescribed procedures and policies of the State(s) where the search area lies.

5.7.3   Parachute flares are normally dropped from fixed-wing aircraft flying above and ahead of the search facilities. In this type of search, vessels and helicopters are the most efficient search facilities. Fixed-wing aircraft will normally be less effective. Parachute flares should not be dropped in such a way that casings or other material could fall on a search facility. It is essential to ensure flight separation between helicopters and fixed-wing aircraft in these situations. If the flare is of the type which falls free after burn-out, the flare must be dropped in such a way that it does not burn out over a search facility. Flares must be handled with care by crewmembers familiar with their use.

(a)   When helicopters are used as primary search facilities, it is essential to ensure a safe separation between them and the illuminating aircraft. Care must be exercised to ensure neither the flares nor debris from them collides with the searching helicopter. The searching helicopter normally flies into the wind or downwind at a height of 150 m (500 ft) and the illuminating aircraft drops the flare at a height which permits flare burn-out below helicopter height. The flare should be dropped well ahead, and well above, the helicopter at the two o'clock or ten o'clock position, so that the observers can search for silhouettes and shadows in addition to searching the area directly illuminated by the flare. The distance between successive flares should be calculated so as to ensure that the area is thoroughly covered. The aircraft dropping flares should be carefully positioned so that it is in position to drop the next flare before the previous flare has burned out. The helicopter pilot should be able to see the flare or flare-dropping aircraft when the flare is dropped. This technique is illustrated in figure 5-15.

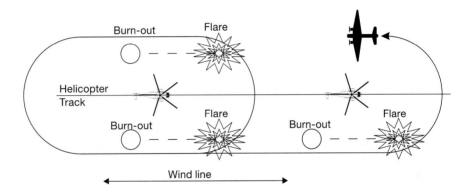

Figure 5-15 – *Parachute flare search using a helicopter*

(b)   When a fixed-wing aircraft is the primary search facility, the chances of success are small even if the search object is large and conspicuous. Fixed-wing aircraft should be used only in extreme emergencies, when no other type of search is available. The search is carried out in a way similar to that for helicopters.

(c)   When a single surface craft is the primary search facility, the search is carried out by having the aircraft drop flares in a systematic pattern. Only large search objects on or near the surface facility's course will have a reasonably good chance of detection. The aircraft should drop the flare upwind of the vessel, off the bow. Flare burn-out should occur on the opposite quarter of the vessel. Illumination may be on one or both sides of the vessel. Figure 5-16 shows this pattern.

(d)   When several surface search facilities are available, this procedure is used with a line-abreast formation. The spacing between the surface facilities depends on the size of the search object and on-scene conditions. The aircraft flies a racetrack pattern over the formation, dropping a set of flares upwind so that they are over the formation during the middle of the burning period, and a new set is dropped as the previous set burns out. The number of flares to be dropped will depend on the length of the line of surface facilities. This pattern is shown in figure 5-17.

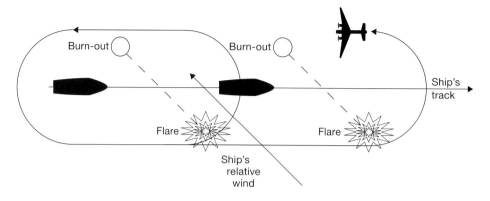

Figure 5-16 *– Parachute flare search using a surface facility*

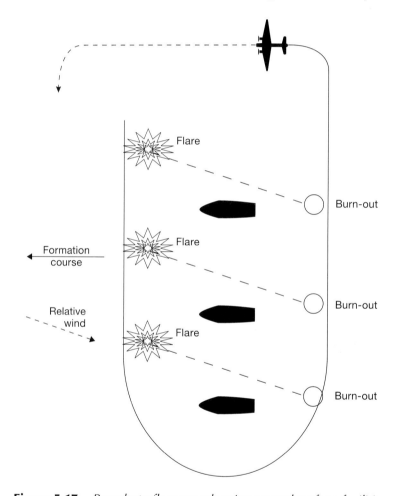

Figure 5-17 *– Parachute flare search using several surface facilities*

Search by infrared devices

5.7.4 Infrared (IR) devices, such as IR TV cameras or Forward-Looking Infrared Radar (FLIR), are passive detection systems used to detect thermal radiation. They operate on the principle of detecting temperature differences to produce a video picture. Therefore, IR devices can often detect survivors by their body heat.

5.7.5 IR devices are normally preferred for night use. For aircraft, search height should normally be from 70 m to 150 m (200 ft to 500 ft) for small search objects such as persons in the water and up to a maximum of approximately 450 m (1,500 ft) for larger search objects or those having a stronger heat signature. The sweep width can be estimated based on the effective detection range as provided by the manufacturer.

Night vision goggles

5.7.6   Use of night vision goggles (NVGs) can be effective in searches carried out by helicopters, fixed-wing aircraft, rescue vessels, utility boats, and ground search parties.

5.7.7   The following factors may influence the effectiveness of NVGs for searching:

–   NVG quality;

–   crew training and experience;

–   environmental conditions (meteorological visibility, moisture, moonlight, cloud coverage, precipitation, etc.);

–   level and glare effects of ambient light (including natural light like moonlight and starlight, and artificial light like illumination from search, navigation and other lights, inside and outside the search facility), and whether the light sources are within the NVG wearer's field of view;

–   search-craft speed;

–   height of the observers above the surface;

–   surface conditions (like the presence of snow) and sea state;

–   size, illumination, and reflectivity of the search object (reflective tape on survivors or their craft can significantly improve the chances of detection with NVGs); and,

–   types of survival equipment or light sources (like signalling devices and pyrotechnics) used by the survivors.

5.7.8   Glare should be minimized as much as possible within the facility's environment where the NVG users are stationed. This may involve opening or removing windows where practicable. Also, proper scanning techniques are important for reducing the adverse effects of moonlight or artificial light sources like light-houses, offshore rigs, ships, anti-collision lights, etc.

5.7.9   Visible moonlight can significantly improve detection of unlighted search objects when using NVGs. Search object light sources, like strobe or similar lights, or even cigarettes, can greatly improve detection even in poor visibility conditions such as light snowfall.

5.7.10   RCC staffs should be aware that sweep width estimates should take into account local conditions and the advice of the facility on scene.

5.8   Land search patterns

5.8.1   The normal functions of land rescue facilities are to care for and evacuate survivors after they have been located. Search of large areas by ground parties alone is normally impracticable but may be used when aerial search is not possible or is ineffective, or when a closer examination of an area is desirable. Searching on the ground can be particularly effective in heavy forest or mountainous area. Land search parties may also be used to locate survivors who have left the site of a crashed aircraft or grounded vessel.

Visual search patterns for land search parties

5.8.2   Whenever possible, obvious natural or artificial landmarks such as rivers, roads, etc., should be used to delimit search sub-areas. This will help the search party considerably. Leaders of search parties should be equipped with large-scale topographical maps, preferably with a scale of 1:50000 or, when these are not available, 1:100000. The search areas should be marked on these maps prior to commencing the search.

5.8.3   The search patterns used by land search parties are normally parallel sweeps or contour searches using a line-abreast formation. Variations and modifications of these patterns may be necessary to accommodate local terrain.

5.8.4 The parallel sweep search is the most common and effective type of land search pattern. Track spacing for lost persons is normally between five and eight metres. Search progress through wooded areas should be conducted at a slow pace so each thicket and depression may be checked. One square kilometre of woods can be searched by a land party of 20 to 25 persons in slightly more than 1.5 hours.

(a) A search party requires a team leader, two flankers and as many searchers as the terrain will allow. The team leader and the flankers should be equipped with large-scale topographic maps and a means of keeping in contact with one another and the on-scene co-ordinator.

(b) The search line is first formed along the search area boundary, with individual searchers positioned one track spacing apart. The control of the operation rests with the team leader, who must ensure that the line is as straight as possible. To do that, the team leader must keep the pace equal to that of the slowest person in the line. If part of the team encounters an obstacle, or item of interest, they should investigate it while the rest of the team continues just past that point and stops to wait. When the investigators have rejoined the search line, the entire search line again moves forward on the team leader's signal.

(c) Boundary control of each successive sweep through an area is assigned to the pivoting flanker. During the first leg of the search, one flanker will try to follow a natural boundary or predetermined compass course while the other flanker marks the trail at the other end of the line. When the first leg has been completed, the line pivots about the number two flanker and proceeds in the opposite direction on the second leg. This procedure is continued until the search area has been completely covered.

(d) The distance between each individual searcher (track spacing) is determined by the distance a person can effectively search while keeping adjacent searchers in visual and audible contact. This will ensure full coverage as well as give protection to inexperienced searchers. The track spacing will depend on the search object size and colour, weather, and terrain. The team leader will make the final determination on what track spacing to use.

(e) Whenever contact with a searcher is lost, the team leader must be notified immediately. The search line will then stop until complete team contact is re-established.

5.8.5 The contour search is a modification of the parallel sweep search and is adopted when mountainous features can be circled completely.

(a) The search begins with one flanker at the highest level and the other flanker at the low end of the line. When the mountain has been circled once, the line is re-formed on the lower side of the bottom flanker and the process is repeated until the search is concluded.

(b) The contour search is normally performed by one team leader, two flankers and up to 25 searchers.

(c) The team leader maintains overall control of the team, with the sweep boundary control assigned to the upper flanker.

(d) The general procedures as outlined in 5.8.4 above are also followed when making a contour search.

5.9 Search object motion

Effects of search object motion on search patterns

5.9.1 Search object motion is an important consideration, especially in the marine environment. It has two primary effects.

(a) Search areas and patterns are normally based on the search object's estimated location (datum) for the time at which search activities are scheduled to begin. If a search facility's arrival in its assigned search sub-area is delayed for any reason, the datum on which it is based is no longer valid because the search object has continued to move during the delay. Similarly, a search facility may experience mechanical or other difficulties and depart the search area before completing its assigned pattern, leaving a portion to be completed later.

(b) Search patterns, when plotted relative to a moving object, may appear distorted. *The effectiveness of a search pattern depends on how well the actual pattern, when plotted relative to the search object, matches the intended pattern.* For static search objects, the geographic plot of the pattern and the relative motion plot are always identical. For moving search objects, however, the geographic and relative motion plots can be quite different.

5.9.2 If a search facility is going to experience a significant delay in starting its assigned search pattern, or must depart the search area without completing its assigned search pattern, the OSC and SMC should be informed as soon as possible. Depending on the sub-area affected and its POC value as compared to those of the other search sub-areas, it may be necessary for the OSC or SMC to re-assign the search responsibilities to ensure the high-probability areas are covered first. For this reason, sub-areas should be prioritized in advance whenever possible. Ranking sub-areas in order of POC value will make any necessary reassignment decisions easier and more efficient and will reduce the impacts of delays and interruptions. It may also be necessary to move a delayed sub-area in the downdrift direction an appropriate distance if this can be done safely while maintaining adequate separation of the search facilities.

5.9.3 For patterns that employ parallel tracks, maintaining the correct track spacing *relative to the search object* at all times is crucial to search effectiveness. Failing to account for the relative motion between the search facility and the search object can lead to non-parallel tracks and uncovered areas relative to the search object. Figure 5-18 shows a PS pattern as it would appear relative to an object moving perpendicular to the search legs. If the search object had been in the area marked "Not Searched" (270 NM^2 or 37.5% of the intended search area) when the aircraft arrived at the commence search point, it would not have been found. The adverse impact on the POS for the search is likely to be significant. The reduced area that was covered had a higher coverage factor but a lower probability of containing (POC) the search object. Unless the search object probability density in the missed area was very low compared to that in the covered area, the decrease in POC from not covering all of the intended area will outweigh any increase in POD that might have been attained in the portion that was covered. The resulting POS value will be lower, perhaps much lower, than intended.

Note: An error in the estimate of the crosswind used in aeronautical navigation computations could also distort the search pattern in the same way relative to a fixed object.

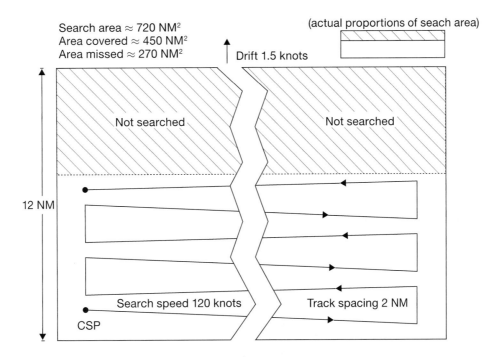

Figure 5-18 – *Relative motion plot for a search object moving perpendicular to the search legs*

Note: The search legs in the covered area were neither parallel nor equally spaced relative to the moving search object. Both these conditions are required for the "Ideal Search Conditions" curve on the POD graph in figure N-10 to be valid, even when applied to just that portion of the sub-area actually searched. For search patterns distorted in this way, the lower POD curve should be used and applied only to the area actually covered.

Minimizing the impact of search object motion on search effectiveness

5.9.4   The simplest method for keeping search legs parallel and equally spaced relative to a moving search object is to ensure the search legs are parallel to the search object's predicted direction of motion. This minimizes the impact of search object motion on track spacing when the pattern is plotted relative to the search object. Figure 5-19 shows the relative motion plot of a PS pattern with search legs parallel to the direction of the search object's motion. It should be noted that the area of the parallelogram in figure 5-19 is exactly equal to the area of the original rectangle. However, at one end of the intended search area, a small triangular portion was not searched. Note that the area missed (27 NM^2 or 3.75% of the intended search area) was only one tenth of that missed in figure 5-18. If the survivors had been in the missed portion, they would not have been found. On the other hand, a triangular area of equal size was effectively covered outside the intended search area at the other end. The impact on the POS for the search will depend on the POC for the triangular area that was missed as compared to the POC for the triangular area that was added at the opposite end. In any event, the impact will be much, much smaller than for the situation where search legs are perpendicular to the direction of motion.

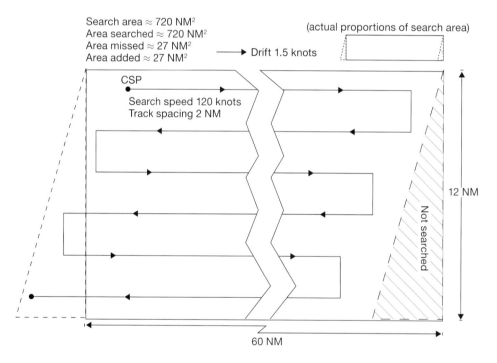

Search area ≈ 720 NM^2
Area searched ≈ 720 NM^2
Area missed ≈ 27 NM^2
Area added ≈ 27 NM^2

(actual proportions of search area)

Drift 1.5 knots

CSP

Search speed 120 knots
Track spacing 2 NM

12 NM

Not searched

60 NM

Figure 5-19 – *Relative motion plot for a search object moving parallel to the search legs*

Note: Because the search legs remained parallel and equally spaced, either of the POD curves in figure N-10 may be applied to the parallelogram that was covered. The choice of POD curve will depend on other factors, as discussed in section 5.3.

5.9.5   When the search area has high-probability cells near a side that lies in the direction of search object motion as viewed from the centre of the search area, the search planner should consider moving or extending the search area in the direction of motion by an appropriate amount to ensure these cells do not leave the intended search area before a search facility has a chance to search them. The amount of search area movement or expansion required will be determined by the search object's rate of motion and the amount of time it will take to cover the search area. Figure 5-20 shows how a search area could be extended in the direction of the search object's predicted movement.

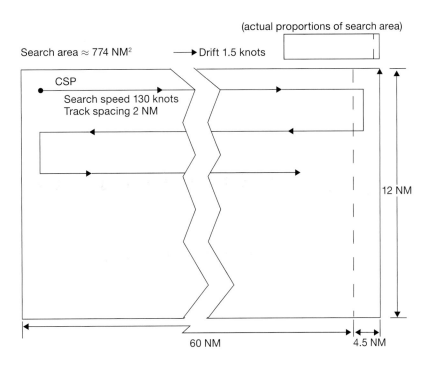

Figure 5-20 *– Geographic plot for a sub-area extended in the direction of search object movement*

5.10 Assignment of search sub-areas to individual facilities

5.10.1 When planning a search involving several search facilities, the search planner has to simultaneously balance a number of interrelated factors. These factors include, but are not limited to, the following:

- size, shape, and orientation of sub-areas so the desired search area is covered;

- type of search (visual or electronic) and coverage factors;

- track spacing and orientation of search patterns;

- maintaining safe separations between search facilities;

- search endurances, operating ranges, required fuel reserves, and alternate aerodromes for aircraft;

- transit times to and from the search area; and,

- search speeds.

5.10.2 Because all these factors are more or less equally important and modifying one impacts the others, there is no order of discussion or consideration which is preferable to all others. The search planner must consider all of the factors discussed in the following paragraphs to develop a practical search plan.

Search area coverage

5.10.3 In chapter 4, the optimal area to search (*A*) was determined from the available search effort (*Z*) and the type of search object location probability distribution that was estimated or assumed. Using the universal definition of coverage factor (*C*) given in section 4.6, it is possible to compute the optimal coverage factor by:

$$C = Z/A$$

When search facilities are given an area to search, however, they are not normally given the amount of area and the desired coverage factor. Instead, they are normally given a specific, detailed description of the search sub-area they are to cover and an equally specific, detailed search pattern to follow.

Standard search patterns were described section 5.8 above. The description and designation of search sub-areas are discussed in section 5.11.

Track spacing

5.10.4 Most of the search patterns described in this chapter consist of equally spaced parallel search legs (tracks). The distance between adjacent search legs is called the track spacing. For these patterns, the coverage factor (C) may be computed as:

$$C = W/S$$

where W is the sweep width and S is the track spacing. For parallel sweep searches, this formula is equivalent to the one in paragraph 5.10.3. If the sweep width and optimal coverage factor are known, the optimal track spacing may be found by:

$$S = W/C$$

Before a track spacing is assigned to a facility, care must be taken to ensure the facility is capable of accurately locating and following search legs at that spacing.

Adjusting track spacing

5.10.5 Increasing the track spacing increases the area which can be searched, but reduces the coverage factor and the probability of detection (POD). Decreasing the track spacing has the opposite effects. It decreases the area and increases the coverage factor and POD. Guidance was provided in sections 4.6 and 4.7 for determining the optimal area to search with the available effort. As shown in paragraphs 5.10.3 and 5.10.4 above, this information can be used to find the optimal coverage factor and track spacing. However, the optimal track spacing from a theoretical perspective may not be the best choice from a practical perspective. Normally, some adjustment of the optimal track spacing will be required. Sometimes the computed optimal track spacing is too small for the search facility to follow. Also, since it is desirable to have the widths of rectangular search sub-areas equal to a whole number of track spacings, adjustments are sometimes necessary, especially when the search planner needs to divide a search area into several adjacent sub-areas. If the optimal track spacing is used as a starting point, the adjustments needed to account for practical considerations will usually make the resulting search plan only slightly sub-optimal.

Size of a search sub-area

5.10.6 To determine the maximum search area that may be assigned to an individual facility, the pilot in command of the facility if it is an aircraft, or the master of the facility if it is a vessel, must be consulted. Some of the factors to consider are listed below.

(a) The search planner should consider facility characteristics, such as:

– facility's search endurance and time available on task;

– aircraft range at normal cruise power setting;

– aircraft required fuel reserve (alternate aerodromes, destination);

– time to and from the search area; and

– search speed (to determine time required to cover the area).

Note: Pilots in command of aircraft should be cautioned that fuel consumption during search missions may be higher than normal, particularly in mountainous terrain.

(b) The distance to the search area is important because the greater the distance, the shorter the time available for search.

(c) The size of search area and track spacing determine how much time on scene will be required for the facility to complete its assigned search sub-area. Alternatively, the facility's search endurance and the track spacing determine how much area can be covered.

(d) The type of search (visual or electronic) affects the choice of pattern and track spacing.

Note: For contour searches, the time required to complete the search area can be computed only by tracing the actual flight path on a map.

5.10.7 When all these factors are known, it is possible to determine the area that can be covered by an individual facility in a given time. It is extremely important that each facility is allocated only an area that it can cover on that sortie. The following formula can be used to determine the search endurance (*T*) required to search an individual sub-area:

$$T = A/(V \times S)$$

where *A* is the area of the search sub-area, *V* is the speed of the search facility, and *S* is the track spacing. For several search facilities covering equal portions of the search area using the same search speed and track spacing, the search endurance required to cover the total search area (A_t) is given by the following formula:

$$T = A_t/(V \times N \times S)$$

where *N* is the number of search facilities. If several search facilities are used which do not have the same search endurance, search speed, or track spacing, the time required to complete the search is equal to the longest of the times required to complete the search sub-areas. The area which can be searched by a facility based on its search endurance, search speed, and assigned track spacing may be found by the following formula:

$$A = T \times V \times S$$

The total amount of area which can be covered by several search facilities is the sum of the areas which can be covered by each of the individual search facilities.

5.10.8 The search area planning graph in figure N-9 may be used instead of the above formulas to find either the time required to search a given area or the area that can be searched in a given time. In using either the formulas or this graph, the following items should be considered.

(a) At low levels, the indicated airspeed (IAS) for aircraft is approximately the same as ground speed.

(b) At altitudes up to 600 m (2,000 ft) and a temperature ranging from +5°C to +35°C, true airspeed (TAS) for aircraft is approximately the same as IAS (when temperatures are higher or lower than this, the TAS should be used).

(c) For the purpose of computing how much area can be covered, wind effects on aircraft are usually negligible because the tracks in most search patterns are reciprocal to each other. (When actually flying the search pattern, however, aircraft must correctly compensate for all wind effects, especially crosswind effects, to avoid search pattern distortions similar to those shown in figures 5-18 and 5-19.)

Allocation of search areas for individual facilities

5.10.9 When sub-areas are allocated to individual facilities, care should be taken to ensure that each facility is used only in searches for which it is technically and operationally suitable.

(a) Short-range or medium-range facilities should be used for areas not far from a suitable base.

(b) Fast, long-range facilities should be used for distant areas or far offshore.

(c) Facilities with poor navigational ability should be used for searches with constant, or at least frequent, visual references.

(d) Fast aircraft should be assigned search patterns which they can perform, for example, electronic or visual search along the intended track.

(e) Craft with the ability to rescue or assist survivors should be assigned to the higher probability sub-areas.

(f) The widths of rectangular areas to be covered with a PS pattern and the lengths of rectangular areas to be covered with a CS pattern should equal a whole number of track spacings.

5.10.10 When assigning search patterns, care should be taken to ensure that each facility is assigned a pattern it can safely and accurately follow. Things the search planner should consider are listed below.

(a) Facilities should not normally be assigned search patterns with a track spacing less than the facilities' minimum turning radius. If a high coverage is needed in a sub-area and attaining that coverage on a single search requires a track spacing that is smaller than the facility can follow, the search planner should consider having the search facility cover the area twice at a larger track spacing that is within the facility's capability.

(b) Whenever possible, search patterns should be oriented so the search legs are parallel to the expected motion of the search object during the search. Other factors which may influence search leg orientation are the method(s) of navigation used by the search facility, sun angle, swell or ridge direction, wind direction, etc. The search planner should decide which factor is likely to have the greatest impact on POS and orient the search area, patterns, and legs accordingly.

Search facility separation

5.10.11 Safe separations among the search facilities must be assured at all times. This is particularly critical for searching aircraft due to their high speed. Adjacent search sub-areas, the search patterns used to cover them, and commence search points should be planned so that all search craft of the same general type (surface or air) are following parallel tracks and creeping in the same direction to ensure horizontal separation. Aircraft in adjacent sub-areas should also be assigned different search altitudes to provide vertical separation. Vertical separation of aircraft in adjacent search sub-areas should be at least 150 m (500 ft). An aircraft co-ordinator (ACO) should be assigned whenever multiple aircraft are operating in close proximity.

5.11 Designation and description of search sub-areas

5.11.1 The following paragraphs describe various methods that may be employed by search planners to designate and describe search areas.

Designation of search sub-areas

5.11.2 For ease of reference in assigning search sub-areas and reporting search results, each search sub-area should be given a unique designation. One method for doing this is to use a letter and number combination, where the letter denotes the search day ("A" for the first day of search, "B" for the second day, etc.) and the number distinguishes sub-areas searched on the same day from one another. Using this method, search sub-areas would be given designations such as A-1, B-3, C-2, etc. Almost any method may be used as long as it is understood by all participants.

Description of search sub-areas

5.11.3 A number of methods exist for describing search sub-areas, depending on the type of datum, the type of pattern, whether the search is being conducted over land or water, the navigational capabilities of the search facility, etc.

5.11.4 *Geographical co-ordinate method.* This is the normal method of describing an area. The corners of the area are defined by geographical co-ordinates of latitude and longitude. An advantage of this method is that areas of any shape can be described easily. However, the method is lengthy and subject to errors in transmission. For example:

AREA   CORNER POINTS
A-1   1547N 06512W, 1559N 06500W, 1500N 06403W, 1447N 06415W

Adding a *checksum digit* to each co-ordinate can make use of geographical co-ordinates more reliable by providing an opportunity to detect errors in transmission. Checksum digits are computed by adding all the digits in the co-ordinate and recording the last (least significant) digit of the result following the hemisphere designator (N, S, E, W). For example, the sum of the digits of the first latitude above is

$1 + 5 + 4 + 7 = 17$ so the checksum digit is 7. The co-ordinates for area A-1 would appear as follows if checksum digits were used:

AREA   CORNER POINTS
A-1   1547N7 06512W4, 1559N0 06500W1, 1500N6 06403W3, 1447N6 06415W6

If the receiving facility finds an incorrect checksum digit, an error has occurred and a retransmission of the co-ordinates should be requested. Most military facilities will recognize this checksum technique but civilian facilities may require an explanation the first time it is used.

5.11.5   *Centre point method.* Any rectangular or square area can be described by giving the geographical co-ordinates of the centre of the area, the direction of the longer axis, the lengths of the longer and shorter axes and the direction of creep. For example:

CENTRE POINT	LENGTH	WIDTH	MAJOR AXIS	TRACK SPACING	CREEP
3417N 13622W	80 NM	40 NM	025T	5.0 NM	115T

5.11.6   *Track line method.* A track line search area may be described by giving the relevant points on the track and the width of coverage. For example:

SEARCH AREA: 2406N 05855W to 2450N 05546W, WIDTH 50 NM.

5.11.7   *Landmark method.* Description of search areas by natural and artificial boundaries is particularly suitable for searches in mountainous areas and for areas assigned to search facilities with limited navigational capability.

5.11.8   *Grid method.* Many areas are divided into grids on local grid maps. Use of these grids permits accurate positioning and small area referencing without transmitting lengthy geographical co-ordinates and reduces the possibility of transmission errors. Such grids also often provide a convenient grid for probability maps (see sections 4.6 and 4.7) and it is efficient to use the same grid for both purposes.

5.11.9   *Grid overlay method.* The advantages of the grid method (see paragraph 5.11.8) may also be obtained by using a grid overlay for search facilities requiring the description of search areas. Grid overlays are most useful when all ships and aircraft involved in a search have a previously prepared grid overlay that is consistent with those of the other search facilities.

5.11.10   Various types of grid overlays can be used, made of transparent plastic material, for example, and placed on top of a map. Figure 5-21 shows a simple version of a 64-cell grid overlay. As mentioned above, it is often both convenient and efficient to use the same grid for both probability maps and designation of search areas.

5.11.11   The centre of the grid overlay should be placed over the most probable location (datum point) of the missing aircraft or vessel. If all search aircraft or vessels have on board previously prepared grid overlays, the search planner may direct them to orient the overlay on a given true bearing line, such as the probable track of the missing aircraft or vessel. Should another type of grid overlay than the type described above be used, it is at times more convenient to orient it north–south.

5.12   Planning on-scene co-ordination

5.12.1   When planning on-scene co-ordination, the SMC must try to maximize the efficiency of the operation while ensuring the safety of all facilities concerned.

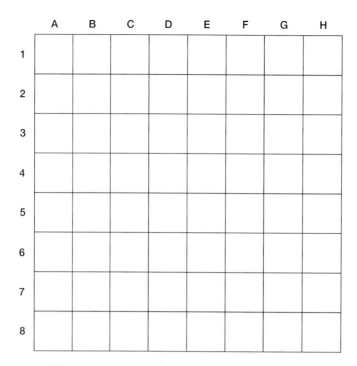

Figure 5-21 – *Simple version of a grid overlay*

5.12.2 In planning on-scene co-ordination, the following actions should be taken:

- designate the SMC;

- designate the OSC;

- designate ACO, as appropriate;

- determine the on-scene time for search facilities;

- assign search facilities, areas and patterns;

- issue co-ordination instructions to the OSC and ACO;

- request airspace reservations;

- request air and marine safety notices be issued as appropriate;

- activate appropriate pre-arranged mutual assistance agreements;

- designate primary and secondary communications channels; and,

- establish a situation report (SITREP) schedule between the OSC and SMC.

Safety considerations for aircraft

5.12.3 Air search, except possibly electronic search, is normally carried out in visual flight conditions (as opposed to instrument flight conditions). The SMC is responsible for developing a search action plan that provides for adequate separation among searching aircraft. It is the responsibility of the OSC and each pilot in command to ensure adequate separation is actually maintained during the search unless performance of this function is done by the ATS unit responsible for the airspace in which the search aircraft are operating. To ensure that the necessary separation from other traffic can be provided while search aircraft enter, operate in, and leave the search area, the SMC must co-ordinate the search action plan with the ATS unit concerned and ensure flight plans are submitted for the search aircraft. Aircraft passing through the search area but not participating in the search should be directed to maintain an altitude that is at least 700 m (2,000 ft) above the highest altitude assigned to searching aircraft. The SMC or, if that is not practicable, the OSC, may designate an aircraft co-ordinator (ACO) to assist in maintaining flight safety as discussed in chapter 1. Considerations as to whether an ACO is designated may include, but are not limited to, multiple aircraft in the search area, aircraft from different countries, weather conditions, communications problems and logistic problems.

5.12.4 For large-scale searches and searches in controlled airspaces, the SMC should obtain a temporary airspace reservation or flight restrictions to limit aircraft not involved in the search from the appropriate authority. It may then be the responsibility of the SMC, OSC or ACO to make arrangements for separation among the search aircraft if they are unable to provide their own separation. Horizontal and/or vertical separation should be provided for aircraft conducting visual searches in adjacent areas as described in paragraph 5.10.11 above. Aircraft conducting an electronic search may be separated only vertically. Vertical separation in this situation should be at least 300 m (1000 ft).

5.12.5 The SMC should consider providing a fixed-wing escort for SAR helicopters whenever circumstances require these helicopters to operate:

– offshore or in remote areas, especially if near their operational range limits;

– in marginal weather conditions (e.g., high winds, reduced visibility, icing, etc.);

– in rough terrain where significant turbulence may exist;

– near their maximum operational altitude for the situation (loading, air temperature, etc.); or

– in any unusually hazardous situation.

5.12.6 The primary advantage of a fixed-wing escort is increased safety. Specific advantages contributing to increased safety may include:

– increased navigational accuracy;

– added communications capability;

– the ability to immediately locate the helicopter in the event of a forced landing, drop survival gear, alert the SMC and possibly locate assistance (e.g., a passing ship);

– the ability to fly ahead, locate the survivors, and direct the helicopter to them, thus reducing the helicopter's on-scene and total sortie times; and

– the ability to fly ahead, observe environmental conditions and report them to the helicopter.

5.13 Search action plans

5.13.1 After an attainable search action plan is developed for accomplishment by the OSC and facilities on scene, it is provided to them in a search action message. Potential parts of the message are given below. An example of a search action message is provided in appendix L with the Search Action Plan Worksheet. The message should include a situation summary of the on-scene situation, including the nature of the emergency, the last known position, search object description, types of detection aids and survival equipment which survivors may have, present and forecast weather, and search facilities on scene. The message should include a listing of the search area(s) and sub-areas that can be searched by the search facilities in the allotted time. The message should assign primary and secondary control channels, on scene, monitor and press channels, and special radio procedures, schedules, or relevant communication factors. It is better to release the message early. If a "first light" search is being planned, parent agencies providing search facilities should typically receive the message at least six hours before departure time. The message can always be expanded or amended later.

5.13.2 The message normally includes six parts:

(a) *Situation:* includes a brief description of the incident, position, and time; number of persons on board (POBs); primary and secondary search objects, including the amount and types of survival equipment; weather forecast and period of forecast; and search facilities on scene.

(b) *Search area(s):* presented in column format with headings for area, size, corner points, other essential data.

(c) *Execution:* presented in column format with headings for area, search facility, parent agency or location, pattern, creep direction, commence search points, and altitude.

(d) *Co-ordination:* designates the SMC, OSC and ACO; search facility on-scene times; track spacings and coverage factors desired; OSC and ACO instructions, such as on the use of datum marker buoys; airspace reservations; aircraft safety instructions; search facility change of operational control information if pertinent; parent agency relief instructions; and authorizations for non-SAR aircraft in the area.

(e) *Communications:* prescribes control channels; on-scene channels; monitor channels; method to identify OSC, ACO and search facilities (such as radar transponder codes); and press channels.

(f) *Reports:* requirements for OSC and ACO reports of on-scene weather, progress, and other SITREP information; and for parent agencies to provide at the end of daily operations, such as sorties, hours flown, hours and area(s) searched, and coverage factor(s).

A sample search action message is provided in appendix L.

5.14 Conduct of the search

5.14.1 There are a number of activities which are important to the conduct of search operations. These activities include briefing of search personnel, procedures to be followed when entering, operating in, and departing the search area, and debriefing search personnel.

5.14.2 The importance of briefings, debriefings and following standard or prescribed procedures should not be underestimated, especially when several facilities will be operating simultaneously in adjacent search sub-areas. For safety reasons, each facility should be briefed on the intended locations of all other nearby facilities at all times, including periods of transit to or from the search area. Look-outs will be more effective if they have a precise description of the search object. Often detailed descriptions, drawings, photographs, etc., of the same or similar objects can be most effectively communicated in briefings. Any last minute co-ordination details or questions about procedures can be resolved at briefings. Debriefings are essential for obtaining detailed information about any clues that were sighted and getting an accurate description of the actual search conditions encountered for the purpose of estimating search effectiveness (POS and POS_c).

5.15 Briefings

5.15.1 Briefing of SAR personnel should, if possible, be held in sufficient time before departure. SAR personnel should be given all relevant details of the distress and all instructions for the SAR operation. Time permitting, this may be done by issuing a search operation briefing/tasking form to the crew, giving as much information as possible (see appendix H). Situation updates should be provided to the search facility *en route*. Descriptive information regarding merchant vessels and small craft is given in the Maritime Search and Rescue Code (MAREC) in appendix I. If the SMC receives additional pertinent information after the briefing, the information should be passed to facilities *en route* or on scene.

Briefing of air search personnel

5.15.2 Briefings should include all items detailed on the briefing form and any other important information available, and should include:

– a full description and nature of distress;

– full details of the search area(s) and any description of clues that may indicate the presence of the search object, including:

  – distress signals and visual signal codes (listed in appendix A) that survivors might use to attract attention or communicate their status or direction of movement;

  – broken tree tops;

  – wreckage;

- dye markers, burnt patches, oil slicks;

- smoke;

- signs of a landslide or other unusual occurrence affecting the terrain;

- coloured or white objects; and

- reflections from metal or glass;

Note: Details that are already known to be of no significance for the present search, such as locations of wreckage from previous unrelated incidents, should also be pointed out.

- type and method of search and method to record areas searched;

- details of other SAR facilities engaged and their search areas;

- communication procedures and frequencies to be used;

- frequencies to be guarded for transmissions from survivors;

- special instructions concerning the flight to and from the search area, including routes and levels;

- details of droppable supplies to be carried and any special dropping procedures;

- action to be taken on sighting the search object;

- flight separation instructions;

- precautions to be taken when dropping pyrotechnics;

- present and forecast weather conditions to, from and in the search area, and at destination and alternate aerodromes; and

- designation of OSC and ACO.

These details are included in the Briefing Form in appendix H. Trained and experienced search crews will not normally require details on search procedures; however, untrained or volunteer searchers may require additional information concerning search procedures to optimize their search effort.

Briefing of surface search personnel

5.15.3 Briefing of surface search personnel should cover all items similar to that of air personnel, except that emphasis should be given to matters of interest to surface facilities. To ensure effective co-ordination of surface searches, radiocommunication equipment should be used to exchange information during the search operation.

5.16 Aircraft search procedures

5.16.1 Aircraft are the most capable facilities for searching a large area quickly. As each aircraft has its operational and technical limitations, the urgency of a situation should never cause an aircraft to be used beyond these limits or on operations for which it is not suitable. Reliable communications between aircraft and the controlling agency are essential to keep all parties aware of the progress of the search. In areas of poor radio reception or when working beyond the range of CRSs, a high-flying aircraft or a surface craft with an appropriate communications capability can serve as a central communications facility. Situation reports (SITREPs) should be sent to the controlling RCC at the intervals specified in the search action plan. An example of a SITREP is provided in appendix I. Detailed in-flight procedures, including scanning techniques, are included in the *International Aeronautical and Maritime SAR Manual for Mobile Facilities*.

5.17 Surface facility search procedures

5.17.1 When surface facilities are used for search operations, they must be capable of carrying out the operation in the prevailing and forecast sea and weather conditions for the search area. Complete procedures for surface craft, including scanning techniques, are found in the *International Aeronautical and Maritime SAR Manual for Mobile Facilities*.

5.18 Search by land facilities

5.18.1 The same basic theory of search applies on land as well as in the marine environment. In both cases, the goal is to increase the cumulative POS as quickly as the available resources will allow. However, the planning methods and search techniques used on land are often different from those used in the marine environment. If the initial search object is a forced landing site, then search object motion is not likely to be an issue. If the search object is a lost or missing person, whether from a forced landing site or some other circumstance such as a lost hiker, hunter or child, search object motion may be an issue. However, in these cases, the influences of the lost person's behaviour, weather, terrain and vegetation take the place of winds, currents and drift. Aerial search effectiveness is reduced over areas that are mountainous or covered with significant amounts of vegetation. Searching with land facilities may be the only alternative. Land facility search procedures are covered in the IAMSAR Manual, volume III, *Mobile Facilities*.

5.18.2 Searching for lost persons with ground parties may involve large numbers of searchers. Logistics (keeping track of searchers and providing food and shelter for them) can become quite complex, especially in remote areas. Search environments, and hence sweep width values, can vary dramatically over short distances such as when pasture lands and dense forests are adjacent to one another. Search assignments normally involve small teams of persons. Search areas are based on terrain, vegetation, a corresponding estimated search speed, sweep width, etc. Decisions about which areas to search when there are insufficient search facilities should be determined by where the cumulative POS can be increased at the greatest rate. Search area boundaries are normally defined by physical features such as ridgelines, water boundaries, roads, trails, fences, visible power lines and pipelines, etc. These search areas may have irregular shapes. Decisions about the best balance between team size (number of persons) and assigned area size must be made. Additional "search" techniques include searching for signs of the lost person's passage (footprints, discarded items, disturbed vegetation, etc.), the use of trackers, both human and animal, and establishing a perimeter around the overall search area, then patrolling it for signs that the lost person crossed the perimeter and left the original search area.

5.18.3 Search effectiveness can be improved by combining air assets with ground parties.

5.19 Debriefing of search personnel

5.19.1 A timely and comprehensive debriefing of search crews is as important as the briefing. A careful debriefing and evaluation of the reports of search crews is necessary for an accurate evaluation of the search activities. This evaluation in turn will determine if and where further searching should be done. Areas covered during the search should be recorded on the plot in the RCC. The information obtained should be entered on the Search Operation Debriefing Form (see appendix H).

5.19.2 All relevant debriefing information should be plotted on a chart showing the search area or areas. A careful study of the data will enable the SMC to update probability of containment (POC), probability of success (POS), and cumulative probability of success (POS_c) values (see chapter 4), and use them together with other information to determine whether an area has been sufficiently searched.

5.20 Continuation of search

5.20.1 The SMC should continue the search until all reasonable hope of rescuing survivors has passed. As the search progresses it may be necessary to re-evaluate scenarios and redefine the search area. Plots of search sub-areas covered should be maintained so that a progressive record of the search is built up. Before terminating or suspending search activities, the SMC should review the following factors:

- the possibility that survivors might still be alive, given the temperature, wind, and sea conditions prevalent since the distress incident;

- the cumulative probability of success (POS_c); and

– the availability of search facilities to continue the search.

5.20.2 Recommended procedures to follow during the conclusion of SAR operations are discussed in chapter 8.

5.21 Geographic referencing

5.21.1 If position information is communicated in latitude and longitude format in the planning and conduct of a SAR operation, it is recommended that the degrees, minutes, decimal minutes (DD° MM.mm′) format be used.

5.21.2 Geographic referencing refers to the ability to locate a point on the earth's surface, either physically or on a chart or map. A system of co-ordinates is used to define a location in physical space. Mariners and aviators typically use latitude and longitude to define their position but these co-ordinates can be displayed in different ways and people on land may use a different co-ordinate system, such as a grid system. On land, after a major disaster or in undeveloped areas, landmarks and navigational aids, such as roads, may not be recognizable so the use of a co-ordinate system may be the only way to find specific locations. Search facilities must have a good geographic reference system to conduct an effective search as well as to safely operate near each other, especially to avoid airspace traffic conflicts.

5.21.3 Charts and maps have two primary difficulties in providing a location:

(a) showing the earth's spherical shape as a flat surface, and

(b) the earth is not a perfect sphere. Another complication is States using a different basis or datum for developing charts. Also, land maps may use a local reference point to show positions on the basis of grid distances (usually east and north in metres) from the reference point. These concerns usually do not interfere with routine, local SAR operations but they can become significant concerns when assisting other States or co-ordinating with local authorities during disasters. Search planners and SAR facilities need to be aware of these differences and, when feasible, should be using the same charts and maps as well. If it is not possible for all personnel and facilities to use the same co-ordinate system and maps or charts, the SMC should be prepared to convert position data from one system to another and ensure positions are provided in the appropriate form for use. SAR facilities and personnel using electronic navigation systems (e.g., GNSS) must ensure their navigation devices are set to the appropriate datum and co-ordinate system.

5.21.4 For routine SAR operations, mass rescue operations or large scale disasters, SAR agencies must be able to understand how geographic information is communicated among the SMC, OSC, ACO and various SAR facilities. This becomes an even greater challenge when SAR facilities transition between maritime and land-based SAR operations or in large-scale disaster operations that involve many different SAR facilities that may have different ways to communicate position information. In the development of State and regional SAR plans, States should consider concerns such as:

– How does the SMC effectively use position information from external sources (e.g., general public, other agencies (non-emergency and emergency), etc.) and communicate that position information accurately and efficiently to various aeronautical, marine or land-based SAR facilities in forms they can use?

– Do States have unique, national co-ordinate systems that may not be familiar to other international SAR facilities requested to assist in a SAR, MRO or disaster response operation?

– What is the "right" reference system that should be used for a specific SAR, MRO or disaster response operation?

– Is there only one reference system that satisfies the requirements of all SAR facilities? If there is more than one reference system, how is the data translated and sent to the various SAR facilities?

– How and when is position information in one reference system converted to another?

> – How is position information received in non-standard formats (street addresses, landmark names, etc.) converted to a standard reference format?

> – In large scale MRO and disaster operations, how do SAR facilities navigate when landmarks such as street signs and homes are destroyed?

> – How do multiple SAR facilities safely and efficiently operate in the same area, particularly for mass rescue operations? For aeronautical SAR facilities, avoiding airspace traffic conflicts is a major safety issue to prevent mid-air collisions. The safe operation of multiple aviation SAR facilities in the same area may be highly dependent on all units having a common and accurate sense of their location in relation to other aviation units.

5.21.5 Latitude and longitude are angular measurements in degrees (the symbol, "°"), minutes (the apostrophe symbol, " ' "), and seconds (the quotation symbol, " " "). However, latitude and longitude can be read and written in different formats such as:

> – degrees, minutes, decimal minutes (DD° MM.mm');

> – degrees, minutes, seconds (DD° MM' SS"); and

> – degrees, decimal degrees (DD.DDDD°).

The SC should standardize how position information is communicated by the SMC, OSC, ACO and SAR facilities to limit confusion in assignments (e.g., search areas, survivor locations, etc.) and SAR planning.

Chapter 6

Rescue planning and operations

6.1 General

6.1.1 When the search object has been located, the SMC (or the OSC or master or pilot in command of the SAR facility as the case may be) must decide on the method of rescue to be followed and the facilities to be used. The following factors should be considered:

- action taken by the sighting craft and the SAR action which can be taken by other craft on scene;

- location and disposition of the survivors;

- condition of survivors and medical considerations;

- number of persons reported to be on board the distressed craft and the number who have been located;

- environmental conditions, observed and forecasted;

- available SAR facilities and their state of readiness (to reduce delay, the SAR facilities which are likely to be used should be alerted and deployed to a suitable location while the search is in progress);

- effect of weather conditions on SAR operations;

- time of day (remaining daylight) and other factors relating to visibility; and

- any risks to SAR personnel, such as hazardous materials.

6.1.2 In times of armed conflict, SAR services will normally continue to be provided in accordance with the Second Geneva Convention of 1949 (Geneva Convention for the Amelioration of the Condition of Wounded, Sick and Shipwrecked Members of the Armed Forces at Sea, of 12 August 1949) and Additional Protocol I to the Conventions.

    (a) The SAR services recognized by their Administrations are afforded protection for their humanitarian missions so far as operational requirements permit. Such protection applies to coastal rescue craft, their personnel, and fixed coastal SAR installations, including RCCs and RSCs as far as these centres are located in coastal areas and are used exclusively to co-ordinate search and rescue operations. SAR personnel should be informed about their Administration's status regarding, and views on the implementation of, the Second Geneva Convention and its Additional Protocol I.

    (b) Chapter XIV of the *International Code of Signals* illustrates the different means of identification that shall be used to provide effective protection for rescue craft.

    (c) The above-mentioned coastal installations should, in time of armed conflict, display the distinctive emblem (red cross or red crescent), according to regulations issued by their competent authorities.

    (d) It is recommended that Parties to a conflict notify the other Parties with the name, description and locations (or area of activity) of their above-mentioned rescue craft and coastal installations in the area they are located.

6.2   Sighting and subsequent procedures

6.2.1   When the search object has been located, ensure that the search facility (or rescue team if it is a land-based facility) understands that the rescue of survivors may be even more difficult and hazardous than the search. The search facility should indicate to the survivors that they have been sighted, by any of the following methods:

–   flashing a signalling lamp or searchlight; or

–   firing two, preferably green, signal flares a few seconds apart; or

–   if the search facility is an aircraft, the pilot may be able to fly low over the survivors with landing lights on or rocking the wings.

6.2.2   If the search facility is unable to effect an immediate rescue, ensure that it knows it may consider other steps such as:

–   dropping communications and survival equipment;

–   keeping the distress scene in sight at all times, thoroughly surveying the scene and accurately plotting its location, and marking it with a dye marker, smoke float or floating radio beacons;

–   reporting the sighting to the SMC with available information on:

    –   time of sighting – time zone to be specified;

    –   position of the search object;

    –   description of the distress scene;

    –   number of sighted survivors and their apparent condition;

    –   apparent condition of the distressed craft;

    –   supplies and survival equipment required by survivors (in general, supply of water should take priority over that of food);

    –   all messages, including radio transmissions, received from survivors;

    –   weather and, if applicable, sea conditions;

    –   type and location of nearby surface craft;

    –   action taken or assistance already given, and future actions required;

    –   remaining fuel and on-scene endurance of search facility or land facility making the report; and

    –   apparent risks involved in the rescue, including hazardous materials.

6.2.3   The SMC may also request the search facility to:

–   establish the location of stretches of land or water suitable for use by aircraft, pararescuers, and paramedics and the best route for use by a land facility;

–   direct rescue facilities and other aircraft to the distress scene;

–   if the search facility is an aircraft, take photographs of the distressed craft from normal search heights and directions, from a low level, and from an angle, taking in prominent landmarks, if possible; and

–   remain on scene until relieved, forced to return to base, or rescue has been effected.

6.3   Delivery of rescue personnel and equipment

6.3.1   Maritime SRUs are a reliable means of delivering supplies, equipment, and personnel to the scene of a distress. Equipment may include bilge pumps, towing equipment, fire-fighting equipment, and medical supplies. Personnel delivery is usually limited to medical personnel or repair parties.

6.3.2 Air delivery of supplies, equipment, or personnel to the scene is the most expeditious method. Helicopters are particularly suitable for this purpose and are usually the primary means for delivering personnel. Personnel delivery by fixed-wing aircraft is limited to pararescue personnel.

6.3.3 SRUs should carry a variety of rescue equipment at all times, but SAR boats and helicopters are limited due to their size. An SRU should be provided with rescue equipment suitable for individual operations. A supply of commonly required equipment should be maintained at the permanent bases of SRUs. This includes equipment designed for supply-dropping by aircraft.

6.3.4 Illumination of the scene of operation is required at night. All SRUs should be capable of providing this. Illumination could involve the use of parachute flares or high-intensity searchlights. Section 5.7 provides additional information.

6.4 Supplies and survival equipment

6.4.1 Supplies and survival equipment are carried by air and maritime SAR facilities to aid survivors, and facilitate their rescue. The type and number to be carried depend on the circumstances on scene. Maritime facilities and helicopters generally can deliver this equipment directly to survivors. Fixed-wing aircraft can deliver supplies to survivors if suitable landing areas exist nearby or if the supplies can be dropped at the scene. The packing of supplies and survival equipment should be adapted to the manner of delivery.

6.4.2 Packs of supplies and survival equipment must be adapted to the circumstances of the SRR in which they are used. Appendix G provides a guide of recommended supplies and survival equipment that SRUs may be expected to provide. Other SAR facilities may not have such supplies and equipment.

6.4.3 *Droppable containers and packages.* The type and dimensions of droppable containers or packages will vary with the type and quantities of equipment to be dropped (dictated by the number of survivors and their requirements); the size and type of the delivering aircraft; the manner of delivery (e.g., parachute or free-drop from wing racks or through hatches, let down from helicopters, etc.); and the surface conditions. Containers and packages of supplies and survival equipment should be strong, easy to open, of a highly visible colour, waterproof, and buoyant. Containers are normally cylindrical and can be made economically of a light metal alloy, such as aluminium, or of plastic-coated three-ply corrugated cardboard. Packages may consist of bags made of heavy canvas reinforced with webbing and cardboard stiffeners. If it is necessary to drop large quantities of liquids separately from other items, suitable containers should be filled to no more than nine-tenths of capacity to prevent bursting. Drinking water may be free-dropped in suitable containers. Other considerations include:

   (a) Items of a non-fragile and robust nature may be free-dropped into water or other favourable areas provided their packing will be able to withstand the shock and are watertight and buoyant. It is usually better to attach parachutes. The parachutes need not be of the same standard as those used by air crews and may be economically made from obsolete aircrew parachutes, or from a suitable and inexpensive cloth.

   (b) The contents of each container or package should be clearly indicated in print in English and two or more other languages or using self-explanatory symbols, and may also be indicated by colour-coded streamers and pictograms discussed in appendix G, section G-7.

   (c) Instructions on the use of survival equipment should be enclosed in each of the droppable containers or packages. They should be printed in English and one or more other languages appropriate for the area, using self-explanatory diagrams and symbols wherever possible.

6.4.4 *Storage and inspection.* Since it may not be economical to provide all facilities with supplies and survival equipment, storage depots may be established at appropriate locations. These depots could also be used to store equipment that should be available to SRUs if not already carried by them as discussed in chapter 5.

(a) An adequate number of packs of supplies and survival equipment should be kept at aerodromes and ports from which SRUs normally operate. In addition, packs may be stored at redeployment bases and at aerodromes and ports where SRUs are not normally available, but where the packs could be easily picked up during a SAR operation. If this is not possible, arrangements should be made to ensure rapid delivery from a nearby depot.

(b) Used stocks of packing material and supplies and survival equipment should be replenished immediately. Unused stocks should be inspected and repacked at regular intervals and replaced if necessary.

6.4.5 For air SAR facilities:

(a) All fixed-wing search aircraft should carry supplies and survival equipment for dropping to survivors as soon as they have been found. This will be important when survivors are found to be in a weakened condition, or, after being located, must sustain themselves for extended periods.

(b) Liferafts packed for dropping should be available for use when:

– survival craft have not been launched successfully or have been damaged in launching;

– survival craft have become unserviceable;

– survivors are overcrowded in the survival craft in use; or

– survivors are in the water.

Liferafts, supplies, and equipment may be dropped together in a chain (ideally with liferafts at each end).

(c) An airborne droppable lifeboat may contribute to the rescue, but the need for a particular type of aircraft, handling, and dropping procedures makes it an item which can only be used by specialized SRUs.

6.4.6 For maritime SAR facilities:

(a) The supplies and survival equipment carried on rescue boats and other inshore craft need not be extensive when medical attention, blankets, clothing, hot drinks, etc., are available ashore. Additional equipment should be taken if the rescue boats are limited in number or the climate is severe. Hot liquids, covering for survivors, and insulating blankets for hypothermic survivors should always be carried.

(b) Rescue vessels likely to operate some distance offshore should carry an adequate quantity of the items referred to above, including equipment for artificial respiration, first aid, and advanced life support to the extent of the crew's training.

6.5 Supply dropping

6.5.1 When deciding whether or not supplies should be dropped, consider whether communications have been established with the survivors, and if so, whether:

– the needed supplies have been identified;

– suitable aircraft are available; and

– the crew has adequate training and experience.

6.5.2 Pilot and crew should understand and be able to account for factors that affect an air drop, such as:

– correct release point;

– drift effect of the wind;

-   aircraft speed;

-   aircraft height;

-   relative locations of the distress site and the rescue facility's base;

-   time before rescue can be effected; and

-   danger of exposure.

6.5.3 *Type of aircraft.* Military aircraft designed for dropping containers or specially designed civil aircraft should be used when supplies are to be dropped. If such aircraft are not available, supplies should be dropped only in extreme emergencies. Selection of other aircraft should be made in advance by personnel knowledgeable in this type of operation, and accounted for in the plans of operation.

6.5.4 When necessary, a supply-dropping operation should be co-ordinated with the appropriate ATS unit as far in advance of the mission as possible to avoid any undue delay in the issuance of an air traffic control clearance.

6.6 Medical personnel

6.6.1 In formulating any rescue plan, the SMC should consider establishing a forward medical base to enable triage by competent medical staff. Once the search object has been sighted, the SMC must consider whether to send medical personnel to the scene. Another consideration is the mental trauma that both survivors and rescuers may endure. Plans and procedures should be developed for post-traumatic stress syndrome debriefings.

6.7 Rescue by aircraft

6.7.1 In some cases aircraft may be used for rescue. Each aircraft has operational and technical limitations and should not be used on operations for which it is not suitable. When possible, a rescue operation by aircraft should be backed up by a surface facility, particularly for a large number of survivors.

6.7.2 Fixed-wing aircraft may drop equipment to survivors and direct rescue facilities. They can mark the position as long as they can remain on scene, by serving as a radio and radar beacon, showing lights, dropping flares, and providing radio signals for direction finding and homing by other rescue facilities.

6.7.3 The use of a landplane as a rescue aircraft is limited to instances where there is a suitable landing site at or near the distress scene or where the aircraft is designed to operate from rough and improvised strips. This can be done, for instance, in cold climates where landplanes fitted with skis operate from frozen lakes and rivers or snow-covered surfaces. Landing in unknown terrain may, even under ideal conditions, be hazardous, and the urgency of the situation should be carefully considered by the pilot before it is attempted. It may be possible to have one qualified person parachuted in to survey the area.

6.7.4 Seaplanes and amphibians are able to operate from lakes, rivers, and in-shore waters and can land close to survivors located in such areas. However, a landing in unknown waters may be risky.

    (a) Under favourable weather and sea conditions, seaplanes and amphibians can be used for rescue operations in inland seas, large lakes, bays, or coastal waters. This should only be considered when no other means of rescue are immediately available.

    (b) Open-sea landings should only be contemplated with aircraft designed for the purpose. A landing in the open sea should not be attempted when rescue can be assured through other means.

6.7.5 Helicopters can be used to rescue survivors by winching or by landing on a ship if a suitable location exists. Water landings are possible when amphibious helicopters are used. Due to their unique flying capabilities, they should be used whenever possible. They are particularly suitable for rescues in heavy seas or at locations where surface facilities are unable to operate. However, there are special concerns of which the SMC must be aware:

(a) Operations by surface parties may be hampered by the noise and rotor wash produced by helicopters. To facilitate the co-ordination between helicopters and surface rescue facilities and to minimize the risk of collision associated with helicopters operating in a confined space, their operations should be co-ordinated by a facility in communication with them, and preferably by the OSC.

(b) The number of survivors that a helicopter may take aboard each trip is limited. Therefore, it may be necessary to reduce its weight by removal of non-essential equipment or fuel. Fuel loads at the scene may be reduced by use of advance bases with fuelling capabilities.

(c) The route followed by the helicopter as well as the location where the survivors are to disembark should be known to the SMC.

(d) Due to the generally limited fuel reserves of helicopters, and their susceptibility to icing in some locations, it may be advantageous to dispatch a fixed-wing aircraft in advance to confirm the suitability of *en route* weather, and ensure that the craft requiring assistance is properly briefed in advance on helicopter hoisting procedures.

(e) Recovery by landing of the helicopter creates additional concerns. Factors like turbulence, level terrain, clearing, loose debris, altitude, and landing and take-off paths must be considered when selecting a landing site. Operations in a high-altitude environment will reduce helicopter performance and severely affect hovering capability. When conditions are marginal, landings should be carried out only as a last resort.

(f) A typical recovery is carried out by hovering over the survivors and taking them aboard using a winch with a sling, rescue basket, rescue net, rescue seat, or rescue stretcher. Selection of the site is the same as for recovery by landing. However, the cable and rescue device being lowered may have a large static electricity charge. No one should touch the cable or rescue device until it has made contact with the surroundings.

6.8 Rescue by maritime facilities

6.8.1 When both maritime rescue facilities and helicopters are dispatched to the scene, it may be advisable to transfer survivors to the helicopters for a more rapid delivery to medical facilities. All surface SRUs should be equipped to lift survivors from the water without help from the survivors, as they may be injured, exhausted, or suffering from hypothermia. Survivors might need to be advised to focus on keeping themselves alive rather than trying to assist in their rescue since this could improve their chances of survival.

6.8.2 When hoisting a person who may be suffering from hypothermia, especially after long-term immersion in water and especially when lifting them some distance such as to the deck of a high-sided vessel or into a helicopter, they should be lifted horizontally or near-horizontally. Hoisting such persons in a vertical position may cause loss of consciousness, severe shock or cardiac arrest. A rescue lifting system, rescue basket or stretcher should be used or two strops or loops with one under the arms and the other under the knees.

6.8.3 Rescue vessel capabilities generally fall into two categories.

(a) Designated SRUs can provide excellent means for rescuing survivors in coastal areas and at sea. Larger vessels are generally capable of radio communication with any ship or craft on all maritime frequencies. The master of a designated SRU of this type is particularly suitable for acting as an OSC. Larger rescue facilities are capable of all SAR operations, including extended search.

(b) If no designated vessels are available, a merchant ship should take over the duties of OSC (see the IAMSAR Manual, volume III, *Mobile Facilities*). Merchant ships may be the only means for an immediate rescue. ARCCs and MRCCs responsible for maritime areas should be able to rapidly obtain the positions of merchant ships within their areas. Section 1.3 provides additional information.

6.8.4 Rescue boats typically are designated SRUs but may include any craft near the scene of the distress. Designated rescue boats are generally small and may not be able to carry many survivors. It may be necessary to send a number of boats to the distress scene if they are available. Each boat should carry additional lifesaving appliances to enable survivors who cannot be rescued immediately to remain afloat while awaiting the arrival of another boat.

6.8.5 An aircraft ditching must be responded to immediately since an aircraft will float for only a very limited time.

6.9 Rescue by land facilities

6.9.1 Land facilities can be used to rescue survivors of aircraft crashes inland and also maritime survivors who may be trapped on shorelines or in estuaries where rescue by sea or air is not possible. Although the location of the distress scene is known, it may be difficult for a land facility to reach it. Therefore, the operation should not be undertaken without sufficient planning.

6.9.2 The land facility should be taken to a location as near as possible to the distress scene by some means of rapid transport. If access to the site is difficult, an aerial survey of the area can help to determine the best route. The equipment carried should be carefully selected and arrangements made for containers to be dropped, should further supplies and equipment be required. A land facility should be equipped with a suitable portable two-way radio.

6.9.3 As soon as the distress scene is located, an attempt should be made to account for all occupants of the distressed craft. The search must continue until all of the occupants have been found, otherwise accounted for, or there is no significant chance of locating additional survivors. Meanwhile, those survivors who have been located must be rescued as soon as possible.

6.9.4 The duties of a land facility at a distress scene include:

–   giving first aid;

–   evacuating survivors by whatever means are available;

–   collecting and preserving medical and technical data to support investigations;

–   establishing identities of casualties/survivors;

–   making a preliminary examination of the wreckage; and

–   reporting to the SMC.

6.10 Use of pararescue teams

6.10.1 A pararescue team becomes a land facility as soon as it has landed.

6.10.2 A pararescue team usually consists of two parachutists with emergency medical care kits, survival kits, and a scuba or forest-penetration parachute kit. They should be trained in parachuting and, ideally, in such skills as mountaineering, survival in all environments, advanced emergency medical care, and scuba diving. They should be able to deploy from aircraft over any type of terrain or water, day or night, to assist survivors. Jumps into isolated areas should, if possible, be made by more than one team simultaneously.

6.10.3 When considering the use of pararescue teams to reach an accident site, the team leader or a designated representative must be involved during the planning stages to ensure that any decision to employ parachutists is made only after due consideration of all factors. A pararescue team may prove to be the only or best means to ascertain that there are survivors. It may be desirable that a team be carried by each SAR aircraft that is suitable for dropping parachutists.

6.10.4 Precautionary measures should include:

–   jumps made only from aircraft approved for this type of operation;

–   precautions similar to those taken for supply-dropping operations (see paragraph 6.5); and

–   pilots experienced in parachute-jumping operations.

6.11   Special requirements at aircraft crash sites

6.11.1   Many military aircraft are fitted with ejection seats and other hazardous material, e.g., bombs or chemicals. National procedures for such incidents should be available to RCCs. When a pilot has to be removed from an aircraft so fitted, extreme care should be taken to avoid triggering the seat mechanism. The activating handles are normally indicated by red or yellow-and-black colouring.

6.11.2   The aircraft wreckage and its surroundings should not be disturbed except to assist in the recovery of survivors. Not only does the wreckage pose dangers, but the position of flight controls, the location of debris and other factors are important to the accident investigation. Rescue facilities should be aware of this policy. Control of access to the crash site should be established as soon as possible.

6.11.3   It is important for the team leader to ensure that the aircraft is not accidentally set on fire. If it is necessary to cut into the aircraft to remove survivors, non-sparking tools should be used and fire extinguishers should be kept ready. Composite material construction of some aircraft and the possible presence of hazardous materials pose additional safety hazards to rescue personnel.

6.11.4   To help investigators, photographs should be taken of the crash site and of the wreckage. A description should be passed on to the SMC as soon as possible.

6.11.5   Measures to preserve as much medical evidence as possible include:

–   photography of bodies before moving them;

–   shielding of bodies from the elements by the best means available;

–   notation of the position of immobilized survivors; and

–   maintenance of a medical log for each survivor.

Note: Except for compelling reasons, human remains should not be moved without authorization from the SMC who should, in turn, obtain authorization from an appropriate authority.

6.12   Ditching assistance

6.12.1   RCC assistance for ditching should include:

–   obtaining the latest position of the aircraft by any means available, e.g., from the aircraft, from its escort (if applicable), by direction finding, or by radar;

–   requesting the maritime RCC or CRSs to alert vessels in the vicinity of the distressed aircraft, asking them to keep a listening watch on frequency 4125 kHz if possible, or on 3023 kHz otherwise;

–   providing the aircraft with the position of the nearest ship (hence, the importance of ship reporting systems to ARCCs), the course to steer, and information on sea condition and ditching heading;

–   requesting the distressed aircraft to communicate with the selected vessel on 4125 kHz or any other suitable frequency (if applicable — if this is not possible, act as a relay station); and

–   if time permits, informing the ship of how it can assist the aircraft.

6.12.2   Assistance provided by ships for ditching depends on the capabilities of the ship. Communications between ships and aircraft are discussed in section 2.8. The nearest vessel to the ditching aircraft will often be a merchant ship. The ship may be limited to the assistance arranged by the RCC, but it can also rescue survivors. The most suitable vessels are SRUs equipped for two-way radio communications with the aircraft, and with crews trained and equipped for SAR incidents including ditching. Assistance from vessels includes:

–   locating the aircraft by radar;

–   providing navigation and homing aids;

–   furnishing weather and sea information;

–   directing the aircraft to the vessel;

–   assisting the aircraft by marking a sea-lane and providing illumination; and

–   effecting rescue after the ditching.

6.12.3   Ditching assistance provided by escort aircraft to distressed aircraft may include:

–   guiding it to the vessel alongside which it plans to ditch;

–   giving advice on ditching procedures;

–   evaluating the sea conditions and recommending a ditching heading;

–   informing the vessel on how it can assist the ditching aircraft;

–   dropping survival and emergency equipment;

–   informing the SMC of the location of the ditching;

–   directing other vessels to the scene; and

–   providing illumination for a night ditching if this cannot be done by the vessel or if the ditching is taking place away from vessels.

6.13   Rescue of persons from inside damaged, capsized, or ditched craft

6.13.1   The rescue of persons from inside damaged, capsized, or ditched craft is typically dangerous, and should normally be attempted only with suitable facilities, equipment, and specially trained personnel. Such operations are generally carried out in three stages:

–   investigation of the situation;

–   prevention of sinking; and

–   lifesaving.

6.13.2   There is always the risk of the craft sinking or shifting. Diving may be required for actions to reduce this risk and for the rescue operation; therefore, these operations must be conducted promptly according to a prudent plan.

Investigation of the Situation

6.13.3   Rescue personnel must conduct an initial investigation and accurately assess the condition of the emergency. A reasonable work plan should then be developed based on the investigation.

6.13.4   *Items of Investigation.* The following items should be investigated.

(a)   Distress area considerations:

–   incident position and depth of water at that location;

–   meteorological and sea conditions (weather, wind direction and velocity, air temperature, sea current direction and velocity, water temperature, visibility both above and below the water surface, waves, swells, etc.);

–   existence of fishing nets or other obstructions;

–   leakage of hazardous material;

–   conditions of other vessels in the vicinity; and

–   existence of sharks or other dangerous marine life.

(b)   Rescue forces considerations:

–   size and number of boats and aircraft;

–   number of divers;

- availability of floating cranes, tugboats, fishing boats, etc.;

- medical assistance; and

- transport for rescue personnel and survivors.

(c) Missing persons considerations:

- number of persons missing;

- position of crew when the accident occurred;

- existence of survivors inside (determine by tapping or other reaction tests); and

- need for emergency measures to sustain survivors trapped inside (i.e., supply of air into the craft, etc.).

(d) Craft structure and stability considerations:

- craft type, tonnage, and cargo, etc.;

- condition of craft and its nearby surroundings;

- amount of the craft exposed above the waterline, and changes;

- list, pitching, and rolling, and their changes and sequence;

- air, hazardous materials, and fuel leakage; and

- lapse of time after capsizing, damage, or ditching.

6.13.5 *Investigation procedures.* The following investigation procedures should normally be used in various situations.

(a) *Conditions on scene.* While approaching the wreck, rescuers should observe circumstances such as meteorological conditions, sea phenomena, conditions of other vessels in the vicinity, and so on. They should also check to see if there is any debris in and under the water.

(b) *Investigation of craft.* The average waterline, list, and leakage of air should be observed at appropriate intervals with video or instant cameras to quickly verify any change of condition. If at least one metre of a floating craft is exposed and the list is insignificant, investigators may consider climbing onto the craft to check for air leakage from the doors, stern tube, etc.

(c) *Existence of survivors.* Investigators may hit the craft with hammers or other items, and then listen for any reaction suggesting the existence of survivors. To hear weak signals from the survivors may require silence among the rescuers. A loudspeaker may be used in an attempt to talk to persons inside. Inboard voices may be audible when the ear is put against the outside of the craft, thus making it possible to talk with survivors inside. If it is difficult to lower a workboat or for investigators to move from a workboat on to the distressed craft due to stormy weather or other hazards, investigating divers should arrive from the leeward side of the craft to reach underneath and hit it with knife grips or similar objects, to see if there is any reaction from persons inside. At this point, it is normally premature and too dangerous to actually swim beneath or enter the craft.

6.13.6 Other matters to be considered during the investigation are listed below.

(a) When a fishing boat has capsized, there are often fishing nets adrift in the nearby sea area, so caution is needed in manoeuvring vessels and carrying out the rescue operation.

(b) The craft may be less likely to sink if the following conditions of the craft exist:

- floating on an even keel;

- not listing;

- existing waterline is one-fifth to one-half the normal draught;

- no opening in the hull leaks air; or

- floating for more than one hour in the same condition.

(c) Even if there was no reaction when the craft was tapped the first time, it is necessary to tap it three or four times at appropriate intervals (i.e., every thirty minutes).

(d) Unless it is known that there are no survivors, work should be performed with the assumption that survivors remain inside.

Prevention of sinking

6.13.7 Measures that could be taken, where practicable, to help prevent the sinking of the craft during rescue operations include:

– preventing air leakage;

– supplying air into the craft;

– fitting floats;

– holding alongside;

– suspending the hull by a floating crane; or

– stranding in a shallow place.

6.13.8 *Prevention of air leakage*. This may be accomplished by:

– closing openings such as doors, ventilators, hatches, pipe, stern tube, etc.; and

– plugging cracks with wooden or metallic wedges.

6.13.9 *Supply of air into the craft*. Air may be introduced into the craft from a lower opening, or by using special tools, e.g., striking a drive pin through to the inside and attaching an air hose.

6.13.10 *Fitting of floats*. Attaching floats is effective when it is not practical or safe to supply air to the inside. However, floats may not fully compensate for the lost buoyancy of the craft and should be considered mainly to minimize the leakage of air and prevent sinking by correcting list or trim. Typical methods of fitting floats are as follows:

(a) *Looping method:* a wire or cable is looped around the lower part of the craft and both ends are fitted to floats.

(b) *Fitting wires to a fixed object*: one end of a wire or cable is fitted to a bollard or some other fixed object and the other end to a float.

6.13.11 *Holding alongside*. This can be accomplished by using one or two vessels.

(a) *Alongside support by two rescue vessels:* two vessels move into position on opposite sides of the craft, but at an appropriate distance from it; wires or cables are then stretched under the craft between both vessels.

(b) *Alongside support by one rescue vessel:* a single vessel may be used to limit list or to support one end of the craft.

Note: Wires or cables used to support the craft may be taken off or cut off immediately as the situation demands.

6.13.12 *Floating crane*. This method is most effective in preventing the sinking of a damaged vessel. It is necessary to immediately arrange use of a floating crane and tugs.

6.13.13 *Stranding in a shallow place*. The craft may be gently grounded in nearby shallow water if the situation permits, and if it appears safer than the present situation.

6.13.14 Other factors to be considered to prevent sinking are listed below.

(a) Supplying air into a craft provides buoyancy, but the air should be introduced into an area where it will improve rather than worsen the craft's stability.

(b) Keeping the craft level improves the chances for survivors and helps to prevent sinking.

(c) Maintaining buoyancy with air and correcting list with side support or floats decreases the possibility of sinking.

(d) A capsized vessel may turn sideways if more than half of its hull comes out of the water.

(e) Alongside support may lead to the sinking or damage of the craft if manoeuvring is done incorrectly, especially in stormy weather.

(f) Supplying fresh air to the subdivisions where survivors are located may be necessary.

Lifesaving

6.13.15 Survivors can be expected to be in state of a panic or shock, and in complete darkness. Rapid rescue is necessary due to the lack of food, water, and fresh air in a capsized craft.

6.13.16 Survivors may be rescued either through an opening made above the waterline, or from under water. Select the method that has the greatest chance for success, taking into account that making an opening can threaten the air pocket in the vessel and survivors may panic if they have to dive under water.

6.13.17 *Measures for prolonging lives.* The following measures may be used to help prolong the lives of survivors.

(a) Periodic tapping on the craft by rescue personnel may reveal the existence of survivors and provide encouragement by keeping them informed of the progress of the rescue operation.

(b) Air hoses or air tanks for divers may be used to feed fresh air to the compartments with survivors.

(c) If survivors are accessible by divers, fresh water and food can be provided until the survivors are rescued.

6.13.18 *Rescue operations by diving.* The following procedures should be followed when attempting to rescue survivors by diving.

(a) To reduce the risks associated with entry into capsized, damaged, or ditched craft, ensure that:

  – the craft is afloat evenly at both ends, there are no obvious air leaks, and there is no change in the draught for at least 30 minutes;

  – measures for the prevention of foundering, such as side support and fitting of floats, have been fully carried out;

  – the craft is sitting on the seabed and there is no danger that it may turn over;

  – the portion above the waterline is more than one metre and the vessel is floating in a stable manner without air leaks;

  – there are no fishing nets or other debris which may hamper diving;

  – leaking hazardous materials and fuel are avoided;

  – the rolling and pitching of the craft is under control so that diving will not be hampered; and

  – no lifting is conducted until the divers return to the surface.

(b) Safety precautions for divers entering the craft include:

  – approaching the entrance to an area likely to contain survivors after having discussed the situation with knowledgeable people who can identify and locate any potential obstacles;

  – using a liaison person so that divers may be immediately refloated when there appears to be a change in the condition of craft;

  – stretching a guide rope from the sea surface to the entrance for use by divers;

- briefing divers about the entrance and the arrangement of the craft inside, taking measures to secure inboard objects which may fall, and understanding the retreat signals to be used in an emergency; and

- arranging for divers inside the craft to use ropes, with at least one diver staying at the entrance holding one end of the ropes for emergency escape and transmission of signals.

(c) After survivors have been discovered, divers should:

- set guide ropes which lead from the entrance to the survivors;

- brief survivors on the rescue operation;

- equip survivors with breathing apparatus with mask, as appropriate;

- position divers behind and in front of survivors to act as an escort along the guide rope; and

- ensure that survivors receive immediate medical care.

6.13.19 *Rescue operations through openings above the waterline.* The following factors should be considered during rescues above the surface of the water.

(a) The following precautions should be used:

- obtaining drawings of the vessel, e.g., general arrangement, to determine the safest areas for cutting;

- selecting areas to cut that do not threaten the air pocket of the survivors, fuel tanks, or other dangerous cargo on board;

- opening a small, airtight section, so that the craft does not sink if it becomes flooded;

- making up for lost buoyancy by side support, fitting of floats, and suspension by a floating crane;

- considering the possibility that gas, sparks, and the like which are generated when the craft is opened may set fire to inboard flammables or may hamper survivors;

- noting the area to be cut and moving the survivors away from the area;

- protecting against possible burns or eye injuries from sparks; and

- understanding the method of signalling (tapping, etc.) in an emergency.

(b) Considerations for opening the compartment include:

- using gas cutters, powered cutters, etc., to cut an opening into the craft;

- spraying water or taking other measures to ensure that sparks from cutting will not spray survivors or set fire to inboard flammables;

- allowing fresh air into the compartment and cooling the opening, as appropriate, before removing survivors.

6.13.20 Other matters to be considered include:

(a) Even when the craft is rolling and pitching, the sea under the craft may be calm, and diving may be conducted in many cases.

(b) Rescue personnel must be wary of falling objects and have a route for emergency exit in mind at all times.

(c) Survivors trapped in a small craft may often be rescued without diving equipment.

6.14 Underwater search and rescue

6.14.1 Many different underwater operations occur within SRRs, such as diving operations or the operation of military or civilian submarines. When accidents occur, survivors may be either on the surface or entrapped in a submarine resting on the sea-bed. Military submarines trapped under the surface may use international distress signals or specific military pyrotechnics, dye markers or beacons. In addition, submarines may pump out fuel, lubricating oil or release air bubbles to indicate their position.

6.14.2 Submarine SAR, (SUBSAR), is a highly specialized and time-critical activity reliant on specific capabilities and training. Medical care requirements for survivors of a submarine accident may also be specialized.

6.14.3 Military submarine-operating States have developed standard SUBSAR procedures, capabilities and training, generally under sponsorship of the North Atlantic Treaty Organization (NATO) for the recovery and care of submarine accidents. RCCs may request support of these resources should the need arise. Relevant information may be obtained from the NATO International Submarine Escape and Rescue Liaison Office.

6.14.4 RCCs should be aware if specialized navy or commercial recovery or treatment facilities (such as the ones with decompression chambers) exist within or near their SRRs and arrange in advance for their use at any time on a 24-hour basis. Similarly, RCCs should liaise with the military to determine mutual assistance that could be provided in the event of military submarine accidents.

6.14.5 Most SAR personnel are poorly prepared to understand or handle medical problems peculiar to underwater activities, such as decompression sickness, air embolism, and nitrogen narcosis. However, they should be trained to recognize the symptoms and know how to obtain competent medical advice. They should also be trained in handling and transporting victims of such problems without worsening their situations. If possible to aid in the treatment of the victim, SAR personnel should obtain information such as time underwater, depth, time at the surface, time of the onset of symptoms, and the symptoms currently being experienced.

6.14.6 Medical advice should be sought before air transport of submarine accident victims.

6.15 Mass rescue operations

MRO overview

6.15.1 A mass rescue operation (MRO) is one that involves a need for immediate assistance to large numbers of persons in distress such that capabilities normally available to SAR authorities are inadequate.

6.15.2 MROs are relatively rare low-probability high-consequence events compared to normal SAR operations, but major incidents leading to the need for MROs have not been infrequent on a world-wide basis, and can occur anywhere at any time. The nature of such operations may be poorly understood due to limited chances to gain experience with major incidents involving MROs.

6.15.3 Flooding, earthquakes, terrorism, casualties in the offshore oil industry and accidents involving releases of hazardous materials are examples which, because of their magnitude, may require the application of the same resources as required for mass maritime or aeronautical rescue operations.

6.15.4 The sequence of priority in major multi-mission incidents must be lifesaving first, generally followed by environmental protection, and then protection of property. Moral and legal obligations and public and political expectations require preparedness to carry out MROs safely and effectively should they become necessary. Since the need for MROs is relatively rare, it is difficult to gain practical experience to help deal with them. Types of potential MRO scenarios vary, but there are certain general principles that can be followed based on lessons of history.

6.15.5 Effective response to such major incidents requires immediate, well-planned and closely co-ordinated large-scale actions and use of resources from multiple organizations. The following are typical MRO demands:

 – intense and sustained high priority lifesaving efforts may need to be carried out at the same time and place as major efforts to save the environment and property;

 – huge amounts of information need to be readily available at the right times and places to support the response efforts and meet the needs of the media, public and families of the persons in distress, which may number in the hundreds or thousands;

- many means of communications need to be available and interlinked amongst organizations at various levels to handle huge amounts of information reliably for the duration of the response (MRO communications are discussed in more detail later in this chapter);

- a surge in the numbers of competent staffing in all key organizations must be made available immediately and be sustainable for up to weeks at a time;

- equipment and logistics demands jump to unprecedented levels; and

- successful MROs depend on the advance provision of flexible and all-level contingency plans. Intense integrated planning and operational efforts must also be carried out in real time throughout actual rescue efforts.

6.15.6 All involved in the overall multi-agency, multi-jurisdiction, multi-mission and possibly international response to major incidents must clearly understand who is in charge, the respective roles of all involved, and how to interact with each other. SAR authorities may be responsible for all or part of the MRO functions, and must be able to co-ordinate their efforts seamlessly with other responders under the overall direction of another authority within or outside their agency.

6.15.7 The broader response environment may involve activities such as:

- hazards mitigation;

- damage control and salvage operations;

- pollution control;

- complex traffic management;

- large-scale logistics efforts;

- medical and coroner functions;

- accident-incident investigation; and

- intense public and political attention.

6.15.8 MRO plans need to be part of and compatible with overall response plans for major incidents. Plans must typically allow for command, control and communications structures that can accommodate simultaneous air, sea and land operations.

6.15.9 The consequences of poor preparations for MROs in terms of loss of life and other adverse results may be disastrous. Major incidents may involve hundreds or thousands of persons in distress in remote and hostile environments. A large passenger ship collision, a downed aircraft, or a terrorist incident could, for example, call for the immediate rescue of large numbers of passengers and crew in poor environmental conditions, with many of the survivors having little ability to help themselves.

6.15.10 Preparedness to mount an extraordinarily large and rapid response is critical to preventing large-scale loss of lives. Such preparedness often depends on strong and visionary leadership and unusual levels of co-operation to achieve.

6.15.11 There will often be resistance to paying the high price in terms of time, effort and funding that preparedness for major incidents entails, particularly as they are rare events. The required levels of co-operation, co-ordination, planning, resources and exercises required for preparedness are challenging and do not happen without the requisite commitment of SAR authorities, regulatory authorities, transportation companies, sources of military and commercial assistance and others.

6.15.12 MRO planning, preparations and exercises are essential since opportunities to handle actual incidents involving mass rescues are rare. Therefore the exercising of MRO plans is particularly important.

6.15.13 Appendix C provides guidance on MRO exercise planning.

General guidance for MROs

6.15.14 For a situation involving large numbers or persons in distress, on-scene responsibilities for the safety of passengers and crew will be shared by the OSC and the craft's pilot in command or master, with the pilot or master assuming as much of this responsibility as possible before or after the aircraft or ship is abandoned.

6.15.15 Pilots and masters are responsible for manoeuvring the aircraft or ship as feasible and appropriate and also have overall responsibility for safety, medical care, communications, fire and damage control, maintaining order and providing general direction.

6.15.16 Unless a ship appears to be in imminent danger of sinking, it is usually advisable for passengers and crew to remain on board as long as it is safe to do so.

6.15.17 In the case of a downed aircraft, whether passengers would be safer on board should be assessed for each situation. Usually they should promptly evacuate the aircraft at sea. On land, this decision must take into account the conditions of the aircraft and the environment, expected time to rescue survivors or repair the aircraft, and whether required passenger care can be best provided inside the aircraft.

6.15.18 The OSC will normally be designated by an SMC. An OSC may be able to handle certain communications on scene and with appropriate remote authorities to help free the pilot or master to retain the integrity of his or her craft. However, these persons are themselves in need of assistance, and anything the OSC can do to help them should be considered, bearing in mind that the OSC's main duty is co-ordinating SAR facilities and rescue efforts under the SMC's general direction.

6.15.19 Unnecessary communications with the master of a ship or pilot in command of an aircraft in distress must be minimized, and this should be taken into account in advance planning.

6.15.20 Exchanges of information during joint planning by use of SAR Plans of Co-operation for passenger ships and other means will reduce the need to ask the pilot or master for this information one or more times during a crisis. Persons or organizations that want this information should be directed to a source ashore or on the ground that is prepared to handle many potential requests.

6.15.21 High priority should be given to tracking and accounting for all persons on board and all lifeboats and rafts, and efforts to keep them together will help in this regard. Availability of accurate manifests and accounting is critical.

6.15.22 The need to relocate survival craft and check for persons in them can waste valuable resources. One option is to sink survival craft once the persons in them have been rescued; however, the potential that other survivors may find and need the craft should be considered.

6.15.23 Navy ships and large passenger ships are often better equipped than other vessels for retrieving people who have abandoned a ship or aircraft; use of any such ships should be considered. Ship reporting systems for SAR may help identify commercial ships available to assist.

6.15.24 Helicopter capabilities should be used if available, especially for retrieval of weak or immobile survivors. Lifeboat crews should be trained in helicopter hoist operations. Lowering a rescue person from the helicopter to assist survivors may be viable.

6.15.25 Ship companies should be encouraged to equip large passenger ships and possibly other types of vessels with helicopter landing areas, clearly marked hoist-winch areas, and onboard helicopters to facilitate more direct transfers of numerous persons.

6.15.26 If a ship with a large freeboard cannot safely retrieve survivors from the water or survival craft, it may be possible to first retrieve them onto small vessels, and then transfer them to progressively larger ones.

6.15.27 Depending on the circumstances, it may be safer to tow survival craft to shore without removing the occupants at sea. Lifeboats could be designed to support passengers for longer periods of time, and to be able to reach shore on their own from longer distances offshore.

6.15.28   To the extent practicable, MROs should be co-ordinated by an SMC in an RCC. However, depending on the magnitude, nature and complexity of an incident, the rescue efforts may be better co-ordinated by an appropriate operations centre higher within the SAR agency or another Government agency. Considerations in this decision might include, among others:

–   extensive rescue support by organizations other than those commonly used for SAR;

–   need for heavy international diplomatic support; and

–   serious problems in addition to potential loss of lives, such as environmental threats, terrorist actions, or national security issues.

6.15.29   The following factors should be considered in MRO planning:

–   use of the Incident Command System (ICS) discussed below, or other effective means of handling multiagency, multi-jurisdiction, multi-mission scenarios;

–   identification of situations within the SRR that could potentially lead to the need for MROs, including scenarios that might involve cascading casualties or outages;

–   mobilization and co-ordination of necessary SAR facilities, including those not normally available for SAR services;

–   ability to activate plans immediately;

–   call up procedures for needed personnel;

–   need for supplemental communications capabilities, possibly including the need for interpreters;

–   dispatching of liaison officers;

–   activation of additional staff to augment, replace or sustain needed staffing levels;

–   recovery and transport of large numbers of survivors (including those unfit, injured or incapable, recovery of bodies, if necessary), accounting for survivors with suspected injuries, guarding against and caring for person with hypothermia, etc.;

–   a means of reliably accounting for everyone involved, including responders, survivors, crew, etc.;

–   care, assistance and further transfer of survivors once delivered to a place of safety and further transfer of bodies beyond their initial delivery point;

–   activation of plans for notifying, managing and assisting the media and families in large numbers;

–   control of access to the RCC and other sensitive facilities and locations;

–   RCC backup and relocation plans, as appropriate; and

–   ready availability to all potential users of plans, checklists and flowcharts.

6.15.30   The ability of an RCC to continue to effectively co-ordinate the MRO and still handle its other SAR responsibilities may become overwhelmed, and another RCC or a higher authority may need to assume responsibility for their other responsibilities.

6.15.31   With these possibilities in mind, MRO plans should provide for various degrees of response, along with criteria for determining which degree of response will be implemented. For example, as local SAR resources are exhausted (or from the outset), SAR resources may need to be obtained from distant national or international sources.

6.15.32   Experiences in responding to major incidents have resulted in the following practical guidance. Authorities should:

–   plan how any agency receiving notification of an actual or potential mass rescue event can immediately alert and conference call other authorities that will potentially be involved, brief them, and enable immediate actions to be taken by all concerned (this will require identification of entities in each agency that can be contacted on a 24-hour basis, and that have authority to immediately initiate actions and commit resources);

–   exercise the above plans;

- co-ordinate all rescue operations effectively from the very beginning;

- begin quickly with a high level of effort stand down as appropriate rather than begin too late with too little effort;

- use capable resources like cruise ships for taking large numbers of survivors on board;

- ensure that MRO emergency plans address communications interoperability or interlinking;

- retrieve and protect debris as evidence for follow on investigation;

- put security plans in place to limit access to the RCC;

- arrange in advance to involve the Red Cross, chaplains, critical incident stress experts and other such support for human needs;

- identify senior agency spokespersons to protect the time of workers directly involved in the response and designate a senior official to provide information to families;

- clearly identify the point at which the SAR response (lifesaving) has ended and the focus shifts to investigation and recovery;

- be prepared to use an Incident Command System (ICS) when appropriate;

- ensure that air traffic and air space can be and is controlled on scene;

- assign additional liaison personnel on scene, as required;

- anticipate development and needs and act early;

- ensure that the scope of SAR plans and other emergency or disaster response plans are co-ordinated to reduce gaps, overlaps and confusion about the person in charge and the procedures to be followed at various times and places;

- control access to the scene, including access by the media;

- determine in advance how private resources can be appropriately used to supplement other SAR resources;

- ensure that SAR plans provide for logistics support for large numbers of rescuers and survivors including pre-arranged accommodations, if possible, and availability of food, medical care and transportation;

- consider requesting assistance from airlines and shipping companies other than the one whose aircraft or ship is involved in the incident, and know the types of assistance that such organizations might provide;

- consider use of bar coded bracelets as an effective means of identifying children before, during and after the emergency;

- attempt to reduce the burden on a pilot or master and crews; if safe and appropriate to do so, place a marine casualty officer on board to assist the master and SAR personnel; and

- share capabilities, expertise and assets among Government and industry to take maximum advantage of the strengths of each.

Communications for mass rescue operations

6.15.33 Communication plans must provide for a heavy volume of communication use as a major incident will normally involve many responding organizations that need to communicate effectively with each other from the beginning.

6.15.34 As necessary, advance arrangements should be made to link means of interagency communications that are not inherently interoperable.

6.15.35 Interagency communications must be based on terminology understood by all involved.

Communications planning for MROs

6.15.36 Efficient MRO responses depend upon efficient communication and efficient communication requires planning, understanding of the plan by those who will have to put it into effect and its rapid implementation at the time of the incident. The following are some of the factors MRO communications planners are recommended to consider:

- Who is likely to be involved in the response to a MRO, including supporting organizations and others with legitimate interest (e.g., officials, family members of victims, the news media, etc.)?

- What are their information needs likely to be?

- Where do they fit in the overall command, control and co-ordination (and, therefore, communications) structure?

- What are the information priorities?

- What communications facilities do the responders have?

- Are there enough people to operate the communications systems, over a potentially long period? The planning should include provision for relief personnel.

- How should these facilities best be used to avoid overload? How should a large amount of data (such as search plans or passenger lists) be communicated?

- Do people know what to say and who to talk to? Do they understand their unit's place in the communications network, other units' roles, and the overall information priorities? Are they aware of the importance of clear procedures and communications discipline?

- Are there likely to be language difficulties, including potential misunderstanding of technical language?

- Who will control and keep order on the various parts of the communications network and do they understand this particularly important role?

- To what extent are different responders' communications systems and procedures interoperable? Can communications hubs be established or liaison officers exchanged to help explain priorities, procedures and technical language?

- How long might the incident last? Distress frequencies may be used for their initial response but the plan should ensure that these frequencies are cleared as soon as practicable.

6.15.37 Appendix C outlines a basic MRO communications plan structure.

Major incident co-ordination

6.15.38 Regardless of the magnitude and priority of the life-saving efforts involved in responding to a major incident, if any other functions are being carried out concurrently on scene by other than SAR personnel, the overall response involving SAR and the other functions, e.g., fire fighting, should be well co-ordinated.

6.15.39 If certain basic concepts and terms are recognized and understood by all emergency responders, they will be much better prepared to co-ordinate joint efforts.

6.15.40 Standard SAR procedures should typically be followed for the SAR part of the response, but these procedures will be largely independent of other efforts. Companies or authorities handling other aspects of the response will follow command, control and communication procedures developed for their respective organizations and duties.

6.15.41 The SAR system can function in its normal manner or use modified SAR procedures established to account for special demands of mass rescues, but it should be appropriately linked and subjected to a scheme for management of the overall incident response.

6.15.42 For major incidents, crisis management for the overall response may also be needed. The Incident Command System (ICS) is one simple and effective means of meeting this need. ICS can be used where no equivalent means of overall incident management is in place. SAR and transportation authorities are likely to encounter use of the ICS within emergency response communities.

6.15.43 The ICS works best with some advance familiarization and exercising.

6.15.44 Appendix C provides general information about ICS.

Industry planning and response

6.15.45 SAR authorities should co-ordinate MRO plans with companies that operate ships and aircraft designed to carry large numbers of persons. Such companies should share in preparations to minimize the chances that MROs will be needed, and to ensure success if they become necessary.

6.15.46 Appendix C provides guidance on industry roles and discusses how companies could arrange for use of field teams and emergency response centres as possible means of carrying out their MRO responsibilities.

6.15.47 For passenger ships, SAR Plans of Co-operation required by the Safety of Life at Sea Convention and developed by SAR authorities and shipping companies are part of MRO plans.

Public and media relations for MROs

6.15.48 Good public and media relations become very demanding and quite important during MROs.

6.15.49 What the media reports may matter more than what SAR services do for shaping public opinion about MROs. The role of the media may be critical in shaping the actions of the public and of those directly involved in the distress situation in a way that contributes to safety, success and panic control. There should be no unwarranted delays in providing information to the media.

6.15.50 Information should be readily available, clear, accurate, consistent and freely exchanged among emergency responders and others concerned, such as the public and families of persons on board.

6.15.51 Designate the person who will speak to the public and the media and develop press releases, and outline what they will say, staying factual. If SAR services do not provide a public spokesperson and information for a major incident, the media likely will, thus denying the Authorities the opportunity to manage the information and emphasize the appropriate points.

6.15.52 A single spokesperson not directly involved in the incident can be valuable in relieving the Incident Commander and SMC of this duty.

6.15.53 Spokespersons should be cautious about speculating on causes of accidents and ensure that the media understands that the main focus of current operations is on saving lives.

6.15.54 Ensure that the media knows who is in charge of co-ordinating rescue operations.

6.15.55 Interviews should be live if possible.

6.15.56 Many entities are involved in a response to a major incident, including ships, aircraft, companies and SAR services. Co-ordination is required to ensure that there is one message with many messengers.

6.15.57 Prompt establishment of a joint information centre at a location distant from the SMC will help to achieve this goal. (A joint information centre is a component of an ICS and is discussed in appendix C). The centre can establish proper procedures for establishing what messages will be released to the public and how those messages will be released. Since the messages may be sensitive, it is critical that everyone communicates the same information. The centre can be responsible for co-ordinating information made available via the internet and perhaps establishing and maintaining a public website.

6.15.58 The media is a 24-hour global market, and its news is broadcast world-wide. The media will find a way to get to the scene for first hand information, pictures and video. By providing transportation to the scene and controlling media access, safety and the information the media reports can be better managed.

6.15.59 Media outlets often have more resources to mobilize on scene than do SAR authorities, and RCC operating plans should account for how to deal with such situations.

6.15.60 Information should be provided to the public on the SAR facilities being used and, if possible, a web address or list of contact phone numbers should be provided for families, media and others to contact for more information.

6.15.61 Preparations should be made so that large numbers of callers can be accommodated without saturating the phone system or crashing the computer server.

6.15.62 Advance preparation of standby web pages by transportation companies and SAR authorities can help in responding to floods of requests for information. These pages can be quickly posted to provide general information for media use. Web information should be timely and accurate.

6.15.63 Once posted, these pages can be easily updated with the status of the incident and could also include:

- contact information;
- basic Government or industry facts;
- industry and SAR definitions;
- photographs and statistics of aircraft, ships and SAR facilities;
- answers to frequently asked questions;
- links to other key sites;
- information on passenger capacity, crew size, vessel plans and fire-fighting capabilities; and
- library footage of a vessel inspection or of the crew performing lifesaving drills.

6.15.64 Besides the media, families and other organizations will also want this information.

MRO follow-up actions

6.15.65 It is very important to develop and share lessons learned from actual MRO operations and exercises. However, concerns about legal liability (often excessive), may discourage staff from highlighting matters that could have been improved.

6.15.66 Since lessons learned can help prevent recurring serious mistakes, agreement should be reached among principal participants on how lessons learned can be depersonalized and made widely available. Lessons learned from MROs should be shared not just locally, but internationally.

6.15.67 Careful accounting for survivors after they have been delivered to a place of safety remains important. They need to be kept informed about plans for them and about the ongoing response operations. With large numbers of persons often staying in different places, keeping track of and working with them can be difficult.

6.15.68 Transportation companies are often best suited to handle and assist survivors during this time.

6.15.69 Crew members may be placed at various locations to record passenger names and locations. Another possibility is for airlines or passenger ships to attach plastic cards to life vests to give passengers phone numbers for contacting the company. Some companies use bar coded bracelets to track children who are passengers.

6.15.70 Communicating with passengers is more difficult in remote areas where phone service may be inadequate or lacking. If phones do exist, calling the airline or shipping company may be the best way to check in and find out information. In more populated areas, local agencies may have an emergency evacuation plan or other useful plan that can be implemented.

6.15.71 To protect passengers from harassment by interviewers and cameras, survivors may be placed in hotels or other places of refuge. However, triage and landing locations must be established and publicized to all rescue personnel and good Samaritans.

6.16 Care of survivors

6.16.1 After rescue, survivors may require hospital treatment. This must be provided as quickly as possible. The SMC should consider having ambulance and hospital facilities ready.

6.16.2 SAR personnel must ensure that, after rescue, survivors are not left alone, particularly if injured or showing signs of hypothermia or of physical or mental exhaustion.

6.16.3 When selecting the method of transport of survivors to medical facilities, the following factors should be considered:

– condition of survivors;

– capability of the rescue facility to reach the survivors in the shortest possible time;

– medical training, qualifications, and operational capabilities of the personnel;

– rescue facilities' capabilities to transport survivors without aggravating injuries or producing new complications;

– difficulties that may be encountered by land parties (e.g., provision of shelter, food, and water; weather conditions, etc.);

– the possible availability of doctors among the survivors, aboard nearby ships, etc.; and

– methods of maintaining communication with the SMC.

6.16.4 When medical advice or assistance is required, the rescue facility should provide the SMC a basic medical assessment. Other information may also be necessary in certain cases. If medical evacuations are being considered, the benefit of such an evacuation must be weighed against the inherent dangers of such operations to both the person needing assistance and to rescue personnel. RCCs should make arrangements to obtain competent medical advice on a 24-hour basis, and should use, when possible, medical advice from personnel familiar with risks peculiar to the environments of the SRR, and with the inherent risks involved with medical evacuations. It may be advisable to involve such personnel in SAR exercises. Medical information provided by the rescue facility to the SMC includes:

– name of the SAR facility and its available means of communications;

– position of the SAR facility, destination, estimated time of arrival, course, and speed;

– names, gender, and age of patients;

– information concerning respiration, pulse, and temperature, and also blood pressure, if possible;

– location of pain;

– nature of illness or injury, including apparent cause and related history;

– symptoms;

– type, time, form, and amounts of all medications given;

– time of last food consumption;

– ability of patients to eat, drink, walk, or be moved;

– whether the rescue facility has a medical kit, and whether a medical professional is with the SAR facility;

– whether a suitable clear area is available for helicopter hoist operations or landing, or a suitable beaching area is available for marine craft; and

– name and point of contact of off-scene persons who hold further details about the distressed craft and its occupants.

6.16.5 Victims of diving accidents may need special consideration. These victims often have compressed-gas injuries that few on-scene SAR personnel understand or are prepared to handle. SAR personnel should be able to recognize the general symptoms of dive-related injuries, be aware of their potential severity, and take basic steps to minimize worsening the medical condition. Other divers with the victim may be excellent sources of information. The RCC should maintain a list of resources that can provide diving medical advice and a list of available recompression chambers.

6.16.6 Divers with decompression sickness or an air embolism require immediate treatment with hyperbaric oxygen in a recompression chamber. These dive-related injuries are worsened by reduced atmospheric pressure. Aircraft transporting these victims should fly at the lowest safe altitude, which may require taking a less direct route.

6.17 Debriefing of survivors

6.17.1 A survivor who has been rescued may be able to give information which will assist the SAR operation. SAR personnel should question survivors and communicate any information received to the RCC.

6.17.2 Information which may be available from survivors includes:

– total number of persons on board the distressed craft, the possibility of other survivors being unaccounted for, and any indication of their position; and

– the survivor's own medical history, in particular, about recurring disease, heart trouble, diabetes, infectious diseases, epilepsy, or similar condition from which they may suffer. This information should be noted, together with any medical attention given, for future attending medical personnel.

6.17.3 The debriefing helps to ensure that all survivors are rescued, to attend to the physical welfare of each survivor, and to obtain information which may assist and improve SAR services. Proper debriefing techniques include:

– due care to avoid worsening a survivor's condition by excessive debriefing;

– careful assessment of the survivor's statements if the survivor is frightened or excited;

– use of a calm voice in questioning;

– avoidance of suggesting the answers when obtaining facts; and

– explaining that the information requested is important for the success of the SAR operation, and possibly for future SAR operations.

6.18 Handling of deceased persons

6.18.1 Searching for and recovering bodies should be conducted according to international and national laws and regulations, and is not normally considered to be part of SAR operations. However, persons in distress may expire either before aid can be rendered to them or after they have been rescued. Handling of human remains by SAR personnel may at times be necessary. Proper handling of such situations may benefit persons affected by the loss of life and improve public relations for the SAR agency.

6.18.2 SAR authorities should make prior arrangements with other authorities concerned with removal and disposal of human remains (often law-enforcement agencies) to co-ordinate transfer of the remains. Where victims are citizens of other States, it may be necessary to use diplomatic channels to co-ordinate transfer of the remains.

6.18.3 Human remains at an aircraft crash site should not be disturbed or removed without authorization from the SMC except for compelling reasons. The SMC would obtain authorization from an appropriate authority, usually associated with aircraft accident investigations.

6.18.4 Without exposing rescuers to danger, an attempt should be made to identify deceased persons. All articles removed from or found near each body must be kept separate, preferably in a container so labelled that it can be correlated later with the body. All these articles should be handed over to the proper authority as soon as possible. Handling of human remains can be traumatic. SAR personnel need to be informed on proper procedures to use, and after their involvement, counselled as appropriate to help meet emotional needs.

6.18.5 When human remains are recovered during a SAR operation, or when a death occurs on board a SAR facility, a waybill should be made out for each deceased person. It should contain the full name and age of the deceased (if known), as well as the place, date, time, and cause of death (if possible). This waybill should be made out in the national language of the SAR facility and, wherever possible, in English.

6.18.6 Considerations for the transport of human remains include:

(a) On vessels, body bags or sailcloth for human remains should be carried. If human remains are kept on board for any length of time, they should be properly wrapped and put in a suitable place on the vessel.

(b) SAR aircraft do not normally transport human remains. However, SAR aircraft may have to carry human remains if no other means are readily available.

(c) Immediately after return to a base specified by the RCC, the remains must be handed over to the appropriate authorities, accompanied by the waybill.

(d) If it is known or suspected that a deceased person had an infectious disease, all material and objects which have been in direct contact with the deceased person must be cleaned and disinfected or destroyed.

6.18.7 SAR operations are conducted only for assisting persons who may be living. However, it is wise to consider the capabilities of existing Disaster Victim Identification (DVI) methods and procedures in the instance of a mass casualty accident.

The DVI operation is a criminal police and forensic science operation carried out according to national policies and legislation in accordance with standards established by INTERPOL. As it is not legally a part of the SAR operation, it is not co-ordinated or supervised by the RCCs.

DVI may be of significant assistance to SAR personnel in those instances where unidentified human remains are recovered in the course of a SAR case, particularly in those instances of multiple casualties. This will assist SAR personnel in accounting for the persons who are the subject of the SAR case, and to verify whether or not additional persons remain missing. This will facilitate closing the SAR case as expeditiously as possible.

SAR and DVI authorities should co-operate in dealing with the families of missing persons. DVI systems can usually be accessed through liaison with local or national police agencies. SAR personnel are encouraged to assist DVI authorities if that is possible based on other operational commitments and organization policies.

6.19 Critical incident stress

6.19.1 Exposure to traumatic events and duties, particularly if they involve dead, mutilated or dismembered bodies, is extremely stressful. SAR personnel may need to cope with such situations during or after a SAR operation. Adverse psychological effects of working in such an environment increase with prolonged exposure, and may be cumulative for personnel involved in multiple events over time.

6.19.2 Aircraft accidents may involve SAR personnel in such operations for a prolonged period, especially if the accident occurs at sea where there are few alternative personnel and facilities to handle recovery of dead, mutilated or dismembered bodies.

6.19.3 Recovery time for persons so exposed is commonly two to three months, but may last over one year and may require professional help a year or more after the event. Even persons experienced in their profession, and with duties such as body recovery, can experience acute or long-term health problems during and after responding to such events. SAR personnel often do not realize how they can be affected.

6.19.4 Situations involving death, severe injuries, etc., usually cause SAR personnel to consider the vulnerability of themselves and others close to them, and to share the anguish of family members and others adversely affected by the tragedy. Event anniversaries may trigger adverse responses.

6.19.5 When SAR authorities assign personnel to on-scene duties, transport or other responsibilities involving handling or viewing of bodies or body parts, or to similar traumatic duties, they should:

(a) After severe events, arrange separate debriefings or counselling sessions for each category of personnel. The demands differ and it is important that the group is small and has an understanding of the incident from their own professional perspective;

(b) Daily or at each shift change, provide information and advice to crews coming on duty to perform such tasks, and counsel them when they are relieved, regardless of whether the persons involved believe they need the assistance;

(c) Conduct a thorough critical incident stress debrief for crews when they will no longer be returning to traumatic duties;

(d) Minimize unnecessary exposure when possible, and in any case, limit assignment to such duties to a maximum of three weeks without subsequently returning them to the operation;

(e) If possible, schedule adequate rest periods to minimize fatigue, a major factor in compounding traumatic stress;

(f) Limit the number of personnel involved when practicable;

(g) After crews have been debriefed and relieved of duty, arrange to follow up with them and their families to monitor needs and assist as appropriate; actively follow up for at least one year, since symptoms and problems are sometimes delayed;

(h) To aid recuperation after exposure, schedule at least 48 hours away from work responsibilities;

(i) Provide access to trained counselling, chaplains, and other human support services during and after the event, and involve spouses or other close persons in follow-up efforts to help the person affected recover more easily; and

(j) Arrange for expressions of appreciation by senior personnel, as well as public expressions of appreciation, as these can help personnel adapt after facing stressful duties.

6.20 Termination of rescue

6.20.1 As soon as the rescue operation has been completed, the SMC should immediately notify all authorities, facilities, or services which have been activated. All information on the conduct of the rescue operation should be added to that on the search operation and a final report prepared. Information of interest to accident investigation and medical authorities should be given to them without delay. Chapter 8 provides guidance on conclusion of SAR operations.

Chapter 7

Emergency assistance other than search and rescue

7.1 General

7.1.1 SAR services may be required to perform operations other than search and rescue, which, if not carried out, could result in a SAR incident, such as:

– assisting a ship or aircraft which is in a serious situation and in danger of becoming a casualty, thereby endangering persons on board;

– broadcasting of maritime safety information (MSI);

– alerting appropriate authorities of unlawful acts being committed against an aircraft or ship; and

– assisting after the ship or aircraft has been abandoned, to minimize future hazards.

7.1.2 Even when a SAR service is not responsible in a given area, it may be called upon to assist other emergency response authorities. For those situations where the assistance of SAR services may be anticipated, suitable operating plans should be developed that include provisions for co-ordination with other authorities, as appropriate. However, in many cases, these requirements cannot be foreseen and SAR personnel may have to provide an appropriate response without any existing plan.

7.2 Intercept and escort services

7.2.1 The main purpose of intercept and escort services is to minimize delay in reaching the scene of distress and to eliminate a search for survivors. Escort service for both aircraft and vessels will normally be provided to the nearest adequate aerodrome or nearest safe haven for vessels (safe mooring and with a means of communications such as a telephone). Escorts can also often provide various types of assistance should the escorted craft be unable to arrive at a safe place under its own power. Procedures to develop intercepts are in appendix J.

7.2.2 The following assistance can be provided by an escort:

– moral support to the persons on board the distressed craft, assuring them that assistance is immediately available;

– navigation and communication functions for the distressed craft, permitting its crew to concentrate on coping with the emergency;

– inspection of the exterior of the distressed craft;

– advice on procedures for aircraft ditching, including ditching heading, or for abandoning or beaching a vessel;

– illumination during aircraft ditching or vessel abandonment, or assistance in the approach procedure at the destination;

– immediate provision of emergency and survival equipment, if any, carried by the escort facility; and

– direction of rescue facilities to the distress scene.

7.2.3 In an uncertainty phase, the SMC may alert SAR facilities capable of providing an escort facility. If the incident progresses to an alert or distress phase, the SMC may then dispatch the escort facility immediately. Even when it appears too late for the intercepting facility to effect the intercept, it should be dispatched to begin the search.

7.2.4   An aircraft may be considered to need an escort when:

–   navigation or radio equipment is suspect;

–   it is unable to maintain altitude;

–   it has suffered structural damage;

–   it is on fire or fire is suspected;

–   the pilot's control of the aircraft is impaired;

–   remaining fuel is suspected to be insufficient;

–   fewer than three out of four, or fewer than two out of three engines are operating normally; or

–   it is threatened by any other grave and imminent danger.

7.2.5   A ship may be considered to need an escort when:

–   its stability is endangered (e.g., taking in water or cargo shifting);

–   it has suffered actual or suspected structural damage;

–   it is on fire or fire is suspected;

–   the master's control of the vessel is impaired;

–   remaining fuel is suspected to be insufficient;

–   its steering gear is defective; or

–   it is threatened by any other grave and imminent danger.

7.2.6   The following information regarding the distressed craft should be given to the intercepting facility:

–   description, including call sign and other identification marks;

–   position at a specified time and type of navigation aids used;

–   heading and drift (or track);

–   speed over the ground or water;

–   if an aircraft, whether maintaining altitude, climbing, or descending;

–   number of persons at risk; and

–   brief description of the emergency.

7.2.7   Accurate navigation by both the distressed craft and the intercepting facility is the most important factor when effecting an intercept.

7.2.8   When visual contact has been made, the intercepting aircraft will normally take up a position slightly above, behind and to the left of the distressed craft. Aircraft can escort ships.

7.2.9   A ship carrying out an interception should stand by the distressed craft until the danger is past, unless given instructions to the contrary.

7.3   Safety information

7.3.1   Maritime safety information (MSI), such as weather forecasts and warnings of hazards to navigation, is promulgated by SAR, meteorological, and navigation authorities. These authorities make arrangements for broadcast of MSI by means that may include NAVTEX, Inmarsat's SafetyNET, and MF, VHF and HF radio. Broadcast of MSI can serve to prevent SAR incidents from occurring. Similar safety information may be promulgated for aircraft and distributed as arranged by aeronautical authorities.

7.4   Unlawful acts

7.4.1   The RCC may become aware of an aircraft known or believed to be subject to unlawful interference. ATS units would usually become aware of the situation first and would be responsible. The RCC should declare an alert phase, advise appropriate authorities (ATS units if not already aware, and response agencies specified in the plans of operation), and begin preparations for possible SAR operations as appropriate.

7.4.2 In situations such as piracy or armed robbery against ships where the ship or crew is in grave and imminent danger, the master may authorize the broadcasting of a distress message, preceded by the appropriate distress alerts (MAYDAY, DSC, etc.), using all available radiocommunications systems. Also, ships subject to the SOLAS Convention are required to carry equipment called the Ship Security Alert System (SSAS) for sending covert alerts to shore for vessel security incidents involving acts of violence against ships (i.e., piracy, armed robbery against ships or any other security incident directed against a ship). The system is intended to allow a covert activation to be made which alerts the competent authority ashore and denies knowledge of its activation to perpetrators of the acts of violence. Under the SSAS concept, national governments should establish a security forces authority to be in charge of providing the response to such security incidents. The RCC, due to it being available on a 24-hour basis, is often the first point of contact between the ship and coastal authorities concerned. Two common systems for transmitting SSAS alerts are Inmarsat and Cospas–Sarsat. (A sample SSAS alert message is found in appendix B, under RCC–Cospas–Sarsat message formats.) National procedures can vary but the role of the RCC, if involved, is usually to receive the SSAS alert and inform the security forces authority that will be in charge of the response. Actions taken by the RCC upon receiving a covert SSAS alert include:

– do not acknowledge receipt of the alert;

– do not attempt to contact the ship originating the alert;

– do not send any communications to other ships in the vicinity of the ship under threat unless directed by the security forces authority;

– if the position of the incident is within its SRR, the RCC should immediately inform its national security forces authority;

– if the position of the incident is outside of its SRR, the RCC should relay the alert to the appropriate RCC using the normal methods of communications; and

– place SAR resources on standby, if appropriate, since it may become a SAR case.

7.5 Search and rescue outside of RCC responsible areas

7.5.1 SAR services may be called upon for assistance by other emergency services in areas that are not in their normal area of responsibility. Examples of these situations include:

– SAR in estuaries, rivers, lakes, harbours, and flooded areas;

– rescue of injured personnel from inaccessible or remote land areas or areas accessible by water but not accessible by land, such as seaside cliffs;

– major incidents where there are large numbers of casualties; and

– medical evacuation when primary services are unable to perform the mission, such as by ship from a small coastal island when weather prohibits the evacuation by aircraft.

7.5.2 In certain exceptional situations, evacuation by sea may be the only way to save persons on land from an imminent danger that has trapped them on the coast or small island. Forest fires, volcanic eruptions, and industrial accidents causing the discharge of hazardous materials are examples of such situations. When these types of situations occur, SAR services may be the only emergency organization capable of performing the evacuation. In most of these cases, harbour installations would probably not be available and hazardous conditions would most likely prevent the use of aircraft or helicopters.

7.6 Assistance to property

7.6.1 The primary concern of SAR operations is assistance to persons in distress. However, chapter 5 of the IAMSAR Manual, volume I, *Organization and Management* points out some factors and reasons for consideration of saving property. Variations of the terms "saving" and "salving" are commonly used internationally regarding removal of property from risk. Commercial salvage companies may become involved during or after SAR operations. SAR personnel on scene are usually in the best position to assess what actions are necessary to minimize future hazards such as pollution from cargo or fuel spills and ships becoming hazards to navigation or vessels, craft or life-saving appliances left adrift at sea that may cause an unnecessary SAR alert in the future. Action such as towing or temporary repairs or recovery by the SAR facility may be able to prevent more complicated problems later. However, SAR facilities typically are not experts in salvage operations, so the SMC must consider their capabilities and the risks to them. Judgements about the stability of a damaged vessel, or whether freeing a grounded vessel will improve or worsen the situation, can be very difficult to make.

7.6.2   When a salvage vessel is at the scene of the distress or *en route* to it, the SRU involved should verify whether the salvage vessel is prepared to effect salvage, and whether this assistance is acceptable to the distressed craft. If not, the SRU should render assistance as necessary to ensure the safety of life.

7.7   Aerodrome emergency plan

7.7.1   Annex 14 of the Convention on International Civil Aviation provides for an Aerodrome Emergency Plan. As recommended in annex 14, the plan should provide for co-operation and co-ordination with the rescue co-ordination centre, as necessary. This Plan is maintained to minimize the number of personal injuries and the extent of property damage resulting from an emergency. These Plans focus on emergency services and resources available to aerodrome and local emergency service organizations. Co-operation and co-ordination between the aerodrome operators and the RCC should be promoted for the provision of mutual assistance. The plan is to include the ready availability of, and co-ordination with, appropriate specialist rescue services to be able to respond to emergencies where an aerodrome is located close to water and/or swampy areas or difficult terrain and where a significant portion of approach or departure operations takes place over these areas.

7.7.2   Aerodromes should make provisions with local SAR service providers for water rescue and mass casualties near aerodromes, as appropriate. The aerodrome emergency plan is required to contain procedures for periodic testing of the adequacy of the plan and for reviewing the results in order to improve its effectiveness. Testing may be by joint exercises conducted so that:

–   aerodrome operators understand the SAR service organization, capabilities, and limitations; and

–   SAR facilities become familiar with the aerodrome layout, support facilities, and access points.

Chapter 8

Conclusion of SAR operations

8.1 General

8.1.1 SAR operations enter the conclusion stage when:

- information is received that the ship, aircraft, other craft, or persons who are the subject of the SAR incident are no longer in distress;

- the ship, aircraft, other craft, or persons for whom SAR facilities are searching have been located and the survivors rescued; or

- during the distress phase, the SMC or other proper authority determines that further search would be to no avail because additional effort cannot appreciably increase the probability of successfully finding any remaining survivors or because there is no longer any reasonable probability that the distressed persons have survived.

8.2 Closing a SAR case

8.2.1 The authority to terminate a case sometimes rests with different levels within the SAR organization depending on the circumstances dictating that the incident be closed or active search suspended. In particular, the responsible SC or other SAR managers may retain the authority to suspend a case when the subjects of a search have not been found, and may delegate to the SMC the authority to close cases in all other circumstances, i.e., when the SMC determines that the craft or people are no longer in distress. In areas not under the responsibility of an RCC, or where the responsible centre is not able to co-ordinate the operations, the OSC may need to take responsibility for deciding when to suspend or close the search.

8.2.2 Most SAR operations typically conclude when those in distress are no longer in distress or are rescued and rescue personnel and facilities are returning to normal duties. The basic steps to closing this type of case are:

- notify immediately all authorities, centres, services, or facilities that have been activated; and

- complete a record of the case.

8.3 Suspending search operations

8.3.1 Some cases may require extended searching. At some point, the proper authority must make the difficult decision to suspend active search operations pending the receipt of additional information. That is, the authority must decide that additional search effort will not result in success. In making this decision, each SAR incident must be considered on its own merits, and care should be taken not to end the search prematurely. The decision to suspend a search involves humanitarian considerations, but there is a limit to the time and effort that can be devoted to each SAR case.

8.3.2 Prior to suspending search operations, a thorough case review should be made. The decision to suspend operations should be based on an evaluation of the probability that there were survivors from the initial incident, the probability of survival after the incident, the probability that any survivors were within the computed search area, and the effectiveness of the search effort as measured by the cumulative probability of success. The reasons for search suspension should be clearly recorded. The case review should also examine:

– search decisions for proper assumptions and reasonable planning scenarios;

– certainty of initial position and any drift factors used in determining search area;

– significant clues and leads re-evaluated;

– data computations;

– the search plan, to ensure that:

  – all assigned areas were searched;

  – the probability of detection is as high as desired; and

  – compensation was made for search degradation caused by weather, navigational, mechanical, or other difficulties; and

– the determination about the survivability of survivors, considering:

  – time elapsed since the incident;

  – environmental conditions (appendix N provides information on some of the environmental factors);

  – age, experience, and physical condition of potential survivors;

  – survival equipment available; and

  – studies or information relating to survival in similar situations.

8.3.3 A search should normally be terminated only when there is no longer any reasonable hope of rescuing survivors from the SAR incident. Considerations for suspending a search include:

– all assigned areas have been thoroughly searched;

– all reasonable probable locations have been investigated;

– all reasonable means of obtaining information about the whereabouts of the ship, aircraft, other craft, or persons who are the subject of the search have been exhausted; and

– all assumptions and calculations used in search planning have been reviewed.

8.3.4 The SMC should advise the relatives of the missing persons that the search has been suspended. Relatives are normally more willing to accept the decision to suspend operations if they have been allowed to follow the progress of the search. The SMC should have maintained regular contact with relatives during the search, as discussed in section 1.10, to provide information and outline future plans. Providing access to the RCC, or if not co-located, to the SMC headquarters, if appropriate, enables relatives to see the search effort. Notification of the decision to terminate should normally be made at least one day prior to suspension of operations, allowing relatives at least one more day of hope, while giving them time to accept that the search cannot continue indefinitely.

8.3.5 When a search has proven unsuccessful and the SMC has suspended search operations, others concerned, e.g., the operating agency of the missing craft, may continue the search. These activities should, if requested, be co-ordinated by the RCC.

8.3.6 The RCC should maintain a suspended case file, which should be periodically reviewed so that the operations can be re-activated without delay if additional information develops which justifies engaging in renewed search efforts.

8.4 Reopening a suspended case

8.4.1 If significant new information or clues are developed, reopening of a suspended case should be considered. Reopening without good reason may lead to unwarranted use of resources, risk of injury to searchers, possible inability to respond to other emergencies, and false hopes among relatives.

8.5 Final reports

8.5.1 When a SAR case is closed or search efforts are suspended, every authority, centre, service, or facility activated should be notified. This is normally done via radio or telephone, and then followed by a final situation report (SITREP) from the RCC. To ensure that search facilities remain under some type of flight or vessel following system, the RCC should not stand down its efforts until all resources have established alternate following plans, where appropriate. Other RCCs involved should be notified of the conclusion of SAR operations, especially if responsibility for the case was assumed from another RCC, such as the first RCC to receive the distress alert.

8.5.2 If the RCC Chief and the responsible managers were not involved in a search suspension decision, they should be informed about the lack of success and the reasons for halting operations.

8.5.3 A record of SAR operations is required to improve methods, evaluate mistakes, if any, and provide statistics for SAR managers to justify SAR system support. This record should include information from debriefing of survivors as discussed in section 6.16. If the SAR service maintains computer files of SAR cases, appropriate information from this case file should be extracted and entered into the database for future analysis.

8.6 Performance improvement

8.6.1 Constant improvement in the performance of the SAR system should be a clearly stated goal of SAR managers. One method to encourage performance improvement is to set up goals whose degree of attainment can be measured by key performance data. This data should be collected, analysed, and published on a routine basis so that individuals can see how the system as a whole is doing, and how their performance is contributing to the achievement of the established goals. Where the SAR case-load is high, some States have established computer databases to aid this analysis. Where the case-load is lower, routine reports from the SMCs to the SCs or other SAR managers can be used for monitoring system performance and highlighting areas where improvement is possible through changes in policies, procedures, or resource allocation.

8.7 Case studies

8.7.1 Sometimes a SAR case has a surprise ending, as when the survivors are found by someone not involved in the search effort in a location outside the search area, or they are found, alive and well, in the search area after the search effort has been suspended. There are also occasions when there seems to have been an unusual number of problems in spite of the best efforts of the SAR personnel. Finally, there may be important and valuable lessons to learn from a SAR incident and the subsequent response of the SAR system that would be revealed only by a careful after-the-fact review.

(a) A SAR case study is an appropriate method for addressing those aspects of an incident that are of particular interest. Individual aspects of interest could include problems with communications, assumptions made, scenario development, search planning, or international co-ordination. SAR case studies or incident reviews also provide opportunities to analyse survivor experiences and lifesaving equipment performance. Survival in hostile environments is affected by many variables, including the physical condition of the survivors, survivor actions, reinforcement given by rescue forces prior to rescue, and the effectiveness of safety or survival equipment. Knowing more about these factors can help the SAR system become more effective.

(b) When used to review and evaluate all aspects of a response to an incident, SAR case studies are one of the most valuable and effective tools for improving SAR system performance. Therefore, SAR case studies or reviews should be performed periodically even when no problems are apparent. There is almost always room for improvement, especially in large, complex cases. The most important outcome, however, is that early detection and correction of apparently small problems or potential problems will prevent them from growing into serious deficiencies later.

8.7.2 The discussion on case review in paragraph 8.3.2 provides topics that typically may be examined during a case study.

8.7.3 To get a balanced view, SAR case studies should be done by more than one person; the case study team should include recognized experts in those aspects of the case being reviewed. To achieve maximum effectiveness, case studies should not assign blame, but rather, should make constructive suggestions for change where analysis shows that such change will improve future performance.

8.8 Archiving case files

8.8.1 All information pertaining to a specific SAR incident should be placed in an easily identified and labelled file folder and then placed in storage. Length of time to retain these records in storage is the decision of the SAR managers. Some States retain all records for a few years and then place files dealing with significant, historically important, or sensitive incidents into permanent secure storage, discarding those involved only with routine situations. Defining which files belong in the "routine" category is, again, a SAR manager matter. Files pertaining to incidents that become the subject of legal proceedings must be retained until those proceedings are complete, including all appeals and legal reviews. Files that are to be permanently retained should be prominently marked so that they are not inadvertently thrown out when the routine files are discarded.

8.9 Incident debriefings

8.9.1 Debriefings, feedback sessions and experience sharing opportunities between the crews of SAR facilities, SMCs and SCs are methods of quality control and continuous improvement to a SAR system. To benefit from this process, SAR authorities should establish a structured and systematic approach to debriefing. Of particular significance would be the following matters:

(a) extent of the debriefings (what experiences need to be shared);

(b) focus of the debriefing (strive to focus on the most important issues);

(c) level of participation at the debriefing;

(d) definition of participants' needs; and

(e) process of information flow from the debriefing (normally from the bottom up).

Although each level of debriefing targets a specific audience, significant benefits can be derived from conducting simultaneous/joint debriefings in which all parties participate. It is important to note that improvements to a SAR system will not be obtained unless recommendations identified by debriefings are reviewed and implemented.

8.9.2 Types of debriefing can be grouped into three categories: operations, liaison and administration. Each category deals with specific segments of an operation that normally includes the following aspects:

(a) Operations:
- operations/response;
- co-ordination;
- communications;
- reporting;
- debriefing; and
- logs and documents.

(b) Liaison:
- participation in briefings/courses held by various SAR providers;
- seminars/workshops/working groups;
- RCC staff visits to sub-units/agencies/groups;
- joint exercises;
- visits to neighbouring countries; and
- participation in international events.

(c) Administration:

- command, communication and control structure;
- policy and regulations;
- personnel; and
- administrative support.

8.9.3 The following methods of debriefings could be used to assist SAR Authorities to improve their system:

(a) *Situation report (SITREP).* As described in chapter 2, this method provides the quickest means to forward issues of concern to the responsible authorities;

(b) *SAR debrief (Search Operation Debriefing Form).* As described in chapter 5, this debriefing form is intended to report actual actions and observations of SAR facilities after each tasking. It provides the opportunity to report areas of concern in a more formal way;

(c) *SAR mission report.* This method requires the primary rescue facilities to prepare a quick description of the tasks and actions taken (see appendix H). This report would provide another avenue for responsible authorities to capture previously undisclosed issues of concern. Concerns may involve issues of broader scope not necessarily apparent at the time of the event;

(d) *Formal debriefing session.* This debriefing method could be initiated by a participating SAR facility, RCC, or a high-level authority and would normally involve an in-depth review of issues of concern. Attendance by representatives of all SAR-participating units would be highly desirable. Findings and proposed changes/amendments to local procedures would be validated and approved by those concerned and promulgated to the responsible authorities for implementation. There would be no requirement for a specific format as the results of this debriefing would be intended for internal use only (distributed among the various emergency service providers); and

(e) *SAR operation report.* This method of debriefing would be required after a significant SAR incident and/or when issues identified in the operation need to be addressed. The report would be prepared by the responsible authority in line with the process described in section 8.7. The report would be intended for a wider audience, which could include government departments, outside agencies, interested groups, owners and operators. Consequently, an established format would be needed to ensure adequacy and consistency of the reports (see appendix H).

8.9.4   The beneficiaries of debriefings and those methods of debriefing best suited to them are described in the following table:

Recipients of debrief (Category of debrief)	Situation report	SAR debrief	SAR mission report	Formal debrief	SAR operation report
SAR facilities (Operations)	•	•	•	•	
SMCs (Operations/Liaison/Administration)	•	•	•	•	•
SAR managers (Operations/Liaison/Administration)	•	•	•	•	•
SAR co-ordinators (Administration)				•	•
International audiences (Operations/Administration)				•	•

Appendices

Appendix A

Distress communications

Morse Code

A	· −	N	− ·
B	− · · ·	O	− − −
C	− · − ·	P	· − − ·
D	− · ·	Q	− − · −
E	·	R	· − ·
F	· · − ·	S	· · ·
G	− − ·	T	−
H	· · · ·	U	· · −
I	· ·	V	· · · −
J	· − − −	W	· − −
K	− · −	X	− · · −
L	· − · ·	Y	− · − −
M	− −	Z	− − · ·

1	· − − − −	6	− · · · ·
2	· · − − −	7	− − · · ·
3	· · · − −	8	− − − · ·
4	· · · · −	9	− − − − ·
5	· · · · ·	0	− − − − −

Procedural words

AFFIRMATIVE means "yes" i.e., that what a person has transmitted is correct.

BREAK is used to separate portions of a message or one message from another.

FIGURES is spoken just before numbers are given in a message.

I SPELL is used just before a phonetic spelling, such as of a proper name.

NEGATIVE means no.

OUT indicates the end of a transmission when no reply is expected or required.

OVER indicates the end of a transmission when an immediate reply is expected.

ROGER means I have received your transmission satisfactorily.

SILENCE is said three times and means cease all transmissions immediately.

SILENCE FINI (pronounced SEE LONSS FEE NEE) means silence is lifted, and is used to signify the end of the emergency and resumption of normal traffic.

THIS IS is said before the station name or call sign which immediately follows.

WAIT means "stand by," i.e., I must pause for a few seconds; stand by for further transmission.

Distress signals

Some basic distress signals are as follows:

- "SOS" in Morse Code by any means;

- a gun or other explosive fired at intervals of about one minute (tracer bullets can be detected up to six miles, but it is difficult to pinpoint survivor location);

- continuous sounding with any fog signalling apparatus;

- a square flag having above or below it a ball or anything resembling a ball;

- flames, e.g., from a burning oil barrel (flames are very effective at night, and have been sighted as far away as 50 miles);

- red flares, which have been sighted up to 35 miles at night, with an average of 10 miles at night, and about 1 to 2 miles during daylight;

- orange smoke, effective up to 12 miles during the day if winds are less than 10 knots, with an average 8 mile range;

- slowly and repeatedly raising and lowering arms outstretched to each side;

- inverted flag;

- flashes from a signal mirror, with an average detection range of five miles, but sometimes detectable up to 45 miles; and

- dye-stained water, normally green or red, has been sighted up to ten miles away, with an average detectability of three miles.

Persons in distress may use any means at their disposal to attract attention, make known their position and obtain help (SOLAS, chapter IV).

The use of an international distress signal, except for the purpose of indicating that a person is or persons are in distress, and the use of any signal which may be confused with an international distress signal are prohibited (SOLAS, chapter V).

Ground-to-air signals

Require assistance	V
Require medical assistance	X
No or negative	N
Yes or affirmative	Y
Proceeding in this direction	↑

Additional visual signals and their meaning are provided in figures A-1 and A-2.

No.	Message	Code Symbol		No.	Message	Code Symbol
1	Operation completed	LLL		5	Have divided into two groups. Each proceeding in direction indicated	
2	We have found all personnel	LL		6	Information received that aircraft is in this direction	→ →
3	We have found only some personnel	++		7	Nothing found. Will continue to searchs direction	NN
4	We are not able to continue. Returning to base	XX				

Figure A-1

Need medical assistance	Our receiver is operating	Use drop message	Affirmative (yes)	Negative (no)	All O.K. do not wait

Do not attempt to land here	Land here	Can proceed shortly - wait if practical	Need mechanical help or parts	Pick us up - plane abandoned

Figure A-2

Air-to-ground signals

The air-to-ground signals are defined in figure A-3.

**Message received and understood
(rocking the wings)**

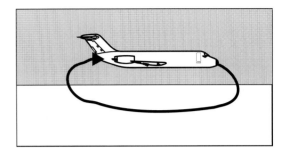

**Message received and not understood
(circling)**

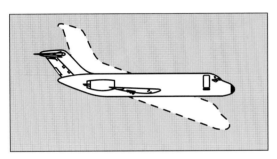

**Affirmative
(pitching nose up and down)**

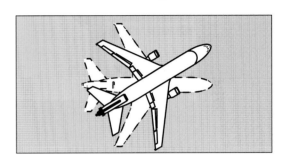

**Negative
(yawning left and right)**

Figure A-3

Panel signals

The panel signals are explained in figure A-4.

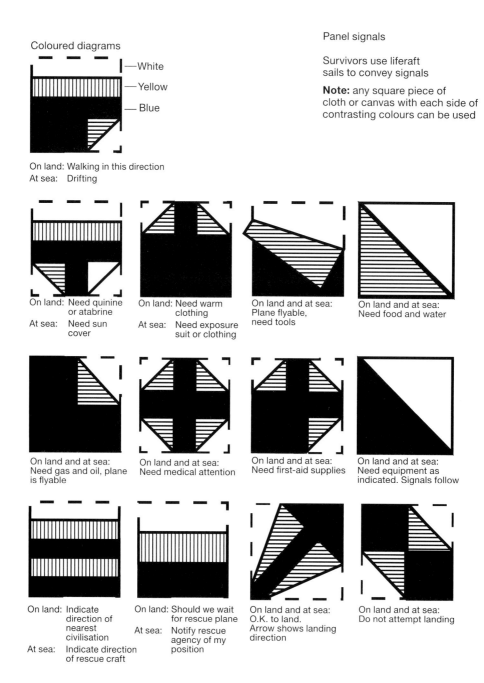

Figure A-4

Appendix B

Message formats

RCC-Cospas–Sarsat message formats

(1)   To send out a distress alert:

        FROM   *(Name of organization/RCC)*
        TO   *(Name of organization/RCC)*
        MESSAGE NUMBER   *(Only if system requirement)*
        1. DISTRESS ALERT   *(System used to signal distress)*

        2. DISTRESS
        (Provide information on the type of information received, system details, etc)
        (Address information, MMSI, system number, etc.) AT TIME *(Time and date of receipt)*

        3. POSITION   Latitude and longitude *(including date and time updated if applicable)*
            COURSE   *(if applicable)*
            SPEED   KTS *(if applicable)*

        4. OTHER/DECODED INFORMATION
        (Include information as applicable to system such as: Inmarsat Region; Receiving Station; communications mode; results of contact; etc.)

        5. *(Include action taken and any information gained, identity of vessel if known; etc.)*

        6. PASSED FOR YOUR CO-ORDINATION.
        PLEASE ACKNOWLEDGE *(Insert RCC contact details)*

(2)   To repeat an unsuccessfully transmitted message:

        FROM   *(Name of organization/RCC)*
        TO   *(Name of organization/RCC)*
        DISTRESS ALERT MESSAGE NUMBER *(number)*
        1. REPEAT REQUESTED

(3)   To advise the MCC that relay of further reports is unnecessary:

        FROM   *(Name of organization/RCC)*
        TO   *(Name of organization/RCC)*
        DISTRESS ALERT MESSAGE NUMBER *(number)*
        1. CASE CLOSED (or SUSPENDED)
        2. BEACON TURNED OFF

(4)   To ask the MCC to monitor a particular area in which the RCC suspects an incident has occurred:

        FROM   *(Name of organization/RCC)*
        TO   *(Name of organization/RCC)*
        REQUEST FOR ALERT DATA
        1. GEOGRAPHIC LOCATION *(location)*
        2. FREQUENCY *(frequency)*
        3. CANCELLATION DATE/TIME *(date and time)*

(5)   To request emergency data which the MCC may have in its database associated with a particular beacon:

        FROM   *(Name of organization/RCC)*
        TO   *(Name of organization/RCC)*
        REQUEST FOR ADDITIONAL DATABASE INFORMATION
        1. BEACON ID CODE *(beacon identity)*

Examples of Cospas–Sarsat Formats

Note: Not all variations have been included in the examples but may be developed using the message field table and examples that follow.

Message Content of a Cospas–Sarsat Alert

Field number	Field name
45	MESSAGE TYPE
46	CURRENT MESSAGE NUMBER
47	MCC REFERENCE
48	DETECTION TIME AND SPACECRAFT ID
49	DETECTION FREQUENCY
50	COUNTRY OF BEACON REGISTRATION
51	USER CLASS OF BEACON
52	IDENTIFICATION
53	EMERGENCY CODE
54	POSITIONS
54a	RESOLVED POSITION
54b	A POSITION AND PROBABILITY
54c	B POSITION AND PROBABILITY
54d	ENCODED POSITION AND TIME OF UPDATE
55	SOURCE OF ENCODED POSITION DATA
56	NEXT PASS TIMES
56a	NEXT TIME OF VISIBILITY OF RESOLVED POSITION
56b	NEXT TIME OF VISIBILITY A POSITION
56c	NEXT TIME OF VISIBILITY B POSITION
56d	NEXT TIME OF VISIBILITY OF ENCODED POSITION
57	BEACON HEX ID & HOMING SIGNAL
58	ACTIVATION TYPE
59	BEACON NUMBER
60	OTHER ENCODED INFORMATION
61	OPERATIONAL INFORMATION
62	REMARKS
63	END OF MESSAGE

Sample 406 MHz Initial Encoded Position Alert
(Standard Location – EPIRB: Serial Number)

1.   DISTRESS COSPAS-SARSAT INITIAL ALERT

2.   MSG NO: 00306 AUMCC REF: 12345

3.   DETECTED AT: 17 APR 07 1627 UTC BY GOES 11

4.   DETECTION FREQUENCY: 406.0250 MHz

5.   COUNTRY OF BEACON REGISTRATION: 316/ CANADA

6.   USER CLASS: STANDARD LOCATION - EPIRB

      SERIAL NO: 05918

7.   EMERGENCY CODE: NIL

8.   POSITIONS:
      RESOLVED - NIL
      DOPPLER A - NIL
      DOPPLER B - NIL
      ENCODED   - 05 00 00 S 178 00 00 E   TIME OF UPDATE UNKNOWN

9.   ENCODED POSITION PROVIDED BY: EXTERNAL DEVICE

10.   NEXT PASS TIMES:
      RESOLVED - NIL
      DOPPLER A - NIL
      DOPPLER B - NIL
      ENCODED   - NIL

11.   HEX ID: 278C362E3CFFBFF HOMING SIGNAL: 121.5 MHZ

12.   ACTIVATION TYPE: NIL

13.   BEACON NUMBER ON AIRCRAFT OR VESSEL: NIL

14.   OTHER ENCODED INFORMATION:

      CSTA CERTIFICATE NO: 0108
      BEACON MODEL – ACR, RLB-33

      ENCODED POSITION UNCERTAINTY: PLUS-MINUS 30 MINUTES OF LATITUDE AND LONGITUDE

15.   OPERATIONAL INFORMATION:

      LUT ID: NZGEO1 WELLINGTON GEOLUT, NEW ZEALAND (GOES 11)

      BEACON REGISTRATION AT [CMCC]

16.   REMARKS: NIL

      END OF MESSAGE

Sample 406 MHz Unlocated Alert
(National Location – ELT)

1.   DISTRESS COSPAS-SARSAT ALERT

2.   MSG NO: 00141 SPMCC REF: 12345

3.   DETECTED AT: 21 FEB 07 0646 UTC BY MSG-2

4.   DETECTION FREQUENCY: 406.0249 MHz

5.   COUNTRY OF BEACON REGISTRATION: 408/ BAHRAIN

6.   USER CLASS: NATIONAL LOCATION - ELT

     SERIAL NO: 000006

7.   EMERGENCY CODE: NIL

8.   POSITIONS:
     RESOLVED - NIL
     DOPPLER A - NIL
     DOPPLER B - NIL
     ENCODED   - NIL UPDATE TIME UNKNOWN

9.   ENCODED POSITION PROVIDED BY: EXTERNAL DEVICE

10. NEXT PASS TIMES:
     RESOLVED - NIL
     DOPPLER A - NIL
     DOPPLER B - NIL
     ENCODED   - NIL

11. HEX ID: 331000033F81FE0 HOMING SIGNAL: 121.5 MHZ

12. ACTIVATION TYPE: NIL

13. BEACON NUMBER ON AIRCRAFT OR VESSEL: NIL

14. OTHER ENCODED INFORMATION: NIL

15. OPERATIONAL INFORMATION:

     BEACON REGISTRATION AT WWW.406REGISTRATION.COM

16. REMARKS: NIL

     END OF MESSAGE

Sample 406 MHz Resolved Position Alert (National Location – PLB)

1.   DISTRESS COSPAS-SARSAT POSITION RESOLVED ALERT

2.   MSG NO: 00812 AUMCC REF: 2DD747073F81FE0

3.   DETECTED AT: 28 APR 07 0920 UTC BY SARSAT S11

4.   DETECTION FREQUENCY: 406.0278 MHz

5.   COUNTRY OF BEACON REGISTRATION: 366/ USA

6.   USER CLASS: NATIONAL LOCATION - PLB

     SERIAL NO: 167438

7.   EMERGENCY CODE: NIL

8. POSITIONS:
    RESOLVED   - 33 27 N 038 56 E
    DOPPLER A - 33 27 N 038 56 E
    DOPPLER B - NIL
    ENCODED   - 33 25 56 N 038 55 40 E
    UPDATE TIME WITHIN 4 HOURS OF DETECTION TIME

9. ENCODED POSITION PROVIDED BY: INTERNAL DEVICE

10. NEXT PASS TIMES:
    RESOLVED   - NIL
    DOPPLER A - NIL
    DOPPLER B - NIL
    ENCODED   - NIL

11. HEX ID: 2DD747073F81FE0 HOMING SIGNAL: 121.5 MHZ

12. ACTIVATION TYPE: NIL

13. BEACON NUMBER ON AIRCRAFT OR VESSEL: NIL

14. OTHER ENCODED INFORMATION: NIL

15. OPERATIONAL INFORMATION:

    LUT ID: FRLUT2 TOULOUSE, FRANCE

16. REMARKS: NIL

    END OF MESSAGE

Sample 406 MHz Initial Position Alert
(Standard Location – ELT: 24-BIT Address)

1. DISTRESS COSPAS-SARSAT INITIAL ALERT

2. MSG NO: 00741 AUMCC REF: 3266E2019CFFBFF

3. DETECTED AT: 22 APR 07 0912 UTC BY SARSAT S10

4. DETECTION FREQUENCY: 406.0247 MHz

5. COUNTRY OF BEACON REGISTRATION: 403/ SAUDI

6. USER CLASS: STANDARD LOCATION - ELT

    AIRCRAFT 24 BIT ADDRESS: 7100CE

7. EMERGENCY CODE: NIL

8. POSITIONS:
    RESOLVED   - NIL
    DOPPLER A - 32 49 N 081 54 E PROB 69 PERCENT
    DOPPLER B - 24 18 N 041 18 E PROB 31 PERCENT
    ENCODED   - NIL UPDATE TIME UNKNOWN

9. ENCODED POSITION PROVIDED BY: EXTERNAL DEVICE

10. NEXT PASS TIMES:
    RESOLVED   - NIL
    DOPPLER A - NIL
    DOPPLER B - NIL
    ENCODED   - NIL

11.   HEX ID: 3266E2019CFFBFF HOMING SIGNAL: 121.5 MHZ

12.   ACTIVATION TYPE: NIL

13.   BEACON NUMBER ON AIRCRAFT OR VESSEL: NIL

14.   OTHER ENCODED INFORMATION:

      AIRCRAFT 24-BIT ADDRESS ASSIGNED TO: SAUDI ARABIA

15.   OPERATIONAL INFORMATION:

      LUT ID: INLUT1 BANGALORE, INDIA

16.   REMARKS: NIL

      END OF MESSAGE

Sample 406 MHz Resolved Update Position Alert
(Standard Location – Ship Security)

1.   SHIP SECURITY COSPAS-SARSAT POSITION RESOLVED UPDATE ALERT

2.   MSG NO: 00192 AUMCC REF: 2AB82AF800FFBFF

3.   DETECTED AT: 03 MAY 07 0853 UTC BY SARSAT S09

4.   DETECTION FREQUENCY: 406.0276 MHZ

5.   COUNTRY OF BEACON REGISTRATION: 341/ ST KITTS

6.   USER CLASS: STANDARD LOCATION – SHIP SECURITY

     MMSI LAST 6 DIGITS: 088000

7.   EMERGENCY CODE: NIL

8.   POSITIONS:
     RESOLVED - 02 15 N 046 00 E
     DOPPLER A - 02 25 N 046 06 E
     DOPPLER B - NIL
     ENCODED   - 01 54 24 N - 045 37 32 E   UPDATE TIME UNKNOWN

9.   ENCODED POSITION PROVIDED BY: EXTERNAL DEVICE

10. NEXT PASS TIMES:
     RESOLVED - NIL
     DOPPLER A - NIL
     DOPPLER B - NIL
     ENCODED   - NIL

11. HEX ID: 2AB82AF800FFBFF

     HOMING SIGNAL: OTHER (NOT 121.5 MHZ) OR NIL

12. ACTIVATION TYPE: NIL

13. BEACON NUMBER ON AIRCRAFT OR VESSEL: 00

14. OTHER ENCODED INFORMATION: NIL

15. OPERATIONAL INFORMATION:

     LUT ID: NZLUT WELLINGTON, NEW ZEALAND

16.   REMARKS:

        THIS IS A SHIP SECURITY ALERT.

        PROCESS THIS ALERT ACCORDING TO RELEVANT SECURITY REQUIREMENTS

        END OF MESSAGE

Sample 406 MHz Initial Alert
(Serial User – EPIRB: Non-Float Free)

1.   DISTRESS COSPAS-SARSAT INITIAL ALERT

2.   MSG NO: 01087 AUMCC REF: ADCE402FA80028D

3.   DETECTED AT: 20 MAY 07 1613 UTC BY SARSAT S08

4.   DETECTION FREQUENCY: 406.0266 MHz

5.   COUNTRY OF BEACON REGISTRATION: 366/ USA

6.   USER CLASS: SERIAL USER – EPIRB (NON-FLOAT FREE)

        SERIAL NO: 0003050

7.   EMERGENCY CODE: NIL

8.   POSITIONS:
        RESOLVED - NIL
        DOPPLER A - 36 38 S 168 58 E PROB 50 PERCENT
        DOPPLER B - 36 39 S 169 01 E PROB 50 PERCENT
        ENCODED   - NIL

9.   ENCODED POSITION PROVIDED BY: NIL

10.   NEXT PASS TIMES:
        RESOLVED - NIL
        DOPPLER A - 21 MAY 07 0812 UTC
        DOPPLER B - 21 MAY 07 0812 UTC
        ENCODED   - NIL

11.   HEX ID: ADCE402FA80028D HOMING SIGNAL: 121.5 MHZ

12.   ACTIVATION TYPE: MANUAL

13.   BEACON NUMBER ON AIRCRAFT OR VESSEL: NIL

14.   OTHER ENCODED INFORMATION:

        CSTA CERTIFICATE NO: 0163

        BEACON MODEL – MCMURDO LTD: G5 OR E5 SMARTFIND

15.   OPERATIONAL INFORMATION:

        RELIABILITY OF DOPPLER POSITION DATA - SUSPECT

        LUT ID: AULUTW ALBANY, AUSTRALIA

16.   REMARKS: NIL

        END OF MESSAGE

**Sample 406 MHz Resolved Alert
(ELT User – Aircraft Registration)**

1. DISTRESS COSPAS-SARSAT POSITION RESOLVED ALERT

2. MSG NO: 00932 AUMCC REF: 9D064BED62EAFE1

3. DETECTED AT: 10 MAY 07 0654 UTC BY SARSAT S11

4. DETECTION FREQUENCY: 406.0246 MHz

5. COUNTRY OF BEACON REGISTRATION: 232/ G. BRITAIN

6. USER CLASS: ELT USER

    AIRCRAFT REGISTRATION: VP-CGK

7. EMERGENCY CODE: NIL

8. POSITIONS:
    RESOLVED - 25 13 N 055 22 E
    DOPPLER A - 25 17 N 055 23 E
    DOPPLER B - NIL
    ENCODED   - NIL

9. ENCODED POSITION PROVIDED BY: NIL

10. NEXT PASS TIMES:
    RESOLVED - NIL
    DOPPLER A - NIL
    DOPPLER B - NIL
    ENCODED   - NIL

11. HEX ID: 9D064BED62EAFE1 HOMING SIGNAL: 121.5 MHZ

12. ACTIVATION TYPE: MANUAL

13. BEACON NUMBER ON AIRCRAFT OR VESSEL: NIL

14. OTHER ENCODED INFORMATION: NIL

15. OPERATIONAL INFORMATION: NIL

16. REMARKS: NIL

    END OF MESSAGE

Inmarsat-C format

FROM *(Name of organization/RCC)*
TO *(Name of organization/RCC)*

1.   DISTRESS ALERT – INMARSAT-C

2.   DISTRESS MESSAGE RECEIVED FROM INMARSAT-C
         NUMBER *(Insert Mobile Number)* AT TIME *(UTC Time and date of receipt)*

3.   POSITION LAT. . . . . LONG. . . . .
         UPDATED AT TIME. . . . . UTC DATE UNKNOWN
         COURSE. . . . .
         SPEED. . . . . KTS

4.   OTHER INFORMATION

         DISTRESS TYPE   NOT SPECIFIED *(Default, change as required)*

         INMARSAT REGION   PACIFIC *(Default, change as required)*

         RECEIVING STATION   LES *(Insert name of Inmarsat LES)*

         PROTOCOL   MARITIME *(Default, change as required)*

         POSITION UPDATED LAST 24 HRS   YES *(Default, change as required)*

         COURSE/SPEED UPDATED LAST 24 HRS   YES *(Default, change as required)*

5.   *(Insert RCC name)* ACKNOWLEDGED MESSAGE VIA INMARSAT-C

         *•   AND MESSAGE DELIVERED TO VESSEL BUT NO REPLY RECEIVED

         *•   BUT MESSAGE COULD NOT BE DELIVERED TO VESSEL

         *•   UNABLE TO IDENTIFY VESSEL FROM OUR RECORDS

         *•   OUR RECORDS IDENTIFY VESSEL AS *(Insert name and call sign of vessel)*

6.   PASSED FOR YOUR CO-ORDINATION. PLEASE ACKNOWLEDGE *(Insert RCC contact details)*

* Delete whichever line does not apply

DSC format

FROM   *(Name of organization/RCC)*
TO   *(Name of organization/RCC)*

1.   DISTRESS ALERT – DIGITAL SELECTIVE CALLING (DSC)

2.   DISTRESS MESSAGE RECEIVED ON   **(Insert frequency)* kHz

        DISTRESS RELAY RECEIVED ON   **(Insert frequency)* kHz

        DISTRESS ACKNOWLEDGMENT RECEIVED ON   **(Insert frequency)* kHz

        AT TIME   *(UTC Time and date of receipt)* UTC

        MMSI NUMBER OF VESSEL IN DISTRESS   *(Insert MMSI number)*

3.   POSITION LAT. . . . . LONG. . . . .
        UPDATED AT TIME. . . . . UTC DATE UNKNOWN

4.   OTHER INFORMATION

        DISTRESS TYPE   NOT SPECIFIED *(Default, change as required)*

        COMMUNICATIONS MODE   VOICE/NBDP *(Delete as required)*

        RELAYED BY   *(Insert MMSI of station)*

        ACKNOWLEDGED BY   *(Insert MMSI of station)*

        RESULT   *(Insert any results from attempts to contact vessel)*

5.   * •   UNABLE TO IDENTIFY VESSEL FROM OUR RECORDS

        * •   OUR RECORDS IDENTIFY VESSEL AS *(Insert name and call sign of vessel)*

6.   PASSED FOR YOUR CO-ORDINATION. PLEASE ACKNOWLEDGE *(Insert RCC contact details)*

* Delete whichever line does not apply

Suggested format for alert information from a commercial locating, tracking and emergency notification service provider to an RCC

(Format based upon Cospas–Sarsat standard format)

Field number	Field name	Field content	Field format
1	Satellite emergency notification device alert	Satellite emergency notification device distress alert	Header
2	Reporting centre	Call centre identity	Agreed alphabetical abbreviation for call centre (e.g., GEOS)
3	Message number	Unique message number	Call centre abbreviation followed by unique message number assigned by call centre (e.g., GEOS/12345)
4	Message date	Year-Month-Day in the Gregorian calendar	YYYY-MM-DD where YYYY is the year, MM is the month of the year between 01 (January) and 12 (December), and DD is the day of the month between 01 and 31
5	Message transmit time	Hours:Minutes:Seconds in Co-ordinated Universal Time (UTC)	hh:mm:ssZ where hh is the number of complete hours that have passed since midnight (00–24), mm is the number of complete minutes that have passed since the start of the hour (00–59), ss is the number of complete seconds since the start of the minute (00–60) and Z indicates the use of UTC time
6	Local time (optional)	Hour:Minutes:Seconds in local time of where device is located	hh:mm:ss(Local) where hh is the number of complete hours that have passed since midnight (00–24), mm is the number of complete minutes that have passed since the start of the hour (00–59), ss is the number of complete seconds since the start of the minute (00–60) and Local is replaced with EST, CST, MST, PST or other local time zone abbreviation. Abbreviation shall include Daylight saving time if applicable
7	Message type	New alert or update (if later include original message no.)	"New" or "Update", as appropriate, plus for updates the original message number as per field number 3

Field number	Field name	Field content	Field format
8	Destination responsible SAR authority	Message destination	Identity of the SAR Authority that the message is intended for in English
9	Message source ID	Message identifier	If alerting device message identifier is different to the message number in field number 3 then insert it here otherwise leave this field blank
10	Device ID	IMEI number (the 15-digit International Mobile Equipment Identity (IMEI) number of the device)	AA-BBBBBB-CCCCCC-D where AA-BBBBBB are the Type Allocation Code (TAC) for the device, CCCCCC is the manufacturer assigned serial number of the device and D is the Luhn check digit
11	Device manufacturer and model number	Identity of the device sending the distress alert	Device manufacturer and model number (e.g., SPOT Satellite GPS Messenger)
12	Satellite system	Identity of the carrier of the distress alert	Identity of satellite system used (e.g., Globalstar, Inmarsat, Iridium, etc.)
13	Message	Complete Message	The complete text of the message as transmitted by the device
14	Latitude	Latitude in degrees and decimal minutes in WGS84 format	sDD° MM.mm' where s indicates if the latitude is North "N" or South "S" of the equator, DD indicates the number of degrees and MM.mm indicates the number of minutes and decimal parts of minutes of latitude (to an accuracy of approximately 2 m (6 ft))
15	Longitude	Longitude in degrees and decimal minutes in WGS84 format	sDDD° MM.mm' where s indicates if the longitude is East "E" or West "W" of the prime meridian, DDD indicates the number of degrees and MM.mm indicates the number of minutes and decimal parts of minutes of longitude (to an accuracy of approximately 2 m (6 ft))
16	Position source and accuracy	Location provided by GPS, GLONASS, Doppler, etc., and estimated accuracy of location	Location source (e.g., GPS, GLONASS, Doppler, etc.) and estimated location accuracy in metres (e.g., GPS:10 m)

Field number	Field name	Field content	Field format
17	Optional position movement and height	If available, speed and course over ground (SOG and COG) and height above sea level	SSS:CCC:HHHHH where SSS is the speed over ground (SOG) in knots (from 1 to 999), CCC is the track made good (course over ground (COG)) in degrees (from 1 to 360) relative to True North and HHHHH is the elevation above ground (height from 1 to 99,999) in metres. If any field is not available, leave blank
18	Device database source	Identity of where database containing user contact details held	Full address and phone numbers (including country, postal/zip code and inter-national telephone dialling codes)
19	Registered name	Name of device owner	Full name of registered device owner
20	Registered address	Owner's address	Full address of device owner including country and postal/ zip code
21	Registered phone numbers	Owner's phone numbers	Phone numbers with full dialling codes for all phones registered by the owner, including land line and mobile/ cell phone
22	Emergency contact details 1	Full name, address and telephone numbers for first emergency contact	Full name, address and phone numbers (including country, postal/zip code and international telephone dialling codes)
23	Emergency contact details 2	Full name, address and telephone numbers for second emergency contact	Full name, address and phone numbers (including country, postal/zip code and international telephone dialling codes)
24	Supporting information	Medical, vehicle, trip plan, numbers in party, etc.	Free text field in which to provide any additional data that may be of use to SAR
25	Call centre contact details	Full address and telephone numbers for call centre	Full address and phone numbers (including country, postal/zip code and inter-national telephone dialling codes)
26	Call centre operative	Name of the person handling the alert at the call centre and their direct telephone number	Full name and phone number (including extension, if applicable)

Field number	Field name	Field content	Field format
27	Remarks	Any additional information that the call centre has on the situation	Free text field
28	End message	End of message	Message ends

Sample of alert from a commercial locating, tracking and emergency notification service provider to an RCC

*** Alert from a commercial locating, tracking and emergency notification
service provider to an RCC ***

Reporting Centre	: GEOS
Message Number	: GEOS/12345
Message Date	: 2011-12-31
Message Transmit Time	: 21:13:39Z
Local Time (optional)	: 15:13:39(EST)
Message Type	: Update to GEOS/12344
SAR Authority	: Jackson County, OR. Sherriff's Department
Message Source ID	:
Device ID	: 49-015420-323751-8
Device Manufacture/Model No.	: SPOT Satellite GPS Messenger
Satellite System	: Globalstar
Message	: "as sent by an emergency notification device"
Latitude	: N42° 06.935'
Longitude	: W122° 42.340'
Position Source and Accuracy	: GPS:10m
Speed:Course:Height (optional)	: 010:034:00500
Device Database Source	: GEOS 1234 Sends Road Springfield, TX. 60092 USA +1 908 145 8389
Registered Name	: John Smith
Registered Address	: 3450 Twin Cedar Drive Ashland, OR 97563 USA
Registered Phone Number	: (541) 772 5899
Emergency Contact Details (1)	: Jane Smith 3450 Twin Cedar Drive Ashland, OR 97563 USA Home (541) 772 5899 Cell (541) 458 9273
Emergency Contact Details (2)	: Jack Smith 8800 Mountain View Drive Phoenix, OR 97543 USA Home (541) 544 5637 Cell(541) 634 9545
Supporting Information	: "Free text field in which to provide any additional data that may be of use to SAR forces"
Call Center Contact Details	: GEOS 1234 Sends Road Springfield, TX. 60092 USA +1 908 145 8389
Call Center Operative	: Max Jones +1 908 145 8389 ext 342
Remarks	: "Any additional information on the situation"

***************************** END MESSAGE *****************************

Appendix C

Mass rescue operations: exercises, industry roles and incident management

MRO exercises

Since opportunities to handle actual incidents involving mass rescues are rare and challenging, exercising MRO plans are particularly important. Mass evacuation and rescue operations are difficult and costly, leading to a tendency to use simulation excessively during exercises rather than physically exercising on-scene efforts.

MRO exercise objectives need not be addressed in a single large exercise, but may be satisfied in part by routine incorporation into multiple drills, some intended mainly to test other systems. However, realistic drills are necessary and costly, and over 1,000 volunteer ship passengers or hundreds of volunteer aircraft passengers will likely be needed to conduct a realistic exercise. Separate rooms can be used to simulate command posts that would normally be in separate locations.

MRO exercises should ideally achieve the following objectives:

- account for:
    - crew and passenger lists,
    - rescued passengers and crew until they can return to their homes. All persons associated with the rescue and aftermath operations,
    - lifeboats, including empty boats or rafts, and
    - exercises should take account of high freeboard issues for likely rescue facilities;
- identify and task available resources:
    - Amver or other ship reporting systems,
    - potential resources ashore and afloat,
    - resources from local agencies (medical personnel, hospital facilities, fire department, general community, transportation resources), and
    - national and regional military and other resources;
- evaluate notification processes, resource availability, timeliness of initial response, real-time elements, conference capabilities and overall co-ordination;
- ensure all agency roles are specified, understood and properly followed;
- test capabilities of potential OSCs and ability to transfer OSC duties;
- evaluate span of control;
- evacuate a ship or aircraft;
- co-ordinate activities and achieve information exchanges:
    - communications (RCC–RCC, Government–industry, RCC–OSC, on-scene, shore–ship, ground–air, ship–air, SAR facility–survival craft, etc.),
    - information for all concerned (identify, merge, purge, retrieve and transfer to the right place in the right form at the right time),
    - new communication and information management technologies, and
    - media and next of kin;
- safely transfer and care for passengers (evacuation, in survival craft, rescue, medical, protection from environment, post-rescue transfers, etc.);
- test all communication links that may be needed for notification, co-ordination and support;
- conduct medical triage and provide first aid;

- assess ship's safety management system effectiveness;

- exercise co-ordination with local response agencies;

- provide food, water, lifejackets and other protective clothing to survivors;

- test mass rescue plans of:

  - SAR services,

  - operating company (including aircraft and ship plans),

  - any relevant emergency response organizations, e.g., disaster response, military, fire fighting and medical, and

  - transportation and accommodation companies;

- assess how effectively earlier lessons learned have been accounted for in updated plans and how well these lessons were disseminated;

- exercise salvage and pollution abatement capabilities;

- carry out emergency relocation of the disabled craft; and

- exercise external affairs, such as international and public relations taking into account:

  - necessary participants involved,

  - joint information centres established quickly and properly staffed,

  - press briefings handled effectively, e.g., consistent information from different sources,

  - notification of the next of kin and family briefings,

  - staff and equipment capacity to handle incoming requests for information, and

  - rescued persons tracked, kept informed and needs monitored, and reunited with belongings.

The following steps are normally carried out during exercise planning:

- agree on the exercise scenario, goals and extent;

- assemble a multi-disciplinary planning team and agree on objectives for each aspect of the exercise;

- develop the main events and associated timetables;

- confirm availability of agencies to be involved, including any media representatives or volunteers;

- confirm availability of transportation, buildings, equipment, aircraft, ships or other needed resources;

- test all communications that will be used, including tests of radio and mobile phones at or near the locations where they will be used;

- identify and brief all participants and people who will facilitate the exercise, and ensure that facilitators have good independent communications with person who will be controlling the exercise;

- ensure that everyone involved knows what to do if an actual emergency should arise during the exercise;

- if observers are invited, arrange for their safety and keep them informed about the exercise progress;

- for longer exercises, arrange for food and toilet facilities;

- use "exercise in progress", signs, advance notifications and other means to help ensure that person not involved in the exercise do not become alarmed;

- schedule times and places for debriefs;

- agree and prepare conclusions and recommendations with the entity responsible for handling each recommendation along with the due date for any actions;

   –   prepare a clear and concise report and distribute it as appropriate to the participating organizations; and

   –   consider the outcome of this exercise in planning future exercises and operations.

MRO industry roles

SAR authorities should co-ordinate MRO plans with companies that operate aircraft and ships designed to carry large numbers of persons. Such companies should share in preparations to minimize the chances that MROs will be needed, and to ensure success if they are. This section provides guidance on industry role, and discusses how companies could arrange for use of company field teams and emergency response centres as possible means of carrying out their MRO responsibilities.

Early notification of potential or developing MROs is critical, due to the level of effort required to mount a very large-scale response. It is much better to begin the response process and abort it should it become unnecessary, than to begin it later than necessary should the actual need exist. Pilots and masters should be advised and trained to notify SAR services at the earliest indication of a potential distress situation.

Company response organizations should be able to help SAR services by organizing support, equipment, advice and liaison with any of their ships or aircraft.

Companies should be prepared to provide information to preclude the need for multiple sources attempting communications with the aircraft pilot in command or ship captain for information that is unavailable or available from another source. Receiving and handling requests for information aboard the distressed craft can interfere with the pilot's or master's ability to handle the emergency and manage critical on-scene leadership needs.

Companies operating large aircraft or ships should be advised to prepare a co-ordinated team that can handle emergency response functions around the clock should the need arise. Such a team might include staff as indicated in the following table.

Typical company field team

Team leader	Maintains overview, directs operations and keeps management informed
Communicator	Maintains open (and possibly sole) line of communications to craft in distress
Co-ordinating representative	Usually a pilot or master mariner, who co-ordinates with SAR and other emergency response authorities, organizes tugs, looks at itineraries, arranges to position ships or ground facilities that may be able to assist and organizes security and suitable delivery points for passengers and crew when they are delivered to safety
Technical representative	Maintains contact with regulatory authorities, classification societies, insurers and investigators and provides liaison and advice for fire fighting, damage control, repairs and other specialized or technical matters
Environmental representative	Involved with environmental impact and spill response
Medical representative	Gives medical advice, tracks casualties and arranges medical and identification services for survivors
Passenger and crew representatives	Provides information and support to whoever is designated to care for next of kin and keep them informed, identifies transportation needs, and may need to deal with various countries, languages and cultures
Media representative	Gathers information, co-ordinates public affairs matters with counterparts in other organizations, prepares press releases, briefs spokespersons and arranges availability of information by phone and web sites
Specialists	From within or outside the company who may facilitate some special aspect of the response or follow up

The company may operate an **emergency response centre (ERC)** to maintain communications with the craft in distress, remotely monitor onboard sensors if feasible, and keep emergency information readily available. Such information might include passenger and crew data, aircraft or ship details, incident details, number of survival craft and status of the current situation. Transportation companies should have readily available contacts with tour companies, shore excursion companies, airlines and cruise lines, hotels, etc., since such resources can be used to address many problems experienced with landing large numbers of survivors into a community. Contingency plans for co-operation should be developed between SAR authorities and transportation companies, and these plans should be sufficiently exercised to ensure they would be effective should an actual mass rescue situation arise. Such plans should identify contacts, co-ordination procedures, responsibilities, and information sources that will be applicable for MROs. These plans should be kept up to date and readily available to all concerned.

Respective functions of the ERC and RCC should be covered in co-ordinated pre-established plans, and refined as appropriate for an actual incident. These centres must maintain close contact throughout the SAR event, co-ordinating and keeping each other appraised of significant plans and developments.

There are other steps the transportation industry could be urged to undertake to improve preparedness for MROs. The following are some examples:

- carry SAR plans on board aircraft or ships;

- provide water and thermal protection for evacuees appropriate for the operating area;

- provide a means of rescue to bring people from the water to the deck of ships;

- use preparation checklists provided by SAR authorities;

- conduct an actual physical exercise in addition to simulations;

- provide the capability to retrieve fully loaded lifeboats and rafts;

- enhance lifeboat lifesaving capabilities;

- provide ways to assist persons in lifeboats who are seasick, injured or weak;

- provide on board helicopter landing areas and helicopters;

- prepare to assist survivors once they have been delivered to a place of safety;

- have aircraft or ship status and specifications readily available, such as inspection records, design plans, communication capabilities, stability calculations, lifesaving appliances, classification society contacts, passenger and cargo manifests, etc., so that such information will not need to be obtained directly from a pilot or master; and

- work with SAR authorities to develop and be able to rapidly deploy air droppable equipment or supplies for survivors, maintain strategically located caches for this purpose.

Acceptance of certain responsibilities by industry demonstrates commitment to passenger safety and can free SAR services to handle critical arrangements relating to SAR resources, co-ordination and communication.

MRO incident management

For major incidents, crisis management for the overall response may also be needed. The **Incident Command System (ICS)**, one widely used means of meeting this need, works best with some advance familiarization and exercising within and among the transportation and emergency response communities. Since SAR and transportation authorities are likely to encounter use of the ICS within emergency response communities, this appendix provides general information for familiarization with ICS.

The following terms are relevant to the ICS:

- **incident commander (IC):** the primary person functioning as a part of the incident command system, usually at or near the scene, responsible for decisions, objectives, strategies and priorities relating to emergency response;

- **incident command post (ICP):** the location at which primary functions are carried out for the Incident Command System;

- **Incident Command System (ICS):** and on-scene emergency management concept that provides an integrated organizational structure adaptable to the complexity and demands of a major incident involving multiple missions, response organizations or jurisdiction;

- **unified command (UC):** the incident commander role of the incident command system expanded to include a team of representatives that manages a major incident by establishing common objectives and strategies and co-operatively directing their implementation.

The ICS is designed for use when multiple organizations and jurisdictions need to be jointly involved in a co-ordinated emergency response activity.

While organizations have their respective systems of command and control or co-ordination, these should be compatible with systems in use by others so that organizations can function jointly and effectively when necessary. Commonality and similarities among crisis management systems locally, regionally and internationally foster effective joint efforts.

The ICS does not take control, responsibility or authority away from SAR services; SAR services remain focused on lifesaving, while the ICS focuses on promoting an effective overall incident response.

The ICS training, advance co-ordination and liaison will be rewarded by better performance and success when a crisis situation arises.

As a tool for managing major incidents, the ICS:

- accommodates all risks and hazards;

- is simple, powerful and flexible;

- can easily expand or contract as the incident warrants;

- relieves the SAR system of co-ordinating non-SAR missions;

- enables SMCs to use the ICS contacts to draw on additional resources; and

- ensures better communication and co-operation between agencies.

The ICS organization can grow or shrink as the situation dictates, and provides a logical process and progression to achieve results. Its organization should be allowed to grow with increased demand and shrink when operations decline, both of which require anticipation.

Advantages of the ICS can be lost when organizations develop their own unique and relatively complex versions of the ICS; it works best when it remains simple, flexible and standardized so everyone on scene from all organizations understands it.

In its basic form a person is designated as the IC to handle overall co-ordination, including setting objectives and priorities.

Support functions (sections supported by one or more persons) can be established as needed and on the scale needed to keep the IC informed and assist in certain areas.

The four support sections in the ICS organization are as follows:

- **operations section:** helps manage resources to carry out the operations;

- **planning section:** helps develop action plans, collect and evaluate information, maintain resource status and arrange to scale up or scale down activities;

- **logistics section:** helps provide resources and services needed to support the incident response, including personnel, transportation, supplies, facilities and equipment; and

- **finance-administration section:** assists with monitoring costs, providing accounting and procurements, keeping time records, doing cost analysis and other administrative matters.

Other additions to directly assist the IC might include:

–   an **information officer:** assists the media and others seeking incident information, ensures the IC has appropriate information available, and helps to provide information to the public and families of persons in distress;

–   a **safety officer:** monitors safety conditions and develops measures to ensure safety and reduce risks; and

–   **liaison officers:** serve as primary contacts for on-scene representatives of their respective organizations.

The following figure illustrates the basic ICS organization:

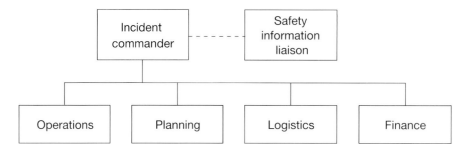

Figure C-1 – *Incident Command System Organization*

The IC usually establishes an **incident command post (ICP)** as a base for ICS activities. For particularly demanding incidents, the ICS organization can be expanded. For example, for operations that are particularly large-scale, sustained or complex, the IC can be augmented by establishment of an actual or virtual (i.e. without everyone co-located) **unified command (UC)** populated by operational managers representing the primary response organizations involved. If the UC is made up of linked independent command posts, a Government post and an industry post for example, ideally there should still be a person from each command post assigned to work at the other post(s) involved.

For a situation like a major passenger aircraft or ship disaster, a **joint information centre (JIC)** should be established, perhaps in association with the Information Officer position, to facilitate and co-ordinate the vast amount of information that will need to be managed internally and shared with the public.

Whether the ICS should be used depends on the duration and complexity of the incident. If it is used, co-ordination of SAR functions with other functions is usually achieved by assigning a representative of the SAR agency or of the SMC to the Operations Section of the ICS organization.

This allows SAR services to be plugged into the ICS and overall operations while still being able to function with relative independence in accordance with normal SAR procedures. The ICS has an overall incident focus, while SAR services must remain focused on lifesaving.

A determination should be made as early as possible regarding the person responsible for overall co-ordination, and how the overall response will be organized and managed. Procedures should be understood by all and overall response managed to ensure mutual support, effort prioritization, and optimal use of available resources, and to enhance on-scene safety and effectiveness.

Inter-agency contingency planning should identify who the IC should be for various scenarios. Typically, the IC will be assigned from the Government organization with primary responsibility for the type of function most prominent in the response to the particular incident. However, with appropriate access to experts and information from all agencies concerned, a key consideration in selecting the IC should be familiarity and experience with the IC function, i.e., the IC should be a person who can best handle the responsibility.

The IC should be someone skilled at managing on-scene operations and should usually be located at or near the scene. Everyone involved, regardless of rank or status, will normally be in a support role for the IC, similar to the SMC support structure within an RCC.

The IC function can be transferred as the situation warrants, although such transfers should be minimized as is the case for transfers of SMC functions during a mission. It is important to designate an IC early, in contingency plans if possible, and to make a transfer later, as appropriate, as delay in designating an IC can be quite detrimental.

Except when functions other than SAR are relatively insignificant to the incident response, the IC should normally be someone other than the SMC. The priority mission will always be lifesaving, and the SMC should normally remain unencumbered by additional non-SAR duties.

Similarly, the IC's command post should normally be at a location other than in the RCC, because the RCC needs to remain focused on, and be vigilant and responsive to, its normal SAR responsibilities in addition to handling SAR aspects of the major incident.

MRO communications in a maritime incident

Efficient communications in major maritime response incidents are best arranged by dividing communications between several different frequencies. The number of frequencies used may vary, depending on the circumstances, but is unlikely to exceed five. The diagram below shows a major incident with numerous surface and air units responding and several different activities taking place on scene and, in support, ashore. The communications plan set up to deal with this incident is relatively simple so that all those responding may readily understand it. It needs to be established from the outset which frequency could include relations to the media (refer to Contact with the media in section 2 of the IAMSAR Manual, volume III).

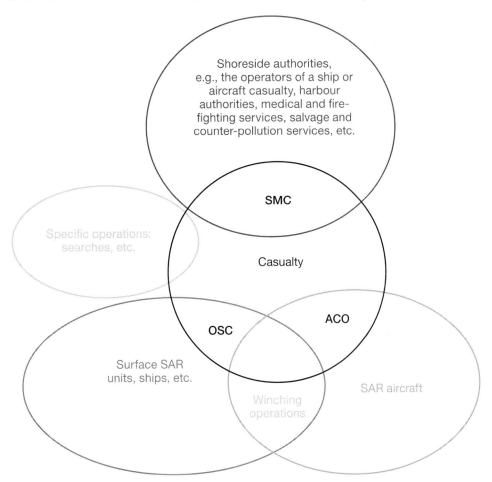

Figure C-2 – *Concept of a communications plan for a major incident*

1   The primary co-ordinating frequency – initially VHF FM channel 16 but a common working frequency may be assigned to ensure channel 16 is available for other distress alerts – is used by the casualty, the OSC, the ACO (if designated) and, if possible, the SMC. If the incident is out of the SMC's VHF range, the SMC will communicate primarily with the OSC by satellite or MF or HF radio communications. Other units on scene should monitor the primary co-ordinating frequency if possible, to be kept up to date by SITREPs, etc., but will not usually transmit on it.

2   Surface SAR units and other surface units such as ships responding to the distress alert will use a second frequency – usually VHF FM channel 6 – controlled by the OSC.

3   Aircraft may also use this second frequency under the OSC's control, if suitably equipped. An ACO should be designated if responding aircraft are not equipped with marine VHF or in cases where it would be more efficient to control them separately (such as multiple aircraft on scene). The aircraft will then use a third frequency – usually VHF AM 123.1MHz – controlled by the ACO.

4   If other activities are taking place on scene, additional frequencies may be used for the necessary communications. If a helicopter, for example, needs to winch to or from a ship, these two units should switch to a mutually compatible frequency not already in use, returning to the main working frequencies after the winching operation is complete. Another example would be a search being conducted as part of the overall SAR operation. In this case, the units assigned to the search will switch to a mutually compatible frequency controlled by a search co-ordinator. This co-ordinating unit reports to OSC or RCC, as appropriate.

5   In a major incident, such as an MRO, there will need to be significant exchange of information with authorities ashore: the operators of a ship or aircraft casualty, harbour and other receiving authorities, shoreside emergency services providing support, authorities and agencies concerned with counter-pollution and salvage operations, and so on. These many organizations should communicate via the RCC, not directly with units on scene. This enables the SMC to maintain a clear overall picture of the response. Efficient procedures for this aspect of the communications plan can and should be pre-planned. The exchange of liaison officers is recommended.

Appendix D

Uncertainty phase data

Uncertainty phase checklist

1   Designate SMC.

2   Verify departure and non-arrival.

3   Assist ATS units with communications search (aircraft).

4   Conduct communications search (vessel).

5   Include information requests in scheduled broadcasts.

6   Co-ordinate news releases to media.

7   Issue appropriate notices.

8   If located and safe:

    (a)   Close case.

    (b)   Cancel broadcasts and notices.

    (c)   Send required reports.

    (d)   Notify all concerned.

9   If not located by a preliminary communications search, execute an extended communications search, consider advancing to the alert phase.

10   Start completing Incident Processing Form.

Communications searches

Communications search for marine craft

1   All SAR facilities in the area should check radio log and records for any information.

2   Checks that give a thorough and rapid coverage of the area should be made, such as:

   (a)   Bridge and lock tenders.

   (b)   Local harbour patrols.

   (c)   Marinas, yacht clubs, and other waterside facilities.

   (d)   Dockmasters.

   (e)   Harbour masters.

   (f)   Local police (for boat launching ramps).

3   If the missing craft is known to have a radio aboard, SAR units should attempt contact. Marine operators in the search areas should be asked to check their logs for traffic to or from the craft. Public correspondence marine operators (MAROP) should be asked to attempt at least one contact.

4   If the departure point of the craft is in the search area, the actual departure and time should be confirmed. The craft's non-arrival should be confirmed and a request made that the nearest SAR facility be notified immediately if it does arrive. These actions should be stated in the SITREP reporting the communications search results to the SMC.

5   Each facility need be contacted only once during the search.

6   A report by SITREP to the SMC should be sent when the communications search is completed.

7   When a vessel is overdue from a long sea voyage, SAR authorities in other States may be requested to assist through their RCCs or through naval or other military channels.

If this search proves unsuccessful, further steps to be taken include:

1   During an extended communications search, facilities checked during first search should normally be rechecked at least every 24 h, and preferably every 8 to 12 h.

2.   Additional facilities to be contacted during an extended search usually are left to the discretion of the unit conducting the communications search. However, a listing of these facilities should be provided to the RCC. An extended search should provide a thorough coverage of the area. Facilities and sources of information may include:

   (a)   Bridge and lock tenders.

   (b)   Vessel/boat agents.

   (c)   Local, county, and State police.

   (d)   Police harbour patrols.

   (e)   Harbour masters, port authorities.

   (f)   Marinas, docks, yacht clubs.

   (g)   Fish companies, fisherman associations.

   (h)   Park service, forest rangers.

   (i)   Fuel suppliers.

   (j)   Ice houses.

    (k)   Ship chandlers, repair yards.

    (l)   Customs, immigration (if applicable).

    (m) Major tug companies (in large ports and rivers).

    (n)   Relatives and neighbours.

3   All facilities and persons contacted during this phase should be asked to maintain a look-out for the search object during the course of their normal operations and to notify the nearest SAR unit if it is sighted. A definite time limit should be set so it will not be necessary to re-contact these numerous sources to de-alert them after the vessel or boat has been located. If information is still desired after this period, another extended communications search should be started.

4   If the missing craft is radio equipped, stations conducting the communications search should attempt contact every four hours for 24 h. If it is known that the vessel has the appropriate frequencies, the marine operator should be asked to call the vessel on the same schedule, and to watch for any pertinent information received from other marine craft.

5   Local press, radio, and television coverage should be made during this phase for further dissemination of, and solicitation for, information on the missing craft.

6   Since numerous facilities must be checked during the search, it is not likely to be completed in a matter of hours, particularly if directed at night or on a weekend. It may be necessary to wait for normal working hours to contact many sources. A listing must be maintained of the facilities contacted that will have to be rechecked. This will ensure a thorough search.

7   SAR facilities conducting an extended search should submit a SITREP as specified by the RCC. The SITREP should indicate the approximate percentage of the communications search completed.

8   A communications search is only as effective as the people making it. Because of this human factor, the SMC should monitor the search as necessary to ensure that it is being conducted effectively.

Communications search for aircraft

1   Contact destination and alternate airports to confirm that aircraft has not arrived. Request physical ramp checks at all uncontrolled airports.

2   Contact departure airport to confirm actual departure, and non-return. Verify flight plan data, weather briefing received, and any other available facts.

3   Request aircraft along or near route to attempt radio contact.

4   Alert airfields, aeronautical radio stations, aeronautical aids to navigation stations, and radar and DF stations within areas through which the aircraft may have flown.

If these attempts are unsuccessful, further measures include:

1   Contact all airfields, aircraft carriers, and other ships as appropriate, aeronautical radio stations, operating agency's radio stations, aeronautical aids to navigation stations, radar and DF stations within 80 km (50 miles) of route and not checked during previous search.

2   Contact the other airfields in the general area where it is reasonably possible that aircraft may have landed.

3   Request aircraft along or near the intended route of flight to attempt contact and monitor appropriate frequencies for possible distress signals.

4   Contact other agencies, facilities, or persons capable of providing additional verifying information.

Man overboard (MOB) checklist

1   Date/time of present position.

2   Craft's course/speed and destination.

3   Date/time of man overboard position.

4   Initial reporting source (parent agency, radio station, name/call sign of craft).

5   Estimated water temperature.

6   Person's name, age, sex.

7   Person's physical condition and swimming capability.

8   Person's clothing amount and colour, including life preserver.

9   Area searched and pattern used by craft on scene.

10   Intentions of craft on scene.

11   Assistance being received.

12   Other pertinent information.

Weather information

1   Visibility and any obscuration such as fog, smoke, or haze, and the time of any recent changes.

2   Water or snow surface conditions such as sea state.

3   Wind direction and velocity, and recent changes.

4   Cloud cover, ceiling, etc., and recent changes.

5   Temperature of air and water.

6   Barometric reading.

7   Whether rain or snow is falling or has fallen, and the time it began and ended.

8   Whether severe weather such as thunderstorms, snow, hail, ice pellets, or freezing rain are occurring or have occurred, and at what times it began or ended.

MEDICO or MEDEVAC checklist

1   Initial reporting source (parent agency, radio station, name/call sign if craft, name/telephone or address if person).

2   Patient name, nationality, age, sex, race.

3   Patient symptoms.

4   Medication given.

5   Standard medicine chest or other medication available.

6   Radio frequencies in use, monitored, or scheduled.

7   Craft description.

8   Vessel's local agent.

9   Craft's last port of call, destination, ETA.

10   Assistance desired, or as recommended by a telemedical assistance service. **Note:** If required, refer to TMAS – TMAS Medical Information Exchange Form. See appendix R.

11   Assistance being received.

12   Other pertinent information.

Lost person checklist

1   Initial reporting source (name/telephone or address).

2   Name of missing person.

3   Location and date/time last seen.

4   Known intentions or possible actions of missing person.

5   Age and physical description of missing person.

6   Clothing, footgear and equipment.

7   Physical and mental condition.

8   Knowledge of area.

9   Outdoor experience.

10   Weather conditions (see Weather information on D-5).

11   Action being taken.

12   Assistance desired, if not obvious.

13   Date/time of initial report.

14   Nearest relative (name/telephone or address).

15   Other pertinent information.

Appendix E

Alert phase data

Alert phase checklist

Note: Ensure uncertainty phase checklist items are considered.

1 Designate SMC if not already done.

2 Issue urgent broadcasts to obtain assistance.

3 Obtain information on positions of ships at sea and request assistance as necessary (see paragraph G.3.2).

4 Dispatch SRU(s) to provide assistance.

5 Alert DF nets.

6 Request ATS unit to obtain assistance from *en-route* aircraft.

7 If disabled unit regains normal operations, monitor until assured of safety.

8 When unit is in no danger, cancel broadcasts and notify all concerned.

9 Close case when assistance has been completed.

10 If situation deteriorates and a unit or person is in grave and imminent danger, advance to distress phase.

Overdue checklists

Overdue aircraft

1   Alert SRU(s).

2   Request ATS units to attempt contact.

3   Review any flight plans filed.

4   Alert radar and DF nets.

5   Have ATS units alert *en-route* aircraft.

6   Alert other agencies.

7   Alert adjacent RCCs or other SAR authorities.

8   Start search planning.

9   Dispatch SRU for initial search.

10   Designate SMC.

11   Use (as appropriate):

    (a)   NOTAMs.

    (b)   News media broadcasts.

12   If located:

    (a)   Close case.

    (b)   Cancel broadcast and notices.

    (c)   Notify all concerned.

13   When situation deteriorates and a unit or person is considered to be in grave and imminent danger, advance to distress phase.

Overdue vessel

1   Alert SRU(s).

2   If submersible, request Navy or other special assistance.

3   Complete preliminary communications search and carry out extended communications search.

4   Alert other agencies.

5   Alert adjacent RCCs or other SAR authorities.

6   Start search planning.

7   Dispatch SRU for initial search.

8   Designate SMC.

9   Use (as appropriate):

    (a)   Urgent broadcasts.

    (b)   Hydros.

    (c)   Notices to Mariners.

(d)   News media broadcasts.

10   If located:

   (a)   Close case.

   (b)   Cancel broadcasts and notices.

   (c)   Notify all concerned.

11   If not located by completion of extended communications search, advance to distress phase.

12   When situation deteriorates and a unit or person is considered to be in grave and imminent danger, advance to distress phase.

Unlawful interference

1   Alert other agencies, such as appropriate law-enforcement and aviation authorities.

2   Alert SRU(s).

3   Alert adjacent RCCs or other SAR authorities.

4   Alert radar and DF nets.

5   Dispatch SRU as requested by other agencies.

6   When it is probable that the aircraft is about to make a forced landing or ditch, or has done so, advance to distress phase.

Appendix F

Distress phase checklist

Note: Ensure uncertainty and alert phase checklists items are considered.

1   Designate SMC if not already done.

2   Notify adjacent RCCs or RSCs or other SAR authorities.

3   Dispatch SRUs if distress location is known.

4   If submersible or underwater habitat, request Navy or other special assistance.

5   Dispatch any specialized units needed.

6   Develop initial search action plan.

7   Provide SRUs with mission information.

8   Designate OSC.

9   Consider use of multiple OSCs.

         (a)   Air OSC.

         (b)   Surface OSC.

         (c)   Geographical OSC.

10   Assign on-scene frequencies.

11   Consider the use of datum marker buoys.

12   Ensure briefing of search crews.

13   Pass instructions to OSC.

14   Request other available agencies provide assistance.

15   Query radar and direction-finding stations.

16   Issue distress broadcasts.

17   Request news media to include urgent requests for information.

18   Determine merchant vessel location, if appropriate. (See ship reporting discussion in paragraph G.3.2.)

19   Have ATS unit alert *en-route* aircraft.

20   Maintain communications link with distressed craft.

21   Inform distressed unit of action taken.

22   Send request for assistance to specific vessels.

23   Begin planning for extended search efforts.

24   Use computer-assisted search planning tools, if available.

25   Establish contact and maintain liaison with distressed craft's operating agency.

26   Notify authorities of country of registry of distressed craft.

27   Notify accident investigation authorities.

28   Maintain records and charts of search activities and estimates of search effectiveness.

29   Send required reports.

30   Ensure debriefing of SAR crews.

31   If search is successful and rescue effected, cancel broadcasts and close case.

32   If search is unsuccessful:

   (a)   Continue operations until all reasonable effort has been made.

   (b)   Obtain management concurrence to suspend search.

33   Notify all concerned of actions taken.

34   Send required final reports.

Appendix G

Facilities and equipment selection

Selection of SAR facilities

G.1 General

G.1.1 There are three broad categories of SAR facilities: aeronautical, maritime, and land. All three will be needed in most parts of the world, but local conditions determine their selection. Facilities selected by a SAR service need to be able to reach the scene of distress quickly and be suitable for the following types of operations:

– providing assistance, e.g., escorting an aircraft or providing guidance on ditching, standing by a ship sinking or on fire;

– conducting a search;

– delivering supplies and survival equipment; and

– rescuing survivors and delivering them to a place of safety and proper medical care.

G.1.2 The range and speed of available search facilities should be considered when the search area is far from their home bases. They should be redeployed to an advance base closer to the scene so that more time will be available for the search and less time will be spent on transits to and from the search area.

G.1.3 The number, placement, and training level of look-outs, their height above the ground or sea, fatigue, and the speed of the search craft are important factors affecting the probability of detection (POD) and probability of success (POS). Altitude is factored into sweep width determinations but the other factors, though important, usually are not included in order to keep the sweep width tables from becoming much larger and more complicated. Search aircraft speed is especially important; slow aircraft flying at low altitudes generally have a significantly better chance of locating search objects visually. Look-out fatigue also can be an important factor, especially for long searches in rough weather.

G.2 Air facilities

G.2.1 Sources of aircraft suitable for SAR include:

– Government department responsible for civil aviation;

– other Government or semi-government departments (e.g., police, fire services);

– military services; and

– commercial or private aircraft operators.

G.2.2 The following abbreviations may be used for aeronautical SAR facilities.

Category	Abbreviation
Short-range (radius of action of 280 km (150 NM) plus $\frac{1}{2}$ hour search remaining)	SRG
Medium-range (radius of action of 740 km (400 NM) plus $2\frac{1}{2}$ hours search remaining)	MRG
Long-range (radius of action of 1,390 km (750 NM) plus $2\frac{1}{2}$ hours search remaining)	LRG
Very-long-range (radius of action of more than 1,850 km (1,000 NM) plus $2\frac{1}{2}$ hours search remaining)	VLR
Extra-long-range (radius of action of 2,780 km (1,500 NM) or more, plus $2\frac{1}{2}$ hours search remaining)	ELR

Helicopters	Abbreviation
Light helicopter (radius of action, for rescue purposes, up to 185 km (100 NM) and capacity for evacuating one to five persons)	HEL-L
Medium helicopter (radius of action, for rescue purposes, 185 to 370 km (100 to 200 NM) and capacity for evacuating six to 15 persons)	HEL-M
Heavy helicopter (radius of action, for rescue purposes, more than 370 km (200 NM) and capacity for evacuating more than 15 persons)	HEL-H

Note: The categories light, medium, and heavy refer to the load-carrying capabilities. Some military helicopters may have an air refuelling capability which extends their range. Hoist capability may also be included.

G.2.3   Aircraft are particularly suitable for any of the following functions in SAR tasks:

Search   Aircraft are the most efficient search units because they can reach distant areas quickly and cover a large area within a given time. Fixed-wing aircraft normally fly at higher speeds than helicopters and can therefore be used in larger areas and at greater range. Helicopters are excellent search aircraft, but their normally limited endurance and speed reduce the area they can search effectively. *En-route* aircraft may be able to give valuable assistance in locating survivors. They may be asked to keep a look-out or listening watch for signals from survival beacons or other signalling devices, to report positions where they were first detected and, if possible, the position of greatest detected signal strength. Vessels and aircraft fitted with direction-finding (DF) equipment should be requested to report their own position and the DF bearing of the signals.

Support   Aircraft may be used for delivering supplies, survival equipment, and SAR and medical personnel at the distress scene, guiding other units on scene, and relaying communications.

Rescue   Helicopters are a prime means for recovering survivors from a distress scene.

G.2.4   Many types of aircraft will be suitable for these tasks with little or no modification. However, even in an emergency, flight safety is the primary consideration. The SMC should be familiar with normal operational and technical limitations of an aircraft and crew. For instance, an aircraft without adequate instrumentation or a pilot without an instrument rating should not undertake flights under instrument meteorological conditions.

G.2.5   SAR planners must consider the trade-off between aircraft speed and visual search effectiveness. Generally, the slower an aircraft flies, the better it is for conducting a visual search; small and partially hidden search objects are easily missed at higher speeds. The faster the aircraft flies, the greater the area that can be covered. For fixed-wing aircraft, the maximum search speed should be no greater than 275 km/h (150 kts) unless the search object is very large. Normally, the slower the aircraft the lower the search height should be, to a minimum of 150 m (500 ft). Lower search heights should be at pilot discretion. Faster aircraft may have operational limitations making them unsuitable for low-level flight. Nevertheless, fast or high-flying aircraft can play an important part in search operations, by carrying out:

–   radio searches to home on distress signals transmitted from downed aircraft, vessels in distress, and ELTs and EPIRBs;

–   exploratory sweeps of a large area, simultaneously with searches by slower aircraft flying at lower levels. This method is particularly effective over the sea or other flat and unobstructed areas; and

–   radio communication relays over areas of poor radio reception or beyond the range of coastal radio stations.

G.2.6 The suitability and efficiency of an aircraft for search, support, and rescue operations will depend on the following features:

- – operational characteristics:
  - – safe, low speed and low-level flight capability;
  - – short landing and take-off;
  - – sufficient range to cover the area, with due regard to the location of redeployment bases;
  - – good manoeuvrability, especially for searches in mountainous areas; and
  - – substantial payload capacity;
- – equipment:
  - – suitable navigation and instrument flying aids;
  - – radio equipment capable of receiving and homing on emergency radio signals; and
  - – adequate communications equipment for SAR purposes;
- – availability of good observation posts, including some rear-looking;
- – sensors for aiding in search object detection;
- – suitability for the delivery of supplies, emergency equipment, and personnel;
- – air refuelling capability; and
- – facilities for treatment and berthing of survivors.

G.2.7 Land-based fixed-wing aircraft can search and carry droppable supplies or parachute rescue personnel. Large aircraft must normally operate from prepared surfaces but many small aircraft can operate from grass strips or frozen lakes or rivers. Where suitable landing grounds are near the distress scene, the landplane can accelerate the evacuation of survivors rescued by other means.

G.2.8 The seaplane is as useful as the landplane for carrying droppable supplies and personnel. Its use as a rescue plane or carrier of non-droppable supplies and personnel is generally limited to operations in lakes, rivers, sheltered waters, and bays. Under favourable weather and sea conditions, suitable seaplanes could carry out rescue operations in protected waters, e.g., large lakes, but those on open water or at sea should be restricted to large seaplanes designed for rough-water work.

G.2.9 The amphibian combines the advantages of both landplane and seaplane. However, the weight penalty for carrying both a rugged hull and landing wheels reduces its range and restricts its water-landing and take-off performance and its manoeuvrability on water.

G.2.10 Helicopters are the most versatile SAR aircraft because:

- – their slow speed and ability to hover make them suitable for search as well as rescue operations, particularly where small search objects are sought or close scrutiny of terrain or sea is required; and
- – their ability to land in a confined area and to operate from vessels enable them to rescue survivors from inaccessible places and rough seas long before surface units can arrive.

Helicopters should be equipped with rescue equipment for the evacuation of survivors, e.g., winching equipment, slings, baskets.

G.2.11 Small helicopters sometimes are only equipped for flight under visual meteorological conditions or, in some cases, during daylight. SAR helicopters should normally be instrumented for flight in instrument meteorological conditions and at night. Turbulence, gusty winds, or icing conditions may limit helicopter use.

G.2.12 Providing a fixed-wing escort, also known as top cover, would improve safety and communications and may reduce SAR incident time for the helicopter. Top cover should be considered for a helicopter when it is operating in conditions such as at night, in remote areas, in extreme weather, or off the coast near its range limits.

G.2.13 Due to the potential hazard of collision and the noise problem associated with helicopters operating in a confined space during rescue operations, it is essential that their operations be co-ordinated by the unit best suited for this function. This may be the RCC, OSC, or one of the helicopters or a fixed-wing aircraft. This unit should provide operating areas and altitudes for the helicopters and be responsive to the requirements of surface rescue units whose operations may be hampered by helicopter noise and rotor wash.

G.2.14 Carrier-based aircraft can give the SAR system great flexibility because they have a well-equipped and mobile base. Furthermore, the aircraft carrier is well equipped to carry out rescue operations and to receive and care for survivors.

G.2.15 Equipment for aircraft participating in SAR operations includes:

– *Navigation equipment.* Accurate navigation is essential for maximizing the probability of success in search operations and for determining the exact position of survivors or wreckage. Since long- and medium-range aircraft may need to search far from their bases over isolated or ocean areas, extensive navigation equipment is essential. Precise navigation equipment such as the Global Positioning System (GPS) or GLONASS can be helpful in covering a search area carefully or locating a datum, especially when operating over terrain or water with few navigation references. Short-range aircraft normally will not require extensive navigation equipment if used to search areas familiar to the pilot close to their bases. Aircraft tasked for SAR operations should be equipped to receive and home on radio signals, emergency locator transmitters (ELTs), emergency position-indicating radio beacons (EPIRBs), and if practical, SAR radar transponders (SARTs).

– *Communications equipment.* All aircraft should be equipped to maintain good communications with their RCC and RSC (either directly or indirectly) and other SAR facilities. SAR aircraft, particularly those engaged in oceanic searches, should be equipped to communicate with vessels or survival craft. They also should be able to communicate with survivors on VHF-FM channel 16 (156.8 MHz) and VHF-AM on 121.5 MHz and 123.1 MHz. SAR co-ordinators should consider the possible need for communications between aircraft and surface units within their SAR Regions, and ensure that this need can be met even for aircraft that cannot communicate directly on maritime frequencies. Typically, the RCC should be able to provide a communication link between the aircraft and surface units directly or by making other arrangements. SAR and government vessels should be encouraged to fit equipment to be able to communicate directly on aeronautical frequencies. Passenger ships subject to the SOLAS Convention are required to have this capability.

– *Auxiliary fuel tanks.* Where practicable, auxiliary fuel tanks should be available for SAR aircraft, to be readily fitted when increased range or endurance would benefit operations.

– *Miscellaneous.* The following equipment, not normally carried by aircraft, should be readily available for SAR operations:
  – binoculars;
  – a copy of the *International Code of Signals*;
  – signalling equipment, e.g., lamps, mounted loudspeakers, pyrotechnics;
  – buoyant VHF/UHF marker beacons, floating lights, smoke floats, dye markers, etc., to mark position of survivors;
  – air-deployable supplies and equipment for survivors;
  – fire-fighting equipment;
  – cameras for photographing wreckage and the location of survivors;
  – first-aid supplies, including resuscitation equipment for immediate use;
  – loudhailers and containers for dropping written messages;
  – portable dewatering pumps and bailers;
  – inflatable liferafts; and
  – lifejackets and lifebuoys.

G.3 Maritime facilities

G.3.1 Vessels suitable for oceanic SAR operations can be provided by:

– Government departments responsible for merchant and fishing vessel safety;

– military services;

– lifesaving institutions;

– commercial shipping companies, and

– other public and private authorities, operators and owners of small vessels, e.g., police, customs and port authorities, fishing fleet and tugboat operators, pleasure boat owners, and oil companies with off-shore installations.

G.3.2 Knowing the positions of merchant ships is often of considerable value in SAR operations. They are frequently the closest available means of search or rescue in a SAR incident on or over the high seas. It is very important that RCCs fully use Inmarsat, GMDSS, CRS, VTS, and other means of communication described in chapter 2 of this volume to contact vessels in or near the search area to determine their locations and capabilities. Another, often faster and more efficient, means to obtain this information is via merchant vessel ship reporting systems. One such system is the Automated Mutual-assistance Vessel Rescue System (Amver).

Note: Amver is a global, voluntary merchant vessel reporting system open to ships of all flags. It is operated by the U.S. Coast Guard as a humanitarian service to promote safety of life at sea. By U.S. law and international agreement, Amver information may be used only for search and rescue purposes. Amver information is made available to any RCC in the world for use in responding to a search and rescue incident. Amver information may be obtained by contacting any U.S. Coast Guard RCC. Amver may be used to determine positions, courses, speeds, and capabilities (including medical) of participating vessels within a specified radius about a point, within an area, or within some distance of a track line. Given a missing vessel's international radio call sign, Amver can provide the vessel's intended track, projected position, and date and time of its last Amver report if it is an Amver participant.

G.3.3 The International Convention for the Safety of Life at Sea contains an obligatory provision for the master of a vessel to proceed with all speed to the assistance of persons in distress at sea. However, the master of a vessel is wholly responsible for the safety of his/her ship and therefore should be requested (not directed) to undertake a specific action. The SMC should ensure that all pertinent information is given to any masters who are requested to divert their vessels to the scene of a distress.

G.3.4 The following abbreviations may be used for maritime SAR facilities.

Category	Abbreviation
Rescue boat – short-range coastal and/or river craft	RB
Rescue vessel – long-range seagoing craft	RV

Note: The boat and vessel speed in knots should be inserted, e.g., RB(14) or RV(10).

G.3.5 Vessels are usually suitable for both search and rescue operations at sea, particularly those which have adequate speed, range, and seagoing qualities. The type of vessel assigned to an incident will depend upon the location of the distress scene, the number of survivors, the weather conditions, the speed, range and seagoing qualities required, and availability. Rescue vessels can sustain operations far from base. Warships, offshore lifeboats, seagoing tugs, customs and pilot launches, and patrol boats, are most suitable on account of their special equipment and trained personnel. Agreements to secure the services of these vessels should be a priority.

G.3.6 Other potential SAR vessels include:

– icebreakers, which some States operate in colder climates for research purposes and to open navigation routes for other vessels;

     – merchant vessels; their importance as a SAR facility is improved if they participate in a vessel reporting system; and

     – offshore oil rig supply vessels, fishing vessels, private yachts, and launches.

G.3.7 Rescue boats are short-range vessels, e.g., lifeboats, patrol boats and crash boats, which are capable of operating to a limited distance offshore. Pleasure craft, yachts, and inflatable boats fitted with an outboard engine also can be used for SAR, provided they carry appropriate equipment (see G.3.9).

G.3.8 Enough rescue boats should be available in areas with large numbers of pleasure craft and at aerodromes where the take-off or approach paths are over water so that they may go immediately to the scene of an accident. If boats of the type mentioned above are not available for rescue work from local owners or operators and owners, or if the area is distant from harbour or lifeboat station, special rescue boats may have to be provided. Other vessels which could serve as rescue boats include:

     – hydrofoils, capable of speeds in the range of 55 to 150 km/h (30 to 80 kts). They are best used in coastal or semi-sheltered water when fast response is desired; and

     – hovercraft, which have a similar speed range to hydrofoils. Their amphibious capability and high speed make them ideal for rescue in ice-covered areas, swamps, and shallow or flat coastal areas. Most can maintain a hover one to two metres off the surface and are unaffected by moderate seas, floating debris, or small obstructions.

G.3.9 Equipment for vessels participating in SAR operations includes:

     – *Navigation equipment.* Although larger vessels generally carry adequate navigation equipment, small craft may not. Owners of such craft assigned to SAR should be encouraged to install lightweight, easy-to-operate navigation equipment to enable them to reach a rendezvous or to carry out a given search pattern accurately, without visual reference points.

     – *Communications.* The communications requirements for SAR vessels are generally the same as those for SAR aircraft. Good direct or indirect communications with the RCC, RSC, and other SAR units are essential. All SAR units must have radio communications to guard and communicate on the international distress frequency being used by the ship or other craft in distress. Radio equipment should be capable of operating on MF/HF and VHF/UHF to communicate with the RCC and rescue units. SAR co-ordinators should consider the possible need for communications between aircraft and surface units within their SAR Regions, and ensure that this need can be met even for aircraft that cannot communicate directly on maritime frequencies. Typically, the RCC should be able to provide a communication link between the aircraft and surface units with their own equipment or by making other arrangements. SAR and government vessels should be encouraged to fit equipment to be able to communicate directly on aeronautical frequencies. Passenger ships subject to the SOLAS Convention are required to have this capability. Chapter 2 discusses selection of radio frequencies.

     – *Miscellaneous equipment.* The equipment listed in G.2.12 and the following equipment should be carried aboard maritime SAR units. For smaller vessels or those which only operate inshore this may not be practical, in which case the equipment should be readily available ashore. This equipment includes:

          – lifesaving and rescue equipment:

               – lifeboat with oars;

               – line-throwing apparatus, buoyant lifelines, and hauling lines;

               – non-sparking boat-hooks or grappling hooks and hatchets; and

               – rescue baskets, litters, boarding ladders, and/or scrambling nets;

          – signalling equipment:

               – lamps, searchlights, and torches (flashlights);

               – buoyant VHF/UHF marker beacons, floating lights, smoke generators, flame and smoke floats, dye markers; and

          – exposure suits for the crew.

G.4   Coastal facilities

G.4.1   Personnel and equipment for coastal SAR operations can be drawn from several sources:

–   military and coastguard services;

–   lifesaving institutions; and

–   police, fire departments, and other local authorities.

G.4.2   Facilities provided vary according to local prevailing conditions. They include:

–   shelter huts equipped with emergency rations, means of communication, etc.;

–   SAR teams provided with cliff rescue, breeches buoys, and similar equipment;

–   first aid and medical teams; and

–   accommodations for survivors.

G.5   Land facilities

G.5.1   Sources of personnel and equipment for land SAR operations include:

–   military services (trained personnel, equipped and mobile);

–   police or fire departments (trained and equipped to search for, rescue, and transport missing and injured persons);

–   public or commercial enterprises operating in the field or in remote areas and employing people and equipment capable of providing SAR assistance, e.g.,

–   forestry departments;

–   transportation departments;

–   railway, telephone, telegraph, and hydro-electric companies;

–   disaster-response organizations;

–   engineering and road-building enterprises; and

–   health departments (medical stations);

–   sports clubs and similar organizations specializing in activities useful to SAR, e.g., parachute jumping, diving, scouting, hiking, mountain climbing, cave spelunking, skiing, or potholing; and

–   specialized international teams, e.g., search dogs and collapsed structure task forces.

G.5.2   Land facilities, unlike air and marine facilities, are difficult to classify. However, abbreviations for five specialist facilities, parachute rescue unit (PRU), mountain rescue unit (MRU), urban search and rescue (USAR), cave rescue unit (CRU), and desert rescue unit (DRU), may be used. USAR teams specialize in rescue of survivors from collapsed structures.

G.5.3   Search by land facilities alone is usually impractical for large areas but they can be used in most weather conditions and can provide complete coverage of the area searched. They are mainly used when a confined area cannot be thoroughly searched from the air, and in operations where the search is carried out by aircraft and the rescue is performed by land facilities.

G.5.4   Land rescue facilities need highly mobile vehicles in order to reach an accident site quickly and initiate rescue action. For road transport, the land facility will normally use vehicles at its disposal, such as ambulances, four-wheel-drive vehicles, trucks, buses, or cars belonging to its members. Military units can usually provide rough-terrain vehicles, such as high traction vehicles and troop-carriers. In areas where motor transport is unsuitable, transport by horses, mules, dog-sleds, canoe, boats, or on foot may be required.

G.5.5 Equipment for land facilities includes:

– *Navigation equipment.* The navigation equipment needed by land facilities need not be elaborate, but at least the following should be carried by each member or team:

  – large-scale maps (1:50000 or 1:100000);

  – reliable magnetic compass and watch; and

  – a protractor and a pair of dividers.

– DF equipment for radio signals, listening devices for collapsed structures, and GPS equipment for three-dimensional positioning can be useful.

– *Communications.* Each land facility should be able to communicate with the RCC, either directly or through its base camp. In combined air/surface operations the land facility must be able to communicate with the SAR aircraft. Portable lightweight radio equipment is available for this purpose. The selection of appropriate radio frequencies for the different communications functions is dealt with in chapter 2.

– *Personal equipment.* Each member of a land SAR facility should be properly clothed and equipped for the mission. This may include rations for two or three days to reduce the need for air-drops, and sufficient personal medical supplies. If not part of the permanent equipment carried by the land facility, the following should be readily available:

  – binoculars;

  – signalling equipment, e.g., loudhailers, pyrotechnics, whistles;

  – non-sparking tools;

  – cameras;

  – supplies and survival equipment as required;

  – portable lights operated from vehicle batteries and flashlights and spare batteries to be carried by each team member; and

  – fire-fighting equipment.

G.5.6 Proper equipment is particularly important for those facilities which require additional gear for specialist work, such as:

– special equipment for a PRU, in addition to parachutes, will vary according to the nature of the terrain in which it will operate, i.e.,

  – crash helmets fitted with protective visor;

  – protective suits of tough material;

  – stout boots; and

  – ropes or other devices for climbing down from trees;

– special equipment for an MRU will include mountain-climbing gear such as ropes, slings, ice axes, and crampons;

– special equipment for USAR teams will include dogs and electronic locating equipment, equipment suitable for cutting and removing various types of structural material and debris;

– special equipment for CRUs includes climbing equipment, lights, litters, and helmets; and

– special equipment for a DRU will include:

  – sunshades and extra drinking water;

  – four-wheel-drive winch-fitted vehicle;

  – sand shovel; and

  – mats, boards, and other material to ensure that the vehicle does not get stuck.

Supplies and survival equipment guide

G.6 Packs of supplies and survival equipment

G.6.1 The word "pack" is used here as a collective term. A pack may consist of several parcels. The lists of supplies and survival equipment which follow are not all-inclusive but are intended to serve as a guide. The lists indicate which items should be considered for inclusion in a basic pack.

– *Rations:* subsistence pack of concentrated food or assorted containers of food, water in sealed containers or screw-top polythene containers, condensed milk, coffee, sugar, and salt. In general, provision of water to survivors should take priority over food.

– *Signalling:* portable radio transmitter/receiver, pyrotechnic signals (smoke candles and red flares), flare pistol and colour-coded signal flares, flashlight, whistle, signalling mirror, and signal code card.

– *Medical:* first-aid kit, insect repellent and head net, aspirin, sunburn lotion, and sunglasses or glare goggles.

– *Covering:* tent, sleeping bag, blanket, waterproof clothing, socks, gloves, protective foot covering, wool hat, and compact foil emergency ("space") blanket.

– *Fire and lighting:* water- and wind-proof matches, burning lens, fire kindling tablets, emergency stove, candles, and flashlight with spare batteries and bulbs.

– *Sundry:* can opener, cooking and eating utensils, fishing kit, lock-blade knife, axe, rope, compass, writing pad, pencil, soap, towelling and toilet tissues, and booklet with survival hints.

G.6.2 A sufficient number of packs should be held in stock for immediate delivery to SRUs setting out on a SAR operation. There should be enough of each item to enable survivors to subsist until rescue may be effected.

G.6.3 In areas with more severe climates the basic items will have to be supplemented. The areas for which these items are listed below do not cover the entire world, but the items may be needed in maritime areas from the polar regions to the tropics.

– *Maritime areas:*
Rations: extra fluids, desalination and water purification kits;
Signalling: dye markers, smoke floats;
Medical: sea-sickness medication; and
Sundry: fishing kit, additional liferafts, liferaft repair kit, shark repellent and lifejackets.

– *Desert areas:*
Rations: extra fluids;
Covering: wide-brimmed hat, shade sheets; and
Medical: additional sunscreen and antiseptic ointment.

– *Forest and jungle areas:*
Rations: water purification tablets;
Medical: anti-malaria tablets, antiseptic ointment, snakebite kit, adhesive plaster, insect repellent; and
Sundry: fishing kit, bush axe, and bush saw.

– *Arctic and sub-arctic areas:*
Covering: arctic tent, arctic clothing; and
Sundry: fishing kit, snow shovel, snow saw, heater and fuel.

– *Mountainous areas:*
Sundry: rope and mountain-climbing equipment.

G.6.4   Additional items that may be required include:

– *Hunting and self protection:* firearms and ammunition, knives.

– *Care of injured:* extra dressings and bandages, air mattresses, stretchers, splints, morphine, antibiotic drugs.

– *Leaving scene of accident for recovery point:* litters (for the injured), rucksacks, walking boots, snow-shoes, skis, additional signalling equipment.

– *Necessary equipment for survival in polar and subpolar areas.*

G.7   Supply colour coding and pictograms

G.7.1   Containers or packages containing survival equipment for dropping to survivors should have the general nature of their contents indicated by a colour code, printed indication (in English and two or more other languages), and self-explanatory symbols.

G.7.2   The colour identification of the contents of droppable containers and packages of survival equipment should have streamers coloured according to the following code:

RED: Medical supplies and first-aid equipment.

BLUE: Food and water.

YELLOW: Blankets and protective clothing.

BLACK: Miscellaneous equipment such as stoves, axes, compasses, and cooking utensils.

G.7.3   Bands of suitable pictograms in retro-reflective material should also be used. Pictograms are shown in figure G-1.

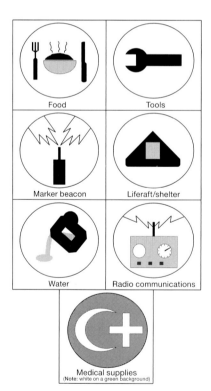

Figure G-1

Appendix H

Operation briefing and tasking forms

SAR Briefing and Debriefing Form

Briefing

SAR _____

Date _____

A/C type and number _____ Unit _____ Captain _____

Details as to nature of distress or emergency _____

Description of Search Object

(1)   Type of aircraft or vessel _____

(2)   Number or name of craft _____

(3)   Length _____ Width (wingspan) _____

(4)   Number on board _____

(5)   Full description of craft, including colour and markings _____

          _____

          _____

          _____

(6)   Frequencies of missing craft _____

          _____

Assigned search areas

Area _____

Type of search _____ Altitude/visibility _____

Time on task _____

Commence search at (position) _____ and track (N–S)(E–W) _____

Frequencies

(1) Controlling agency _____ (2) Aircraft _____

(3) Surface vessels _____ (4) Others _____

Progress reports

To be passed to _____ every _____ hours with weather report included every _____ hours.

Special Instructions:

_____

Debriefing

SAR _____ A/C No. _____

Date _____

Point of departure _____ Point of landing _____

Time off _____ On task _____ Off task _____ Landed _____

Area actually searched _____

_____

_____

Type of search _____ Altitude/visibility _____

Terrain or sea state _____ Number of observers _____

Weather conditions in search area (visibility, wind velocity, ceiling, etc.)

_____

_____

Object of search (located) at position _____

_____

Number and condition of survivors _____

_____

_____

Sightings and/or other reports _____

_____

_____

_____

Telecommunications (Note quality of communications and/or any changes other than briefed)

_____

_____

Remarks (to include any action taken on search, any problems, criticism, suggestions)

_____

_____

_____

_____

_____

_____   _____
        Date/time (local)   Captain

Abbreviated SAR Briefing and Debriefing Form

Briefing

SAR _____

Date _____

A/C type and number _____ Captain _____

Take-off time _____

Search area _____

_____

_____

Search height _____ Scanning range _____

Type of search _____

Remarks _____

_____

_____

_____

Debriefing

Area actually searched _____

_____

_____

_____

Search time _____ Transit time _____

Effectiveness of search: _____ %   Percent of area covered _____ %

Remarks _____

_____

_____

_____

SAR Briefing and Tasking Form — Marine

1   DTG

2   SAR (incident name)

3   Search object

    (a)   Type (aircraft/vessel/other – delete as necessary)

    (b)   Name _____

    (c)   Registration _____

    (d)   Tonnage _____

    (e)   Description (colour, markings, superstructure, characteristics) _____

        _____

        _____

    (f)   Owner/operator/agent _____

    (g)   POB _____

    (h)   Emergency equipment carried _____

        _____

4   Nature of distress or emergency (brief description) _____

    _____

5   Search area

    (a)   Area corner points (latitude and longitude) _____

    (b)   CSP (commence search point) _____

    (c)   Direction of creep _____

    (d)   Requested coverage factor _____

    (e)   Requested track spacing _____

    (f)   Requested search pattern _____

6   Other SAR facilities to be engaged in adjacent areas

    Aircraft/height _____

    Vessels _____

    Land parties _____

7   Frequencies and call signs to be used for communication with

    (a)   RCC/MRSC/ARSC/OSC (delete as necessary) _____

    (b)   Other search aircraft _____

    (c)   Other search vessels _____

    (d)   Land parties _____

    (e)   Ship or craft in distress/survivors _____

8   Action on sighting the search object (delete as necessary)

       Report to _____

       If unable to effect rescue, direct other vessels and/or aircraft to the scene.

       Remain on scene until relieved or forced to return or rescue has been effected.

9   Progress reports should be passed to _____

       every _____ hours.

10   Special Instructions

       _____

       _____

       _____

       _____

Sighting Report Form

Case number _____

Name of person reporting _____

Address _____

Telephone _____

Occupation _____

Description of sighting _____

_____

_____

Time of sighting _____ Local date _____

Type _____ Colour _____ Trim _____

. . . .

For aircraft

Wheels/floats/skis _____ High/low wing _____

Number of engines _____ Did engines sound normal _____

Apparent height _____ Direction _____

Turning? _____ Other aircraft sighted _____

Type _____ Description _____ Time _____

Parachutes sighted _____ Number/colour _____

Do aircraft pass regularly _____

. . . .

For vessels

Hull type _____ Superstructure _____

Engines/sails _____ Did engines sound normal _____

Location _____ Direction _____

Turning? _____ Other vessels sighted _____

Type _____ Description _____ Time _____

. . . .

Weather at time of sighting _____

Raining/snowing   _____ Thunderstorm _____

Wind/sea state _____

Remarks _____

. . . .

Date/time received _____ by _____

Received direct or relayed _____

Assessed validity of report _____

Action taken _____

SAR Mission Report – Aircraft/Vessel

SAR case identification _____

Date _____

SAR unit reporting _____

Narratives

Operations (Include narrative account of the conduct of the mission. Amplify factors that affected the mission including location of incident, any delay in responding, terrain/sea and environmental conditions, procedures used, problems encountered during incident, etc.)

Medical (Description of the patient's condition to include vitals, diagnosis and treatment given, etc. on scene and on arrival/release to other medical authority. Attach medical reports if applicable. **Note:** distribution of medical reports and any personal information should be classified)

Equipment report (Comments on the equipment used including any inadequacies, malfunctions, etc. If changes recommended, indicate what follow-up action has been taken)

Attachments (Maps, photographs, etc.)

Distribution list

SAR facilities
SMCs
SAR managers

SAR operation report

Title   (SAR case identification)

Part I   Search object details

(Equipment on board, location of incident, intended route with timings, nature of emergency, weather, etc.)

Part II   Details of SAR operation

1.   RCC action

    a.   Brief narrative of initial actions from log.

    b.   SAR facilities tasked, response times.

    c.   Basic assumptions regarding the search object.

2.   Search operation

    a.   Rationale for the search plan.

    b.   Explanation of any changes to the search plan.

    c.   Brief outline of each day's search activities including areas covered, SAR facilities used and general weather.

    d.   If search object is found, a complete explanation of how to include type of SAR facilities, the position in the facility of the sighting observer, whether the observer was trained, facility altitude and/or distance from the target, the phase of flight, time of day, search conditions, distress beacon details, etc.

    e.   If search object not found, why (in general terms).

3.   Rescue operation

    a.   Condition of survivors.

    b.   SAR facilities used.

    c.   Evacuation details.

    d.   Problems encountered, if any.

Part III   Termination/suspension

1.   Search object located (Date/time, location, survivors, fatalities, missing etc.)

2.   Search suspended (Authority for suspension, survivors, fatalities, missing, etc.)

Part IV   Conclusions/recommendations

1.   SMC conclusions

2.   SMC recommendations (May include recommendations to Government departments, agencies, private companies, etc., to help prevent similar incidents or accidents in the future.)

3.   RCC chief remarks

4.   SAR co-ordinator remarks

Attachments

1.   Weather reports.

2.   Sighting reports.

3.   SAR maps.

4.   SRU utilization (flying/steaming hours).

5.   List of objects recovered.

6.   Photographs (if applicable).

Distribution list

SMCs
SAR managers
SCs
International Authorities

Appendix I

SITREPs and MAREC Code

Situation report formats and examples

Situation reports (SITREPs) are used to pass information about a particular SAR incident. RCCs use them to keep other RCCs, RSCs, and appropriate agencies informed of cases which are of immediate or potential interest or as a briefing tool where an RCC is requesting assistance or action(s) from another RCC or organization. The OSC uses SITREPs to keep the SMC aware of mission events. Search facilities use SITREPs to keep the OSC informed of mission progress. The OSC addresses SITREPs only to the SMC unless otherwise directed. The SMC may address SITREPs to as many agencies as necessary, including other RCCs and RSCs, to keep them informed. SITREPs prepared by an SMC usually include a summary of information received from OSCs. Often a short SITREP is used to provide the earliest notice of a casualty or to pass urgent details when requesting assistance. A more complete SITREP is used to pass amplifying information during SAR operations. Initial SITREPs should be transmitted as soon as some details of an incident become clear and should not be delayed unnecessarily for confirmation of all details.

For SAR incidents where pollution or threat of pollution exists as a result of a casualty, the appropriate agency tasked with environmental protection should be an information addressee on SITREPs.

International SITREP format

A SITREP format has been adopted internationally which is intended for use, along with the standard codes found on pages I-4 to I-6, for international communications between RCCs.

Short form: To pass urgent essential details when requesting assistance, or to provide the earliest notice of casualty, the following information should be provided:

TRANSMISSION	(Distress/urgency)
DATE AND TIME	(UTC or Local Date Time Group)
FROM:	(Originating RCC)
TO:	
SAR SITREP (NUMBER)	(To indicate nature of message and completeness of sequence of SITREPs concerning the casualty)
A. IDENTITY OF CASUALTY	(Name/call sign, flag State)
B. POSITION	(Latitude/longitude)
C. SITUATION	(Type of message, e.g., distress/urgency; date/time; nature of distress/urgency, e.g., fire, collision, medico)
D. NUMBER OF PERSONS	
E. ASSISTANCE REQUIRED	
F. CO-ORDINATING RCC	

Full form: To pass amplifying or updating information during SAR operations, the following additional sections should be used as necessary:

G. DESCRIPTION OF CASUALTY	(Physical description, owner/charterer, cargo carried, passage from/to, life-saving equipment carried , attach photography, if available)

H. WEATHER ON SCENE	(Wind, sea/swell state, air/sea temperature, visibility, cloud cover/ceiling, barometric pressure)
J. INITIAL ACTIONS TAKEN	(By casualty and RCC)
K. SEARCH AREA	(As planned by RCC)
L. CO-ORDINATING INSTRUCTIONS	(OSC designated, units participating, communications , AIS and/or LRIT data available on ships in the vicinity)
M. FUTURE PLANS	
N. ADDITIONAL INFORMATION	(As appropriate, pictures, maps or links to websites where further information is available, include time SAR operation terminated)

Notes

(1)   Each SITREP concerning the same casualty should be numbered sequentially.

(2)   If help is required from the addressee, the first SITREP should be issued in short form if remaining information is not readily available

(3)   When time permits, the full form may be used for the first SITREP, or to amplify it.

(4)   Further SITREPs should be issued as soon as other relevant information has been obtained. Information already passed should not be repeated.

(5)   During prolonged operations, "no change" SITREPs, when appropriate, should be issued at intervals of about 3 hours to reassure recipients that nothing has been missed.

(6)   When the incident is concluded, a final SITREP should be issued as confirmation.

Example SITREP – International Format

```
DISTRESS
152230Z SEP 13
FROM RCC LA GUIRA VENEZUELA
TO SANJUANSARCOORD SAN JUAN PUERTO RICO
BT
SAR SITREP ONE
A. N999EJ (US)
B. 14-20N 064-20W
C. DISTRESS/152200Z/AIRCRAFT DITCHING
D. 4
E. REQUEST SANJUANSARCOORD ASSUME SMC AND CONDUCT SEARCH
F. RCC LA GUIRA VENEZUELA
G. CESSNA CITATION III/EXECUTIVE JETS, INC, MIAMI, FL/ ORIGINATOR
VERIFIED AIRCRAFT ON VFR FLIGHT PLAN DEPARTED PORT OF SPAIN TRINIDAD
152100Z EN ROUTE AGUADILLA, PUERTO RICO/8 PERSON LIFERAFT WITH CANOPY
AND SURVIVAL SUPPLIES/FLARES
H. WEATHER ON SCENE UNKNOWN
J. AIRCRAFT ISSUED MAYDAY BROADCAST ON 121.5 MHZ WHICH WAS HEARD BY
AIR FRANCE 747. PILOT OF DISTRESS AIRCRAFT GAVE POSITION, STATED BOTH
ENGINES FLAMED OUT AND DESCENDING THROUGH 5000 FEET WITH INTENTIONS TO
DITCH.
K. NO SEARCH ASSETS AVAILABLE
BT
```

Alternate SITREP format

Another SITREP format, in common use in certain SAR regions, is presented below. This format uses four main paragraphs and a subject line to convey all essential information.

Identification	(The subject line contains the phase of the emergency, SITREP number, a one- or two-word description of the emergency, and identification of the unit sending the SITREP. SITREPs are numbered sequentially throughout the entire case. When an OSC is relieved on scene, the new OSC continues the SITREP numbering sequence.)
Situation	(A description of the case, the conditions that affect the case, and any amplifying information that will clarify the problem. After the first SITREP, only changes to the original reported situation need be included.)
Action taken	(A report of all action taken since the last report, including results of such action. When an unsuccessful search has been conducted, the report includes the areas searched, a measure of effort such as sorties flown and hours searched, and the track spacing actually achieved.)
Future plans	(A description of actions planned for future execution, including any recommendations and, if necessary, a request for additional assistance.)
Status of case	(This is used only on the final SITREP to indicate that the case is closed or that search is suspended pending further developments.)

Example SITREP – Alternate Format

```
160730Z SEP 13
FROM COGARD AIRSTA BORINQUEN PUERTO RICO
TO SANJUANSARCOORD SAN JUAN PUERTO RICO
BT
SUBJ: DISTRESS, SITREP ONE, N999EJ DITCHED, AIRSTA BQN
A. SANJUANSARCOORD SAN JUAN PR 160010Z SEP 13
1. SITUATION: CGNR 1740 COMPLETED FLARE SEARCH OF AREA A-1 WITH NEGATIVE
RESULTS. O/S WX: CEILING 2000 OVC, NUMEROUS RAIN SHOWERS, VISIBILITY 3NM, SEAS
200T/6-8FT, WINDS 180T/30KTS.
2. ACTION TAKEN:
A. 151905Q INFORMED BY RCC OF DITCHED AIRCRAFT IN POSIT 14-20N 064-20W.
DIRECTED TO LAUNCH READY C-130.
B. 1955Q CGNR 1740 AIRBORNE, CDR PETERMAN.
C. 2120Q CGNR 1740 O/S POSIT 13-50N 064-20W. COMMENCED VECTOR SEARCH, 30NM
LEGS, FIRST LEG 180T, ALTITUDE 1500 FEET, TAS 150KTS.
D. 2135Q CGNR 1740 INSERTED DATUM MARKER BUOY IN POSIT 14-20N 064-20W.
E. 2310Q CGNR 1740 COMPLETED FIRST VS PATTERN, COMMENCED SECOND VECTOR SEARCH
FIRST LEG 150T.
F. 160100Q CGNR 1740 COMPLETED SECOND SEARCH.
G. 0120Q CGNR 1740 RELOCATED DMB IN POSIT 14-22N 064-17W. DEPARTED SCENE.
H. 0230Q CGNR 1740 LANDED BORINQUEN.
3. FUTURE PLANS: LAUNCH CGNR 1742 AT 0645Q FOR SEARCH OF AREA B-1.
BT
```

Maritime Search and Rescue Recognition Code (MAREC Code)

General

1 The purpose of this Code is to facilitate the communication of essential descriptive information regarding merchant vessels and small craft within and between maritime SAR organizations.

2 The MAREC Code is in two parts:

– Part 1 – Merchant vessels

– Part 2 – Small craft

3 All messages should be preceded by the prefix MAREC followed by a local serial number, assigned by the RCC.

4 The message should contain all the lettered identification groups as separate paragraphs. If the information is not known, the symbol UNK should be inserted or alternatively the symbol NA, where the lettered group is not applicable.

Part 1 – Merchant vessels

The message is composed of the following identification groups and will be transmitted in the following sequence:

MAREC – Local serial number

A. Type of vessel – name – call sign or ship station identity

B. Superstructure – location – colour

C. Hull profile – colour

D. Sequence of uprights

E. Length

F. Condition of loading

G. Other characteristics

A. Type of vessel, name and call sign or ship station identity

Merchant ships are classified as follows:

Voice	*TLX*
Passenger ship	PAX
Ferry	FERRY
Tanker	TANK
Bulk carrier	BULK
General cargo ship	GEN
Coaster	COAST
Fishing vessel	FISH
Containership	CONT
Specialized ship	SPEC

The name and call sign, or ship station identity, are added to the above classification.

For specialized vessels, the specific type of vessel should also be given, as appropriate, e.g., gas carrier, tug, or icebreaker.

Example:

Voice: ALFA, SPECIALIZED SHIP GAS CARRIER, FLYING DRAGON, CHARLIE GOLF HOTEL INDIA

TLX: A/SPEC/GAS CARRIER/FLYING DRAGON, CGHI

B.   Superstructure: Location and colour

Superstructures are referred to as being located forward, midships or aft or a combination of these positions, and may be described as long or short.

Colour is given in plain language.

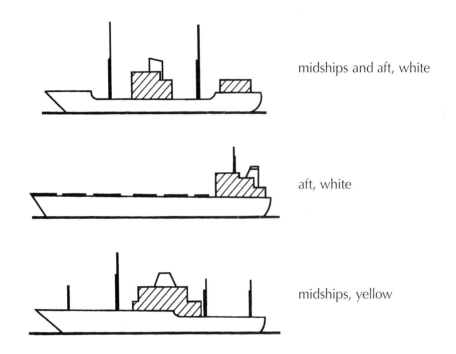

midships and aft, white

aft, white

midships, yellow

Example:

Voice: BRAVO, SUPERSTRUCTURE MIDSHIPS AND AFT, WHITE

TLX: B/MIDSHIPS AND AFT/WHITE

C.   Hull profile and colour

The hull profile is divided into three sections, numbered 1, 2 and 3 from stem to stern.

The existence or otherwise of raised sections (other than superstructures) above the main weather deck of the vessel should be reported numerically as follows:

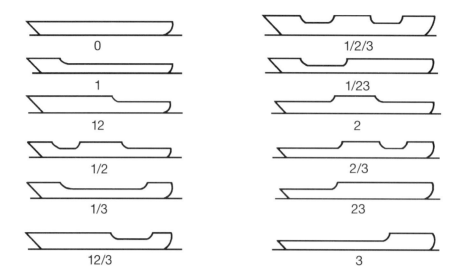

The colour of the hull is given in plain language.

Example:

Voice: CHARLIE, PROFILE ONE TWO SLANT THREE, BLACK

TLX: C/12/3 BLACK

D. Uprights

Uprights include everything, other than the profile and superstructures, which is prominent and can clearly be seen at a distance. The uprights are reported from stem to stern according to the list below:

Voice	*TLX*
Mast	M
Kingpost	K
Funnel	F
Crane	C
Gantry	G

Uprights located close to a superstructure such that they cannot be clearly seen from a distance should not be included. Double kingposts located athwartships (perpendicular to vessel's centreline) are reported as one kingpost.

Example:

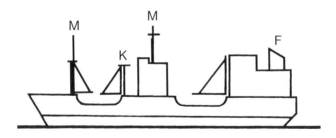

Voice: DELTA, MAST, KINGPOST, MAST, FUNNEL

TLX: D/M K M F

E.   Length

Length is the length overall (LOA) given in metres.

Note: Length can be estimated by observing the vessel's lifeboats, which are normally about 10 metres long, in proportion to the ship's length.

Example:

Voice: ECHO, TWO ZERO METRES

TLX: E/LOA 20

F.   Conditions of loading

The conditions of loading are indicated as follows:

Voice	TLX
Light	LIGHT
In ballast	BALL
Partially loaded	PART
Fully loaded	LOAD

Example:

Voice: FOXTROT, PARTIALLY LOADED

TLX: F/PART

G.   Other characteristics

Other prominent characteristics should be given, e.g., stack insignia, conspicuous deck cargo or other distinguishing marks or colour variations, e.g., name in big letters on vessel's side or company insignia painted on side of hull. In the message, such specific characteristics should be given in full.

Example:

Voice: GOLF, RAILROAD CARS ON DECK

TLX: G/RAILROAD CARS ON DECK

Complete example

The following illustrates a typical merchant vessel and how it would be described in a message according to this system.

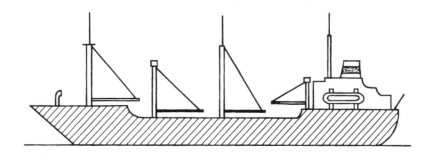

Voice: MAREC, 5/76 RCC STOCKHOLM
ALFA, GENERAL CARGO SHIP, VIKING, ECHO SIERRA DELTA CHARLIE
BRAVO, SUPERSTRUCTURE AFT, WHITE
CHARLIE, PROFILE ONE SLANT THREE, BLACK
DELTA, MAST, KINGPOST, MAST, MAST, FUNNEL
ECHO, EIGHT FIVE METRES
FOXTROT, LIGHT
GOLF, NOT APPLICABLE

TLX: MAREC 5/76 RCC STOCKHOLM
A/GEN/VIKING/ESDC
B/AFT/WHITE
C/1/3/BLACK
D/M K M M F
E/LOA 85
F/LIGHT
G/NA

Part 2 – Small craft

The message is composed of the following identification groups and will be transmitted in the following sequence:

MAREC – Local serial number

A.   Type of craft/number of hulls – name – call sign or ship station identity – use

B.   Make – distinctive markings

C.   Motor installation or rigging

D.   Construction – material – colour

E.   Stem – stern

F.   Type of bottom

G.   Length

H.   Other characteristics

I.   Number of persons on board

A.   Type of small craft/number of hulls, name, call sign or ship station identity and use

Voice	*TLX*
Motor open	MOTO
Motor part cabin	MOTPC
Motor full cabin	MOTFC
Rowing	ROW
Sailing open	SAILO
Sailing part cabin	SAILPC
Sailing full cabin	SAILFC
Motor sail	MOTSAIL
Inflatable	INFLAT

Where the number of hulls is more than one, this should be indicated by adding the words or group as follows:

Two hulls – Catamaran	CAT
Three hulls – Trimaran	TRI

The craft's name, call sign or ship station identity and use should be added to words or groups above. Under *use* indicate the purpose for which the craft is being used, e.g., fishing, pilot boat, or offshore racer.

Example:

Voice: ALFA, MOTOR PART CABIN CATAMARAN, LUCKY LADY, NAVIS ONE THREE, PLEASURE

TLX: A/MOTPC/CAT/LUCKY LADY/NAVIS 13/PLEASURE

B.   Make and distinctive markings

The make and distinctive markings should be given in plain language.

Example:

Voice: BRAVO, MAKE STORTRISS, SAIL MARKINGS TWO OVERLAPPING TRIANGLES WITH POINTS UP AND NUMBER SIERRA ONE THREE EIGHT

TLX: B/STORTRISS/SAILMARKINGS TWO OVERLAPPING TRIANGLES POINTS UP/S138

C.   Motor installation or sail rigging

Motor installation

The motor installation is given according to the figures shown below.

	Voice	TLX
	Outboard motor, if applicable, with the addition	OUTB
	Double	OUTB 2
	or Triple	OUTB 3
	Inboard motor	INB
	Aquamatic, if applicable, with the addition	AQUA
	Double	AQUA 2

Rigging (sailing boats)

Type of rigging is described on sailing boats and motor sailers according to the figures below. (If there is more than one mast, this is indicated by the appropriate number.)

	Voice	**TLX**
	Jib rig	JIB
	Sprit rig	SPRI
	Gaff rig	GAFF
	Lug sail	LUG
	Lateen rig	LAT
	Sloop rig	SLOOP

	Voice	*TLX*

Junk rig   JUNK

Yawl   YAWL

Ketch   KETCH

Schooner   SCHON

Example 1:

Voice: CHARLIE, OUTBOARD MOTOR, DOUBLE

TLX: C/OUTB 2

Example 2:

Voice: CHARLIE, SLOOP RIG

TLX: C/SLOOP

D. Construction – material – colour

Construction

Two different types of construction exist, viz. clinker-built and carvel-built or smooth-sided.

Note: Some glass fibre boats are moulded to resemble clinker-built and should be so described in this Code.

| Clinker | Carvel |

Material

The materials are wood, metal or glass-reinforced plastic (GRP). Construction, material and colour should be given in plain language.

Example:

Voice: DELTA, CLINKER, GLASS FIBRE, WHITE

TLX: D/CLINKER/GRP/WHITE

E. Stem – stern

Stem and stern are described according to the figures shown below.

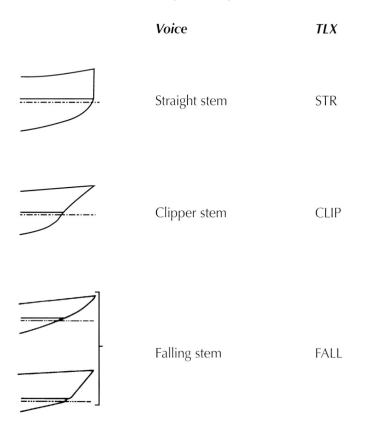

	Voice	*TLX*
	Straight stem	STR
	Clipper stem	CLIP
	Falling stem	FALL

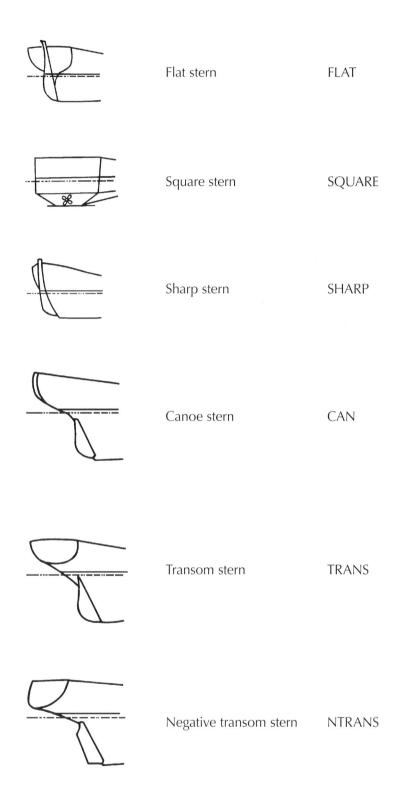

Flat stern	FLAT
Square stern	SQUARE
Sharp stern	SHARP
Canoe stern	CAN
Transom stern	TRANS
Negative transom stern	NTRANS

Example:

Voice: ECHO, FALLING STEM, CANOE STERN

TLX: E/FALL/CAN

F.   Type of bottom

Type of bottom is described according to the figures shown below.

	Voice	*TLX*
	V-bottom	VBOT
	Flat bottom	FLAT
	Round bottom	ROUND
	Ribbed bottom	RIB
	Keel	KEEL
	Fin-keel (where double fin-keel, add the word "double")	FIN
	Centre-board	CB

Example:

Voice: FOXTROT, RIBBED BOTTOM

TLX: F/RIB

G.   Length

Length is the length overall (LOA) given in metres.

Example:

Voice: GOLF, TWO ZERO METRES

TLX: G/LOA 20

H.   Other characteristics

Other characteristics should be included to describe certain details that might facilitate identification, e.g., flying bridge or spinnaker sail colouring.

Example:

Voice: HOTEL, RED SPINNAKER

TLX: H/RED SPINNAKER

I.   Number of persons on board

Example:

Voice: INDIA, THREE

TLX: I/3

Complete example

Motorboat

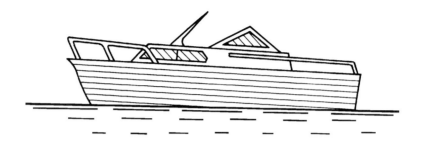

Voice: MAREC 7/76, RCC STOCKHOLM
ALFA, MOTORBOAT PART CABIN, GALANT, NAVIS ONE THREE, PLEASURE
BRAVO, MAKE SOLOE TWO FIVE
CHARLIE, INBOARD MOTOR
DELTA, CLINKER, GLASS FIBRE, WHITE
ECHO, FALLING STEM, SQUARE STERN
FOXTROT, V-BOTTOM
GOLF, SEVEN AND A HALF METRES
HOTEL, PULPIT FORWARD
INDIA, UNKNOWN

TLX: MAREC 7/76 RCC STOCKHOLM
A/MOTPC/GALANT/NAVIS 13/PLEASURE
B/SOLOE/25
C/INB
D/CLINKER/GRP/WHITE
E/FALL/SQUARE
F/VBOT
G/LOA 7.5
H/PULPIT FORWARD
I/UNK

Complete example

Sailing boat

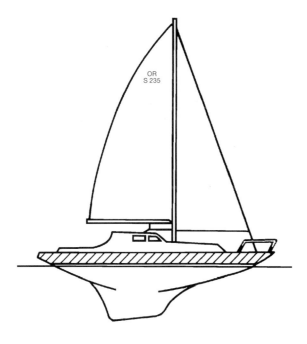

Voice: MAREC 8/76, RCC GOTHENBURG
ALFA, SAILING PART CABIN, ARABESQUE, NAVIS ONE TWO, PLEASURE
BRAVO, MAKE VIVO TWO ZERO, SAIL MARKINGS LETTERS OSCAR ROMEO SIERRA TWO
   THREE FIVE
CHARLIE, SLOOP RIG
DELTA, CARVEL, WOOD, BLACK WITH WHITE CABIN
ECHO, FALLING STEM, NEGATIVE TRANSOM STERN
FOXTROT, KEEL
GOLF, EIGHT METRES
HOTEL, PULPIT FORWARD
INDIA, TWO

TLX: A/SAILPC/ARABESQUE/NAVIS 12/PLEASURE
B/VIVO 20/OR S 235
C/SLOOP
D/CARVEL/WOOD/BLACK WITH WHITE CABIN
E/FALL/NTRANS
F/KEEL
G/LOA 8
H/PULPIT FORWARD
I/2

Appendix J

Intercepts

J.1 Types of intercepts

J.1.1 This appendix provides methods for solving most SAR intercept problems. Intercepts are needed when a distressed craft is still able to move toward a safe haven but there is substantial concern as to whether it will be able to reach safety before it suffers a catastrophic incident. SAR intercepts fall into two broad categories.

(a) Direct intercepts are those where the SAR facility intercepts the distressed craft at some point and then provides assistance, such as rescuing survivors, performing a medical evacuation, escorting the distressed craft to safety, etc. Three types of direct intercept are possible. They are the head-on, overtaking, and offset or beam-on intercepts. For direct intercepts, it is usually assumed that the SAR facility's speed is greater than that of the distressed craft.

(b) Minimum Time To Scene Intercepts (MTTSI) are used when the SAR facility's speed is less than that of the distressed craft. The objective of MTTSI is to launch a SAR facility and have it follow a path that will keep it in the best position relative to the distressed craft so that its transit time to the scene of any ensuing catastrophe (e.g., an aircraft ditching) will be minimised. An example of this situation is when a helicopter is dispatched toward an incoming fixed-wing aircraft that has declared an in-flight emergency. This type of intercept has also been called a "maximum SAR coverage intercept".

J.1.2 The intercept procedures in this appendix may be used for either vessels or aircraft. Some of the examples and figures depict vessel intercepts and some depict aircraft intercepts. It should be noted that the higher speed of aircraft often requires more rapid calculation of the intercept course and speed. Intercept planners should also be aware that winds aloft may affect aircraft intercept calculations and water currents may affect vessel intercept calculations.

J.2 Head-on method

J.2.1 This method is used when the distressed craft is moving directly toward the SAR facility's position. The instructions which follow refer to figure J-1. To establish the intercept course and time and position where the intercept will be made, proceed as follows:

(a) Plot the relative positions of both the distressed craft (A) and the intercepting SAR facility (B) for that time at which the intercepting SAR facility is ready to proceed.

(b) Join the two positions with a line (AB). This line is the course made good of the distressed craft and its reciprocal is the course made good of the intercepting SAR facility.

(c) Lay off a line 90° to the distressed craft's course made good and project it a reasonable distance (AC).

(d) Along this line, measure off the distance it will cover in one hour, based on the speed it is making good, and mark the position with an X.

(e) Lay off a line 90° to the intercepting SAR facility's course made good on the opposite side of AB and project it a reasonable distance (BD).

(f) Along this line, measure off the distance the intercepting SAR facility will cover in one hour, based on the speed it can make good along its intended course, and mark the position with a Y.

(g) Join the positions X and Y with a line. Where it cuts the course line is the intercept position, P.

(h) To find the time for this intercept, measure the distance from the initial position of either craft to the position of intercept and divide this distance by the speed of the chosen craft.

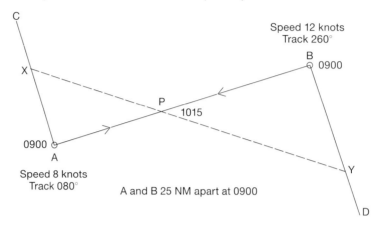

Figure J-1 – *Head-on method*

J.3 Overtaking method

J.3.1 This method is used when the distressed craft is moving directly away from the SAR facility's position. The instructions which follow refer to figure J-2. To establish the intercept course, and the time and position where the intercept will be made, proceed as follows:

(a) Plot the relative positions of both the distressed craft (A) and the intercepting craft (B) for that time at which the intercepting SAR facility is ready to proceed.

(b) Join the two positions with a line and project it a reasonable distance (BC). This line is the course made good of both craft.

(c) Lay off a line at 90° to the intercepting SAR facility's course and project it a reasonable distance (BD).

(d) Along this line, measure off the distance the intercepting SAR facility will cover in one hour, based on the speed it can make good along its intended course, and mark the position with an X.

(e) Lay off a line at 90° to the distressed craft's course and project it a reasonable distance (AE) on the same side as BD.

(f) Along this line, measure off the distance the distressed craft will cover in one hour, based on the speed it is making good, and mark the position with a Y.

(g) Join the positions X and Y with a line and project it until it cuts the course line at F. This is the intercept position.

(h) To find the time for the intercept, measure the distance from the initial position of either craft to the position of the intercept, and divide this distance by the speed of the chosen craft.

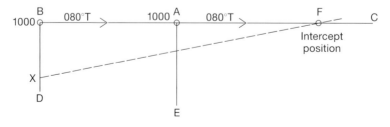

Figure J-2 – *Overtaking method*

J.4 Offset or beam-on intercept: method 1 (no wind/current effects)

J.4.1 This method is used when the distressed craft is not moving directly toward or away from the SAR facility's position and the effects of winds aloft (for aircraft) or currents (for vessels) are not significant. When the distressed craft has the greater ground speed (GS), the SAR facility will have to be closest to the intended destination to make the offset interception possible. (Another technique that is often useful when the SAR facility is slower than the distressed craft is the Minimum Time to Scene Intercept (MTTSI) described in paragraph J.7.) The instructions which follow refer to figure J-3. To establish the intercept course, time of intercept, and position where the intercept will be made, proceed as follows:

(a) Plot the relative positions of both the distressed craft (A) and the intercepting SAR facility (B) for that time at which the intercepting SAR facility is ready to proceed.

(b) Join these two positions with a line (AB).

(c) Lay off the distressed craft's track in the direction of its heading and project it a reasonable distance on the chart (AC).

(d) Along this projected track or course line of the distressed craft, measure off the distance it will cover in one hour, based on its speed through the air (TAS for aircraft) or water (vessels), and mark the position with an X.

(e) Transfer the line joining the two craft through the plotted position, X (XY).

(f) With the centre of the circle being the point of departure of the intercepting SAR facility and using a radius equal to the distance it will cover in the time interval used for the distressed craft, describe an arc and mark the spot where the arc cuts the transferred line (W).

Note: If the speed of the intercepted or intercepting vessel is such that the scale of the chart makes it unreasonable to use a full hour, then it will be necessary to use a proportional interval of time to ensure that the radius of the arc cuts the transferred line.

(g) Draw a line from the position of the intercepting SAR facility through the spot where the arc cuts the transferred line — this is the intercept heading/course for the intercepting SAR facility. By projecting this line until it cuts the projected track or course line of the distressed craft, one finds the position where the intercept will take place (D).

(h) To find the time it will take for the intercept, measure the distance from the initial position of the intercepting vessel to the point of intercept and divide this distance by the speed of the intercepting vessel (BD).

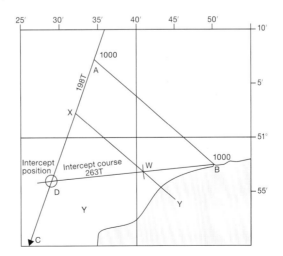

Figure J-3 – *Offset or beam-on intercept: method 1*

J.5 Offset or beam-on intercept: method 2 (with wind/current effects)

J.5.1 This method is used when the distressed craft is making good a known track at a known speed over the ground, the SAR facility is to one side of the track, and winds aloft (for aircraft) or currents (for vessels) are significant. When the distressed craft has the greater ground speed (GS), the SAR facility will have to be closest to the intended destination to make the offset interception possible. (Another technique that is often useful when the SAR facility is slower than the distressed craft is the Minimum Time to Scene Intercept (MTTSI) described in paragraph J.7.) To perform an offset interception (refer to figure J-4):

(a) Plot the simultaneous positions of the distressed aircraft (A) and the SAR aircraft (B). Along the course being made good by the distressed craft, plot its projected positions for ten minutes (C) and one hour and ten minutes (D) later. The ten-minute lead to the position of the distressed craft is allowed for navigational errors. Be certain to use speed (in knots) and course made good over the ground to plot these dead reckoning (DR) positions.

(b) Draw a line of constant bearing (LCB) between positions B and C.

(c) Draw a second LCB, parallel to BC, through point D.

(d) For aircraft, draw a wind vector downwind from the original position of the SAR facility (BF) which is equal to the average expected winds aloft. For vessels, draw a current vector in the down-current direction which is equal to the expected average currents.

(e) Draw an arc equal to the SAR facility's speed (TAS for aircraft, speed through the water for vessels) through the second LCB using the end of the wind/current vector (F) as the centre of origin. Then draw a line between the origin (F) and the point where the SAR facility's speed arc crosses the second LCB (G). This represents the heading to be used by the SAR facility.

(f) The line drawn from the original position of the SAR aircraft (B) to point G represents the intercepting SAR facility's true course and speed made good over the ground. If necessary, this line is extended until it crosses the projected true course of the distressed craft (H).

(g) The distance to intercept the intended track of the distressed craft is measured between the original position of the SAR facility (B) and the point at which the interception course made good crosses the projected course made good of the distressed craft (H). The *en route* time for this distance and closure time for the lead distance are computed and added to determine total time required for a collision point intercept with the distressed aircraft.

(h) Depending on the speed differential, the SAR facility may execute a turn to the reciprocal of the track of the distressed craft when the course of the distressed craft has been intercepted. Interception of the course of the distressed aircraft can be confirmed by direction finding (DF) from the distressed craft.

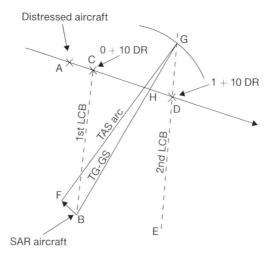

Figure J-4 – *Offset or beam-on intercept: method 2 (not to scale)*

J.6 Offset or beam-on intercept: method 3 (using a direction finder)

J.6.1 This procedure requires that the SAR aircraft have DF equipment that can receive transmissions from the distressed aircraft, and is executed as follows (refer to figure J-5), using magnetic (MAG) bearings:

(a) After the bearing to the distressed aircraft has been determined, the SAR aircraft is turned to a heading 45° from this bearing in the direction the distressed aircraft is flying.

(b) A relative bearing of 45° is maintained by checking DF bearings.

(c) If the DF check reveals that the bearing from the SAR aircraft has increased, the interception course should be increased twice the amount of the change between the last two bearings.

(d) If the check reveals that the bearing from the SAR aircraft has decreased, the interception course should be decreased twice the amount of change between the last two bearings.

(e) By bracketing the bearings as described above, an interception course is determined by maintaining a line of constant bearing.

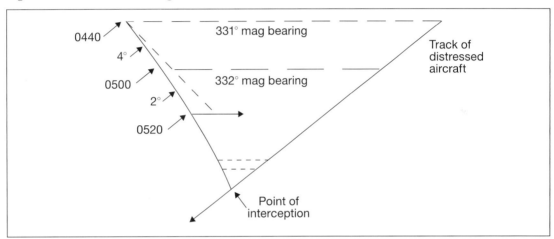

Figure J-5 – *Offset or beam-on intercept: method 3*

J.7 Minimum time to scene intercept (MTTSI)

Introduction

J.7.1 When an aircraft declares an in-flight emergency, it is often prudent for search and rescue (SAR) resources to respond even though the distressed aircraft may be able to reach its destination. The purpose of such a response is to minimise the time required to get a search and rescue unit (SRU) to the scene in the event of a ditching, forced landing, or bailout. Ideally, the SRU would intercept the distressed aircraft and then escort it to its destination. However, this is not always possible. SRUs, especially helicopters, often cannot fly as fast as the distressed aircraft and have a limited endurance and operating distance. When this situation arises, it is necessary to determine when the SRU should be launched toward the distressed aircraft and when it should turn back toward the distressed aircraft's destination so the SRU's transit time to the scene of any ensuing SAR incident is minimised. This is accomplished by having the SRU fly toward the distressed aircraft, turn around before it intercepts the distressed aircraft, and then allow the distressed aircraft to overtake it as both fly toward the destination. Adding complexity to the problem is the fact that the SRU's ground speed on the outbound leg may be significantly different from its ground speed on the inbound leg due to the effects of winds aloft. During the intercept, the distressed aircraft should be constantly informed of the type and the status of the interception being performed.

Assumptions

J.7.2 The three formulas below are based on the following assumptions:

(a) The SRU will depart from and return to the aerodrome that is the distressed aircraft's destination.

(b) The time it takes the SRU to get to the distressed aircraft's position (time to scene) anytime after the SRU makes its turn will be minimised, on average, when the time to scene at the end of the SRU's outbound leg equals the difference in the arrival times of the two aircraft at the destination aerodrome. An intercept procedure where this is true is called a Minimum Time To Scene Intercept (MTTSI).

(c) The distressed aircraft is not expected to be in immediate danger of ditching, crash landing, or bailout before it reaches the SRU's maximum operating distance.

(d) The ground speeds of the SRU on the outbound and inbound legs and the ground speed of the distressed aircraft are all known and remain constant throughout the mission.

(e) The distressed aircraft's ground speed will be greater than that of the SAR aircraft on the inbound leg.

(f) The position of the distressed aircraft is accurately known and it is proceeding from that location directly to the destination aerodrome.

SRU maximum operating distance

J.7.3 The maximum operational endurance of the SRU is an important factor in determining how far it may go from the aerodrome and still have enough fuel to provide some assistance to survivors and return safely. Maximum operational endurance is defined as the maximum endurance of the SRU minus the sum of the minimum useful time on scene and the required fuel reserve. For example, a helicopter might have a maximum endurance of 4+30 (four hours, thirty minutes). If the minimum useful time at the scene is 10 min and a 20 min fuel reserve is required, then its maximum operational endurance is 4+00 or exactly four hours. To compute the maximum operating distance, the following formula may be used:

$$[1] \quad D_{mo} = \frac{(T_{mo} V_{a1} V_{a2})}{V_{a1} + V_{a2}}$$

where:

D_{mo} = The SRU's maximum operating distance in nautical miles,

T_{mo} = The SRU's maximum operational endurance in hours,

V_{a1} = The SRU's ground speed on the outbound leg in knots, and

V_{a2} = The SRU's ground speed on the inbound leg in knots.

For example, if the helicopter mentioned above cruises at 150 knots true air speed (TAS) and there is a 25 knot wind at the helicopter's flight level blowing toward the distressed aircraft, then the SRU's ground speeds will be 175 knots on the outbound leg and 125 knots on the inbound leg. Using these values in formula [1], a maximum operating distance of about 292 NM is computed.

$$\frac{4 \times 175 \times 125}{175 + 125} = 291.67\}$$

Time to launch the SRU

J.7.4 If the distressed aircraft is beyond the SRU's maximum operating distance when the emergency is declared, the time to launch the SRU may be computed using the following formula:

$$[2] \quad T_0 = \left[\frac{D}{V_b} - D_{mo} \frac{V_{a1}^2 + 2V_{a1} + V_{a2} V_b}{V_{a1} V_b (V_{a1} + V_{a2})} \right]$$

where:

T_0 = The time to launch in minutes after the emergency was declared,

D = The distance, in nautical miles, of the distressed aircraft from the aerodrome when the emergency was declared,

V_b = The ground speed of the distressed aircraft in knots.

For example, consider a scenario where the distressed aircraft declares an emergency when it is 600 miles from its destination while maintaining a ground speed of 200 knots, and the SRU is the same helicopter used in the above examples. Using these values in formula [2], it will be found that the helicopter should not be launched until about 14 min after the emergency was declared.

$$\left[60\,\frac{600}{200} - 291.67 \times \frac{175^2 \times 2 \times 175 + 125 \times 200}{175 \times 200 \times (175 + 125)}\right] = 14.375$$

Note: If formula [2] produces a negative value for T_0, it means the distressed aircraft is already close enough for the SRU to be launched immediately.

Note: If it is feared that the distressed aircraft is likely to experience a ditching, forced landing, or bailout situation as soon as it is within the SRU's maximum operating distance or shortly thereafter, then a direct intercept at the SRU's maximum operating distance should be considered. The risk associated with this tactic is that of substantially increasing the SRU's time to scene if the distressed aircraft stays aloft longer than expected. If a second SRU is available, this risk can be eliminated by having it perform a MTTSI intercept in addition to the direct intercept performed by the first SRU.

Time to turn

J.7.5 Once the distressed aircraft's distance from the aerodrome at the time the SRU is launched is known, it is possible to compute how long the SRU should fly before turning back toward the aerodrome. The formula for this computation is

$$[3] \qquad T_{a1} = \frac{60 D_0 V_{a2}(V_{a1} + V_b)}{V_b(V_{a1}^2 + 2V_{a1}V_{a2} + V_{a2}V_b)}$$

where:

T_{a1} = The time in minutes after launch when the SRU should turn back toward the aerodrome, and

D_0 = The distressed aircraft's distance, in nautical miles, from the aerodrome at the time the SRU was launched.

For example, using the same ground speeds as in the previous examples and assuming the distressed aircraft is 500 NM from the aerodrome when the SRU is launched, using formula [3] produces a time to turn of about 71 min after launch.

$$\frac{60 \times 500 \times 125 \times (175 + 200)}{200 \times (175^2 + 2 \times 175 \times 125 + 125 \times 200)} = 70.75$$

Note: In any intercept situation, the SAR Mission Co-ordinator (SMC) should consider other facilities to supplement the capabilities of the intercepting SRU. For example, if the intercept is over the ocean, requesting a list of merchant vessels near the distressed aircraft's intended track from Amver should be considered. If time and circumstances permit, the pilot of the distressed aircraft should be provided such information in case a ditching becomes necessary.

Appendix K

Determining datum

Guidance for establishing probable survivor location

K.1   General

K.1.1   As soon as it is known or suspected that a distress incident has occurred, the SMC must first determine the time and location of the distress as accurately as possible. Sometimes a complete and accurate time and position are given with the initial report. Often, however, only partial information or a few clues are available from which to estimate the time and place of the distress incident.

K.1.2   Whenever a craft is missing and believed to be in distress, the SMC should make every effort to obtain additional information and clues which, when analysed, will reduce the size of the area most likely to contain the survivors and point to a small area that has a high probability of containment (POC) value. Additional information and clues may include any information received from the distressed craft prior to the distress incident or observations by other persons which might be related to the distressed craft or the conditions that led to the distress incident. The effort to obtain more information and clues should continue until all the survivors have been located or otherwise accounted for.

K.1.3   The following sections describe how to estimate the time and location of the distress incident in a few of the more common SAR situations. SMCs should note that the specific scenarios discussed below are only a small sample of the possible situations which may be encountered. Many of the techniques described below may be adapted to other situations not covered here.

K.2   Estimating distress incident time and location

Complete time and position reported

K.2.1   When apparently complete and accurate time and position information about a distress incident are provided, the SMC should immediately plot the position and check for any obvious errors. If the position is not obviously inconsistent with other known information, the SMC should immediately contact and dispatch the most suitable available facilities. As soon as this has been done, steps should be taken to verify the position and reduce its uncertainty. The uncertainty in the reported position will depend upon the method(s) used to determine it. Appendix N contains guidance for estimating probable position errors. If there is continued contact with the distressed craft, its crew should be asked to report any visible landmarks or other information from a second source, such as an alternative means of navigation, to confirm the craft's location. If this is not possible, then a more careful comparison of the reported position with all other known information that might be pertinent should be done. For example, if the initial report was from a vessel sinking in a storm, the position should be compared with the latest available weather information for the reported time and location of the distress. Any inconsistencies which are found must be resolved as quickly as possible.

Time of distress is known, but position is not known

K.2.2   If an *en-route* aircraft or vessel reports a distress without indicating its location, several situations are possible. The following scenarios are just a few of the possibilities that may be considered.

(a)   The craft was following its intended flight or voyage plan at the time of the distress incident. In this situation, the approximate position may be estimated based on data from the flight or voyage plan and any previous position reports along the intended track that may be available. (If previous position reports do not fall on or near the intended track, another scenario should be considered.) The estimated distress position should be based on the last known or reported position, the estimated or intended speed of advance, and the craft's intended track. If there is no conflicting information, this scenario is usually considered the most likely.

(b)   The craft significantly altered its intended course or speed of advance as a result of encountering adverse weather conditions, winds aloft, etc. The SMC should obtain appropriate information about weather conditions along the craft's intended route and attempt to correlate that information with the distress incident. The SMC should then attempt to determine the course(s) of action the master or pilot in command would be most likely to take if those weather conditions were encountered. The estimated position of the distress incident should be based on this information.

(c) The craft significantly altered its intended course or speed of advance to avoid encountering adverse weather conditions. The SMC should obtain appropriate information about weather conditions along the craft's intended route and attempt to correlate that information with the distress incident. The SMC should then attempt to determine the course(s) of action the master or pilot in command would be most likely to take to avoid those weather conditions.

(d) The craft significantly altered its intended course or speed of advance in an attempt to reach the nearest safe port or alternate aerodrome. This includes the possibility of the craft reversing its direction in an attempt to return to its departure point.

K.2.3 To estimate the extent of the possibility area which includes all possible scenarios, perform the following steps:

(a) using the guidance provided in appendix N, or other more accurate information if it is available, estimate the probable error in the last known or reported position;

(b) estimate the maximum distance the distressed craft could have travelled between the time of its last known or reported position and the time of the distress incident;

(c) add the probable error in the last known or reported position to the maximum distance the craft could have travelled and draw a circle of that radius about the last known or reported position to determine the possibility area.

K.2.4 Often the possibility area encompassing all scenarios is too large to search effectively. Whenever several scenarios are possible, and especially when they are about equally likely, the SMC should make every effort to obtain additional information that will eliminate some of the scenarios from consideration and allow refinement of the remaining ones to reduce the size of the possibility area. For example, if a short-range radio was used to transmit the distress signal, determining which stations heard the signal can help reduce the range of possible locations. If a DF bearing was obtained for the distress signal, a line of bearing for the distress position can be established which may eliminate some scenarios. The goal is to eliminate and adjust scenarios until a single scenario emerges which accounts for all the known facts. However, this is not always possible and it may be necessary to choose a specific scenario on which to base the search plan.

K.2.5 For search planning purposes, the estimated area where the distress may have occurred depends on which scenario is most likely to be true. For the scenario described in paragraph K.2.2 (a) above, the datum position and probable error of position are determined as follows:

(a) Determine the distressed craft's last known or reported position and the means used to establish that position, such as a navigational fix and the method of navigation used, radar, etc.

(b) Subtract the time of the last known or reported position from the time of the distress incident.

(c) Multiply the length of this time interval by the estimated speed of advance over the ground prior to the distress incident to get the distance travelled since the last known or reported position.

(d) Advance the last known or reported position along the intended track, based on the distance computed in the previous step. This is the datum point for the distress incident.

(e) If the datum point is in the marine environment, go to the Datum worksheet in this appendix. Otherwise, go to the Total probable error of position worksheet at the end of this appendix. When no maritime drift is involved, the drift error (D_e) is set to zero.

(f) Once the total probable error of position (E) has been estimated, go to the Effort allocation worksheet (datum point or datum line) in appendix L to plan the search. An initial probability map may be prepared by following the instructions provided in appendix M for point datums.

No communication received after the last position report

K.2.6 This is a relatively common situation in search and rescue but it is by far the most difficult because so many scenarios are possible, making the possibility area very large. The possible scenarios are similar to those for which the time but not the position of a distress is known. The only difference is that a range of times for the distress incident are now possible as well as a larger range of locations. The earliest possible time for the distress incident is immediately following the last time when the distressed persons were known to be safe. Usually this is assumed to be the time of the last communication with the craft. The latest possible time for the distress incident is either the time at which all control over the craft's movements must have ceased (usually the time of fuel exhaustion) or the present time, whichever is earlier.

K.2.7 When an aircraft or vessel disappears *en route*, the first assumption is that the aircraft or vessel is in distress on or near the intended track. (There is also the possibility that it is not in distress but has experienced a communications failure and is proceeding in accordance with the current flight or voyage plan.) In the distress scenario, the possible locations of the craft will be concentrated in the immediate vicinity of the craft's intended track. If no other information is available, the datum will normally be assumed to be a line that follows the intended route from the last known or reported position to the destination. An initial probability map for the possible distress incident locations may be prepared using the instructions provided in appendix M for line datums. The Effort allocation worksheet (datum point or datum line) in appendix L may be used to plan the search.

Information, other than position, received since last position report

K.2.8 When the last communication received from an *en-route* aircraft or vessel is not a position report but other communication which did not indicate any distress, three possible scenarios are normally considered and prioritized in the following order:

   (a) *Scenario 1:* The distress incident occurred immediately following the last communication.

   (b) *Scenario 2:* The craft continued along its intended track and the distress incident occurred a significant time after the last communication.

   (c) *Scenario 3:* The craft diverted toward an alternate destination, such as the nearest safe port or an alternate aerodrome, and became distressed a significant time after the last communication. This includes the possibility that the craft reversed direction and the alternate destination was the departure point.

K.2.9 In this situation, it is necessary to prepare a generalized probability map consisting of at least three sub-areas prior to planning any search efforts. The three sub-areas would correspond to the three scenarios.

   (a) The first sub-area is determined by estimating the craft's position at the time of the last communication and centering an area of reasonable size on that point. The total probable error of position may be used as a guide in estimating a reasonable size for this sub-area. This sub-area should be assigned a POC value that makes its probability density higher than that in either of the other two sub-areas.

   (b) The second sub-area extends along the intended track from where the first sub-area ends to the destination and is given a reasonable width. The total probable error of position may be used as a guide for estimating a reasonable width. This sub-area should be assigned a POC value that makes its probability density fall approximately halfway between that of the first and third sub-areas.

   (c) The third sub-area extends along the track the craft would have followed had it diverted to the alternate destination. It begins where the first sub-area (and possibly part of the second as well) ends and extends to the alternate destination. The total probable error of position may be used as a guide for estimating a reasonable width for this sub-area. The POC value for this sub-area should be chosen so that the probability density is less than that of the other two sub-areas.

(d) If it is certain that the survivors are in one of these three areas, their initial POC values should add to 100%. Otherwise, the remainder of the possibility area for these scenarios needs to be defined and assigned a POC value that makes the total equal 100%. It may be advisable to construct a suitable grid for the possibility area and assign POC values to the grid cells based on the sub-area(s) within which they lie. Instructions for preparing generalized probability maps are given in appendix M. The Effort allocation worksheet (generalized distribution) in appendix L should be used to plan the search.

K.3   Estimating survivor location following a distress incident

Aeronautical drift

K.3.1 When an aircraft experiences a serious casualty, such as an engine failure, the pilot will normally attempt to maintain altitude as long as possible. If the casualty cannot be corrected and the pilot is forced to descend, this will be done by either gliding or, if a parachute is available, bailing out.

(a) *Gliding.* The safest descent may involve gliding or flying at greatly reduced power toward the most suitable available site for a forced, off-aerodrome landing. Aircraft can glide a considerable distance. The key factors are power-off rate of descent, glide airspeed, and height above the surface. Since glide ratios vary widely, the manufacturer of the distressed aircraft or pilots experienced with that type of aircraft should be consulted regarding glide and forced landing characteristics.

(b) *Parachute.* If parachutes are available, the pilot in command may elect to use this method of descent. This situation is rare in civil aviation but more common in military aviation. If the survivors leave the aircraft while it is still airborne, their landing site and the crash site of the aircraft may be widely separated from each other and from the bailout position. Drift characteristics for modern civilian parachutes can vary widely. For civilian cases, the manufacturer of the parachute or another knowledgeable source should be consulted for the information needed to determine how far the survivor(s) may have drifted during descent. Drift computations for parachutes may be completed using the Aeronautical drift worksheet in this appendix together with the parachute drift tables provided in appendix N.

Maritime drift

K.3.2 Two types of forces cause survival craft on the ocean to move or drift: wind and current. To compute the area where the survivors may be located, it is necessary to estimate the rate and direction of drift. This requires estimates of the winds and currents in and around the area containing the possible distress locations. The two components of drift are total water current (TWC) and leeway. The Datum worksheet for computing drift in the marine environment and its supporting worksheets describe how to estimate survivor motion due to environmental forces.

(a) Total water current (TWC) can have several components. Some or all of the following may be included:

(1) *Sea current (SC).* This is the main large-scale flow of ocean waters. Sea currents near the surface are of principal interest to search planners. Near shore or in shallow waters, sea current is usually less important than the tidal current or the local wind current. Sea currents are not always steady, so averages should be used with caution. Sea current estimates may be obtained from direct observation at the scene (such as ship set and drift, trajectories of drifting objects having zero leeway), output from computer models of ocean circulation, and hydrographic tables and charts.

(2) *Tidal or rotary currents.* In coastal waters, currents change in direction and speed as the tides change. They may be estimated from tidal current tables, current charts, and pilot charts. However, local knowledge often will be of the greatest value.

(3) *River current.* This should be considered only if the survivors may be in, or near, the mouth of a large river (such as the Amazon).

(4) *Local wind current (WC).* Local wind current is due to the effect of sustained local winds on the water's surface. The exact effect of wind in creating local wind currents is not clear, but it is generally assumed that after 6 to 12 h with the wind in a constant direction, a local surface current is generated. The estimated average wind velocity and direction for the previous 24 to 48 h should be verified by contacting ships which have been in the vicinity of the distress scene. The direction and velocity of local wind current can be estimated using the Local Wind Current Graph in figure N-1.

Vector (direction and speed) values must be obtained for each current which is present and added, vector fashion, to obtain the total water current (TWC). Figure 4-6 in chapter 4 shows how to compute TWC offshore in the open ocean.

(b) *Leeway (LW).* The force of the wind against the exposed surfaces of the craft causes it to move through the water in a generally downwind direction. This is called leeway. A drogue (sea anchor) may be deployed to decrease the rate of leeway. The shapes of the exposed and underwater surfaces can affect the rate of leeway and cause the leeway direction to be somewhat off the downwind direction. Estimates of wind direction and speed may be obtained from direct observation at the scene, output from computer models used for weather prediction, local weather bureaus and, as a last resort, wind roses on pilot charts. Leeway rates may be computed from leeway graphs provided in figures N-2 and N-3.

(c) Once the directions and speeds of the TWC and leeway vectors are estimated, the direction and rate of survivor drift are computed by adding the leeway and TWC vectors as shown in figure 4-7 of chapter 4. Normally, all velocities are computed in nautical miles per hour (knots).

Aeronautical drift worksheet

Case title _____ Case number _____ Date _____

Planner's name _____ Datum number _____ Search plan A B C _____

                                                                           (Circle one)

Search object _____

A   Estimated incident/bailout position

1   Date/time   _____ Z   _____

2   Latitude, longitude   _____ N/S   _____ W/E

B   Aircraft/parachute glide displacement ($d_{a/p}$)

(For both aircraft and parachute glide, use this part twice; once for the aircraft glide and again for the parachute glide. For parachutes with zero glide ratios, go to part C below.)

1   Incident or bailout/opening altitude as appropriate (Alt_{max})   _____ ft

2   Terrain or bailout/opening altitude as appropriate (Alt_{min})   _____ ft

3   Altitude loss ($Alt\ loss = Alt_{max} - Alt_{min}$)   _____ ft

4   Glide ratio (g_r = horizontal distance/vertical distance)
        (from flight manual for aircraft or table N-13 for parachutes)   _____

5   Glide true air speed (TAS_g)   _____ kts

6   Rate of descent ($rate_d$) (($TAS_g \times 101)/g_r$ for aircraft)
        (for parachutes, enter value from table N-13)   _____ ft/min

7   Time of descent ($t_d = Alt\ Loss/rate_d$)   _____ min

8   Glide distance ($d_g = (TAS_g \times t_d)/60$)   _____ NM

9   Descent heading (if unknown, leave blank)   _____ °T

10   Average wind aloft during glide (AWA_g)
        (attach Average wind aloft worksheet)   _____ °T   _____ kts

11   Downwind aircraft/parachute displacement
        due to average wind aloft ($d_d = (t_d \times AWA)/60$)   _____ °T   _____ NM

12   Aircraft/parachute glide displacement
        (d_a = vector sum of d_g and d_d)   _____ °T   _____ NM

13   Date/time at end of glide
        (incident date/time + time of descent)   _____ Z   _____

14   Latitude, longitude at end of glide
        (If descent heading is unknown, leave blank
        and enter the sum of the aircraft and parachute
        glide distances into the **Total probable error
        of position worksheet** at A.5)   _____ Z   _____ W/E

C   Parachute drift (d_p) (for parachutes with a zero glide ratio)

1   Bailout position

             Last known position   LKP
             Estimated incident position   EIP
             Glide position   GP
                       (Circle one)

2   Date/time   _____ Z   _____

3   Latitude, longitude   _____ N/S   _____ W/E

4   Parachute opening altitude (Alt_{max})   _____ ft

5   Terrain altitude (Alt_{min})   _____ ft

6   Altitude loss (Alt loss = Alt_{max} − Alt_{min})   _____ ft

7   Average wind aloft during parachute descent (AWA_p)
   from opening altitude to terrain altitude
   (attach Average wind aloft worksheet)   _____ °T   _____ kts

8   Drift distance from parachute opening altitude to sea level (d_{p1})
   (from table N-14)   _____ NM

9   Drift distance from terrain altitude to sea level (d_{p2})
   (from table N-14)   _____ NM

10   Downwind parachute displacement due to
   winds aloft ($d_p = d_{p1} − d_{p2}$)   _____ °T   _____ NM

11   Time of arrival at the surface
   (incident time + time of descent)   _____ Z   _____

12   Latitude, longitude   _____ N/S   _____ W/E

Aeronautical drift worksheet instructions

Introduction

The Aeronautical drift worksheet is used in conjunction with the Average wind aloft worksheet to compute the probable position of landing when the position of the distress incident is known. Aeronautical drift may consist of either gliding, parachute drift or a combination of the two. There are several things to consider with aeronautical drift, including:

Starting altitude	Terrain altitude
Glide true air speed	Glide ratio
Rate of descent	Average wind aloft

This worksheet assumes the aircraft maintains a constant heading during its descent from the distress incident position and that the parachute, if it has a non-zero glide ratio, also maintains a constant descent heading from the bailout/opening position (not necessarily the same heading as the aircraft's glide). If either of the glide descent headings is unknown, the glide distance should be computed and added to the distressed aircraft's probable position error (X) to give a new (and larger) probable position error value for X on the **Total probable error of position worksheet**.

A   Estimated incident position

1	Date/time	Enter the date time group (DTG) of the incident position. Example: 231140Z FEB 13
2	Latitude, longitude	Enter the estimated incident position.

B   Aircraft/parachute glide displacement ($d_{a/p}$)

For both aircraft and parachute glide, use this part twice; once for the aircraft glide and again for the parachute glide. For parachutes with zero glide ratios, go to part C below.

1	Incident or bailout/opening altitude	For aircraft glide, enter the incident altitude or last known/assigned altitude. For parachute glide, enter the bailout or parachute opening altitude as appropriate. (Alt_{max})
2	Terrain or bailout/opening altitude	For aircraft glide without bailout, enter the terrain altitude. For aircraft glide followed by bailout, enter the bailout altitude. For parachute glide, enter the terrain altitude. (Alt_{min})
3	Altitude loss	Subtract the lower altitude (**B.2**) from the higher altitude (**B.1**).
4	Glide ratio	Enter the glide ratio from the aircraft's flight manual or manufacturer's data or, for parachutes, enter the appropriate value from table N-13.
5	Glide true air speed	If available, enter the actual value provided by the pilot. Otherwise, enter the best glide true air speed from the aircraft's flight manual or manufacturer's data. Leave blank for parachutes.
6	Rate of descent	Multiply the glide true air speed (**B.5**) by 101 and divide the result by the glide ratio (**B.4**). (The value 101 is the conversion factor for converting knots to feet per minute).
7	Time of descent	Divide the altitude loss (**B.3**) by the rate of descent (**B.6**).
8	Glide distance	Multiply the glide true air speed (**B.5**) by the time of descent (**B.7**) and divide the result by 60 to get the glide distance in nautical miles.

9	Descent heading	Enter the descent heading. If unknown, leave blank.
10	Average wind aloft	Enter average wind aloft from the Average wind aloft worksheet for the interval between the higher altitude (**B.1**) and the lower altitude (**B.2**).
11	Downwind displacement	Add (or subtract) 180° to (from) the average wind aloft direction (B.10) to get the downwind direction in degrees true. Multiply the time of descent (B.7) by the speed of the average wind aloft (B.10) and divide the result by 60 to get the downwind distance in nautical miles.
12	Aircraft/parachute glide displacement	If the descent heading is known, compute the vector sum of the descent heading (**B.9**)/glide distance (**B.8**) and the downwind displacement (**B.11**). Otherwise, enter the downwind displacement (**B.11**).
13	Date/time at end of glide	Add the time of descent (**B.7**) to the estimated incident time (**A.1**).
14	Latitude, longitude at end of glide	Plot the end-of-glide position using the incident/bailout position (**A.2**) and the aircraft/parachute glide displacement (**B.12**). If the descent heading is unknown, enter the glide distance (**B.8**) into the **Total probable error of position worksheet** at **A.5**. If both the aircraft and the parachute have non-zero glide distances, enter the larger of the two glide distances.

C Parachute drift (*d*ₚ) (for parachutes with zero glide ratio)

1	Bailout position	Circle the appropriate source of information so it is documented for future reference/review.
2	Date/time	Enter the date time group of the bailout position. Example 231150Z FEB 13.
3	Latitude, longitude	Enter the bailout position.
4	Parachute opening altitude	Enter the altitude at which the parachute opened.
5	Terrain Altitude	Enter the altitude of the terrain below the bailout position.
6	Altitude loss	Subtract the terrain altitude (**C.5**) from the parachute opening altitude (**C.4**).
7	Average wind aloft	Enter average wind aloft from the Average wind aloft worksheet for the interval between the higher altitude (**C.4**) and the lower altitude (**C.5**).
8	Drift distance from parachute opening altitude to sea level	Enter table N-14 with the parachute opening altitude (**C.4**) and average wind aloft (**C.7**) and record the drift distance.
9	Drift distance from terrain altitude to sea level	Enter table N-14 with the terrain altitude (**C.5**) and the average wind aloft (**C.7**) and record the drift distance.
10	Downwind parachute displacement	Enter the downwind direction in degrees true. Subtract the drift distance from terrain altitude to sea level (**C.9**) from the drift distance from parachute opening altitude to sea level (**C.8**) to get the drift distance in nautical miles.
11	Time of arrival at the surface	Add the time of descent from figure N-15 to the time of bailout (**C.2**).
12	Latitude, longitude	Using the bailout position (**C.3**) and downwind parachute displacement (**C.10**), plot the position where the survivor reaches the surface.

Average wind aloft (AWA) worksheet

Case title _____ Case number _____ Date _____

Planner's name _____ Datum number _____ Search plan A B C _____
(Circle one)

Average wind aloft (AWA) worksheet

Altitude of observation	Altitude interval	Thousands of feet (A)	Wind direction (B)	Wind speed (C)	Wind contribution (A × C)
_____	____ – ____	_____	_____ ° T	_____ kts	_____ kts
_____	____ – ____	_____	_____ ° T	_____ kts	_____ kts
_____	____ – ____	_____	_____ ° T	_____ kts	_____ kts
_____	____ – ____	_____	_____ ° T	_____ kts	_____ kts
_____	____ – ____	_____	_____ ° T	_____ kts	_____ kts
_____	____ – ____	_____	_____ ° T	_____ kts	_____ kts
_____	____ – ____	_____	_____ ° T	_____ kts	_____ kts
_____	____ – ____	_____	_____ ° T	_____ kts	_____ kts

Total altitude loss   _____   Vector sum of   _____ °T   _____ kts
(thousands of feet)   (D)   contributions   (E)   (F)

Average wind aloft [(E)°T (F/D) kts]   **AWA** _____ °T _____ **kts**

Average wind aloft (AWA) worksheet instructions

Introduction

The purpose of this worksheet is to compute a weighted average of wind velocity vectors over some range of altitudes. Average wind aloft is used to compute downwind displacement of gliding aircraft and descending parachutes. The contribution of each wind observation or estimate is weighted according to the altitude range where it was in effect. For example, a wind that has been in effect for 2,000 ft will have twice as much influence on the average wind as one that was in effect for only 1,000 ft.

1	Making entries in the worksheet	For each available wind value, enter the altitude of the observation, the starting and ending altitudes of the interval in which that wind value was in effect, the number of feet (in thousands) in the interval (higher altitude minus lower altitude), the wind direction, the wind speed and the wind contribution for that interval (wind speed multiplied by the number of feet (in thousands) in the interval).
2	Computing the total altitude loss	Add all the entries in the "Thousands of feet" column. Usually, when multiplied by 1000, this value should equal the number of feet in the Altitude Loss from **B.3** or **C.6** of the **Aeronautical drift worksheet**. If it doesn't, the difference should be explained.
3	Computing the total wind vector	Using a chart, manoeuvering board, universal plotting sheet or calculator, add all the wind contribution vectors to get the total wind vector.
4	Computing the average wind aloft	The direction of the average wind is the same as the direction of the total wind vector. Divide the magnitude of the total wind vector by the total number of feet (in thousands) in the altitude loss to get the average wind speed.
5	Go to line **B.10** or **C.7** as appropriate of the Aeronautical drift worksheet and record the computed Average wind aloft.	

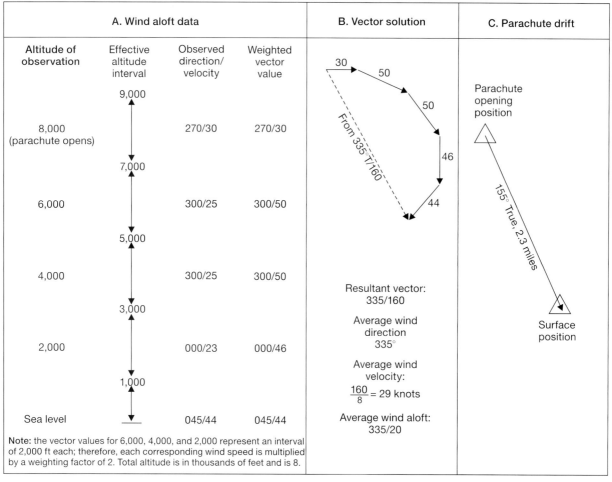

A. Wind aloft data				B. Vector solution	C. Parachute drift
Altitude of observation	Effective altitude interval	Observed direction/ velocity	Weighted vector value		

Note: the vector values for 6,000, 4,000, and 2,000 represent an interval of 2,000 ft each; therefore, each corresponding wind speed is multiplied by a weighting factor of 2. Total altitude is in thousands of feet and is 8.

(Parachute opened at 8,000 feet over ocean)

Figure K-1 – *Average wind aloft example*

Datum worksheet for computing drift in the marine environment

Case title _____ Case number _____ Date _____

Planner's name _____ Datum number _____ Search plan A B C _____

Search object _____

A   Starting position for this drift interval

1   Type of position   Last known position   LKP
     (Circle one)   Estimated incident position   EIP
                                 Previous datum   PD

2   Position Date/time   _____ Z   _____

3   Latitude, longitude of position   _____ N/S   _____ W/E

B   Datum time

1   Commence search date/time   _____ Z   _____

2   Drift interval   _____ hours

C   Average surface wind (ASW)
   (Attach **Average surface wind (ASW) worksheet**)

1   Average surface wind (*ASW*)   _____ °T   _____ kts

2   Probable error of drift velocity due to
     probable error of average surface wind ($ASWDV_e$)   _____ kts

D   Total water current (TWC)
   (Attach **Total water current (TWC) worksheet**)

1   Total water current (*TWC*)   _____ °T   _____ kts

2   Probable total water current error (TWC_e)   _____ kts

E   Leeway (LW)
   (Attach **Leeway (LW) worksheet**)

1   Left of downwind   _____ °T   _____ kts

2   Right of downwind   _____ °T   _____ kts

3   Probable leeway error (LW_e)   _____ kts

F Total surface drift

Use a manoeuvring board or calculator to add Total water current and Leeway vectors.
(See **figure K-1a**)

		(left of downwind)		(right of downwind)	
1	Drift directions	_____	°T	_____	°T
2	Drift speeds	_____	kts	_____	kts
3	Drift distances (**line F.2** × **line B.2**)	_____	NM	_____	NM

4   Total probable drift velocity error (DV_e)

$$DV_e = \sqrt{ASWDV_e^2 + TWC_e^2 + LW_e^2}$$ _____ kts

G Datum positions and divergence distance

Using a chart, universal plotting sheet or calculator, determine the datum positions and divergence distance (DD) (See **figure K-1b**)

1	Latitude, longitude (left of downwind)	_____	N/S	_____	W/E
2	Latitude, longitude (right of downwind)	_____	N/S	_____	W/E
3	Divergence distance (*DD*)			_____	NM

H Total probable error of position (*E*) and separation ratio (*SR*)

(Attach **Total probable error of position (*E*) worksheet**)

1	Total probable error of position squared (E^2)	_____	NM²
2	Total probable error of position (*E*)	_____	NM
3	Separation ratio ($SR = DD/E$)	_____	

4   Go to the **Total available search effort worksheet**.

Datum worksheet (marine environment) instructions

Introduction

The **Datum worksheet** is used to compile information from other worksheets and compute a new Datum position. A **Datum worksheet** should be completed for each initial datum point.

Complete the information at the top of the page, then go to **part A**.

A   Starting position for this drift interval

1	Type of position	Circle the appropriate source of information about the starting position for this drift interval. If the initial position is the last known position (as clearly and accurately reported by the distressed vessel, an eyewitness, or a remote sensor), circle "LKP". If the initial position was estimated by dead reckoning or determined by remote sensing with a large probable error or as ambiguous positions (e.g., pairs of positions sometimes reported by COSPAS/SARSAT), circle "EIP". If the initial position for this drift interval was a datum position computed for a previous drift interval, circle "PD".
2	Position date/time	Enter the date time group (DTG) of the starting position. Example: 231200Z FEB 99.
3	Latitude, longitude of position	Enter the latitude and longitude of the starting position for this drift interval.

B   Datum time

1	Commence search date/time	Enter the date and time when the next search will begin in date time group (DTG) format. This will be the time for which the next datum position is computed.
2	Drift interval	Subtract the starting position date and time (**line A.2**) from the commence search date and time (**line B.1**). If necessary, convert the result from days and hours to get the number of hours between the two date time groups.

C   Average surface wind (ASW)

		If the search object has no leeway and wind current is not a factor, leave **part C** blank and go to **part D**. Otherwise, go to the **Average surface wind (ASW) worksheet** and compute the average surface wind for this drift interval.
1	Average surface wind (ASW)	Enter the average surface wind direction in degrees true and the average surface wind speed in knots from **line A.2** of the **Average surface wind (ASW) worksheet**.
2	Probable error of drift velocity due to ASW_e ($ASWDV_e$)	Enter the estimated probable error of the drift velocity that will be caused by the probable error of the average surface wind from **line B.2** of the **Average surface wind (ASW) worksheet**.

D   Total water current (TWC)

1	Total water current (*TWC*)	Enter the total water current direction in degrees true and the total water current speed in knots from **line A.2** or **line B.5** of the **Total water current (TWC) worksheet**, as appropriate.
2	Probable total water current error (*TWC*$_e$)	Enter the estimated/computed probable error of the total water current from **line A.3** or **line B.6** of the **Total water current (TWC) worksheet**, as appropriate.

E   Leeway (LW)

1	Left of downwind	Enter the leeway direction to the left of the downwind direction in degrees true and the leeway speed in knots from **line 6.a** of the **Leeway (LW) worksheet**.
2	Right of downwind	Enter the leeway direction to the right of the downwind direction in degrees true and the leeway speed in knots from **line 6.b** of the **Leeway (LW) worksheet**.
3	Probable leeway error (*LW*$_e$)	Enter the estimated probable leeway error from **line 7** of the **Leeway (LW) worksheet**.

F   Total surface drift

The total surface drift velocities are the vector sum of the total water current velocity from **line D.1** and each of the leeway velocities from **lines E.1** and **E.2**. Multiplying each of the total surface drift speeds by the drift interval produces the total surface drift distances.

1	Drift directions	Using a manoeuvring board or calculator, add the total water current vector from **line D.1** to each of the leeway vectors from **lines E.1** and **E.2** to compute two resultant surface drift velocity vectors. **Figure K-1a** is an example of how the two drift velocity vectors might appear. Enter the direction of each resultant surface drift velocity vector.
2	Drift speeds	Enter the magnitude of each resultant surface drift velocity vector.
3	Drift distances	Multiply the drift speeds (**line F.2**) by the drift interval (**line B.2**) and enter the results.
4	Total probable drift velocity error (*DV*$_e$) ($DV_e = \sqrt{ASWDV_e^2 + TWC_e^2 + LW_e^2}$)	Compute the probable error of the surface drift velocity vectors by taking the square root of the sum of the squared errors from **lines C.2, D.2** and **E.3**.

G   Datum positions and divergence distance

Determine and plot the datum positions and determine the distance between them. (See **figure K-1b**)

1	Latitude, longitude (left of downwind)	Using a chart, universal plotting sheet, or a calculator, determine the latitude and longitude of the datum position based on the total drift direction (**line F.1**) and distance (**line F.3**) from the starting position (**line A.3**) for the datum that lies to the **left** of the downwind direction. Plot the position.

2	Latitude, longitude (right of downwind)	Using a chart, universal plotting sheet, or a calculator, determine the latitude and longitude of the datum position based on the total drift direction (**line F.1**) and distance (**line F.3**) from the starting position (**line A.3**) for the datum that lies to the **right** of the downwind direction. Plot the position.
3	Divergence distance (*DD*)	Using a chart, universal plotting sheet, or a calculator, determine the divergence distance between the two datums. (See **figure K-1b**)

H Total probable error of position (*E*) and separation ratio (*SR*)

1	Total probable error of position squared (E^2)	Enter the square of the total probable error of position from **line D.1** of the **Total probable error of position worksheet**. This value will be used later with the **Effort allocation worksheet**.
2	Total probable error of position (*E*)	Enter the total probable error of position from **line D.2** of the **Total probable error of position worksheet**. This value will also be used with the **Effort allocation worksheet**.
3	Separation ratio (*SR*)	Divide the divergence distance (*DD*) on **line G.3** by the total probable error of position on **line H.2** and enter the result. Stated as a formula, $SR = DD/E$. This value will also be used with the **Effort allocation worksheet**.
4	Go to the **Total available search effort worksheet**	Proceed to the **Total available search effort worksheet** to continue planning the search.

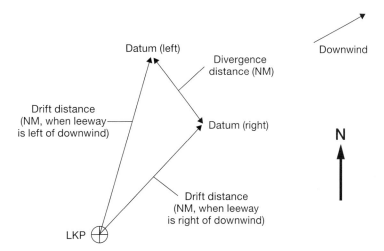

Figure K-1a – *Drift velocity vectors with leeway divergence*

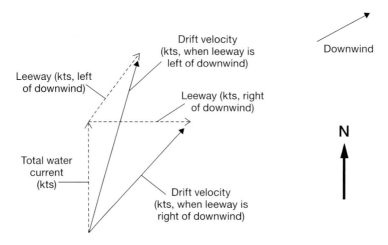

Figure K-1b – *Drift distances and divergence distance*

Average surface wind (ASW) worksheet

Case title _____ Case number _____ Date _____

Planner's name _____ Datum number _____ Search plan A B C _____

A   Average surface wind

1   Surface wind data

Time of observation	Time interval	Number of hours (A)	Wind direction (B)	Wind speed (C)	Wind contribution (A × C)
_____	____ – ____	_____	_____° T	_____ kts	_____ NM
_____	____ – ____	_____	_____° T	_____ kts	_____ NM
_____	____ – ____	_____	_____° T	_____ kts	_____ NM
_____	____ – ____	_____	_____° T	_____ kts	_____ NM
_____	____ – ____	_____	_____° T	_____ kts	_____ NM
_____	____ – ____	_____	_____° T	_____ kts	_____ NM
_____	____ – ____	_____	_____° T	_____ kts	_____ NM
_____	____ – ____	_____	_____° T	_____ kts	_____ NM

Total hours _____ (D)   Vector sum of contributions _____°T (E) _____ NM (F)

2   Average surface wind (ASW) [(E)°T (F/D) kts]   _____ °T _____ kts

B   Probable error

1   Probable error of the average surface wind (ASW_e)   _____ kts

2   Probable error of drift velocity due to probable error of the Average surface wind ($ASWDV_e$)   _____ kts

Go to **part C** on the **Datum worksheet**.

Average surface wind (ASW) worksheet instructions

Introduction

The purpose of this worksheet is to compute a weighted average of wind velocity vectors over some period of time, usually a drift interval. Average surface wind is used to estimate wind current and leeway. The contribution of each wind observation or estimate is weighted according to the amount of time it was in effect. For example, a wind that has been in effect for twelve hours will have twice as much influence on the average wind as one that was in effect for only six hours. In general, wind averages should not be used for intervals exceeding 24 h in length.

Wind observations and estimates are not exact and forecast wind data are even less accurate. Furthermore, the winds experienced by the search object can never be known precisely. Therefore, it is necessary to estimate the probable error of the average surface wind acting on the search object and the amount of probable error this will introduce into the drift computations. This amount will be used to compute the total probable error of position.

A   Average surface wind (*ASW*)

1	Surface wind data	For each available wind value in this drift interval, enter the time of the observation, the starting and ending times of the time interval during which that wind value was in effect, the number of hours in the interval (ending time *minus* starting time), the wind direction, the wind speed, and the wind contribution for that interval (wind speed times the number of hours in the interval).
2	Average surface wind	Add the hours in the "Number of hours" column to get the "Total hours" (D). (The total hours should equal the number of hours in the drift interval from **line B.2** of the **Datum worksheet**. If this is not the case, the difference should be explained.) Use a manoeuvring board or a calculator to compute the direction (E) and speed (F) of the vector sum of all the wind contribution vectors. Copy the direction of this vector sum (E) to the average surface wind direction on **line A.2** of this worksheet. Divide the speed of the vector sum (F) by the total hours (D) and enter the result as the average surface wind speed on **line A.2** of this worksheet. Copy the average surface wind direction and speed to **line C.1** of the **Datum worksheet**.

B   Probable error

1	Probable error of *ASW*	Estimate the probable error of the average surface wind. If no value is available, enter 5 knots for observed winds, 8 knots for forecast winds.
2	Probable error of drift velocity due to probable error of the Average surface wind ($ASWDV_e$)	Estimate the probable error of the drift velocity that will be caused by the probable error of the average surface wind. If no better estimate is available, enter **0.3** knots for observed winds that are either relatively steady or change gradually in speed or direction. Enter **0.5** knots for forecast winds and highly variable observed winds such as winds that suddenly shift during the passage of storms or weather fronts. Copy this value to **line C.2** of the **Datum worksheet**. See note below for more information.

Note: The probable error of the average surface wind (ASW_e) contributes to the total probable drift velocity error (DV_e) in two ways. The ASW_e increases the total probable wind current error and the total probable leeway error. The value recorded on **line B.2** of the **Average surface wind (ASW) worksheet** is an estimate of the combined effects of the increased probable errors in wind current and leeway due to the probable error in the average surface wind. ***Caution:*** The probable wind current error (WC_e) entered on **line 7** of the **Wind current (WC) worksheet** represents **only** the probable error in the wind current estimate that still exists even when the average surface wind is precisely known. It does **not** include any error due to uncertainty about the average surface wind value used to estimate the wind current. Similarly, the probable leeway error (LW_e) entered on **line 7** of the **Leeway (LW) worksheet** represents **only** the probable error in the leeway estimate that still exists even when the average surface wind is precisely known. It also does **not** include any error due to uncertainty about the average surface wind value used to estimate the leeway.

Total water current (TWC) worksheet

Case title _____ Case number _____ Date _____

Planner's name _____ Datum number _____ Search plan A B C _____

A Observed total water current (*TWC*)

1 Source (datum marker buoy (DMB), debris, oil)   _____

2 Observed set/drift   _____ °T   _____ kts

3 Probable error of observation (*TWC*$_e$)   _____ kts

4 Go to **part D** on the **Datum worksheet**.

B Computed total water current

1 Tidal current (*TC*)

     a   Source (tidal current tables, local knowledge)   _____

     b   Tidal current (*TC*) set/drift
         (Attach any tidal current computations)   _____ °T   _____ kts

     c   Probable error of tidal current (TCe)   _____ kts

2 Sea current (*SC*)

     a   Source (atlas, pilot chart, etc.)   _____

     b   Sea current (*SC*) set/drift   _____ °T   _____ kts

     c   Probable error of sea current (*SC*$_e$)   _____ kts

3 Wind current (*WC*)
   (Attach **Wind current worksheet**)

     a   Wind current (*WC*) set/drift   _____ °T   _____ kts

     b   Probable error of wind current (*WC*$_e$)   _____ kts

4 Other water current (*OWC*)

     a   Source (local knowledge, previous incidents, etc.)   _____

     b   Other water current (*OWC*) set/drift   _____ °T   _____ kts

     c   Probable error of other water current (*OWC*$_e$)   _____ kts

5 Computed Total water current (*TWC*) set/drift   _____ °T   _____ kts

6 Computed probable total water current error (*TWC*$_e$)
   ($TWC_e = \sqrt{TC_e^2 + SC_e^2 + WC_e^2 + OWC_e^2}$)   _____ kts

7 Go to **part D** on the **Datum worksheet**.

Total water current (TWC) worksheet instructions

Introduction

Total water current may be determined by observing the drift of objects that have little or no leeway. Total water current may also be determined or estimated using data from tidal current tables, sea current atlases, a wind current graph or computational procedure, and other sources. Often the Total Water Current will be the vector sum of two or more of these values.

None of the values will be exact and each will have at least some probable error. It is necessary to estimate the sizes of these probable errors. If two or more current vectors are added to determine the total water current, then the probable error of the total water current must be computed from the probable errors of the individual currents. This value will then be used to compute the total probable error of position.

If available, observed total water current at or near the scene is preferable to computed or estimated values. If total water current observations are available, complete **Part A** of this worksheet and record the result in **Part D** of the **Datum worksheet**. If total water current observations are not available, complete the applicable sections of **Part B** of this worksheet and record the result in **Part D** of the **Datum worksheet**.

A	**Observed total water current**	Datum marker buoys (DMBs) and debris with little freeboard tend to drift with the surface current. Early observations derived from relocating identifiable objects may be questionable due to navigational error. Self-locating DMBs are generally very accurate although the data returned may require some processing to be useful.
1	Source	Enter the type of object whose drift was observed to determine the total water current.
2	Observed set/drift	Enter the true direction and drift of the observed object.
3	Probable error of observation (TWC_e)	Enter the estimated probable error of the observed total water current as it relates to the search object's probable starting position. Factors to consider include the probable position errors of the observations, the distance between the observations and the search object's probable starting position, the amount of time since the last observation, and the amount of variability of the currents in the area of interest. If the observations are considered to be of good to excellent quality and representative of the current at the search object's (unknown) location, enter **0.1** knots. Otherwise, enter **0.2** knots.
4	Go to **Part D** of the **Datum worksheet**	Enter the true direction and speed (**line A.2**) on **line D.1** of the **Datum worksheet**. Enter the probable error (**line A.3**) on **line D.2** of the **Datum worksheet**.
B	**Computed total water current**	Enter values only for those currents that are present at the search object's location. For any current that is not present, leave the set, drift, and probable error blank.
1	Tidal current (*TC*)	General Rule: In coastal waters, tidal currents will usually be important. To compute tidal current, search planners should consult published tidal current tables, if available, for the vicinity of the datum position. Local knowledge is also often of great value in dealing with drift due to tidal currents.
	a Source	Enter the source of the tidal current information.

	b	Tidal current (*TC*) set/drift	Enter the true direction and speed of the average, or net, tidal current for the drift interval.
	c	Probable error of tidal current (*TC*$_e$)	Enter the estimated probable error of the computed or estimated tidal current as it relates to the search object's approximate location. Factors to consider include the distance between the reference location shown in the tidal current tables and the search object's probable starting position and the amount of variability of the currents in the area of interest. If no better estimate is available, enter **0.3** knots.
2		Sea current (*SC*)	General rule: Sea currents derived from long-term seasonal averages taken over a wide area (e.g., currents taken from a pilot chart or atlas of surface currents) are most useful in areas that are well off shore. Currents from these sources generally should not be used when computing total water current in coastal waters, especially when the distance from the shore of a large land mass is less than 25 miles **and** the water depth is less than 300 feet (100 metres, 50 fathoms). If local and regional data on short-term coastal surface currents are available, or if such data are available from a validated computerized circulation model, these values should be used. If not, sea current should be ignored and *TWC* should be calculated using only the wind current (*WC*) and tidal current (*TC*).
	a	Source	Enter the source of the sea current information.
	b	Sea current (*SC*) set/drift	Enter the true direction and speed of the sea current from the information source.
	c	Probable error of sea current (*SC*$_e$)	Enter the estimated probable error of the sea current as it relates to the search object's approximate location. Consider the amount of variability of the currents in the area of interest. If no better estimate is available, enter **0.3** knots.
3		Wind current (*WC*)	Go to the **Wind current worksheet**, compute the wind current, and attach the worksheet.
	a	Wind current (*WC*) set/drift	Enter the true direction and speed of the wind current from **line 6** of the **Wind current worksheet.**
	b	Probable error of wind current (*WC*$_e$)	Enter the estimated probable error of the wind current from **line 7** of the **Wind current worksheet.**
4		Other water current (*OWC*)	General rule: Other water current is current that does not fall into one of the other categories. For example, the discharge of large rivers into the sea can affect the currents many miles from shore.
	a	Source	Enter the source of this current information.
	b	Other water current (*OWC*) set/drift	Enter the true direction and speed of this current from the information source.
	c	Probable error of other water current (*OWC*$_e$)	Enter the estimated probable error of this current as it relates to the search object's approximate location. Consider the amount of variability of the currents in the area of interest. If no better estimate is available, enter **0.3** knots.

5	Computed total water current set/drift	Using a manoeuvring board or calculator, compute the vector sum of all the above water currents. Enter the resultant direction (set) and speed (drift) in the spaces provided.
6	Computed total probable water current error (TWC_e)	Compute the probable error of the total water current by taking the square root of the sum of all the squared water current errors. Stated as a general formula:

$$TWC_e = \sqrt{TC_e^{\,2} + SC_e^{\,2} + WC_e^{\,2} + OWC_e^{\,2}}$$

Usually only some of these terms will be used. For example, if the object is well out to sea beyond tidal influence, then the term TC_e is removed from the formula above.

7	Go to **Part D** of the **Datum worksheet**	Enter the computed total water current true direction and speed (**line B.5**) on **line D.1** of the **Datum worksheet**. Enter the probable total water current error (line B.6) on **line D.2** of the **Datum worksheet**.

Wind current (WC) worksheet

Case title _____ Case number _____ Date _____

Planner's name _____ Datum number _____ Search plan A B C _____

Wind current (*WC*)

1   Average surface wind (*ASW*)
     (From **Datum worksheet, line C.1**)   _____ °T   _____ kts

2   Downwind direction (ASW direction ± 180°)   _____ °T

3   Wind current drift
     (from **figure N-1**)   _____ kts

4   Divergence of wind current
     (from **figure N-1**)   ± _____ °

5   Wind current set
     (Downwind direction ± divergence of wind current)
     (add divergence in northern hemisphere,
     subtract in southern hemisphere)   _____ °T

6   Wind current (*WC*) set/drift   _____ °T   _____ kts

7   Probable error of wind current (*WC*$_e$)   _____ kts

8   Go to **line B.3** on the **Total water current (TWC) worksheet**.

Wind current (WC) worksheet instructions

Introduction

Local wind blowing over the ocean's surface generates a current in the water. Usually this current is in addition to the average sea current found in atlases and on pilot charts. Therefore, it is necessary to estimate this current and the probable error of the estimated value.

Wind current (WC)

Caution: In areas where the wind is nearly constant over long periods, like the trade winds, it may not be appropriate to add wind current to the average sea current. Also, the sea current values estimated by some computer models include the local wind current. Search planners should not compute and add wind current to this type of data.

1	Average surface wind (*ASW*)	Enter the computed average surface wind from the **Datum worksheet** (**line C.1**).
2	Downwind direction	Add (or subtract) 180° to (from) the average surface wind direction to get the downwind direction.
3	Wind current drift	Go to **figure N-1**, **Local wind current graph and table**, find the wind current that corresponds to the speed of the average surface wind on **line 1**.
4	Divergence of wind current	Go to **figure N-1** and find the appropriate value for the divergence of the wind current from the downwind direction based on the approximate latitude of the search object.
5	Wind current set	In the northern hemisphere, add the divergence from **line 4** to the downwind direction from **line 2**. If the result is greater than 360°, subtract 360°. In the southern hemisphere, subtract the divergence on **line 4** from the downwind direction on **line 2**. If the result is less than zero, add 360°.
6	Wind current (*WC*) set/drift	Enter the set from **line 5** and the drift from **line 3**.
7	Probable wind current error (*WC$_e$*)	Enter the estimated probable error of the wind current. Factors to consider include the distance between the wind observations and the search object's probable starting position, the amount of time since the last wind observation, and the amount of variability of the winds in the area of interest during the drift interval. Wind current estimates based on the average of highly variable winds tend to have larger probable errors than those based on steady winds. If no better estimate is available, enter **0.3** knots. See note below for more information.
8	Go to **line B.3** on the **Total water current (TWC) worksheet**	Enter the wind current set and drift (**line 6**) on **line B.3.a** of the **Total water current (TWC) worksheet**. Enter the probable error of the wind current (**line 7**) on **line B.3.b** of the **Total water current (TWC) worksheet**.

Note: The relationship between wind and wind current is not precisely understood, especially when there is significant variation in the wind over the interval of interest. For this reason the wind current estimate has some probable error that is independent of the probable error in the average surface wind. The probable wind current error (*WC$_e$*) entered on **line 7** of the **Wind current (WC) worksheet** represents **only** the probable error in the wind current estimate that is still present even when the average surface wind is precisely known. It does not include any error due to uncertainty about the average surface wind value used to estimate the wind current. The additional error due to uncertainty about the average surface wind is included in the Probable error of drift velocity due to Probable error of the average surface wind (*ASWDV$_e$*) entered on **line B.2** of the **Average surface wind (ASW) worksheet** and **line C.2** of the **Datum worksheet**.

Leeway (LW) worksheet

Case title _____ Case number _____ Date _____

Planner's name _____ Datum number _____ Search plan A B C _____

Search object _____

1   Average surface wind (*ASW*)
     (from **Datum worksheet, line C.1**)   _____ °T   _____ kts

2   Downwind direction (*ASW* direction ± 180°)   _____ °T

3   Leeway speed
     (from **figure N-2 or N-3**)   _____ kts

4   Leeway divergence angle
     (from **figure N-2 or N-3**)   ± _____ °

5   Leeway directions

     a   Left of downwind (**line 2 – line 4**)   _____ °T

     b   Right of downwind (**line 2 + line 4**)   _____ °T

6   Leeway (*LW*)

     a   Left of downwind   _____ °T   _____ kts

     b   Right of downwind   _____ °T   _____ kts

7   Probable leeway error (*LW*$_e$)
     (from **figure N-2 or N-3**)   _____ kts

8   Go to **Part E** on the **Datum worksheet**.

Leeway (LW) worksheet instructions

Introduction

Leeway is the movement of an object through the water due to wind and waves acting on the object. Leeway speeds for various types of objects may be estimated by using the graphs in **figures N-2** and **N-3**. Estimating leeway direction is more difficult. Lack of symmetry in the search object's shape either above or below the waterline may cause it to have leeway in a direction that is not directly downwind. The leeway divergence angles given in **figures N-2** and **N-3** are the average differences between the object's direction of leeway and the downwind direction. For example, an object with a leeway divergence of $\pm 45°$ has a leeway that is, on average, either 45° to the left of the downwind direction or 45° to the right of the downwind direction. Since the leeway of objects that tend to diverge from the downwind direction is equally likely to be to the left or right of the downwind direction, it is necessary to account for both possibilities. It is also necessary to account for the probable error of the leeway estimate.

The leeway values obtained from **figures N-2** and **N-3** are not exact. They are average values for the types of objects shown. All the values have at least some probable error. It is necessary to estimate the size of this probable error so the total probable drift error may be computed.

1	Average surface wind (*ASW*)	Enter the value for the average surface wind direction and speed from the **Datum worksheet**, **line C.1**.
2	Downwind direction	Add (or subtract) 180° to (from) the average surface wind direction to get the downwind direction.
3	Leeway speed	Find the description in **figure N-2** or **N-3** that most closely corresponds to the search object. Use the corresponding line on the graph and the average surface wind speed (**line 1**) to find the leeway speed. Enter this value in the blank provided.
4	Leeway divergence angle	Use the same description as the one used for **line 3** to find the search object's leeway divergence angle on **figure N-2** or **N-3**. Enter the leeway divergence angle that appears in parentheses ( ) next to the search object's description.
5	Leeway directions	
	a Left of downwind	Subtract the leeway divergence angle (**line 4**) from the downwind direction (**line 2**). If the result is less than zero, add 360°.
	b Right of downwind	Add the leeway divergence angle (**line 4**) to the downwind direction (**line 2**). If the result is greater than 360°, subtract 360°.
6	Leeway (*LW*)	
	a Left of downwind	Enter the direction from **line 5.a** and the speed from **line 3**.
	b Right of downwind	Enter the direction from **line 5.b** and the speed from **line 3**.
7	Probable leeway error	Using the same description as the one used for **line 3**, find the probable error of the search object's leeway estimate on **figure N-2** or **N-3**. Enter the probable leeway error that appears in brackets [ ] next to the search object's description. Copy this value to **line E.3** of the **Datum worksheet**. See note below for more information.
8	Go to **line E** on the **Datum worksheet**	Enter the "left" direction and speed from **line 6.a** on **line E.1** of the **Datum worksheet**. Enter the "right"' direction and speed from **line 6.b** on **line E.2** of the **Datum worksheet**. Enter the probable leeway error from **line 7** on **line E.3** of the **Datum worksheet**.

Note: Figures N-2 and **N-3** are based on the best and latest information from leeway experiments. However, the values obtained from the graphs are not exact and are still subject to some probable error. The probable leeway error (LW_e) entered on **line 7** of the **Leeway (LW) worksheet** represents **only** the probable error in the leeway estimate that still exists even when the average surface wind is precisely known. It does **not** include any error due to uncertainty about the average surface wind value used to estimate the leeway. The additional error due to uncertainty about the average surface wind is included in the Probable error of drift velocity due to probable error of the average surface wind ($ASWDV_e$) entered on **line B.2** of the **Average surface wind (ASW) worksheet** and **line C.2** of the **Datum worksheet**.

Total probable error of position (E) worksheet for land and marine environments

Case title _____ Case number _____ Date _____

Planner's name _____ Datum number _____ Search plan A B C _____

A Probable distress incident/initial position error (X)

(Go to **line 1** to compute probable error of the distress incident position. Go to **line 6** if the starting position for this drift interval is a previous datum.)

1 Navigational fix error
   (from **table N-1** or **N-2**)   _____ NM

2 Dead reckoning (DR) error rate
   (from **table N-3**)   _____ %

3 DR distance since last fix   _____ NM

4 DR navigational error
   (**line A.2** × **line A.3**)   _____ NM

5 Glide distance (if aircraft/parachute descent heading
   is unknown)   _____ NM

6 Probable initial position error (X)
   (X = **line A.1** + **line A.4** + **line A.5**) or
   (X = Total probable error of position from **line H.2**
   of previous **Datum worksheet**)   _____ NM

B Total probable drift error (D_e)

1 Drift interval
   (from **line B.2** of the **Datum worksheet**)   _____ hours

2 Probable drift velocity error (DV_e)
   (from **line F.4** of the **Datum worksheet**)   _____ kts

3 Total probable drift error (D_e)
   (D_e = **line B.1** × **line B.2**)   _____ NM

C Probable search facility position error (Y)

1 Navigational fix error
   (from **table N-1** or **N-2**)   _____ NM

2 Dead reckoning (DR) error rate
   (from **table N-3**)   _____ %

3 DR distance since last fix   _____ NM

4 DR navigational error
   (**line C.2** × **line C.3**)   _____ NM

5 Probable search facility position error (Y)
   (Y = **line C.1** + **line C.4**)   _____ NM

D Total probable error of position (*E*)

1 Sum of squared errors
$(E^2 = X^2 + D_e{}^2 + Y^2)$ _____ NM^2

2 Total probable error of position
$(E = \sqrt{X^2 + D_e{}^2 + Y^2})$ _____ NM

Total probable error of position (E) worksheet instructions

Introduction

The total probable error of position is a measure of the uncertainty about the search object's location and the ability of the search facilities to locate their assigned search areas accurately. Total probable error of position is used to determine the size of the optimal area to search with the available search effort. The new datum position and total probable error of position data are carried forward to the **Effort allocation worksheet**.

A	**Probable distress incident/initial position error (X)**	If this is the first **Total probable error of position worksheet** for this case, complete **lines A.1** through **A.6**. Otherwise, go directly to **line A.6** and enter the total probable error of position (E) from **line H.2** of the previous **Datum worksheet.**
1	Navigational fix error	Enter the probable fix error based on the navigational capability of the distressed craft. **Tables N-1** and **N-2** provide estimates of probable navigational fix error based on the type of navigation and size of the distressed craft. These values may be used when more accurate information is not available.
2	Dead reckoning (DR) error rate	Enter the probable error in DR position as a percentage of the distance travelled since the last navigational fix. **Table N-3** provides estimates of DR error rates based on the type and size of the distressed craft. These values may be used when more accurate information is not available.
3	DR distance since last fix	Enter the estimated distance travelled by the distressed craft since its last navigational fix.
4	DR navigational error	Convert the percentage on **line A.2** to a decimal fraction and multiply it by the value on **line A.3** to get the DR navigational error.
5	Glide distance (aircraft/parachute)	If the incident involves an aircraft and the descent heading is unknown for either the aircraft, a parachute with a non-zero glide ratio or both, enter the maximum estimated glide distance (aircraft glide or parachute glide as appropriate). Otherwise, enter zero.
6	Probable initial position error (X)	If **lines A.1** through **A.5** were completed, compute the Probable Initial Position Error as the sum of **lines A.1**, **A.4**, and **A.5**. Otherwise, enter the total probable error of position from **line H.2** of the previous **Datum worksheet**.

B	**Total probable drift error (D_e)**	
1	Drift interval	Enter the drift interval in hours from **line B.2** of the **Datum worksheet.**
2	Probable drift velocity error (DV_e)	Enter the probable drift velocity error from **line F.4** of the **Datum worksheet**.
3	Total probable drift error (D_e)	Multiply the drift interval on **line B.1** by the probable drift velocity error on **line B.2** to get the total probable drift error.

C   Probable search facility position error (*Y*)

1	Navigational fix error	Enter the probable fix error based on the navigational capability of the search facility. **Tables N-1** and **N-2** provide estimates of probable navigational fix error based on the type of navigation and size of the search facility. These values may be used when more accurate information is not available.
2	Dead reckoning (DR) error rate	Enter the probable error in DR position as a percentage of the distance travelled by the search facility between navigational fixes. **Table N-3** provides estimates of DR error rates based on the type and size of the search facility. These values may be used when more accurate information is not available.
3	DR distance since last fix	Enter the estimated distance travelled by the search facility between navigational fixes.
4	DR navigational error	Convert the percentage on **line C.2** to a decimal fraction and multiply it by the value on **line C.3** to get the DR navigational error.
5	Probable search facility position error (*Y*)	Compute the Probable search facility position error as the sum of **lines C.1** and **C.4**.

D   Total probable error of position (*E*)

1	Sum of squared errors (E^2)	Square the values on **lines A.6**, **B.3**, and **C.5**. Add the squared values together to get the sum of the squared errors (E_2). This value will be used in the **Effort allocation worksheet**.
2	Total probable error of position (*E*)	Compute the square root of the value on **line D.1** to get the total probable error of position (*E*). This value will be used for search effort allocation and as the probable initial position error for the next drift interval.

Appendix L

Search planning and evaluation worksheets

Total available search effort (Z_{ta}) worksheet

Case title _____ Case number _____ Date _____

Planner's name _____ Datum number _____ Search plan A B C _____

Datum _____ _____ Datum _____ _____
(left)   Latitude   Longitude   (right)   Latitude   Longitude

Search object _____ Date/time _____

Total Available Effort Computations

		1	2	3	4	5
1	Search sub-area designation	___	___	___	___	___
2	Search facility assigned	___	___	___	___	___
3	Search facility speed (V)	___	___	___	___	___
4	On-scene endurance	___	___	___	___	___
5	Daylight hours remaining	___	___	___	___	___
6	Search endurance (T) (T = 85% of lesser of **line 4** or **5** above)	___	___	___	___	___
7	Search altitude (metres/feet) *(circle one)*	___	___	___	___	___
8	Uncorrected sweep width	___	___	___	___	___
9	Weather, terrain correction factor (f_w, f_t)	___	___	___	___	___
10	Velocity correction factor (f_v) (aircraft only)	___	___	___	___	___
11	Fatigue correction factor (f_f)	___	___	___	___	___
12	Corrected sweep width (W)	___	___	___	___	___
13	Search effort ($Z = V \times T \times W$)	___	___	___	___	___

14   Total available search effort ($Z_{ta} = Z_{a1} + Z_{a2} + Z_{a3} + ...$)   _____ NM^2

15   Separation ratio (SR) (leeway divergence datums only) (from **line H.3** of the **Datum worksheet**)   _____

15   Relative effort ($Z_r = Z_{ta}/f_z$)   _____

16   If the separation ratio (SR) on **line 15** is greater than four ($SR > 4$), go to the **Widely diverging datums worksheet**. Otherwise, go to the **Effort allocation worksheet**.

Total available search effort (Z_{ta}) worksheet instructions

Introduction

This **Total available search effort worksheet** is used to determine the total amount of search effort that will be available on scene. This worksheet is based on a DAYLIGHT VISUAL SEARCH.

Enter the case title, case number, planner's name, datum number, search designator, datum latitudes, longitudes and time, and the primary search object in the spaces provided. All of this information may be found on the **Datum worksheet** except possibly the planner's name. The name that appears on this worksheet should be that of the person responsible for completing this worksheet, who may be different from the person who completed the **Datum worksheet**.

Total available search effort computations

1	Search sub-area designation	Use standard sub-area designators, such as A-1, B-3, etc.
2	Search facility assigned	Enter name, hull or tail number, or other identifier that uniquely identifies the search facility assigned to the corresponding search sub-area.
3	Search facility speed (*V*)	Enter the average speed made good over the ground for each search facility while searching. For aircraft, the True Airspeed (TAS) while searching is usually a satisfactory approximation.
4	On-scene endurance	Enter the total amount of time the search facility can provide on scene. Do not include the transit time to and from the area.
5	Daylight hours remaining	Enter the number of hours between the search facility's estimated time of arrival on scene (start of searching) and sunset.
6	Search endurance (*T*)	Compute 85% of the value on **line 4** or **line 5**, whichever is smaller. This figure represents the "productive" search time. It provides a 15% allowance for investigating sightings and navigating turns at the ends of search legs.
7	Search altitude	Determine the search altitude options available (See note below) and enter a preliminary altitude assignment.

Note: Recommended guidelines for determining search altitude options:

(a) Stay at least 150 m (500 ft) below cloud bases.

(b) Stay at least 60 m (200 ft) above the water or ground.

(c) Use at least 150 m (500 ft) of vertical separation between aircraft that share a common search sub-area boundary.

(d) In most cases, use altitudes in increments of 150 m (500 ft).

(e) Additional guidance is provided in **table N-11**.

8	Uncorrected sweep width	Enter the appropriate value from the Sweep width tables in appendix N. Based on the type of search facility, use **table N-4**, **N-5**, or **N-6** for maritime searches. Use **table N-9** for searches over land.
9	Weather, terrain correction factor (f_w, f_t)	For maritime searches, enter the appropriate value (f_w) from **table N-7**. For searches over land, enter the appropriate value (f_t) from **table N-10**.

10	Velocity correction factor (f_v)	For searches conducted by aircraft over water, enter the appropriate velocity correction factor (f_v) from **table N-8**. For searches conducted by vessels and for searches over land, enter **1.0**.
11	Fatigue correction factor (f_f)	If there are indications that the search facility crew is or will be suffering significantly from fatigue during the search, enter **0.9**. If crew fatigue is not considered a significant factor for the assigned search facility, enter **1.0**.
12	Corrected sweep width (W)	Multiply the values in each column on **lines 8**, **9**, **10**, and **11** (uncorrected sweep width, weather/terrain correction factor, velocity correction factor and fatigue correction factor) to get the corrected sweep width.
13	Search effort (Z)	Multiply the search facility's speed (**line 3**) by the search facility's endurance (**line 6**) and multiply the result by the corrected sweep width (**line 12**), or use **figure N-4**.
14	Total available search effort (Z_{ta})	Add the individual search effort values listed on **line 13** and enter the total.
15	Separation ratio (SR)	Enter the separation ratio (SR) from **line H.3** of the **Datum worksheet**.

16   In most cases, the separation ratio (SR) will be less than or equal to four ($SR \leq 4$) and the search planner may go directly to the **Effort allocation worksheet**. However, if the separation ratio (SR) entered on **line 15** is greater than four ($SR > 4$), an initial effort allocation decision must be made between the following two choices:

- The two datums may be treated as separate single point datums, each with its own search area. Two separate search areas with no overlap will be the usual result.

- A line may be drawn between the two datums and treated as the base line portion of a datum line. In this case a single search area centred on the datum line will be the result.

The **Widely diverging datums worksheet instructions** provide guidance to help the search planner decide which alternative to use. The Widely diverging datums worksheet helps the search planner make the necessary preparations for entering the Effort allocation worksheet(s).

The following conditions can lead to leeway divergence datums becoming so widely separated in comparison to their total probable errors of position that separate search areas should be considered:

- The leeway divergence angle is large ($> 30°$).

- The leeway rate is moderate to large (> 1 knot).

- The time adrift is significant (> 12 h).

- The probable errors of the initial and search facility positions are small (< 1 NM).

- The probable errors of the factors affecting drift (winds, currents, leeway) are all small (< 0.3 knot).

- The cumulative relative search effort is small to moderate (< 10).

Usually all of these conditions must be met before the separation ratio will become greater than four ($SR > 4$) and the divergence distance (DD) will be large enough to justify dividing the available search effort into two portions assigned to separate, non-contiguous search areas. Only rarely will enough of these conditions be met to create such a situation.

Widely diverging datums worksheet

Case title _____ Case number _____ Date _____

Planner's name _____ Datum number _____ Search plan A B C _____

Datum _____ _____ Datum _____ _____
(left)   Latitude   Longitude   (right)   Latitude   Longitude

Search object _____ Date/time _____

1   Total available search effort (Z_{ta})
       (from **line 14** of the **Total available search effort worksheet**)   _____ NM^2

2   Divergence distance (DD)
       (from **line G.3** of the **Datum worksheet**)   _____ NM^2

3   Total probable error of position (E)
       (from **line H.2** of the **Datum worksheet**)   _____ NM^2

4   Type of datum to use for planning this search
       (Circle one)

       a   Two separate point datums (Go to **line 5**)

       b   A line datum between two point datums (Go to **line 6**)

5   Two separate point datums

       a   Available search effort for the left datum ($Z_{a(left)}$)   _____ NM^2

       b   Available search effort for the right datum ($Z_{a(right)}$)   _____ NM^2

       c   Total available search effort ($Z_{ta} = Z_{a(left)} + Z_{a(right)}$)
             (must equal value on **line 1**)   _____ NM^2

       d   Go to the **Effort allocation worksheets** (one for each datum) and follow the instructions for single point datums.

6   A line datum between two point datums

       a   Length of the datum line [$L = DD + (2 \times E)$]   _____ NM

       b   Go to the **Effort allocation worksheet** and follow the instructions for a line datum.

Widely diverging datums worksheet instructions

Introduction

It is possible for objects that have leeway divergence to have two widely separated datums whose associated probability density distributions have little or no overlap. When the distance between the datums is large in comparison to the probable error of each datum position, the search planner must decide whether they should be treated as two separate single point datums or as the end points of the base line portion of a datum line.

Experimental evidence indicates that once an object starts to have a leeway to the left of the downwind direction it tends to remain on that tack indefinitely. The same is true if the object starts to have a leeway to the right of the downwind direction. If the initial and search facility probable position errors are small, the leeway divergence angle is large ($> 30°$), the probable errors of the winds, currents and leeway are all small (each contributing less than 0.3 knot to the drift velocity error), etc., the divergence distance (DD) may become greater than four times the probable error of position (E). This is an unlikely situation. However, if it occurs, the search planner should seriously consider applying a portion of the available search effort to each datum rather than applying the total available search effort to a single large area that includes both datums and the area between them. Objects that have large divergence angles will tend toward locations on the line connecting the left and right datums only if they jibe or tack downwind. There has been very little evidence of jibing behaviour in the leeway experiments done to date. This means that when the probable errors are small and the divergence angle is large, there is very little chance of the search object being halfway between the left and right datums. If this is the case, then the area that is near the midpoint of the line connecting the left and right datums will not be a very productive area to search.

If the search planner decides to treat the two datums separately, then it is necessary to divide the total available search effort into two portions and plan two single point datum searches. Unless there is some reason to favour one datum over the other, the total available search effort should be divided into two equal portions. One example of a situation where one datum should be favoured over the other is the following: Suppose a drifting search object was located by an aircraft and observed long enough to determine its leeway was to the right of the downwind direction, but then contact was lost before a homing beacon could be deployed or a rescue facility could arrive on scene. In this case, the datum for the next search that was to the right of the downwind direction probably should be assigned most of the total available search effort. Whenever search effort is to be allocated separately to two datums, an **Effort allocation worksheet** should be completed for each datum, using the instructions for a single point datum.

In situations where the wind has shown large and sudden changes in direction, when the sea is confused, etc., the search planner may decide that the probability of the search object jibing or tacking downwind is larger than usual. The search planner may have other reasons for covering all of the area between the left and right datums. In these cases, the search planner should consider drawing a line between the left and right datums and using it as the base line portion of a datum line. When the total available search effort is to be allocated in this fashion, a single **Effort allocation worksheet** should be completed following the instructions for a datum line.

1	Total available search effort (Z_{ta})	Enter the total available search effort (Z_{ta}) from **line 14** of the **Total available search effort worksheet**.
2	Divergence distance (DD)	Enter the divergence distance (DD) from **line G.3** of the **Datum worksheet**.
3	Total probable error of position (E)	Enter the total probable error of position from **line H.2** of the **Datum worksheet**. (**Note:** The value of DD on **line 2** should be more than four times the value of E on this line ($DD > 4 \times E$). If this is **not** true, discard this worksheet and go directly to the **Effort allocation worksheet**.)

4	Type of datum	Decide whether to plan the next search around two separate datums or along a datum line that passes through the left and right datums. Circle "a" or "b" as appropriate. If "a" is circled, go to **line 5**. If "b" is circled, go to **line 6**.
5	Two separate point datums	In this case, the total available search effort is to be divided into two parts. One part will be applied to a search area centred on one of the datums while the other part will be applied to a search area centred on the other datum.
a	Available search effort for the left datum ($Z_{a(left)}$)	Enter the amount of search effort that will be applied to the left datum. This amount must be between zero and the total available search effort ($0 \leq Z_{a(left)} \leq Z_{ta}$).
b	Available search effort for the right datum ($Z_{a(right)}$)	Enter the amount of search effort that will be applied to the right datum. This amount must be between zero and the total available search effort ($0 \leq Z_{a(right)} \leq Z_{ta}$).
c	Total available search effort ($Z_{ta} = Z_{a(left)} + Z_{a(right)}$)	Add the search effort available for the left datum (**line 5.a**) to the search effort available for the right datum (**line 5.b**). The result should equal the total available search effort (**line 1**). If this is not true, adjust the efforts for the left and right datums so their sum equals the total available search effort (**line 1**).
d	Go to **Effort allocation worksheets**	Complete an **Effort allocation worksheet** for each datum. Enter the search effort available for the left datum ($Z_{a(left)}$) on **line 1** of the **Effort allocation worksheet** for the left datum. On a second **Effort allocation worksheet**, enter the search effort available for the right datum ($Z_{a(right)}$) on **line 1**.
6	A line datum between two point datums	In this case, a single search area is to be centred on the line connecting the left and right datums.
a	Length of the datum line (L)	Compute the length of the datum line by adding twice the total probable error of position (E) from **line 3** to the divergence distance (DD) from **line 2**. Stated as a formula, $L = DD + (2 \times E)$.
b	Go to the **Effort allocation worksheet**	Go to the **Effort allocation worksheet**. Enter the total available search effort (Z_{ta}) from **line 1** of this worksheet as the available search effort (Z_a) on **line 1** of the **Effort allocation worksheet**. Enter the length of the datum line (L) from **line 6.a** as the length of the datum line (L) on **line 2.b** of the **Effort allocation worksheet**. Follow the effort allocation instructions for line datums.

Effort allocation worksheet for optimal search of single point, leeway divergence or line datums

Case title _____ Case number _____ Date _____

Planner's name _____ Datum number _____ Search plan A B C _____

Datum _____ _____ Datum _____ _____
(left)   Latitude   Longitude   (right)   Latitude   Longitude

Search object _____ Date/time _____

Effort allocation computations

1   Available search effort (Z_{ta}, $Z_{a(left)}$, or $Z_{a(right)}$)
     (from **line 14** of the **Total available search effort worksheet** or
     line 5.a or **line 5.b** of the **Widely diverging datums worksheet**) _____ NM^2

2   Effort factor (f_Z)

    a   Total probable error of position (E)   _____ NM

    b   Length of datum line (L)   _____ NM

    c   Effort factor (f_Z) ($f_{Zp} = E_2$ or $f_{Zl} = E \times L$)   _____ NM^2

3   Relative effort ($Z_r = Z_a/f_z$)   _____

4   Cumulative relative effort (Z_{rc} = previous $Z_{rc} + Z_r$)   _____

5   Optimal search factor (f_s)   Ideal_____ Normal _____ (f_s) _____

6   Optimal search radius ($R_o = f_s \times E$)   _____ NM

7   Optimal search area (A_o)   _____ NM^2

    a   Single point datum ($A_o = 4 \times R_o^2$)

    b   Leeway divergence datums [$A_o = (4 \times R_o^2) + 2 \times R_o \times DD)$]

    c   Line datum ($A_o = 2 \times R_o \times L$)

8   Optimal coverage factor ($C_o = Z_a/A_o$)   _____

			1	2	3	4	5
9	Optimal track spacing ($S_o = W/C_o$)		___	___	___	___	___
10	Nearest assignable track spacing (S) (within limits of search facility navigational capability)		___	___	___	___	___
11	Adjusted search areas ($A = V \times T \times S$)		___	___	___	___	___

12   Total adjusted search area ($A_t = A_1 + A_2 + A_3 + ...$)   _____ NM^2

13   Adjusted search radius (R)   _____ NM

    a   Single point datum $R = \dfrac{\sqrt{A_t}}{2}$

    b   Leeway divergence datums $R = \dfrac{\sqrt{DD^2 + (4 \times A_t)} - DD}{4}$

    c   Line datum $R = \dfrac{A_t}{2 \times L}$

14   Adjusted search area dimensions

    a   Length   Length _____ NM

          i)   Single point datum   *Length* $= 2 \times R$

          ii)   Leeway divergence datums   *Length* $= (2 \times R) + DD$

          iii) Line datum   *Length of the Base Line* (L_b)   _____ NM

               a)   No extensions   *Length* $= L_b$

               b)   One extension   *Length* $= R + L_b$

               c)   Two extensions   *Length* $= (2 \times R) + L_b$

    b   Width $= 2 \times R$ Width _____ NM

15   Plot the adjusted search area on a suitable chart   (Check when done)_____

16   Divide the adjusted search area into search sub-areas
according to the values on **line 11**   (Check when done)_____

17   Go to the **Search action plan worksheet**.

Effort allocation worksheet instructions for optimal search of single point, leeway divergence or line datums

Introduction

This **Effort allocation worksheet** is used to determine the optimal way to allocate the available search effort around a single datum point, over two divergent datum points or along a datum line. It considers the search effort that several dissimilar search facilities can provide. The worksheet also aids in computing the optimal area to search and the optimum uniform coverage factor. Finally, the worksheet provides guidance for determining the actual search sub-area dimensions for each available search facility. This worksheet is based on a DAYLIGHT VISUAL SEARCH.

Enter the case title, case number, datum number, search designator, datum latitude, longitude and time, and the primary search object from the Datum worksheet. In the space labelled "Planner's Name", enter the name of the person responsible for completing this worksheet.

Effort allocation computations

1	Available search effort (Z_a)	Enter the total available search effort (Z_{ta}) from **line 14** of the **Total available search effort worksheet** unless the left and right datums are to be treated as separate searches. In that case, two **Effort allocation worksheets** will be required. Enter the available effort for the left datum ($Z_{a(left)}$) on one worksheet and the available effort for the right datum ($Z_{a(right)}$) on the other worksheet.
2	Effort factor (f_Z)	The effort factor (f_Z) provides a standard method for characterizing the size of the area where the search object is probably located. Although the effort factor has units of *area*, its value is only a fraction of the area where the search object may be located.
(a)	Total probable error of position (E)	Enter the total probable error of position (E) from **line H.2** of the **Datum worksheet**.
(b)	Length of datum line (L)	**For line datums only:** Measure or compute the length of the base line (L_b) connecting two points, such as the last known position of a vessel or aircraft and the next point at which a report was expected but not received. When appropriate, extend the base line in one or both directions by an amount equal to E to form the datum line (L).

Examples:

(i) A vessel's intended track lies between two ports, the LKP was the port of departure and the vessel is overdue at its destination. The base line is not extended over land in either direction and $L = L_b$.

(ii) A vessel's intended track lies between its last reported position at sea and its next port of call, where it is overdue. In this situation, the seaward end of the base line is extended by E and $L = L_b + E$.

(iii) Both the last reported position and the next position where the vessel or aircraft was expected to report might be in error. In this situation, both ends of the base line are extended by E and $L = L_b + (2 \times E)$. **Figure L-4** depicts this situation.

			(iv) The length of the datum line was computed on **line 6.a** of the **Widely diverging datums worksheet**. In this situation, the divergence distance (*DD*) was used as the length of the base line (L_b) that was then extended in both directions to form the datum line, as shown in **figure L-4**.

Enter the value of *L* on **line 2.b** if this effort allocation is for a datum line. Otherwise, leave blank.

	(c)	Effort factor (f_Z)	For single and diverging point datums, enter the total probable error of position squared (E^2) from **line H.1** of the **Datum worksheet** or square the total probable error of position (*E*) from **line 2.a**. Stated as a formula, $f_{Zp} = E^2$. For line datums, multiply the total probable error of position (*E*) from **line 2.a** by the length of the datum line (*L*) from **line 2.b**. Stated as a formula, $f_{Zl} = E \times L$.
3		Relative effort (Z_r)	The relative effort (Z_r) shows the relationship between the available search effort (Z_a) and the size of the area where the search object may be located. The relative effort (Z_r) is computed as the ratio of the available effort (Z_a) to the effort factor (f_Z). Divide the available effort (Z_a) from **line 1** by the effort factor (f_Z) from **line 2.c**.
4		Cumulative relative effort (Z_{rc})	Add the relative effort (Z_r) on **line 3** to the cumulative relative effort (Z_{rc}) from **line 4** of the previous **Effort allocation worksheet**. If this is the first search, enter the value of Z_r from **line 3** above. If this is the first time two leeway divergence datums are being treated separately, assume one half of the relative effort (Z_{rc}) from **line 4** of the previous **Effort allocation worksheet** was applied to each datum.
5		Optimal search factor (f_s)	Check "Ideal" or "Normal" search conditions, as appropriate. If any of the correction factors on **lines 9**, **10** or **11** of the **Total available search effort worksheet** are less than **1.0**, or if any probable search facility position error exceeds the corresponding corrected sweep width, check "Normal" search conditions. Otherwise, check "Ideal" search conditions. Enter the optimal search factor (f_s) from the appropriate graph and curve in appendix N (**figure N-5** or **N-6** for single point and leeway divergence datums, **figure N-7** or **N-8** for line datums).
6		Optimal search radius (R_o)	Multiply the optimal search factor (f_s) from **line 5** by the total probable error of position (*E*) from **line 2.a.**
7		Optimal search area (A_o)	The optimal search area depends on whether the type of datum is (a) a single point datum, (b) two leeway divergence datums, or (c) a line datum.
	a	Single point datum	For a single point datum, square the optimal search radius (R_o) from **line 6** and multiply by four. Stated as a formula, $A_o = 4 \times R_o^2$.
	b	Leeway divergence datums	For two leeway divergence datums, copy the divergence distance (*DD*) between the two datums from **line G.3** of the **Datum worksheet** to **line 7.b** of this worksheet. Compute the optimal search area (A_o) using the following formula: $$A_o = (4 \times R_o^2) + (2 \times R_o \times DD).$$
	c	Line datum	For a line datum, multiply twice the optimal search radius (R_o) from **line 6** by the length of the datum line (*L*) from **line 2.b**. Stated as a formula, $A_o = 2 \times R_o \times L$.

8	Optimal coverage factor (C_o)	Divide the available search effort (Z_a) from **line 1** by the optimal search area (A_o) from **line 7**.
9	Optimal track spacing (S_o)	Divide the corrected sweep widths (W) from **line 12** of the **Total available search effort worksheet** by the optimal coverage factor (C_o) from **line 8**.
10	Nearest assignable track spacing (S)	Round the optimal track spacing (S_o) from **line 9** to a value that the corresponding search facility can navigate safely and accurately.
11	Adjusted search areas (A)	Multiply the search facility's speed from **line 3** of the **Total available search effort worksheet** by the search facility's endurance from **line 6** of the **Total available search effort worksheet** and multiply the result by the nearest assignable track spacing from **line 10** of this worksheet. Stated as a formula, $A = V \times T \times S$. **Figure N-9** may also be used to find the adjusted search areas.
12	Total adjusted search area (A_t)	Add the individual adjusted search area values listed on **line 11** and enter the total.
13	Adjusted search radius	The adjusted search radius (R) depends on whether the type of datum is (a) a single point datum, (b) two leeway divergence datums, or (c) a line datum.
	a Single point datum	For single point datums, the adjusted search radius (R) is one-half the square root of the total adjusted search area (A_t) from **line 12**. Stated as a formula: $$R = \frac{\sqrt{A_t}}{2}$$
	b Leeway divergence datums	For two diverging point datums, the search planner must adjust the search radius so the area of the actual search rectangle equals the total adjusted search area (A_t) from **line 12**. The following formula is used to compute an adjusted search radius (R) for the circles around each datum: $$R = \frac{\sqrt{DD^2 + (4 \times A_t)} - DD}{4}$$
	c Line datum	For a line datum, divide the total adjusted search area (A_t) from **line 12** by twice the length of the datum line (L) from **line 2.b** to get the adjusted search radius. Stated as a formula: $$R = \frac{A_t}{2 \times L}$$
14	Adjusted search area dimensions	Choose the correct type of datum below, compute the length of the adjusted search area on **line 14.a** and the width of the adjusted search area on **line 14.b** using the formulas provided.
	a Length	The formula used to find the length of the adjusted search area depends on whether the type of datum is (i) a single point datum, (ii) two leeway divergence datums, or (iii) a line datum.
	i Single point datum	The adjusted search area is a square with its length equal to twice the adjusted search radius from **line 13**. Stated as a formula, *Length = 2 × R*
	ii Leeway divergence datums	The length of the adjusted search area is found by adding twice the adjusted search radius (R) from **line 13** to the divergence distance (DD). Stated as a formula, *Length = (2 × R) + DD*

iii Line datum		Enter the length of the base line portion (L_b) of the datum line. The length of the adjusted search area depends on whether the datum line was formed with zero, one, or two extensions as described in the instructions for **line 2.b**.
	a) No extensions	If the base line was not extended in either direction to form the datum line, then the length of the adjusted search area is the same as the length of the base line (L_b). *Length* = L_b
	b) One extension	If only one end of the base line was extended to form the datum line, then the length of the adjusted search area is the adjusted search radius (R) plus the length of the base line (L_b). *Length* = $R + L_b$
	c) Two extensions	If the base line was extended in both directions to form the datum line, then the length of the adjusted search area is twice the adjusted search radius (R) plus the length of the base line (L_b). *Length* = $(2 \times R) + L_b$
b Width		The formula used to find the width of the adjusted search area is the same in all cases. The width is always equal to twice the adjusted search radius (R). Stated as a formula, *Width* = $2 \times R$
15 Plot the adjusted search area on a suitable chart		Using a suitable chart, plot the adjusted search square(s) or rectangle centred on the datum(s).
a Single point datum		Using the datum position as the centre, draw a circle with its radius equal to the adjusted search radius (R) from **line 13**. Estimate the direction of search object drift during the search. Circumscribe a square around the circle and orient the square so the search legs will be parallel to the predicted direction of drift during the search. In **figure L-1** it is assumed the direction of drift during the search will be the same as the average direction of drift from the last known position.
b Leeway divergence datums		Using each of the datum positions as a centre, draw a circle around each datum with its radius equal to the adjusted search radius (R) from **line 13**. Based on the distance separating the circles, decide whether to use a single rectangle as shown in **figure L-2** or two squares as shown in **figure L-3**. Estimate the directions of search object drift during the search. Orient the search sub-areas so the search legs are as nearly parallel as possible to the predicted directions of search object drift during the search. However, do not compromise safety of search facility navigation in adjacent search sub-areas.
c Line datum		Instructions for plotting the adjusted search area depend on whether the datum line was formed with zero, one, or two extensions as described in the instructions for **line 2.b**.
i No extensions		If the base line was not extended in either direction to form the datum line, draw lines perpendicular to the base line at each end. On each of these perpendicular lines, use a compass or dividers to measure a distance equal to the adjusted search radius (R) in each direction from the datum line. Using these four points as the corner points, plot the rectangular adjusted search area. (**See figure L-5.**)

ii	One extension	If the base line was extended in only one direction to form the datum line, draw a line perpendicular to the base line at the end that was not extended. Measure a distance equal to the adjusted search radius (*R*) in each direction from the datum line along the perpendicular line. These two points will be two of the corner points of the rectangular adjusted search area. Using the other end of the **base line** as the centre, draw a circle with its radius equal to the adjusted search radius (*R*). Draw a rectangle that includes the previous two corner points and the circle. (See **figure L-6**.)
iii	Two extensions	If the base line was extended in both directions to form the datum line, draw a circle with a radius equal to the adjusted search radius (*R*) around each end point of the base line. Be certain to use the end points of the **base line** as the centres of the circles, not the end points of the datum line. Circumscribe a single rectangle around both circles. (See **figure L-7**.)

16   Adjust the locations, lengths and widths of the search sub-areas so they fill the total adjusted search area as nearly as possible. The following guidelines may be used:

(a)   The width of each search sub-area must equal a whole number of track spacings. Some adjustment of track spacings may be made, but care must be taken to ensure all track spacings remain within the usable limits of the assigned search facility's navigational capability.

(b)   The search legs should be parallel to the search object's anticipated direction of movement during the search.

(c)   For fixed-wing aircraft, a flying time of about 30 minutes per search leg is recommended. For rotary-wing aircraft, a flying time of about 20 minutes is recommended.

Note 1: POS values tend to be very stable near the point of perfectly optimal effort allocation. This allows search planners the freedom needed to adapt the optimal allocation of effort to account for practical considerations imposed by the environment and the capabilities of the search facilities. Normally, small changes from the optimal values indicated in lines 10–14 that are needed to make the search plan practical will not have a large impact on search effectiveness (POS).

Note 2: Do not use the POS graphs (**figures N-11** and **N-12**) for searches of leeway divergence datums. The variations in the relationship between divergence distance and the probable error of position create a situation that is too complex to represent on a graph. For the same reason, no templates for constructing probability maps for two leeway divergence datums are provided in appendix M.

17   Go to the **Search action plan worksheet** where the plotted search sub-areas of **line 16** will be specified in one of the standard formats (methods) such as the corner-point method. The search action plan will also provide all necessary co-ordination instructions such as assigning specific search

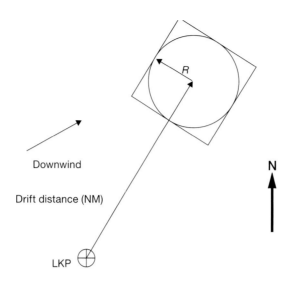

Figure L-1 – *Search area for a single point datum*

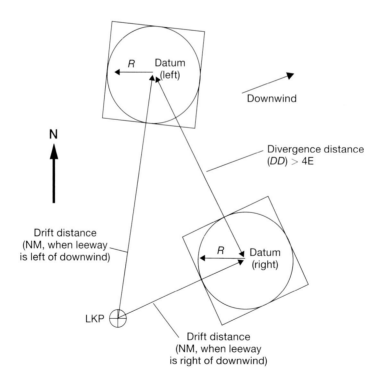

Figure L-2 – *Search area for two leeway divergence datums when the leeway divergence distance (DD) is less than 4 × E*

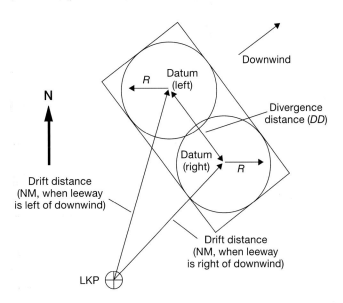

Figure L-3 – *Search area for two leeway divergence datums when the leeway divergence distance (*DD*) is greater than 4 × E*

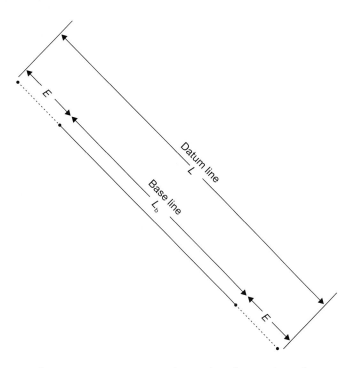

Figure L-4 – *Forming a datum line from a base line*

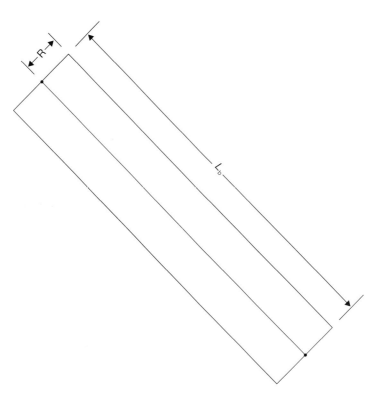

Figure L-5 – *Search area for a line datum (neither end extended)*

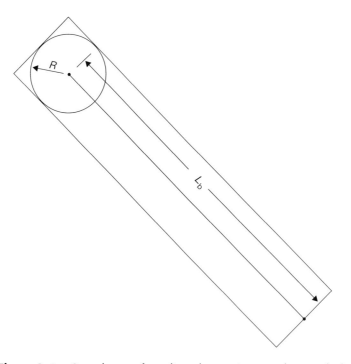

Figure L-6 – *Search area for a line datum (one end extended)*

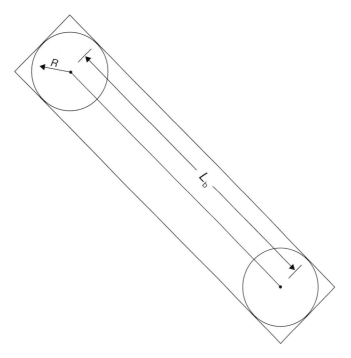

Figure L-7 – *Search area for a line datum (both ends extended)*

Effort allocation worksheet for optimal search of a generalized distribution

Case title _____ Case number _____ Date _____

Datum _____ _____ _____ _____
$\quad\quad\quad\quad$ Latitude $\quad\quad\quad\quad\quad$ Longitude $\quad\quad\quad\quad$ Time $\quad\quad\quad$ Total probable error of position (E)

Effort allocation computations $\quad\quad\quad\quad$ Search object _____

1 $\quad\quad$ Total available search effort (Z_{ta}) $\quad\quad\quad\quad\quad\quad\quad\quad\quad\quad\quad\quad$ _____

2 $\quad\quad$ Prepare probability map $\quad\quad\quad\quad\quad\quad\quad$ (Check when done) _____

3 $\quad\quad$ Probability map cell size $\quad\quad\quad\quad\quad\quad\quad\quad\quad\quad\quad$ _____ × _____

4 $\quad\quad$ Area of one cell of the probability map (a) $\quad\quad\quad\quad\quad\quad$ _____

5 $\quad\quad$ First trial area ($A_{1\text{-}t} \approx Z_t$, $a \times$ number of cells in first trial area) $\quad\quad$ _____

6 $\quad\quad$ First trial coverage ($C_{1\text{-}t} = Z_t/A_{1\text{-}t} \approx 1.0$) $\quad\quad\quad\quad\quad\quad$ _____

7 $\quad\quad$ First trial POD ($POD_{1\text{-}t}$) $\quad\quad\quad\quad$ Ideal _____ Normal _____ $\quad\quad\quad$ _____

8 $\quad\quad$ First trial POC ($POC_{1\text{-}t}$) $\quad\quad\quad\quad\quad\quad\quad\quad\quad\quad\quad\quad$ _____

9 $\quad\quad$ First trial POS ($POS_{1\text{-}t} = POC_{1\text{-}t} \times POD_{1\text{-}t}$) $\quad\quad\quad\quad\quad$ _____

10 $\quad\quad$ Second trial area ($A_{2\text{-}t} \approx 2 \times Z_t$) $\quad\quad\quad\quad\quad\quad\quad\quad$ _____

11 $\quad\quad$ Second trial coverage ($C_{2\text{-}t} = Z_t/A_{2\text{-}t} \approx 0.5$) $\quad\quad\quad\quad\quad$ _____

12 $\quad\quad$ Second trial POD ($POD_{2\text{-}t}$) $\quad\quad\quad$ Ideal _____ Normal _____ $\quad\quad$ _____

13 $\quad\quad$ Second trial POC ($POC_{2\text{-}t}$) $\quad\quad\quad\quad\quad\quad\quad\quad\quad\quad\quad$ _____

14 $\quad\quad$ Second trial POS ($POS_{2\text{-}t} = POC_{2\text{-}t} \times POD_{2\text{-}t}$) $\quad\quad\quad$ _____

15 $\quad\quad$ Third trial area ($A_{3\text{-}t} \approx 0.67 \times Z_t$) $\quad\quad\quad\quad\quad\quad\quad$ _____

16 $\quad\quad$ Third trial coverage ($C_{3\text{-}t} = Z_t/A_{3\text{-}t} \approx 1.5$) $\quad\quad\quad\quad\quad$ _____

17 $\quad\quad$ Third trial POD ($POD_{3\text{-}t}$) $\quad\quad\quad\quad$ Ideal _____ Normal _____ $\quad\quad$ _____

18 $\quad\quad$ Third trial POC ($POC_{3\text{-}t}$) $\quad\quad\quad\quad\quad\quad\quad\quad\quad\quad\quad\quad$ _____

19 $\quad\quad$ Third trial POS ($POS_{3\text{-}t} = POC_{3\text{-}t} \times POD_{3\text{-}t}$) $\quad\quad\quad\quad$ _____

20 $\quad\quad$ Best trial (highest POS) $\quad\quad\quad\quad\quad\quad$ Circle one: 1 $\quad\quad\quad\quad$ 2 $\quad\quad\quad\quad$ 3

21 $\quad\quad$ Optimal search area (A_o = Total area of best trial rectangle(s)) $\quad\quad$ _____

22 $\quad\quad$ Optimal coverage factor ($C_o = Z_{ta}/A_o$) $\quad\quad\quad\quad\quad\quad\quad$ _____

23 $\quad\quad$ Optimal track spacing ($S_o = W/C_o$) $\quad\quad\quad\quad\quad\quad\quad\quad$ _____

24   Nearest assignable track spacing (S)
(within usable limits of search facility
navigational capability)   ____ ____ ____ ____ ____

25   Adjusted search areas $(A = V \times S \times T)$ ____ ____ ____ ____ ____

26   Divide the search area into search sub-areas according to values on line 25 _____

                                            (check when done)

27   Go to the **Search action plan worksheet**.

Effort allocation worksheet instructions for optimal search of a generalized distribution

Introduction

This Effort allocation worksheet is used to determine the optimal way to allocate the available search effort for a generalized distribution of search object location probabilities. It considers the search effort that several dissimilar search facilities can provide. The worksheet also aids in computing the optimal area to search and the optimum uniform coverage factor. Finally, the worksheet provides guidance for determining the actual search sub-area dimensions for each available search facility. This Worksheet is based on a *daylight visual search* which does not continue beyond sunset.

Effort allocation computations

1	"Total available search effort"	Obtain from **line 14** of the **Total available search effort worksheet**.
2	"Prepare probability map"	To plan the first search, prepare a probability map using an appropriate, convenient grid. If an appropriate grid does not already exist, it will be necessary to create one. In either situation, a probability value must be assigned to each grid cell based on the known facts and the search planner's best judgement. The sum of all cell probabilities on the first probability map should be 100%. See instructions on page M-8.
		For the second and later searches, ensure cell probabilities have been adjusted for all previous searching and that cell locations, shapes, and sizes reflect the effects of the search object's probable motion, if any. Appendix M contains instructions for preparing probability maps.
3	"Probability map cell size"	Record the dimensions of one cell of the probability map.
4	"Area of one cell of the probability map"	Multiply the dimensions recorded on **line 3** and record the result.
5	"First trial area"	Plot one or more rectangles whose total area is approximately equal to the total available search effort from **line 1** on the probability map. The size, shape, and placement of the rectangle(s) should be that which maximizes the amount of probability contained in the rectangle(s). If desired, the rectangle(s) may be adjusted so a whole number of cells is covered. Compute the actual total area of the plotted rectangle(s) and enter it on this line.
6	"First trial coverage"	Divide the total available effort from **line 1** by the first trial area from **line 5** and record the result.
7	"First trial POD"	Indicate with a check mark whether search conditions are ideal or normal. Use the appropriate curve from **figure N-10** to determine the POD and record the result on this line.
8	"First trial POC"	Using the probability map, add the probabilities of all the cells and portions of cells contained in the first trial area and record the result.
9	"First trial POS"	Multiply the first trial POD from **line 7** by the first trial POC from **line 8** and record the result.

10	"Second trial area"	Plot one or more rectangles whose total area is approximately equal to twice the total available search effort from **line 1** on the probability map. The size, shape, and placement of the rectangle(s) should be that which maximizes the amount of probability contained in the rectangle(s). If desired, the rectangle(s) may be adjusted so a whole number of cells is covered. Compute the actual total area of the plotted rectangle(s) and enter it on this line.
11	"Second trial coverage"	Divide the total available effort from **line 1** by the second trial area from **line 10** and record the result.
12	"Second trial POD"	Indicate with a check mark whether search conditions are ideal or normal. Use the appropriate curve from **figure N-10** to determine the POD and record the result on this line.
13	"Second trial POC"	Using the probability map, add the probabilities of all the cells and portions of cells contained in the second trial area and record the result.
14	"Second trial POS"	Multiply the second trial POD from **line 12** by the second trial POC from **line 13** and record the result.
15	"Third trial area"	Plot one or more rectangles whose total area is approximately equal to two-thirds of the total available search effort from **line 1** on the probability map. The size, shape, and placement of the rectangle(s) should be that which maximizes the amount of probability contained in the rectangle(s). If desired, the rectangle(s) may be adjusted so a whole number of cells is covered. Compute the **actual total area** of the plotted rectangle(s) and enter it on this line.
16	"Third trial coverage"	Divide the total available effort from **line 1** by the third trial area from **line 15** and record the result.
17	"Third trial POD"	Indicate with a check mark whether search conditions are ideal or normal. Use the appropriate curve from **figure N-10** to determine the POD and record the result on this line.
18	"Third trial POC"	Using the probability map, add the probabilities of all the cells and portions of cells contained in the third trial area and record the result.
19	"Third trial POS"	Multiply the third trial POD from **line 17** by the third trial POC from **line 18** and record the result.
20	"Best trial"	Compare the trial POS values on **lines 9**, **14**, and **19**. Circle the number (1, 2, or 3) corresponding to the trial having the highest POS.
21	"Optimal search area"	Record the area corresponding to the trial circled on **line 20**.
22	"Optimal coverage factor"	Divide the total available search effort from **line 1** by the optimal search area on **line 21**.
23	"Optimal track spacing"	Divide the corrected sweep widths (*W*) from **line 12** of the **Total available search effort worksheet** by the optimal coverage factor (C_o) from **line 22**.
24	"Nearest assignable track spacing"	Round the optimal track spacing on **line 23** to a value that the corresponding search facility can navigate safely and accurately.

| 25 | "Adjusted search areas" | Multiply the search facility's speed from **line 3** of the **Total Available search effort worksheet** by the search facility's endurance from **line 6** of the **Total available search effort worksheet** and multiply the result by the nearest assignable track spacing from **line 24** of this worksheet. Stated as a formula, $A = V \times T \times S$. **Figure N-9** may also be used to find the adjusted search areas. |

26 Using the adjusted search areas from **line 25** and a suitable chart, plot corresponding search sub-areas to fill the rectangle(s) corresponding to the best trial from **line 20** as nearly as possible. Use the following guidelines:

(a) The width of each search sub-area must be a whole number of track spacings. Some adjustment of track spacings may be made, but care must be taken to ensure all track spacings remain within the usable limits of search facility navigational capability.

(b) The search legs should be parallel to the search object's anticipated direction of movement during the search.

(c) For fixed-wing aircraft, search legs should require about 30 minutes flying time. For rotary-wing aircraft, search legs should require about 20 minutes flying time.

Note: POS values tend to be very stable near the point of perfectly optimal effort allocation. This allows the search planner the freedom needed to adapt the theoretically optimal allocation of effort to the realities imposed by the environment and the capabilities of the search facilities. Normally, the small changes from the nearly optimal values indicated in line 25 for the purpose of developing a practical search plan will not have a large impact on search effectiveness (POS). Therefore, the search planner may make such changes with confidence.

27 Go to the **Search action plan worksheet**, where the plotted search sub-areas of **line 26** will be specified in one of the standard formats (methods) such as the corner-point method. The search action plan will also provide all necessary co-ordination instructions, such as assigning specific search facilities to specific sub-areas, search patterns, altitudes to each aircraft search facility, commence search points, direction of creep (for parallel sweep and creeping line search patterns), etc.

Search action plan worksheet

Search action plan message

(Precedence and date/time group of the message)
FROM *(RCC or RSC responsible for the search)*
TO *(All agencies/facilities tasked with conducting the search)*
INFO *(Agencies concerned, but not participating, in the search)*
BT

(Emergency Phase, i.e., DISTRESS, ALERT, UNCERTAINTY), (Identification of the search object, e.g., M/V NEVERSEEN) (Two-letter abbreviation for the flag of the search object, e.g., (PN)) (One or two word description of the SAR cause, e.g., UNREPORTED, SUNK, DITCHED, etc.), (General description of the search location, e.g., GULF OF OMAN, CABO SAN ANTONIO TO KEY WEST, etc.)

SEARCH ACTION PLAN FOR *(Date)*

A   *(References)*

1   SITUATION:

A   SUMMARY: *(A brief summary of the case, without repeating information previously provided to all addressees.)*

B   DESCRIPTION: *(Description of the missing craft, e.g., MOTOR VESSEL, 150 METRES, BLACK HULL, WHITE SUPERSTRUCTURE AFT)*

C   PERSONS ON BOARD: *(Number)*

D   SEARCH OBJECTS:

         PRIMARY: *(Description of the primary search object, e.g., 8-PERSON ORANGE LIFERAFT WITH CANOPY)*

         SECONDARY: *(Description of secondary search object(s), e.g., POSSIBLE SURVIVORS IN WATER, WRECKAGE/DEBRIS, 121.5 MHZ EPIRB, MIRROR FLASH, ORANGE SMOKE, FLARES)*

E   ON-SCENE WEATHER FORECAST PERIOD *(date/time)* TO *(date/time)*: CEILING *(in feet, with cloud cover, e.g., 8000 OVERCAST)*, VISIBILITY *(in nautical miles)*, WIND *(direction from which the wind is blowing in degrees true/speed in knots, e.g., 190T/30KTS)*, SEAS *(direction from which the seas are coming in degrees true/height range and unit of measure, e.g., 210T/3-6 FEET)*

2   ACTION:

A   *(Specific tasking for a particular SAR agency or facility)*

B   *(A separate subparagraph should be used for each agency or facility participating in the search)*

3   SEARCH AREAS (READ IN TWO COLUMNS):

         AREA   CORNER POINTS

(Search area designations may follow a "Letter hyphen number" format, e.g., A-4, C-1. The first day's searches use the letter "A" and are sequentially numbered, the second day's searches use the letter "B", and so forth.) (Corner points are given in degrees and minutes of latitude and longitude, e.g., 38-52.0N 077-14.0W. Usually, search areas are rectangular with the four corner points listed in clockwise order.)

4   EXECUTION (READ IN SEVEN COLUMNS. ALTITUDES IN FEET):

AREA	SAR FACILITY	LOCATION	PATTERN	CREEP	COMMENCE SEARCH POINT	ALT

(Search area designations will be identical to those specified in paragraph 3 of the Search Action Plan message: (SAR facility identification) (Home base or location from which each SAR facility is operating) (Letter abbreviation for the desired search pattern, found in section 5.5 of this volume) (Direction towards which the search facility will move as it completes successive legs of the search) (Latitude and longitude of the point where the search of each area is to begin) (The search altitude, in feet. For ships this will be "SURFACE")) #A complete example follows:

AREA	SAR FACILITY	LOCATION	PATTERN	CREEP	COMMENCE SEARCH POINT	ALT
B-1	ATLANTIQUE	MARTINIQUE	PS	225T	15-00.0N 64-00.9W	1000

5   CO-ORDINATION INSTRUCTIONS:

A   *(The SMC should be identified)*

B   *(If two or more search facilities will be used, an on-scene co-ordinator should be designated)*

C   *(The time that the search is to begin should be specified)*

D   *(The desired track spacing should be specified. The maximum search speed for aircraft should be given; for fixed-wing aircraft, a maximum of 150 knots is recommended.)*

E   *(OSC authorizations, responsibilities, and instructions should be clearly specified. See the sample message on the next page for examples.)*

F   *(Other co-ordinating instructions as needed)*

6   COMMUNICATIONS:

A	CONTROL CHANNEL	PRIMARY	SECONDARY
	HF:	*(NNNN)* KHZ USB	*(NNNN)* KHZ USB

B	ON-SCENE FREQUENCIES	PRIMARY	SECONDARY
	HF:	*(NNNN)* KHZ	*(2182)* KHZ
	VHF-AM:	*(NNN.N)* MHZ	*(121.5)* MHZ
	VHF-FM:	CH *(NN)*	CH *(16)*
	UHF-AM	*(NNN.N)* MHZ	*(243.0)* MHZ

C	AIR/GROUND FREQUENCIES	PRIMARY	SECONDARY
	HF:	*(NNNN)* KHZ	*(NNNN)* KHZ
	VHF-FM	CH *(NN)*	CH *(NN)*

D	AIR/AIR FREQUENCIES	PRIMARY	SECONDARY
	UHF-AM:	*(NNN.N)* MHZ	*(243.0)* MHZ

7   REPORTS:

A   *(Instructions to the OSC about the desired times for submitting SITREPs)*

B   *(Reporting instructions for participating search facilities)*

C   *(Reporting instructions for parent activities of search facilities)*

D   *(See the sample message on the next page for examples)*

BT

Sample search action plan message

```
FROM SANJUANSARCOORD SAN JUAN PUERTO RICO
TO COGARD AIRSTA BORINQUEN PUERTO RICO//OPS//
MARINE FORT DE FRANCE MARTINIQUE//MRCC//
RCC CURACAO NETHERLANDS ANTILLES
INFO CCGDSEVEN MIAMI FLORIDA//CC/OSR//
MRCC ETEL
RCC LA GUIRA VENEZUELA
ATC SAN JUAN PUERTO RICO
BT
```

ATTN: COMMAND DUTY OFFICER

DISTRESS N999EJ (US) DITCHED - EASTERN CARIBBEAN

SEARCH ACTION PLAN FOR 17 SEPTEMBER 1996

A   TELCON LTJG BASS/LT LAFAYETTE (MARTINIQUE) 162115Z SEP 96

B   TELCON LTJG BASS/LTC VAN SMOOT (CURACAO) 162130Z SEP 96

C   TELCON LTJG BASS/MR. C. SMITH 162145Z SEP 96 (ATC SAN JUAN)

1   SITUATION:

A   SUMMARY: N999EJ (US REGISTERED) EN ROUTE FROM PORT OF SPAIN TRINIDAD
        TO AGUADILLA PUERTO RICO REPORTED ENGINE FAILURE AND DESCENDING
        THROUGH 5000 FEET IN POSITION 14-20N 64-20W AT 152200Z WITH INTENTIONS
        TO DITCH. NIGHT FLARE SEARCHES 15 AND 16 SEP AND DAY SEARCH 16 SEP.
        NEGATIVE SIGHTINGS.

B   DESCRIPTION: CESSNA CITATION III, WHITE WITH BLUE TRIM.

C   PERSONS ON BOARD: 4

D   SEARCH OBJECTS:

PRIMARY: 8-PERSON ORANGE RAFT WITH CANOPY.

SECONDARY: POSSIBLE SURVIVORS IN WATER, WRECKAGE/DEBRIS, 121.5 MHZ
                ELT, MIRROR FLASH, ORANGE SMOKE, FLARES.

E   ON-SCENE WEATHER FORECAST PERIOD 171200Z TO 172400Z: CEILING 8000
        BROKEN, VISIBILITY 16 NM, WIND 190T/30KTS, SEAS 300T/3-6 FEET.

2   ACTION:

A   AS PER REFERENCE A, REQUEST MRCC FORT DE FRANCE PROVIDE ATLANTIQUE
        AIRCRAFT TO SEARCH SUB-AREA C-1.

B   HERCULES CGNR 1742, CALL SIGN RESCUE 1742, SEARCH SUB-AREA C-2 AND
        ASSUME OSC DUTIES.

C   AS PER REFERENCE B, REQUEST RCC CURACAO PROVIDE ORION AIRCRAFT TO
        SEARCH SUB-AREA C-3.

3   SEARCH AREA (READ IN TWO COLUMNS):

AREA   CORNER POINTS

C-1   15-46.7N 65-13.1W, 15-59.4N 65-00.0W, 15-00.0N 63-58.8W, 14-47.3N 64-11.9W

C-2   15-23.4N 65-37.0W, 15-46.7N 65-13.1W, 14-47.3N 64-11.9W, 14-24.0N 64-35.8W

C-3   15-00.0N 66-01.0W, 15-23.4N 65-37.0W, 14-24.0N 64-35.8W, 14-00.6N 65-00.0W

4   EXECUTION (READ IN SEVEN COLUMNS. ALTITUDES IN FEET):

AREA	SAR FACILITY	LOCATION	PATTERN	CREEP	COMMENCE SEARCH POINT	ALT
C-1	ATLANTIQUE	MARTINIQUE	PS	225T	15-00.0N 64-00.9W	1000
C-2	HERCULES	PUERTO RICO	PS	225T	15-44.6N 65-13.1W	500
C-3	ORION	CURACAO	PS	225T	15-21.3N 65-37.0W	1000

5   CO-ORDINATION INSTRUCTIONS:

A   SAN JUAN SAR COORDINATOR IS SMC.

B   HERCULES CGNR 1742, CALL SIGN RESCUE 1742, DESIGNATED OSC.

C   COMMENCE SEARCH TIME IS 170800Q.

D   TRACK SPACING 3 NM DESIRED. MAXIMUM SEARCH SPEED 150 KNOTS.

E   OSC AUTHORIZED TO ALTER SEARCH PLAN AS NECESSARY BASED ON SITUATION ON-SCENE PROVIDED SMC IS KEPT FULLY INFORMED. ORDER OF SEARCH PRIORITY IS C-2, C-1, C-3 IF UNABLE TO COVER ALL SUB-AREAS. ENSURE ALTITUDE SEPARATION MAINTAINED FOR ALL AIRCRAFT. OSC DEPLOY DATUM MARKER BUOY (DMB). DATUM FOR THIS SEARCH IS 15-00N 65-00W. ENSURE FREQUENCY SEPARATION FROM ANY PREVIOUSLY DEPLOYED DMBS. ENSURE DMB OPERATING PROPERLY. RELOCATE ALL DEPLOYED DMBS WHEN ENTERING AND DEPARTING SEARCH AREAS. OSC PASS EXACT TIME OF INSERTION/RELOCATION AND POSITION TO SMC VIA FASTEST MEANS.

F   AS PER REFERENCE C, SAN JUAN CENTER APPROVED SAR OPERATIONS WARNING AREA TO 6000 FT FROM 14-00N TO 16-00N BETWEEN 64-00W AND 66-00W.

G   AIRCRAFT CHECK IN WITH OSC UPON ARRIVAL IN SEARCH AREA, CHECK OUT WITH OSC AND CHECK IN WITH SAN JUAN CENTER UPON DEPARTING SEARCH AREA.

H   ONE AIRCRAFT CARRYING PRESS AUTHORIZED IN SAR WARNING AREA. IDENTIFICATION N-1768-C. PRESS AIRCRAFT DIRECTED TO CONTACT OSC PRIOR TO ENTERING SAR WARNING AREA.

6   COMMUNICATIONS:

A   CONTROL CHANNEL

	PRIMARY	SECONDARY
HF:	5680 KHZ USB	8983 KHZ USB

B   ON-SCENE FREQUENCIES

	PRIMARY	SECONDARY
HF:	5680 KHZ	2182 KHZ
VHF-AM:	123.1 MHZ	282.8 MHZ
VHF-FM:	CH 81A	CH 16
UHF-AM	282.8 MHZ	243.0 MHZ

C   AIR/GROUND FREQUENCIES

	PRIMARY	SECONDARY
HF:	5696 KHZ	8983 KHZ
VHF-FM	CH 23A	CH 16

D   AIR/AIR FREQUENCIES

	PRIMARY	SECONDARY
UHF-AM:	381.8 MHZ	243.0 MHZ

E   PRESS CHANNEL AT OSC DISCRETION

7   REPORTS:

A   OSC SEND SITREP TO SMC UPON ARRIVAL ON-SCENE THEN HOURLY THEREAFTER. INCLUDE WEATHER IN ALL SITREPS.

B   ALL PARTICIPATING SEARCH CRAFT PASS ON-SCENE WEATHER TO OSC HOURLY OR WHEN CONDITIONS CHANGE. OSC COLLATE WEATHER DATA AND RESOLVE ANY DISCREPANCIES IN OBSERVATIONS PRIOR TO REPORTING TO SMC. REPORT ALL SIGHTINGS IMMEDIATELY.

C   PARENT ACTIVITIES NOTIFY SMC WHEN AIRCRAFT DEPART. ALSO NOTIFY SMC AS SOON AS POSSIBLE OF ANY DEPARTURE THAT IS TO BE DELAYED BY MORE THAN 30 MINUTES.

D   AT END OF DAYS OPERATIONS, SEARCH FACILITIES OR PARENT ACTIVITIES REPORT TO SMC BY MESSAGE THE NUMBER OF SORTIES, TIMES OF ON-SCENE ARRIVAL AND DEPARTURE, HOURS FLOWN, HOURS SEARCHED, AREA SEARCHED (SQUARE NAUTICAL MILES), ACTUAL TRACK SPACING, ACTUAL SEARCH ALTITUDE, CORNER POINTS OF ACTUAL AREA COVERED IF DIFFERENT FROM ASSIGNED SUB-AREA, ANY MODIFICATIONS TO SUB-AREA ASSIGNED, AND OBSERVED NAVIGATION ERRORS BETWEEN FIXES. SEND REPORTS VIA MOST RAPID MEANS.

BT

Search evaluation worksheet for updating probability maps and computing POS and POS$_c$

Search evaluation computations

1   Search sub-area designation   _____ _____ _____ _____ _____

2   Search facility assigned   _____ _____ _____ _____ _____

3   Standard probability map (A – J), if used   _____

4   Probability map cell size   _____ $\times$ _____

5   Map or chart scale (such as 1 inch = 5 nautical miles) used for the probability map   _____ = _____

6   Total starting POC (POC$_{t\text{-old}}$)   _____

7   Plot search sub-areas on the probability map   (Check when done)   _____

8   Actual sweep widths (W)   _____ _____ _____ _____ _____

9   Actual track spacings (S)   _____ _____ _____ _____ _____

10   Coverage factors ($C = W/S$)   _____ _____ _____ _____ _____

11   Probabilities of detection (PODs)
(Circle "I" for ideal or "P" for poor search conditions)   I P   I P   I P   I P   I P

12   POC update multipliers ($M_{POC} = 1 - POD$)   _____ _____ _____ _____ _____

13   Update POCs for grid cells in search sub-areas
(POC$_{new} = M_{POC} \times$ POC$_{old}$)   (Check when done)   _____

14   Total probability of containment after searching (POC$_{t\text{-new}}$)   _____

15   Probability of success (POS = POC$_{t\text{-old}}$ – POC$_{t\text{-new}}$)   _____

16   Cumulative probability of success (POS$_c$ = previous POS$_c$ + POS)   _____

Search evaluation worksheet instructions

Introduction

The results of each search must be evaluated before the next search for the survivors is planned. Even if nothing is found by the search facilities, the fact that a sub-area was searched changes the search planner's estimate of the survivors' most probable location. The procedure described below allows the search planner to update the probability map so it accurately reflects the search results. It also allows the search planner to compute the probability of success for each search and the cumulative probability of success for all searches done to date.

1	"Search sub-area designation"	Use standard sub-area designators, such as A-1, B-3, etc.
2	"Search unit assigned"	List type of search facility, agency or owner, and call sign, if known.
3	"Standard probability map"	For point or line datums, enter the letter from **line 5** of the **Preparing initial probability maps** worksheet. For area datums, leave blank.
4	"Probability map cell size"	Enter the length and width of a cell. (It is assumed that all cells have the same dimensions and are therefore the same size as one another.) For point datums, cells are usually square and the cell width may be found on **line 6** of the **Preparing probability maps for point datums worksheet**. For line datums, the cell width is also found on **line 6** while the cell length is found on **line 8** of the **Preparing initial probability maps for line datums worksheet** (page M-4).
5	"Map or chart scale"	Enter the scale of miles (or other measure) for the probability map if it is not plotted on a map or chart overlay. Otherwise, enter the scale of the chart or map for which the overlay was prepared. For point datums, the scale appears on **line 7** of the **Preparing probability maps for point datums worksheet**.
6	"Total starting POC"	Add the POC values from all the grid cells contained in the probability map. If no searching has been done, then the total starting POC should be 100%.
7	"Plot search sub-areas"	Using the scale from **line 5**, plot the search sub-areas on the probability map.
8	"Actual sweep widths"	Using each search facility's reported on-scene conditions, re-compute the sweep width for that facility's search sub-area.
9	"Actual track spacings"	For each search facility, enter the actual track spacing used, including any adjustments made by the SMC, OSC or search facility.
10	"Actual coverage factors"	Divide **line 8** by **line 9**.
11	"Probabilities of detection"	Using the coverage factors in **line 10** and **figure N-10**, enter the POD for each sub-area. Be sure to use the correct curve ("Ideal" or "Poor") depending on the search conditions at the scene.
12	"POC update multipliers"	Subtract each of the PODs in **line 11** from 1.0 (100%).

13	"Update POCs"	For each cell or portion of a cell actually searched, multiply the last computed POC in that cell or portion of the cell by the POC multiplier from **line 12** for the sub-area containing the cell or portion. Record the POC_{new} for that cell on a fresh probability map. Complete the new probability map by copying the POC values for the remaining (un-searched) cells from the previous probability map. See the note at the end of these instructions for proper handling of partially covered cells.
14	"Total POC after searching"	Add the POC values from all cells on the new probability map to get the total probability of containment remaining after the latest search.
15	"Probability of success"	Subtract **line 14** from **line 6**.
16	"Cumulative probability of success"	Add the POS on **line 15** to the sum of all previous POS values. (In other words, add this POS to the previous POS_c value.) For point and line datums, if the optimal search recommendations have been followed, then the value of POS_c computed here should be close to that estimated from the appropriate Cumulative POS graph. For point datums, the Cumulative POS graph is **figure N-11**; for line datums, the Cumulative POS Graph is **figure N-12**.

Note: If a cell is only partially contained in a search sub-area, assume the probability in the cell is uniformly distributed and include the appropriate fraction of its value in the POC and POS computations. For example, if one-third of a cell's area is contained in the search sub-area and the POC value for the whole cell is 6%, then the POC for the portion inside the search sub-area is 2% and the POC for the portion outside is 4%. If the POD for that search sub-area is 50%, then the adjusted POC for the portion inside the search sub-area is:

$$POC_{1/3\text{-new}} = POD \times POC_{1/3\text{-old}}$$

or

$$POC_{1/3\text{-new}} = 0.50 \times 0.02 = 0.01 \text{ or } 1\%$$

To get the POC_{new} value for the entire cell, it is necessary to add the value just computed (1%) to the POC of the unsearched portion (4%) to get the correct value of 5%. That is, for the cell as a whole:

$$POC_{new} = POC_{1/3\text{-new}} + POC_{2/3\text{-old}}$$

or

$$POC_{new} = 0.01 + 0.04 = 0.05 \text{ or } 5\%$$

If the cell was divided between two or more search sub-areas having different PODs, then each portion must be updated separately and the resulting POC_{new} for the cell computed as the sum of the POC_{new} values for each portion.

If many cells on a probability map are only partially covered, the need for computations like those illustrated above can substantially increase the computational burden on the search planner. Whenever possible, probability maps and search sub-areas should be adjusted so the number of cells only partially covered is minimized.

Appendix M

Preparing initial probability maps

Preparing initial probability maps for single point datums

Case title _____ Planner's name _____ Date ____

Datum _____ _____ _____ _____
　　　　　　Latitude　　　　　　Longitude　　　Time　　Total probable error of position (E)

Computation of probability map parameters

Search object _____

1　Total probable error of position (E)
　　(from **line H.2** of the **Datum worksheet**)　　　　　　　　　_____

2　Adjusted search area width
　　(from **line 14.b** of the **Effort allocation worksheet**)　　_____

3　Adjusted search radius (R_a = Width/2.0)　　　　　　　　　　_____

4　Adjusted search factor ($f_{sa} = R_a/E$)　　　　　　　　　　　_____

5　Standard probability map (A – J)
　　(from table M-1)　　　　　　　　　　　　　　　　　　　　　_____

6　Cell width
　　(from table M-2)　　　　　　　　　　　　　　　　　　　　　_____

7　Probability map scale　　　　　　　　　　_____ = _____

8　Record the total probable error of position, scale,
　　and cell width on a copy of the selected standard
　　probability map.　　　　　　　　　　　　Check when done　_____

9　Plot the probability map on an appropriate
　　map or chart, using the correct scale.　　Check when done　_____

Preparing initial probability maps for single point datums instructions

Introduction

Before the results of the first search can be fully evaluated, a probability map must be prepared. The following steps describe how to prepare an initial probability map for a point datum using the standard point datum probability maps in this appendix. (Full evaluation of the second and later searches depends on keeping the probability map updated to reflect all searching that has been done and any search object motion that has been estimated. Procedures for updating probability maps are provided with the **Search evaluation worksheet**.)

There are two methods for preparing point datum probability maps. The first and simplest method is to determine which of the standard probability maps is best for the situation and make a photocopy for direct use. The disadvantage is that the search planner must determine the appropriate scale (miles per inch, kilometres per centimetre, etc.) to use for plotting information on the probability map. Search sub-areas and any other important geographic information must be properly scaled and plotted on the probability map for it to be useful.

The second, and preferred, method is to plot a similar grid, drawn to the proper scale, on a tracing paper or plastic overlay for the map or chart being used to plan the search. The advantage of doing this is that, apart from plotting the grid and entering the POC values in the appropriate cells, all other geographic information is either already on the chart or would normally be plotted on an overlay (such as search sub-areas).

1	"Total probable error of position"	Enter the total probable error of position (E) from **line H.2** of the **Datum worksheet**.
2	"Adjusted search area width"	Enter the width of the adjusted search area from **line 14.b** of the **Effort allocation worksheet**.
3	"Adjusted search radius"	Divide **line 2** by 2.0 and enter the result.
4	"Adjusted search factor"	Divide **line 3** by **line 1** and record the result.
5	"Standard probability map"	Enter table M-1 in with the adjusted search factor from **line 4**, find the nearest value in the first column and enter the letter which appears in the second column. If more than one letter appears, choose one of the alternatives. Usually, the first letter will be the best choice. When the adjusted search factor is the same as the search factor in column 1, the width of the adjusted search area will correspond to a whole number of cell widths.
6	"Cell width"	Enter table M-2 with the letter from **line 5**, perform the multiplication indicated in column 2, and record the result.
7	"Probability map scale"	Enter the scale of miles (or other measure). All of the grids printed in this volume are based on a scale of:

Two centimetres = E nautical miles or
One centimetre = $E/2$ nautical miles

Other scales are:
One inch = $1.27 \times E$ nautical miles
and
One centimetre = $0.926 \times E$ kilometres.

8	For direct use, select the probability map indicated by the letter on **line 5** from this appendix, make a working copy, and record the total probable error of position (E), cell width, and scale on the working copy.

9   To plot the probability map on an overlay for the chart or map being used to plan the search, follow these steps:

(a)   Draw a circle, centred on the datum point for the first search, with a radius of $3.0 \times E$.

(b)   Draw (circumscribe) a square around the circle so its sides are parallel to those of the adjusted first search area.

(c)   Divide the square into the same number of cells as the selected standard probability map which corresponds to the letter on **line 5**.

(d)   Enter the probability of containment value for each cell from the corresponding cell of the selected standard probability map.

The probability map is now ready for use in evaluating the first search.

Preparing initial probability maps for line datums

Case title _____ Planner's name _____ Date _____

Datum _____ _____ _____ _____
               Latitude   Longitude   Time   Total probable error of position (*E*)

Computation of probability map parameters

Search object _____

1	Total probable error of position (*E*) (from **line H.2** of the **Datum worksheet**)	_____
2	Adjusted search area dimensions (from **line 14.b** of the **Effort allocation worksheet**) Length_____ Width_____	
3	Adjusted search radius (R_a = Width/2.0)	_____
4	Adjusted search factor ($f_{sa} = R_a/E$)	_____
5	Standard probability map (A – J) (from table M-1)	_____
6	Cell width (from table M-2)	_____
7	Number of divisions along the datum line	_____
8	Cell length (search area length/ number of divisions)	_____
9	Plot the probability map on an appropriate map or chart, using the correct scale.	Check when done _____

Preparing initial probability maps for line datums instructions

Introduction

Before the results of the first search can be fully evaluated, a probability map must be prepared. The following steps describe how to prepare an initial probability map for a line datum, using the standard line datum probability cross-sections in this appendix. (Full evaluation of the second and later searches depends on keeping the probability map updated to reflect all searching that has been done and any search object motion that has been estimated. Procedures for updating probability maps are provided with the **Search evaluation worksheet**.)

1	"Total probable error of position"	Enter the total probable error of position (E) from **line H.2** of the **Datum worksheet**.
2	"Adjusted search area dimensions"	Enter the length and width of the adjusted search area from line 14.b of the **Effort allocation worksheet**.
3	"Adjusted search radius"	Divide the **Width** from **line 2** by 2.0 and enter the result.
4	"Adjusted search factor"	Divide **line 3** by **line 1** and record the result.
5	"Standard probability map"	Enter table M-1 with the adjusted search factor from **line 4**, find the nearest value in the first column, and enter the letter which appears in the second column. If more than one letter appears, choose one of the alternatives. Usually, the first letter will be the best choice. When the adjusted search factor is the same as the search factor in column 1, the width of the adjusted search area will correspond to a whole number of cell widths.
6	"Cell width"	Enter table M-2 with the letter from **line 5**, perform the multiplication indicated in column 2, and record the result.
7	"Number of divisions along the datum line"	Enter the desired number of divisions along the datum line. This value will determine how many probability map cells will be required to match the length of the adjusted search area.
8	"Cell length"	Divide the Length from **line 2** by the number of divisions from **line 7**.

9   To plot the probability map on an overlay for the chart or map being used to plan the search, follow these steps:

    (a)   At each end point of the datum line, draw a line perpendicular to the datum line.

    (b)   On these perpendicular lines, mark the points which are a distance of $3.0 \times E$ from the datum line on either side. Connect these four points to form a rectangle.

    (c)   Divide the rectangle into the same number of strips as the selected standard probability cross-section which corresponds to the letter on **line 5**. Note the probability of containment for each strip, which is found by using figure M-13. Figure M-1 shows how this is done for standard probability cross-section C.

1.7%
22.3%
Datum line
52.0%
22.3%
1.7%

Figure M-1

(d)   Divide the strips into the desired number of divisions from **line 7** to form a grid.

(e)   Divide the probability of containment for each strip by the number of divisions from **line 7** to get the POC value for each cell in that strip. Figure M-2 shows a completed probability map for a line datum.

0.2%	0.2%	0.2%	0.2%	0.2%	0.2%	0.2%	0.2%
2.8%	2.8%	2.8%	2.8%	2.8%	2.8%	2.8%	2.8%
			Datum line				
6.5%	6.5%	6.5%	6.5%	6.5%	6.5%	6.5%	6.5%
2.8%	2.8%	2.8%	2.8%	2.8%	2.8%	2.8%	2.8%
0.2%	0.2%	0.2%	0.2%	0.2%	0.2%	0.2%	0.2%

Figure M-2

The probability map is now ready for use in evaluating the first search.

Preparing initial probability maps for area datums with a uniform distribution of search object location probabilities instructions

Introduction

Before the results of the first search can be fully evaluated, a probability map must be prepared. The following steps describe how to prepare an initial probability map for an area datum when the search object is equally likely to be anywhere in the area. In this situation the distribution of search object location probabilities is uniform. (Full evaluation of the second and later searches depends on keeping the probability map updated to reflect all searching that has been done and any search object motion that has been estimated. Procedures for updating probability maps are provided with the **Search evaluation worksheet**.)

1   Plot the scenario's datum (possibility) area on a tracing paper or plastic overlay for an appropriate map or chart.

2   Plot a grid that divides the area into rectangular cells of equal size and count or compute the number of cells.

Number of cells _____

3   Divide 100% by the number of cells from line 2 to get the probability of containment (POC) value for one cell.

Cell POC _____

4   Enter the cell POC value from **line 3** in each cell of the probability map.

The probability map is now ready for use in evaluating the first search.

Preparing initial probability maps for area datums with a generalized distribution of search object location probabilities instructions

Introduction

Before the results of the first search can be fully evaluated, a probability map must be prepared. The following steps describe how to prepare an initial probability map for an area datum when the search object is more likely to be in some parts of the area and less likely to be in other parts. In this situation the distribution of search object location probabilities is not uniform. (Full evaluation of the second and later searches depends on keeping the probability map updated to reflect all searching that has been done and any search object motion that has been estimated. Procedures for updating probability maps are provided with the **Search evaluation worksheet**.)

1   Plot the scenario's datum (possibility) area on a tracing paper or plastic overlay for an appropriate map or chart.

2   Plot a grid on the overlay that divides the area into rectangular cells of equal size.

3   Based on the facts and assumptions used to develop the scenario, estimate the initial probability of containment (POC) for each cell in the datum area and record that value in the cell as plotted on the overlay.

The probability map is now ready for use in evaluating the first search.

Grid finder

Matching optimal search factors and probability maps/cross-sections for initial point/line datum probability maps

Search factor	Probability map/ cross-section	Width (number of cells)
0.27	I	11
0.33	G	9
0.43	E	7
0.50	J	12
0.60	H, C	10, 5
0.75	F	8
0.82	I	11
1.00	J, G, D, A	12, 9, 6, 3
1.20	H	10
1.29	E	7
1.36	I	11
1.50	J, F, B	12, 8, 4
1.67	G	9
1.80	H, C	10, 5
1.91	I	11
2.00	J, D	12, 6
2.14	E	7
2.25	F	8
2.33	G	9
2.40	H	10
2.45	I	11
2.50	J	12
3.00	All	

Table M-1

Matching probability maps/cross-sections with cell widths

Probability map/ cross-section	Cell width
A	$2.00 \times E$
B	$1.50 \times E$
C	$1.20 \times E$
D	$1.00 \times E$
E	$0.86 \times E$
F	$0.75 \times E$
G	$0.67 \times E$
H	$0.60 \times E$
I	$0.55 \times E$
J	$0.50 \times E$

Table M-2

Point datum grids

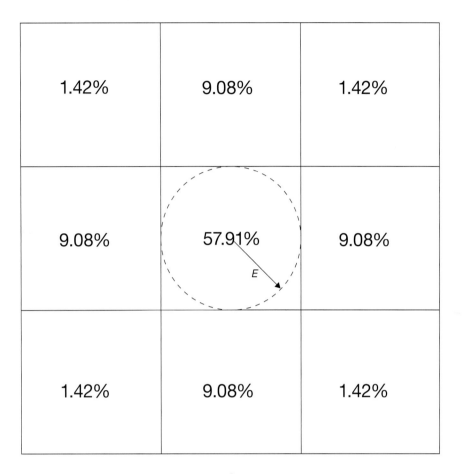

A

(3 × 3)

Total probable error
of position (*E*) _____

Cell width   _____

Scale   _____ = _____

Figure M-3

0.15%	1.78%	1.78%	0.15%
1.78%	21.28%	21.28%	1.78%
1.78%	21.28%	21.28%	1.78%
0.15%	1.78%	1.78%	0.15%

B

(4 × 4)

Total probable error
of position (*E*) _____

Cell width _____

Scale _____ = _____

Figure M-4

0.03%	0.38%	0.88%	0.38%	0.03%
0.38%	4.97%	11.59%	4.97%	0.38%
0.88%	11.59%	27.05%	11.59%	0.88%
0.38%	4.97%	11.59%	4.97%	0.38%
0.03%	0.38%	0.88%	0.38%	0.03%

C

(5 × 5)

Total probable error
of position (*E*) _____

Cell width _____

Scale _____ = _____

Figure M-5

0.01%	0.10%	0.34%	0.34%	0.10%	0.01%
0.10%	1.22%	4.19%	4.19%	1.22%	0.10%
0.34%	4.19%	14.48%	14.48%	4.19%	0.34%
0.34%	4.19%	14.48%	14.48%	4.19%	0.34%
0.10%	1.22%	4.19%	4.19%	1.22%	0.10%
0.01%	0.10%	0.34%	0.34%	0.10%	0.01%

D

(6 × 6)

Total probable error
of position (*E*) _____

Cell width   _____

Scale   _____ = _____

Figure M-6

0.00%	0.03%	0.14%	0.22%	0.14%	0.03%	0.00%
0.03%	0.35%	1.43%	2.29%	1.43%	0.35%	0.03%
0.14%	1.43%	5.85%	9.34%	5.85%	1.43%	0.14%
0.22%	2.29%	9.34%	14.91%	9.34%	2.29%	0.22%
0.14%	1.43%	5.85%	9.34%	5.85%	1.43%	0.14%
0.03%	0.35%	1.43%	2.29%	1.43%	0.35%	0.03%
0.00%	0.03%	0.14%	0.22%	0.14%	0.03%	0.00%

E

(7 × 7)

Total probable error
of position (*E*) _____

Cell width   _____

Scale   _____ = _____

Figure M-7

0.00%	0.01%	0.06%	0.12%	0.12%	0.06%	0.01%	0.00%
0.01%	0.12%	0.52%	1.08%	1.08%	0.52%	0.12%	0.01%
0.06%	0.52%	2.25%	4.67%	4.67%	2.25%	0.52%	0.06%
0.12%	1.08%	4.67%	9.70%	9.70%	4.67%	1.08%	0.12%
0.12%	1.08%	4.67%	9.70%	9.70%	4.67%	1.08%	0.12%
0.06%	0.52%	2.25%	4.67%	4.67%	2.25%	0.52%	0.06%
0.01%	0.12%	0.52%	1.08%	1.08%	0.52%	0.12%	0.01%
0.00%	0.01%	0.06%	0.12%	0.12%	0.06%	0.01%	0.00%

F

(8 × 8)

Total probable error
of position (E) _____

Cell width _____

Scale _____ = _____

Figure M-8

0.00%	0.01%	0.03%	0.06%	0.09%	0.06%	0.03%	0.01%	0.00%
0.01%	0.05%	0.21%	0.50%	0.67%	0.50%	0.21%	0.05%	0.01%
0.03%	0.21%	0.90%	2.16%	2.89%	2.16%	0.90%	0.21%	0.03%
0.06%	0.50%	2.16%	5.19%	6.96%	5.19%	2.16%	0.50%	0.06%
0.09%	0.67%	2.89%	6.96%	9.32%	6.96%	2.89%	0.67%	0.09%
0.06%	0.50%	2.16%	5.19%	6.96%	5.19%	2.16%	0.50%	0.06%
0.03%	0.21%	0.90%	2.16%	2.89%	2.16%	0.90%	0.21%	0.03%
0.01%	0.05%	0.21%	0.50%	0.67%	0.50%	0.21%	0.05%	0.01%
0.00%	0.01%	0.03%	0.06%	0.09%	0.06%	0.03%	0.01%	0.00%

G

(9 × 9)

Total probable error
of position (*E*)   _____

Cell width   _____

Scale   _____ = _____

Figure M-9

0.00%	0.00%	0.01%	0.03%	0.06%	0.06%	0.03%	0.01%	0.00%	0.00%
0.00%	0.02%	0.09%	0.24%	0.38%	0.38%	0.24%	0.09%	0.02%	0.00%
0.01%	0.09%	0.38%	1.00%	1.61%	1.61%	1.00%	0.38%	0.09%	0.01%
0.03%	0.24%	1.00%	2.60%	4.19%	4.19%	2.60%	1.00%	0.24%	0.03%
0.06%	0.38%	1.61%	4.19%	6.76%	6.76%	4.19%	1.61%	0.38%	0.06%
0.06%	0.38%	1.61%	4.19%	6.76%	6.76%	4.19%	1.61%	0.38%	0.06%
0.03%	0.24%	1.00%	2.60%	4.19%	4.19%	2.60%	1.00%	0.24%	0.03%
0.01%	0.09%	0.38%	1.00%	1.61%	1.61%	1.00%	0.38%	0.09%	0.01%
0.00%	0.02%	0.09%	0.24%	0.38%	0.38%	0.24%	0.09%	0.02%	0.00%
0.00%	0.00%	0.01%	0.03%	0.06%	0.06%	0.03%	0.01%	0.00%	0.00%

H
(10 × 10)

Total probable error
of position (*E*)   _____

Cell width   _____

Scale   _____ = _____

Figure M-10

0.00%	0.00%	0.01%	0.02%	0.04%	0.04%	0.04%	0.02%	0.01%	0.00%	0.00%
0.00%	0.01%	0.04%	0.12%	0.21%	0.26%	0.21%	0.12%	0.04%	0.01%	0.00%
0.01%	0.04%	0.18%	0.48%	0.86%	1.06%	0.86%	0.48%	0.18%	0.04%	0.01%
0.02%	0.12%	0.48%	1.29%	2.34%	2.86%	2.34%	1.29%	0.48%	0.12%	0.02%
0.04%	0.21%	0.86%	2.34%	4.26%	5.20%	4.26%	2.34%	0.86%	0.21%	0.04%
0.04%	0.26%	1.06%	2.86%	5.20%	6.34%	5.20%	2.86%	1.06%	0.26%	0.04%
0.04%	0.21%	0.86%	2.34%	4.26%	5.20%	4.26%	2.34%	0.86%	0.21%	0.04%
0.02%	0.12%	0.48%	1.29%	2.34%	2.86%	2.34%	1.29%	0.48%	0.12%	0.02%
0.01%	0.04%	0.18%	0.48%	0.86%	1.06%	0.86%	0.48%	0.18%	0.04%	0.01%
0.00%	0.01%	0.04%	0.12%	0.21%	0.26%	0.21%	0.12%	0.04%	0.01%	0.00%
0.00%	0.00%	0.01%	0.02%	0.04%	0.04%	0.04%	0.02%	0.01%	0.00%	0.00%

I
(11 × 11)

Total probable error
of position (*E*) _____

Cell width _____

Scale _____ = _____

Figure M-11

0.00%	0.00%	0.00%	0.01%	0.02%	0.03%	0.03%	0.02%	0.01%	0.00%	0.00%	0.00%
0.00%	0.01%	0.02%	0.06%	0.12%	0.17%	0.17%	0.12%	0.06%	0.02%	0.01%	0.00%
0.00%	0.02%	0.09%	0.24%	0.47%	0.65%	0.65%	0.47%	0.24%	0.09%	0.02%	0.00%
0.01%	0.06%	0.24%	0.65%	1.28%	1.79%	1.79%	1.28%	0.65%	0.24%	0.06%	0.01%
0.02%	0.12%	0.47%	1.28%	2.51%	3.52%	3.52%	2.51%	1.28%	0.47%	0.12%	0.02%
0.03%	0.17%	0.65%	1.79%	3.52%	4.93%	4.93%	3.52%	1.79%	0.65%	0.17%	0.03%
0.03%	0.17%	0.65%	1.79%	3.52%	4.93%	4.93%	3.52%	1.79%	0.65%	0.17%	0.03%
0.02%	0.12%	0.47%	1.28%	2.51%	3.52%	3.52%	2.51%	1.28%	0.47%	0.12%	0.02%
0.01%	0.06%	0.24%	0.65%	1.28%	1.79%	1.79%	1.28%	0.65%	0.24%	0.06%	0.01%
0.00%	0.02%	0.09%	0.24%	0.47%	0.65%	0.65%	0.47%	0.24%	0.09%	0.02%	0.00%
0.00%	0.01%	0.02%	0.06%	0.12%	0.17%	0.17%	0.12%	0.06%	0.02%	0.01%	0.00%
0.00%	0.00%	0.00%	0.01%	0.02%	0.03%	0.03%	0.02%	0.01%	0.00%	0.00%	0.00%

J
(12×12)

Total probable error
of position (E)   _____

Cell width   _____

Scale   _____ = _____

Figure M-12

Probability cross-sections for line datums

A (3)
11.9%
76.1%
11.9%

B (4)
3.9%
46.1%
46.1%
3.9%

C (5)
1.7%
22.3%
52.0%
22.3%
1.7%

D (6)
0.9%
11.0%
38.1%
38.1%
11.0%
0.9%

E (7)
0.6%
5.9%
24.2%
38.6%
24.2%
5.9%
0.6%

F (8)
0.4%
3.5%
15.0%
31.1%
31.1%
15.0%
3.5%
0.4%

G (9)
0.3%
2.2%
9.5%
22.8%
30.5%
22.8%
9.5%
2.2%
0.3%

H (10)
0.2%
1.5%
6.2%
16.1%
26.0%
26.0%
16.1%
6.2%
1.5%
0.2%

I (11)
0.2%
1.0%
4.2%
11.4%
20.6%
25.2%
20.6%
11.4%
4.2%
1.0%
0.2%

J (12)
0.1%
0.8%
2.9%
8.1%
15.9%
22.2%
22.2%
15.9%
8.1%
2.9%
0.8%
0.1%

Figure M-13

Appendix N

Tables and graphs

Local wind current graph and table

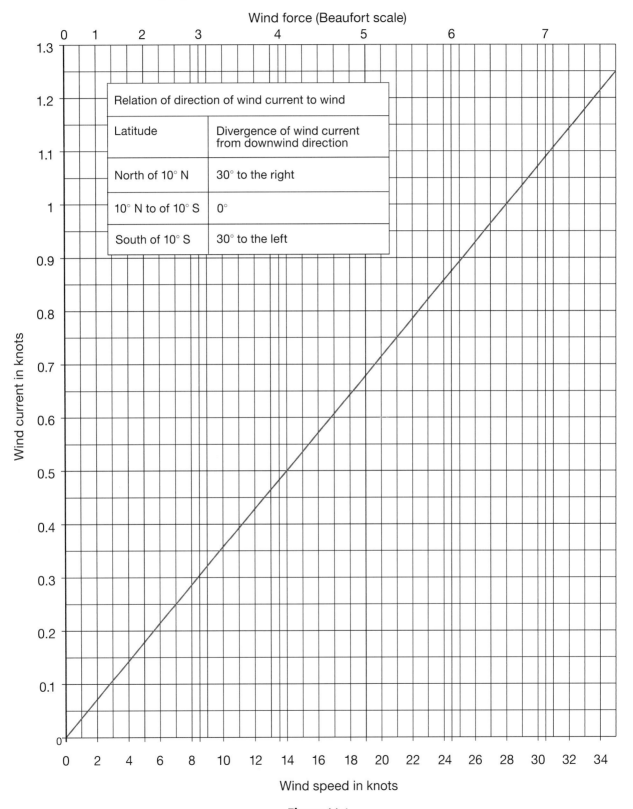

Figure N-1

Leeway charts

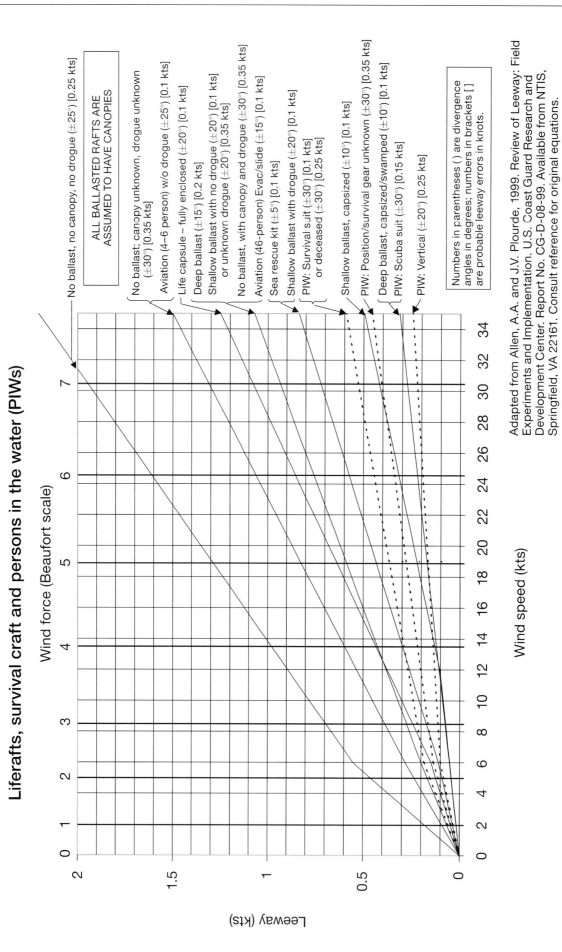

Figure N-2 – *Leeway of liferafts, survival craft and persons in the water (PIWs)*

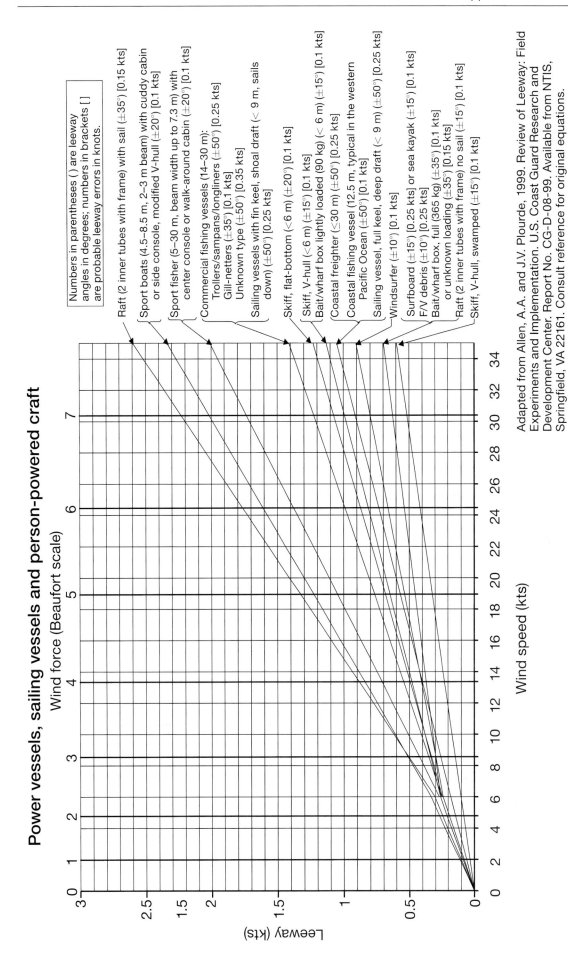

Figure N-3 – *Leeway rates for various craft*

Probable errors of position

Initial position error (*X*) and Search craft position error (*Y*) are the estimated errors of position based on navigational accuracy of the distressed craft and of the search facilities.

If information on the means of navigation used by the distressed craft or by a search facility is available, the navigational fix errors (Fix$_e$) listed in table N-1 may be used for positions reported as navigation fixes (*X* = Fix$_e$ or *Y* = Fix$_e$).

Table N-1 – *Navigational fix errors*

Means of navigation	Fix errors (NM)
GNSS	0.1 NM
Radar	1 NM
Visual fix (3 lines)*	1 NM
Celestial fix (3 lines)*	2 NM
Marine radio beacon	4 NM (3-beacon fix)
LORAN C	1 NM
INS	0.5 NM per flight hour without position update
VOR	±3° arc <u>and</u> 3% of distance or 0.5 NM radius, whichever is greater
TACAN	±3° arc <u>and</u> 3% of distance or 0.5 NM radius, whichever is greater

* Should be evaluated upward according to circumstances.

If the means of navigation used by the distressed craft or by a search facility is unknown, then Fix$_e$ is equal to:

Table N-2 – *Fix errors by craft type*

Type of craft	Fix$_e$
Ships, military submarines, and aircraft with more than two engines	5 NM
Twin-engine aircraft	10 NM
Boats, submersibles, and single-engine aircraft	15 NM

When the initially reported position of the distressed craft is based on dead reckoning (DR) or the search facility must use DR navigation, an additional error is assumed for the distance travelled since the last fix. The position error is the sum of the fix error (Fix$_e$) plus the DR error (DR$_e$). Table N-3 gives DR$_e$ for various craft.

Table N-3 – *Dead reckoning errors*

Type of craft	DR$_e$
Ship	5% of the DR distance
Submarine (military)	5% of the DR distance
Aircraft (more than two engines)	5% of the DR distance
Aircraft (twin-engine)	10% of the DR distance
Aircraft (single-engine)	15% of the DR distance
Submersible	15% of the DR distance
Boat	15% of the DR distance

Sweep width tables

Search object	Meteorological visibility (km (NM))				
	6 (3)	**9 (5)**	**19 (10)**	**28 (15)**	**37 (20)**
Person in water	0.7 (0.4)	0.9 (0.5)	1.1 (0.6)	1.3 (0.7)	1.3 (0.7)
4-person liferaft	4.2 (2.3)	5.9 (3.2)	7.8 (4.2)	9.1 (4.9)	10.2 (5.5)
6-person liferaft	4.6 (2.5)	6.7 (3.6)	9.3 (5.0)	11.5 (6.2)	12.8 (6.9)
15-person liferaft	4.8 (2.6)	7.4 (4.0)	9.4 (5.1)	11.9 (6.4)	13.5 (7.3)
25-person liferaft	5.0 (2.7)	7.8 (4.2)	9.6 (5.2)	12.0 (6.5)	13.9 (7.5)
Boat <5 m (17 ft)	2.0 (1.1)	2.6 (1.4)	3.5 (1.9)	3.9 (2.1)	4.3 (2.3)
Boat 7 m (23 ft)	3.7 (2.0)	5.4 (2.9)	8.0 (4.3)	9.6 (5.2)	10.7 (5.8)
Boat 12 m (40 ft)	5.2 (2.8)	8.3 (4.5)	14.1 (7.6)	17.4 (9.4)	21.5 (11.6)
Boat 24 m (79 ft)	5.9 (3.2)	10.4 (5.6)	19.8 (10.7)	27.2 (14.7)	33.5 (18.1)

Table N-4 – *Sweep widths for merchant vessels (km (NM))*

Table N-5 – Sweep widths for helicopters (km (NM))

Search object (metres (feet))	Altitude 150 metres (500 feet) Visibility (km (NM))						Altitude 300 metres (1000 feet) Visibility (km (NM))						Altitude 600 metres (2000 feet) Visibility (km (NM))					
	1.9 (1)	5.6 (3)	9.3 (5)	18.5 (10)	27.8 (15)	>37.0 (>20)	1.9 (1)	5.6 (3)	9.3 (5)	18.5 (10)	27.8 (15)	>37.0 (>20)	1.9 (1)	5.6 (3)	9.3 (5)	18.5 (10)	27.8 (15)	>37.0 (>20)
Person in water*	0.0 (0.0)	0.2 (0.1)	0.2 (0.1)	0.2 (0.1)	0.2 (0.1)	0.2 (0.1)	0.0 (0.0)	0.2 (0.1)	0.2 (0.1)	0.2 (0.1)	0.2 (0.1)	0.2 (0.1)	0.0 (0.0)	0.0 (0.0)	0.0 (0.0)	0.0 (0.0)	0.0 (0.0)	0.2 (0.1)
Raft 1-person	0.7 (0.4)	1.7 (0.9)	2.2 (1.2)	3.0 (1.6)	3.3 (1.8)	3.3 (1.8)	0.7 (0.4)	1.7 (0.9)	2.2 (1.2)	3.0 (1.6)	3.3 (1.8)	3.3 (1.8)	0.4 (0.2)	1.5 (0.8)	2.2 (1.2)	3.0 (1.6)	3.3 (1.8)	3.3 (1.8)
Raft 4-person	0.9 (0.5)	2.2 (1.2)	3.0 (1.6)	4.1 (2.2)	4.8 (2.6)	5.2 (2.8)	0.9 (0.5)	2.2 (1.2)	3.1 (1.7)	4.3 (2.3)	4.8 (2.6)	5.4 (2.9)	0.6 (0.3)	2.2 (1.2)	3.1 (1.7)	4.3 (2.3)	5.0 (2.7)	5.6 (3.0)
Raft 6-person	0.9 (0.5)	2.6 (1.4)	3.5 (1.9)	5.0 (2.7)	5.9 (3.2)	6.5 (3.5)	0.9 (0.5)	2.6 (1.4)	3.7 (2.0)	5.2 (2.8)	5.9 (3.2)	6.5 (3.5)	0.6 (0.3)	2.6 (1.4)	3.7 (2.0)	5.2 (2.8)	6.1 (3.3)	6.7 (3.6)
Raft 8-person	1.1 (0.6)	2.8 (1.5)	3.7 (2.0)	5.2 (2.8)	6.1 (3.3)	6.9 (3.7)	0.9 (0.5)	2.8 (1.5)	3.9 (2.1)	5.4 (2.9)	6.3 (3.4)	7.0 (3.8)	0.6 (0.3)	2.8 (1.5)	3.9 (2.1)	5.6 (3.0)	6.7 (3.6)	7.2 (3.9)
Raft 10-person	1.1 (0.6)	3.0 (1.6)	4.1 (2.2)	5.7 (3.1)	6.7 (3.6)	7.4 (4.0)	0.9 (0.5)	3.0 (1.6)	4.1 (2.2)	5.9 (3.2)	6.9 (3.7)	7.6 (4.1)	0.6 (0.3)	3.0 (1.6)	4.3 (2.3)	6.1 (3.3)	7.2 (3.9)	7.8 (4.2)
Raft 15-person	1.1 (0.6)	3.1 (1.7)	4.3 (2.3)	6.1 (3.3)	7.4 (4.0)	8.1 (4.4)	1.1 (0.6)	3.1 (1.7)	4.4 (2.4)	6.5 (3.5)	7.6 (4.1)	8.3 (4.5)	0.6 (0.3)	3.1 (1.7)	4.6 (2.5)	6.7 (3.6)	8.0 (4.3)	8.7 (4.7)
Raft 20-person	1.1 (0.6)	3.3 (1.8)	4.8 (2.6)	7.0 (3.8)	8.5 (4.6)	9.4 (5.1)	1.1 (0.6)	3.3 (1.8)	5.0 (2.7)	7.2 (3.9)	8.7 (4.7)	9.6 (5.2)	0.7 (0.4)	3.3 (1.8)	5.0 (2.7)	7.4 (4.0)	9.1 (4.9)	10.0 (5.4)
Raft 25-person	1.1 (0.6)	3.5 (1.9)	5.0 (2.7)	7.6 (4.1)	9.3 (5.0)	10.4 (5.6)	1.1 (0.6)	3.5 (1.9)	5.2 (2.8)	7.8 (4.2)	9.4 (5.1)	10.6 (5.7)	0.7 (0.4)	3.5 (1.9)	5.4 (2.9)	8.0 (4.3)	9.8 (5.3)	10.9 (5.9)
Power boat < 5 (15)	0.9 (0.5)	2.2 (1.2)	2.8 (1.5)	3.5 (1.9)	4.1 (2.2)	4.3 (2.3)	0.9 (0.5)	2.2 (1.2)	3.0 (1.6)	3.9 (2.1)	4.3 (2.3)	4.6 (2.5)	0.6 (0.3)	2.4 (1.3)	3.1 (1.7)	4.3 (2.3)	4.8 (2.6)	5.0 (2.7)
Power boat 6 (20)	1.3 (0.7)	3.7 (2.0)	5.4 (2.9)	8.0 (4.3)	9.6 (5.2)	10.7 (5.8)	1.3 (0.7)	3.9 (2.1)	5.6 (3.0)	8.1 (4.4)	9.8 (5.3)	10.9 (5.9)	0.7 (0.4)	3.9 (2.1)	5.6 (3.0)	8.3 (4.5)	10.2 (5.5)	11.3 (6.1)
Power boat 10 (33)	1.5 (0.8)	4.6 (2.5)	7.2 (3.9)	11.5 (6.2)	14.4 (7.8)	16.7 (9.0)	1.3 (0.7)	4.8 (2.6)	7.2 (3.9)	11.7 (6.3)	14.6 (7.9)	16.9 (9.1)	0.9 (0.5)	4.8 (2.6)	7.4 (4.0)	11.9 (6.4)	14.8 (8.0)	17.2 (9.3)
Power boat 16 (53)	1.5 (0.8)	5.7 (3.1)	9.4 (5.1)	17.0 (9.2)	22.8 (12.3)	27.2 (14.7)	1.3 (0.7)	5.7 (3.1)	9.6 (5.2)	17.0 (9.2)	22.8 (12.3)	27.4 (14.8)	0.9 (0.5)	5.6 (3.0)	9.6 (5.2)	17.2 (9.3)	23.0 (12.4)	27.6 (14.9)
Power boat 24 (78)	1.5 (0.8)	6.1 (3.3)	10.6 (5.7)	20.0 (10.8)	27.8 (15.0)	34.1 (18.4)	1.5 (0.8)	6.1 (3.3)	10.6 (5.7)	20.2 (10.9)	27.8 (15.0)	34.3 (18.5)	0.9 (0.5)	5.9 (3.2)	10.6 (5.7)	20.2 (10.9)	28.0 (15.1)	34.3 (18.5)
Sail boat 5 (15)	1.3 (0.7)	3.5 (1.9)	5.0 (2.7)	7.2 (3.9)	8.7 (4.7)	9.6 (5.2)	1.1 (0.6)	3.5 (1.9)	5.2 (2.8)	7.4 (4.0)	8.9 (4.8)	10.0 (5.4)	0.7 (0.4)	3.5 (1.9)	5.2 (2.8)	7.8 (4.2)	9.3 (5.0)	10.4 (5.6)
Sail boat 8 (26)	1.5 (0.8)	4.4 (2.4)	6.9 (3.7)	10.6 (5.7)	13.1 (7.1)	15.2 (8.2)	1.3 (0.7)	4.6 (2.5)	6.9 (3.7)	10.7 (5.8)	13.5 (7.3)	15.4 (8.3)	0.9 (0.5)	4.6 (2.5)	7.0 (3.8)	11.1 (6.0)	13.9 (7.5)	15.9 (8.6)
Sail boat 12 (39)	1.5 (0.8)	5.6 (3.0)	9.1 (4.9)	15.4 (8.3)	20.9 (11.3)	25.0 (13.5)	1.3 (0.7)	5.6 (3.0)	9.1 (4.9)	15.9 (8.6)	21.1 (11.4)	25.0 (13.5)	0.9 (0.5)	5.6 (3.0)	9.1 (4.9)	16.1 (8.7)	21.1 (11.4)	25.2 (13.6)
Sail boat 15 (49)	1.5 (0.8)	5.7 (3.1)	9.6 (5.2)	17.6 (9.5)	23.5 (12.7)	28.3 (15.3)	1.3 (0.7)	5.7 (3.1)	9.8 (5.3)	17.6 (9.5)	23.7 (12.8)	28.5 (15.4)	0.9 (0.5)	5.7 (3.1)	9.8 (5.3)	17.8 (9.6)	23.9 (12.9)	28.7 (15.5)
Sail boat 21 (69)	1.5 (0.8)	5.9 (3.2)	10.2 (5.5)	19.3 (10.4)	26.1 (14.1)	32.0 (17.3)	1.5 (0.8)	5.9 (3.2)	10.4 (5.6)	19.3 (10.4)	26.3 (14.2)	32.0 (17.3)	0.9 (0.5)	5.9 (3.2)	10.4 (5.6)	19.4 (10.5)	26.5 (14.3)	32.2 (17.4)
Sail boat 25 (83)	1.5 (0.8)	6.1 (3.3)	10.6 (5.7)	20.4 (11.0)	28.2 (15.2)	34.6 (18.7)	1.5 (0.8)	6.1 (3.3)	10.6 (5.7)	20.4 (11.0)	28.3 (15.3)	34.8 (18.8)	0.9 (0.5)	5.9 (3.2)	10.6 (5.7)	20.6 (11.1)	28.5 (15.4)	35.0 (18.9)
Ship 27–46 (90–150)	1.5 (0.8)	6.3 (3.4)	11.1 (6.0)	22.6 (12.2)	32.2 (17.4)	40.6 (21.9)	1.5 (0.8)	6.3 (3.4)	11.1 (6.0)	22.6 (12.2)	32.2 (17.4)	40.6 (21.9)	0.9 (0.5)	6.1 (3.3)	11.1 (6.0)	22.6 (12.2)	32.4 (17.5)	40.7 (22.0)
Ship 46–91 (150–300)	1.5 (0.8)	6.3 (3.4)	11.7 (6.3)	25.2 (13.6)	37.8 (20.4)	49.3 (26.6)	1.5 (0.8)	6.3 (3.4)	11.7 (6.3)	25.2 (13.6)	37.8 (20.4)	49.3 (26.6)	0.9 (0.5)	6.3 (3.4)	11.7 (6.3)	25.2 (13.6)	37.8 (20.4)	49.3 (26.6)
Ship > 91 (300)	1.5 (0.8)	6.5 (3.5)	11.9 (6.4)	26.5 (14.3)	40.9 (22.1)	55.2 (29.8)	1.5 (0.8)	6.5 (3.5)	11.9 (6.4)	26.5 (14.3)	41.1 (22.2)	55.2 (29.8)	1.1 (0.6)	6.3 (3.4)	11.9 (6.4)	26.5 (14.3)	41.1 (22.2)	55.2 (29.8)

* For seach altitudes of 150 metres (500 feet) only, the sweep width values for a person in water may be multiplied by 4, if it is known that the person is wearing a personal flotation device.

Table N-6 – *Sweep widths for fixed-wing aircraft (km (NM))*

Search object (metres (feet))	Altitude 150 metres (500 feet) Visibility (km (NM)) 1.9 (1)	5.6 (3)	9.3 (5)	18.5 (10)	27.8 (15)	>37.0 (>20)	Altitude 300 metres (1000 feet) Visibility (km (NM)) 1.9 (1)	5.6 (3)	9.3 (5)	18.5 (10)	27.8 (15)	>37.0 (>20)	Altitude 600 metres (2000 feet) Visibility (km (NM)) 1.9 (1)	5.6 (3)	9.3 (5)	18.5 (10)	27.8 (15)	>37.0 (>20)
Person in water*	0.0 (0.0)	0.2 (0.1)	0.2 (0.1)	0.2 (0.1)	0.2 (0.1)	0.2 (0.1)	0.0 (0.0)	0.2 (0.1)	0.2 (0.1)	0.2 (0.1)	0.2 (0.1)	0.2 (0.1)	0.0 (0.0)	0.0 (0.0)	0.0 (0.0)	0.0 (0.0)	0.0 (0.0)	0.0 (0.0)
Raft 1-person	0.6 (0.3)	1.3 (0.7)	1.7 (0.9)	2.2 (1.2)	2.6 (1.4)	2.6 (1.4)	0.6 (0.3)	1.3 (0.7)	1.7 (0.9)	2.2 (1.2)	2.6 (1.4)	2.6 (1.4)	0.2 (0.1)	1.1 (0.6)	1.7 (0.9)	2.2 (1.2)	2.6 (1.4)	2.6 (1.4)
Raft 4-person	0.7 (0.4)	1.9 (1.0)	2.4 (1.3)	3.3 (1.8)	3.7 (2.0)	4.1 (2.2)	0.6 (0.3)	1.9 (1.0)	2.4 (1.3)	3.3 (1.8)	3.9 (2.1)	4.3 (2.3)	0.4 (0.2)	1.7 (0.9)	2.4 (1.3)	3.5 (1.9)	4.1 (2.2)	4.3 (2.3)
Raft 6-person	0.7 (0.4)	2.0 (1.1)	2.8 (1.5)	4.1 (2.2)	4.6 (2.5)	5.2 (2.8)	0.7 (0.4)	2.0 (1.1)	3.0 (1.6)	4.1 (2.2)	4.8 (2.6)	5.2 (2.8)	0.4 (0.2)	2.0 (1.1)	3.0 (1.6)	4.3 (2.3)	5.0 (2.7)	5.4 (2.9)
Raft 8-person	0.7 (0.4)	2.2 (1.2)	3.0 (1.6)	4.3 (2.3)	5.0 (2.7)	5.4 (2.9)	0.7 (0.4)	2.2 (1.2)	3.1 (1.7)	4.4 (2.4)	5.2 (2.8)	5.6 (3.0)	0.4 (0.2)	2.2 (1.2)	3.1 (1.7)	4.6 (2.5)	5.4 (2.9)	5.9 (3.2)
Raft 10-person	0.7 (0.4)	2.2 (1.2)	3.1 (1.7)	4.6 (2.5)	5.4 (2.9)	5.9 (3.2)	0.7 (0.4)	2.4 (1.3)	3.3 (1.8)	4.8 (2.6)	5.6 (3.0)	6.1 (3.3)	0.4 (0.2)	2.2 (1.2)	3.3 (1.8)	5.0 (2.7)	5.7 (3.1)	6.5 (3.5)
Raft 15-person	0.9 (0.5)	2.4 (1.3)	3.5 (1.9)	5.0 (2.7)	6.1 (3.3)	6.7 (3.6)	0.7 (0.4)	2.6 (1.4)	3.7 (2.0)	5.2 (2.8)	6.3 (3.4)	6.9 (3.7)	0.4 (0.2)	2.6 (1.4)	3.7 (2.0)	5.6 (3.0)	6.5 (3.5)	7.2 (3.9)
Raft 20-person	0.9 (0.5)	2.8 (1.5)	3.9 (2.1)	5.9 (3.2)	7.0 (3.8)	7.8 (4.2)	0.7 (0.4)	2.8 (1.5)	4.1 (2.2)	5.9 (3.2)	7.2 (3.9)	8.0 (4.3)	0.7 (0.4)	2.8 (1.5)	4.1 (2.2)	6.3 (3.4)	7.4 (4.0)	8.3 (4.5)
Raft 25-person	0.9 (0.5)	3.0 (1.6)	4.3 (2.3)	6.3 (3.4)	7.6 (4.1)	8.5 (4.6)	0.7 (0.4)	3.0 (1.6)	4.3 (2.3)	6.5 (3.5)	7.8 (4.2)	8.7 (4.7)	0.6 (0.3)	3.0 (1.6)	4.4 (2.4)	6.7 (3.6)	8.1 (4.4)	9.1 (4.9)
Power boat < 5 (15)	0.7 (0.4)	1.7 (0.9)	2.2 (1.2)	2.8 (1.5)	3.1 (1.7)	3.3 (1.8)	0.7 (0.4)	1.9 (1.0)	2.4 (1.3)	3.1 (1.7)	3.3 (1.8)	3.7 (2.0)	0.4 (0.2)	1.9 (1.0)	2.4 (1.3)	3.3 (1.8)	3.7 (2.0)	4.1 (2.2)
Power boat 6 (20)	0.9 (0.5)	3.1 (1.7)	4.4 (2.4)	6.7 (3.6)	8.0 (4.3)	8.9 (4.8)	0.9 (0.5)	3.1 (1.7)	4.6 (2.5)	6.9 (3.7)	8.1 (4.4)	9.3 (5.0)	0.6 (0.3)	3.1 (1.7)	4.6 (2.5)	7.0 (3.8)	8.5 (4.6)	9.4 (5.1)
Power boat 10 (33)	1.1 (0.6)	3.9 (2.1)	6.1 (3.3)	9.8 (5.3)	12.4 (6.7)	14.3 (7.7)	0.9 (0.5)	4.1 (2.2)	6.3 (3.4)	10.0 (5.4)	12.6 (6.8)	14.4 (7.8)	0.6 (0.3)	4.1 (2.2)	6.3 (3.4)	10.2 (5.5)	12.8 (6.9)	14.8 (8.0)
Power boat 16 (53)	1.1 (0.6)	5.0 (2.7)	8.3 (4.5)	15.0 (8.1)	20.2 (10.9)	24.3 (13.1)	1.1 (0.6)	5.0 (2.7)	8.3 (4.5)	15.2 (8.2)	20.2 (10.9)	24.3 (13.1)	0.7 (0.4)	4.8 (2.6)	8.3 (4.5)	15.4 (8.3)	20.4 (11.0)	24.6 (13.3)
Power boat 24 (78)	1.1 (0.6)	5.2 (2.8)	9.3 (5.0)	18.1 (9.8)	25.0 (13.5)	30.9 (16.7)	1.1 (0.6)	5.2 (2.8)	9.4 (5.1)	18.1 (9.8)	25.2 (13.6)	30.9 (16.7)	0.7 (0.4)	5.2 (2.8)	9.3 (5.0)	18.1 (9.8)	25.2 (13.6)	31.1 (16.8)
Sail boat 5 (15)	0.9 (0.5)	3.0 (1.6)	4.1 (2.2)	5.9 (3.2)	7.2 (3.9)	8.0 (4.3)	0.9 (0.5)	3.0 (1.6)	4.3 (2.3)	6.1 (3.3)	7.4 (4.0)	8.1 (4.4)	0.6 (0.3)	3.0 (1.6)	4.3 (2.3)	6.5 (3.5)	7.6 (4.1)	8.3 (4.5)
Sail boat 8 (26)	1.1 (0.6)	3.7 (2.0)	5.7 (3.1)	9.1 (4.9)	11.3 (6.1)	13.0 (7.0)	0.9 (0.5)	3.9 (2.1)	5.9 (3.2)	9.3 (5.0)	11.5 (6.2)	13.1 (7.1)	0.6 (0.3)	3.9 (2.1)	6.1 (3.3)	9.6 (5.2)	11.9 (6.4)	13.5 (7.3)
Sail boat 12 (39)	1.1 (0.6)	4.8 (2.6)	8.0 (4.3)	14.1 (7.6)	18.5 (10.0)	22.0 (11.9)	1.1 (0.6)	4.8 (2.6)	8.0 (4.3)	14.1 (7.6)	20.2 (10.9)	22.2 (12.0)	0.7 (0.4)	4.6 (2.5)	8.0 (4.3)	14.3 (7.7)	18.7 (10.1)	22.4 (12.1)
Sail boat 15 (49)	1.1 (0.6)	5.0 (2.7)	8.5 (4.6)	15.6 (8.4)	20.9 (11.3)	25.4 (13.7)	1.1 (0.6)	5.0 (2.7)	8.5 (4.6)	15.7 (8.5)	21.1 (11.4)	25.4 (13.7)	0.7 (0.4)	5.0 (2.7)	8.5 (4.6)	15.9 (8.6)	21.3 (11.5)	25.7 (13.9)
Sail boat 21 (69)	1.1 (0.6)	5.2 (2.8)	9.1 (4.9)	17.2 (9.3)	23.5 (12.7)	28.7 (15.5)	1.1 (0.6)	5.2 (2.8)	9.1 (4.9)	17.2 (9.3)	23.7 (12.8)	28.9 (15.6)	0.7 (0.4)	5.0 (2.7)	9.1 (4.9)	17.4 (9.4)	23.9 (12.9)	29.1 (15.7)
Sail boat 25 (83)	1.1 (0.6)	5.2 (2.8)	9.4 (5.1)	18.3 (9.9)	25.4 (13.7)	31.5 (17.0)	1.1 (0.6)	5.2 (2.8)	9.4 (5.1)	18.3 (9.9)	25.6 (13.8)	31.5 (17.0)	0.7 (0.4)	5.2 (2.8)	9.4 (5.1)	18.5 (10.0)	25.7 (13.9)	31.7 (17.1)
Ship 27–46 (90–150)	1.1 (0.6)	5.4 (2.9)	10.0 (5.4)	20.6 (11.1)	29.4 (15.9)	37.2 (20.1)	1.1 (0.6)	5.4 (2.9)	10.0 (5.4)	20.6 (11.1)	29.4 (15.9)	37.2 (20.1)	0.7 (0.4)	5.4 (2.9)	10.0 (5.4)	20.6 (11.1)	29.6 (16.0)	37.2 (20.1)
Ship 46–91 (150–300)	1.1 (0.6)	5.6 (3.0)	10.6 (5.7)	23.2 (12.5)	35.0 (18.9)	45.7 (24.7)	1.1 (0.6)	5.6 (3.0)	10.6 (5.7)	23.2 (12.5)	35.0 (18.9)	45.7 (24.7)	0.7 (0.4)	5.6 (3.0)	10.6 (5.7)	23.2 (12.5)	35.0 (18.9)	45.7 (24.7)
Ship > 91 (300)	1.3 (0.7)	5.6 (3.0)	10.7 (5.8)	24.4 (13.2)	38.2 (20.6)	51.7 (27.9)	1.1 (0.6)	5.6 (3.0)	10.7 (5.8)	24.4 (13.2)	38.2 (20.6)	51.7 (27.9)	0.9 (0.5)	5.6 (3.0)	10.7 (5.8)	24.4 (13.2)	38.3 (20.7)	51.7 (27.9)

* For seach altitudes of 150 metres (500 feet) only, the sweep width values for a person in water may be multiplied by 4, if it is known that the person is wearing a personal flotation device.

Table N-7 – *Weather correction factors for all types of search facilities*

Weather: Winds km/h (kt) or seas m (ft)	Search object	
	Person in water, raft or boat < 10 m (33 ft)	Other search objects
Winds 0–28 km/h (0–15 kts) or seas 0–1 m (0–3 ft)	1.0	1.0
Winds 28–46 km/h (15–25 kts) or seas 1–1.5 m (3–5 ft)	0.5	0.9
Winds > 46 km/h (> 25 kts) or seas > 1.5 m (> 5 ft)	0.25	0.9

Table N-8 – *Speed (velocity) correction factors for helicopter and fixed-wing aircraft search facilities*

Search object	Fixed-wing speed km/h (kts)			Helicopter speed km/h (kts)			
	≤ 275 (≤ 150)	330 (180)	385 (210)	≤ 110 (≤ 60)	165 (90)	220 (120)	255 (140)
Person in Water	1.2	1.0	0.9	1.5	1.0	0.8	0.7
Raft 1–4 person	1.1	1.0	0.9	1.3	1.0	0.9	0.8
Raft 6–25 person	1.1	1.0	0.9	1.2	1.0	0.9	0.8
Power boat < 8 m (< 25 ft)	1.1	1.0	0.9	1.2	1.0	0.9	0.8
Power boat 10 m (33 ft)	1.1	1.0	0.9	1.1	1.0	0.9	0.9
Power boat 16 m (53 ft)	1.1	1.0	1.0	1.1	1.0	0.9	0.9
Power boat 24 m (78 ft)	1.1	1.0	1.0	1.1	1.0	1.0	0.9
Sail boat < 8 m (< 25 ft)	1.1	1.0	0.9	1.2	1.0	0.9	0.9
Sail boat 12 m (39 ft)	1.1	1.0	1.0	1.1	1.0	0.9	0.9
Sail boat 25 m (83 ft)	1.1	1.0	1.0	1.1	1.0	1.0	0.9
Ship > 27 m (> 90 ft)	1.0	1.0	1.0	1.1	1.0	1.0	0.9

Table N-9 – *Sweep widths for visual land search (km (NM))*

Search object	Height (m (ft))	Visibility (km (NM))				
		6 (3)	**9 (5)**	**19 (10)**	**28 (15)**	**37 (20)**
Person	150 (500)	0.7 (0.4)	0.7 (0.4)	0.9 (0.5)	0.9 (0.5)	0.9 (0.5)
	300 (1,000)	0.7 (0.4)	0.7 (0.4)	0.9 (0.5)	0.9 (0.5)	0.9 (0.5)
	450 (1,500)	—	—	—	—	—
	600 (2,000)	—	—	—	—	—
Vehicle	150 (500)	1.7 (0.9)	2.4 (1.3)	2.4 (1.3)	2.4 (1.3)	2.4 (1.3)
	300 (1,000)	1.9 (1.0)	2.6 (1.4)	2.6 (1.4)	2.8 (1.5)	2.8 (1.5)
	450 (1,500)	1.9 (1.0)	2.6 (1.4)	3.1 (1.7)	3.1 (1.7)	3.1 (1.7)
	600 (2,000)	1.9 (1.0)	2.8 (1.5)	3.7 (2.0)	3.7 (2.0)	3.7 (2.0)
Aircraft less than 5,700 kg	150 (500)	1.9 (1.0)	2.6 (1.4)	2.6 (1.4)	2.6 (1.4)	2.6 (1.4)
	300 (1,000)	1.9 (1.0)	2.8 (1.5)	2.8 (1.5)	3.0 (1.6)	3.0 (1.6)
	450 (1,500)	1.9 (1.0)	2.8 (1.5)	3.3 (1.8)	3.3 (1.8)	3.3 (1.8)
	600 (2,000)	1.9 (1.0)	3.0 (1.6)	3.7 (2.0)	3.7 (2.0)	3.7 (2.0)
Aircraft over 5,700 kg	150 (500)	2.2 (1.2)	3.7 (2.0)	4.1 (2.2)	4.1 (2.2)	4.1 (2.2)
	300 (1,000)	3.3 (1.8)	5.0 (2.7)	5.6 (3.0)	5.6 (3.0)	5.6 (3.0)
	450 (1,500)	3.7 (2.0)	5.2 (2.8)	5.9 (3.2)	5.9 (3.2)	5.9 (3.2)
	600 (2,000)	4.1 (2.2)	5.2 (2.9)	6.5 (3.5)	6.5 (3.5)	6.5 (3.5)

Table N-10 – *Correction factors — vegetation and high terrain*

Search object	15–60% vegetation or hilly	60–85% vegetation or mountainous	Over 85% vegetation
Person	0.5	0.3	0.1
Vehicle	0.7	0.4	0.1
Aircraft less than 5,700 kg	0.7	0.4	0.1
Aircraft over 5,700 kg	0.8	0.4	0.1

Table N-11 *– Recommended altitudes according to nature of search object and terrain*

Search object	Terrain	Recommended altitudes
Person, light aircraft	Moderate terrain	60–150 m (200–500 ft)
Large aircraft	Moderate terrain	120–300 m (400–1,000 ft)
Person, one-person raft, light aircraft	Water or flat terrain	60–150 m (200–500 ft)
Medium-sized liferaft and aircraft	Water or flat terrain	300–900 m (1,000–3,000 ft)
Pyrotechnical signal at night	Night	450–900 m (1,500–3,000 ft)
Medium-sized aircraft	Mountainous terrain	150–300 m (500–1,000 ft)

Distance to horizon

The distance to the horizon is equal to a constant multiplied by the square root of the altitude, as shown in these two formulas:

$$H_{NM} = 1.17 \times \sqrt{Altitude_{feet}}$$

$$H_{km} = 3.83 \times \sqrt{Altitude_{metres}}$$

Table N-12 *– Horizon range table*

Altitude in feet	Distance in nautical miles	Altitude in metres	Distance in kilometres
500	26	150	47
1,000	37	300	66
2,000	52	600	94
3,000	64	900	115
4,000	74	1,200	133
5,000	83	1,500	148
10,000	117	3,000	210
15,000	143	4,550	257
20,000	165	6,100	297
25,000	185	7,600	332
30,000	203	9,150	363
35,000	219	10,650	392
40,000	234	12,200	420

Available search effort graph

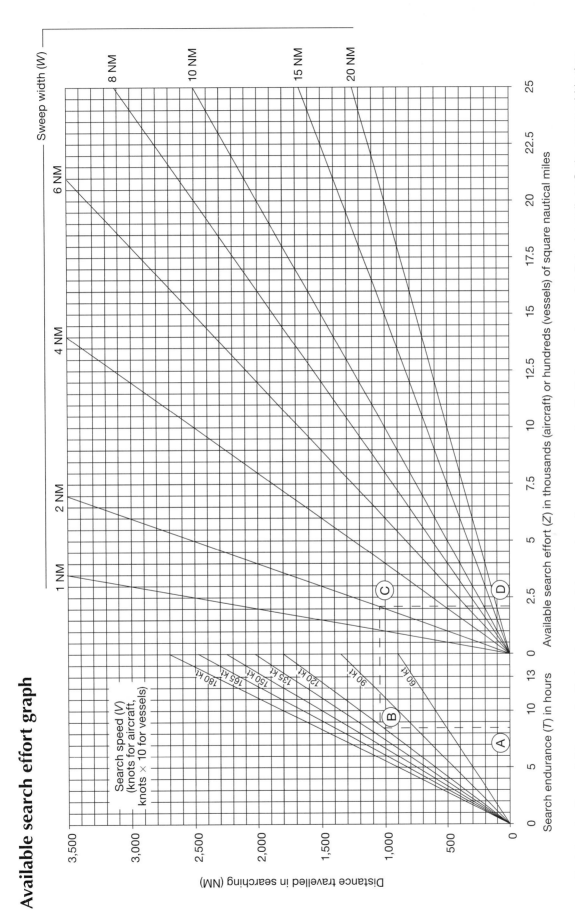

Figure N-4

To determine the available search effort, enter graph at A, search endurance; proceed vertically to search speed at B; horizontally to C, the sweep width; then downwards to find area, D. (8.5 h × 120 kts × 2 NM = 2040 NM² or 8.5 h × 12 kts × 2 NM = 204 NM²). Reverse the procedure to determine the search endurance required to provide a given amount of search effort.

Optimal search factor graphs for point datums

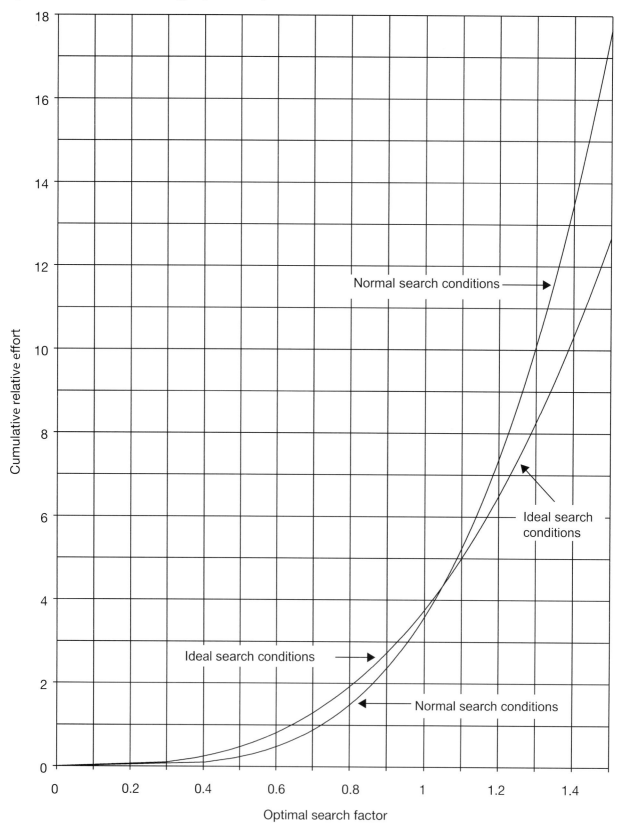

Figure N-5

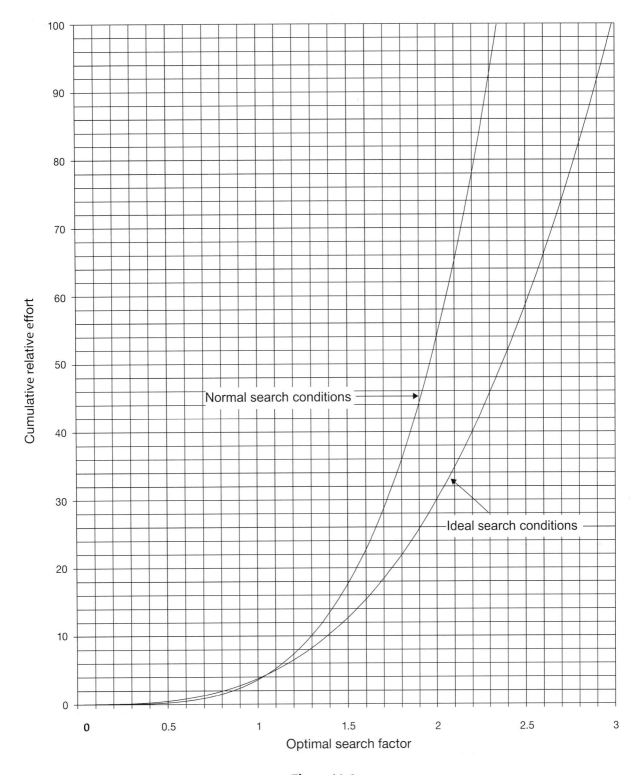

Figure N-6

Optimal search factor graphs for line datums

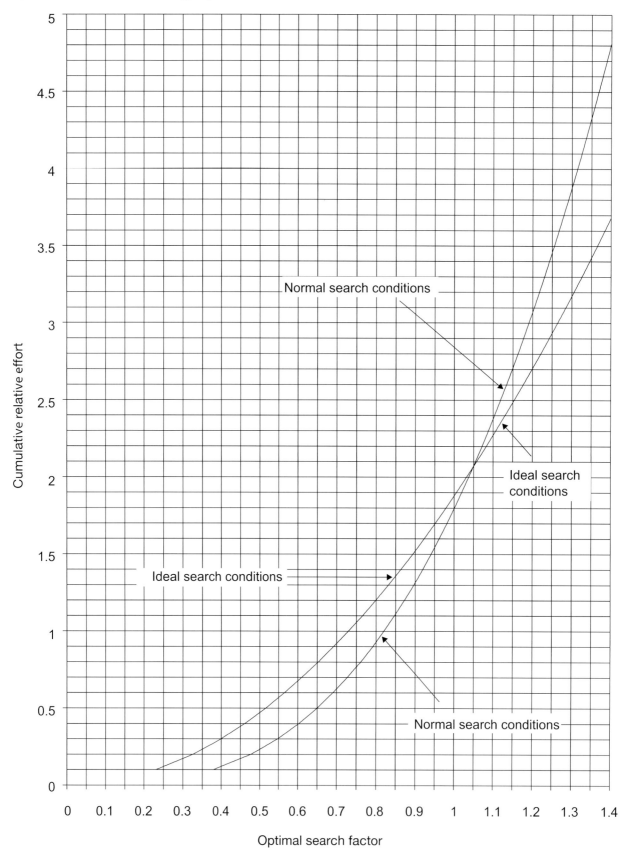

Figure N-7

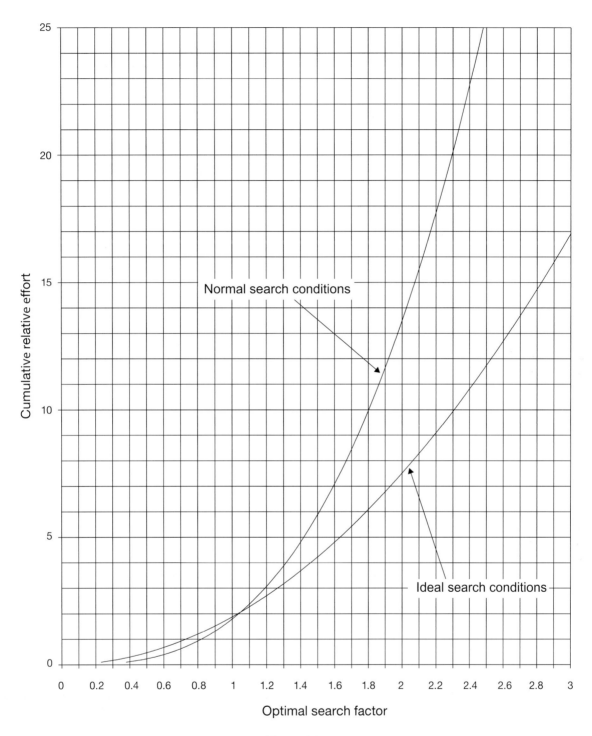

Figure N-8

Search area planning graph

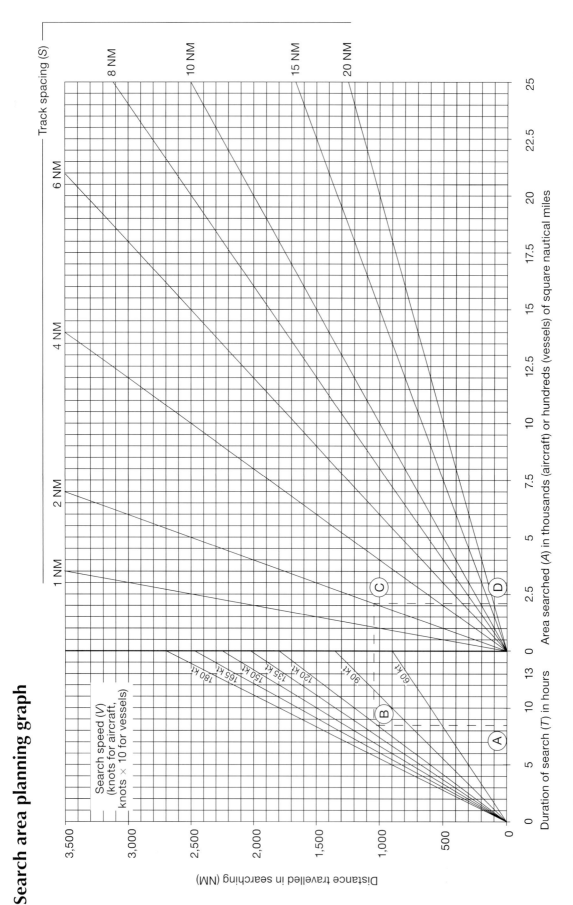

To determine the area that can be searched in a given time, enter graph at A, duration of search; proceed vertically to search speed at B; horizontally to C, the track spacing; then downwards to find area, D. (8.5 hours × 120 kts × 12 kts × 2 NM = 2040 NM² or 8.5 hours × 12 kts × 2 NM = 204 NM²). Reverse the procedure to determine the time required to search a given area.

Figure N-9

POD graph

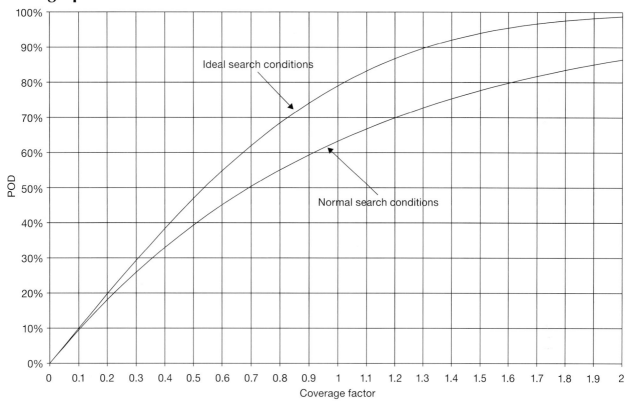

Figure N-10 – *Average probabilities of detection (POD) over an area for visual searches using parallel sweeps*

Cumulative POS graphs

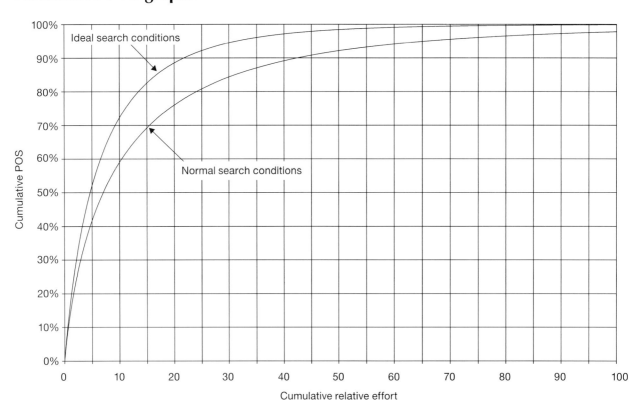

Figure N-11 – *Cumulative probability of success for optimal searches of point datums*

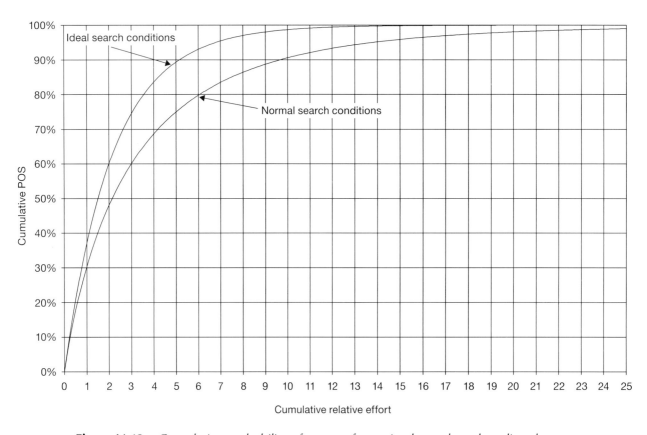

Figure N-12 – *Cumulative probability of success for optimal searches along line datums*

Environmental curves

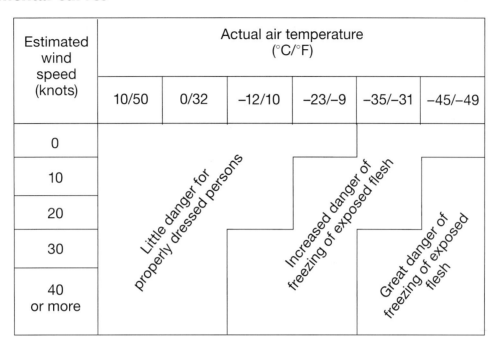

Figure N-13 – *Wind chill and frostbite*

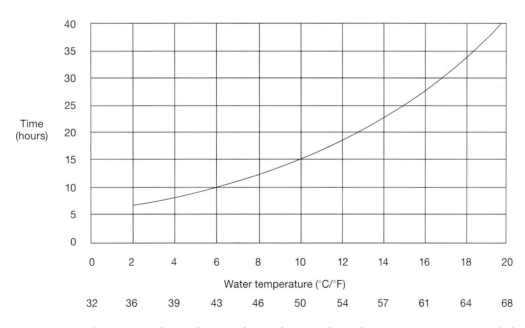

Figure N-14 – *Realistic upper limit of survival time for people in the water wearing normal clothing, from time of entry into the water (refer to the IAMSAR Manual, volume II, chapter 3, for details)*[*]

---

[*] Based on expert medical opinion and the latest scientific data.

Parachute tables

Parachute type	Rate of descent at sea level (feet per minute)	Rate of descent at 7,000 feet (feet per minute)	Glide ratio (horizontal/ vertical)
28 feet (C-9), escape	1,176	1,284	0
28 feet (C-9), with 4 suspension line release, escape	1,146	1,260	0.40
24 feet, paratroop reserve	1,362	1,494	0
24 feet, Martin-Baker system	1,440		0
35 feet (T-10), Army paratroop	918	1,008	0
35 feet (HALO), AF and Army special paratroop	960	1,038	0.35
Skysail (Navy), escape	1,212	1,320	0
Paracommander, AF special paratroop	1,080	482	1.16
Parawing (experimental)	600–900		3.0
Parafoil (experimental)	600–900		3.0
Parasail (experimental)	600–900		2.7
Apollo, 2 each (83 feet diameter)	2,100	2,232	0
Apollo, 3 each (83 feet diameter; deployed at 24,000 feet)	1,800	1,950	0

Table N-13 – *Parachute descent data (300 lb person, except Apollo)*

Parachute opening height	Wind in knots						
	10	**20**	**30**	**40**	**50**	**60**	**70**
30,000 ft (9,000 m)	3.7	7.4	11.1	14.7	18.4	22.1	25.8
20,000 ft (6,000 m)	2.7	5.3	8.0	10.7	13.3	16.0	18.7
14,000 ft (4,300 m)	1.9	3.8	5.7	7.7	9.5	11.4	13.3
10,000 ft (3,050 m)	1.4	2.8	4.2	5.7	7.0	8.3	9.7
8,000 ft (2,400 m)	1.2	2.3	3.5	4.6	5.8	6.9	8.1
6,000 ft (1,800 m)	0.9	1.7	2.6	3.5	4.4	5.2	6.1
4,000 ft (1,200 m)	0.6	1.2	1.8	2.4	3.0	3.5	4.1
2,000 ft (600 m)	0.3	0.6	0.9	1.2	1.5	1.8	2.1

Table N-14 – *Parachute drift distance (zero glide ratio)*
(Distance in miles of landing position downwind from position of parachute opening)

Descent data

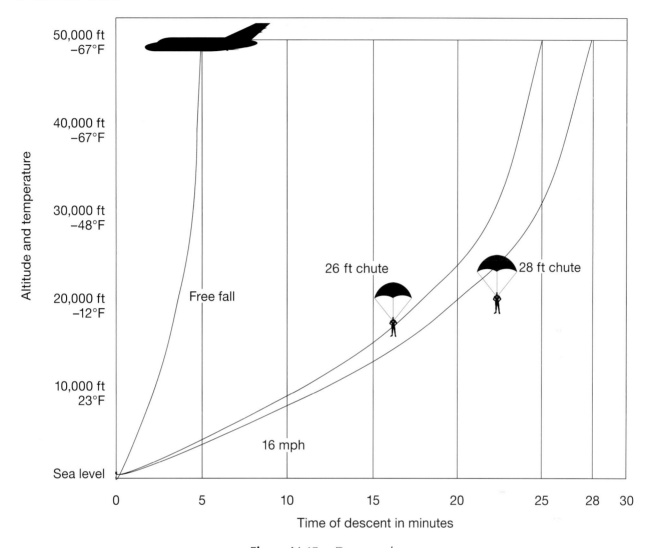

Figure N-15 – *Descent data*

Appendix O

Ship reporting systems for SAR

System name and country (if applicable)	Operating authority	General reporting area description	Voluntary or mandatory participation	Categories of ships entitled to participate	Reporting interval	System purpose/ objective	Where/how to send reports
Amver United States and world shipping	United States Coast Guard (USCG)	World-wide	Voluntary	Merchant vessels of all nations making offshore voyages.	When departing port and at intervals not exceeding 48 h.	To provide an RCC the predicted location and SAR characteristics of vessels known to be within an area of interest during a maritime emergency.	Via selected radio stations (see list in ALRS, Volume 1, Parts 1 and 2) or via Inmarsat. Details of charges (if applicable) are included in the services of each station.
Argentina SECOSENA	The Prefectura Naval Argentina	Argentine waters	Mandatory	Mandatory for all vessels greater than 24 m in length. This requirement may be extended to smaller vessels in certain circumstances.	When entering and departing the area and at 0000 and 1200 UTC while within the area.	*Not stated in the Admiralty List of Radio Signals (ALRS)*	Reports should be sent to the nearest SECOSENA Coast Radio Station or a public correspondence Coast Radio Station if necessary. **Messages should be sent in Spanish or using the International Code of Signals.**

System name and country (if applicable)	Operating authority	General reporting area description	Voluntary or mandatory participation	Categories of ships entitled to participate	Reporting interval	System purpose/ objective	Where/how to send reports
Australia AUSREP	Australian Maritime Safety Authority through RCC AUSTRALIA	The coverage area is the same as for the Australian SAR area. Precise details are in ALRS, Volume 1, Part 2.	Mandatory and voluntary	Mandatory for Australian registered vessels and for foreign vessels on voyages between Australian ports, and voluntary for foreign vessels transiting through the AUSREP area and also for fishing vessels and small craft which comply with certain criteria.	When entering and departing the area and at intervals not exceeding 24 h.	To aid SAR operations by: – limiting the time between the loss of a vessel and the start of a SAR action in cases where no distress signal is transmitted. – limiting the size of a search area, and – providing up-to-date information of shipping in the vicinity of a SAR incident. AUSREP is a positive reporting system. This means that if a report becomes overdue, then a SAR response will be started and may include world-wide communication checks as well as search action.	Reports are to be addressed to RCC AUSTRALIA and can be sent free of charge through any Australian Coast Radio Station or via Inmarsat-C via LES Perth and using Special Access Code 43. For further details, refer to the ALRS, Volume 1, Part 2.
Brazil SISTRAM	Naval Command for the Control of Maritime Traffic (COMCONTRAM)	Coverage area stretches east of Brazil to 10°W and from approximately 04.5°N to 34.5°S. Exact details are shown in ALRS, Volume 1, Part 2.	Mandatory and voluntary	Mandatory for Brazilian registered vessels, and voluntary for other vessels.	When entering and departing the area and if there are any changes to the planned route.	To know the position of vessels within the Brazilian SAR area in case of a SAR incident.	Reports can be sent free of charge to COMCONTRAM RIO through any Brazilian Coast Radio Station. Reports sent via telex to 21366931 or 21303933 will be charged.

System name and country (if applicable)	Operating authority	General reporting area description	Voluntary or mandatory participation	Categories of ships entitled to participate	Reporting interval	System purpose/ objective	Where/how to send reports
Canada Amver	United States Coast Guard (USCG)	World-wide	Mandatory	Mandatory for Canadian vessels and vessels involved in the Canadian coasting trade (with certain exceptions).	When departing port and at intervals not exceeding 48 h.	To provide (to SAR agencies and persons in distress) predicted location and SAR characteristics of vessels known to be within an area of interest during a maritime emergency.	Reports should be addressed to "Amver Vancouver" or "Amver Halifax" and can be sent through any Canadian Coast Radio Station or through a Canadian Coast Guard vessel.
Canada ECAREG	Canadian Coast Guard (CCG)	East Coast Canadian waters south of 60°N and east of 66°W	Mandatory	All vessels ≥ 500 GRT	Entry into or departing the area, at selected points and if there are any changes to information previously submitted.	To ensure compliance with Canadian regulatory requirements.	To ECAREG CANADA via any CCG Marine Communications and Traffic Services Station.
Canada NORDREG	*As above*	Canadian waters north of 60°N including all waters of Ungava, James and Hudson Bays	Voluntary	*As above*	*As above*	*As above*	To NORDREG CANADA via any CCG Marine Communications and Traffic Services Station.
Combined US/ Canada Vessel Traffic Services Area (CVTS OFFSHORE)	*As above*	Canadian waters on the west coast of Canada	Mandatory	All vessels ≥ 300 GRT	24 h prior to entry into Canadian waters.	*As above*	CVTS OFFSHORE via any CCG Marine Communications and Traffic Services Station.

System name and country (if applicable)	Operating authority	General reporting area description	Voluntary or mandatory participation	Categories of ships entitled to participate	Reporting interval	System purpose/ objective	Where/how to send reports
Chile CHILREP	General Directorate of the Maritime Territory and Merchant Marine, which is a directorate of the Chilean Navy.	The coverage area is the same as for the Chilean SAR area. Precise details of area are in ALRS, Volume 1, Part 2.	Voluntary	*Not stated in the ALRS*	When entering and departing the area and once a day between 1200 and 1600 UTC so that a report is received every 24 h.	To aid SAR operations by: – limiting the time between the loss of a vessel and the initiation of a SAR action in cases where no distress signal is sent out – limiting the size of a search area for a rescue action, and – providing up-to-date information of shipping resources available in the area, in the event of a SAR incident.	Reports are to be sent through Chilean Coast Radio Stations that accept public correspondence. Reports should be addressed to DIRECTEMAR VALPARAISO.
Denmark SHIPPOS	SHIPPOS Aarhus	Danish waters of the Baltic Sea, including 17 m minimum-depth transit route known as Route T.	Voluntary	All vessels of 20,000 GRT and over. All loaded oil, gas, and chemical tankers of 1,600 GRT and over. All vessels with a draught of 13 m or more. All vessels carrying radio-active material. All vessels with a draught of 10 m or more may participate when transiting the ferry routes S of Sprogoe. Vessels of 40,000 DWT are recommended to participate in this service while passing through the entrances to the Baltic Sea	When entering and departing the area and when crossing reporting lines (details in ALRS, Volume 1, Part 1).	*Not stated in the ALRS*	Reports will be accepted through any Danish Coast Radio Station.

System name and country (if applicable)	Operating authority	General reporting area description	Voluntary or mandatory participation	Categories of ships entitled to participate	Reporting interval	System purpose/ objective	Where/how to send reports
Ecuador	Coast Guard	Within 200 NM of Ecuador and between the mainland and the Archipelago de Colon.	Mandatory	Vessels navigating in the reporting area.	When entering or departing the area and position reports as required.	*Not stated in the ALRS*	Reports should be sent through Guayaquil (HCG) and addressed to Coast Guard (COGUAR).
Fiji	*Not stated in the ALRS*	See diagram in ALRS, Volume 1, Part 2.		For all vessels, including small craft.	Send reports at least once daily.	This is a maritime surveillance safety service involving ship reporting.	Reports should be sent to Suva (3DP) Coast Radio Station or by telex to HOMSEC Fiji.
Greenland GREENPOS	GRØNLANDS-KOMMANDO	For vessels *en route* to or from Greenland and in the area north of the 57°N and within 250 NM of the Greenland coast.	Mandatory	All ships on voyages to or from Greenland ports and places of call.	On entry and departure for the area, and position reports are to be sent four times daily at times depicted in ALRS, Volume 1, Part 2.	Designed to assist in the co-ordination of SAR operations.	Reports can be sent free of charge in the form of a radio telegram direct to GRØNLAND-KOMMANDO (GLK) via Grønnedal Flåde Radio (OVC) or through a Coast Radio Station.
Greenland KYSTKONTROL	GRØNLANDS-KOMMANDO	For vessels on passage between harbours and ports on the coast of Greenland.	Mandatory	All ships of 20 gross tonnage and more and fishing vessels, on voyages between Greenland ports and places of call.	On entry and departure from a port or harbour. Position reports are to be sent at least every 24 h if the voyage exceeds 24 h.	Designed to assist in the co-ordination of SAR operations.	Reports can be sent free of charge and should be addressed to SKIBSKONTROL and the name of the appropriate control station as listed in ALRS, Volume 1, Part 2. They can also be sent via a Coast Radio Station.
Iceland	The Icelandic Lifesaving Association	*Not stated in the ALRS*	Mandatory	Compulsory for all Icelandic vessels.	When entering or leaving harbour and twice a day at sea.	*Not stated in the ALRS*	Through Icelandic Coast Radio Stations.

System name and country (if applicable)	Operating authority	General reporting area description	Voluntary or mandatory participation	Categories of ships entitled to participate	Reporting interval	System purpose/ objective	Where/how to send reports
India INSPIRES	*Not stated in the ALRS*	As detailed in ALRS, Volume 1, Part 1 but broadly covers from India-Pakistan border to the African coast, then to 30°S (excluding Madagascar) across to 95°E and northwards to coast.	Mandatory and voluntary	Mandatory for all Indian merchant vessels, including coastal and fishing vessels of more than 300 GRT. Other vessels within the reporting areas are encouraged to participate.	When entering and departing the area and daily according to the schedule depicted in ALRS, Volume 1, Part 1.	To provide data for SAR operations, vessel traffic management, weather forecasting, and the prevention and containment of marine pollution.	Reports are free if sent through Indian Naval Communications Centres Bombay (VTF) or Vishakhapatnam (VTO). Reports sent through Bombay Radio (VWB) or Madras Radio (VWM) are chargeable.
Italy ARES	*Not stated in the ALRS*	Not specifically stated in the ALRS but appears to be for vessels in the Mediterranean or outside it.	Mandatory	Mandatory for all Italian merchant vessels of over 1,600 GRT except for those vessels making national voyages of less than 24 h and international voyages of less than 12 h. Other vessels in the Mediterranean are encouraged to participate in the system.	When entering and departing the area and daily at 1200 local time if in the Mediterranean and every 48 h if outside.	To provide data that will ensure the efficiency of SAR operations.	Reports are accepted free of charge by Italian Coast Radio Stations.
Japan JASREP	Japanese Maritime Safety Agency (JMSA)	The sea area bounded by the mainland of Asia, the parallel of latitude 17°N, and the meridian of longitude 165°E.	Voluntary	All suitably equipped vessels are invited to participate	When entering and departing the area and at intervals not exceeding 24 h.	To assist in the co-ordination of SAR operations. SAR action may be initiated if an expected report is not received.	Reports should be send to Tokyo (JNA) or to any of the Coast Radio Stations listed in ALRS Volume 1, Part 1.
Madagascar	Cencorsau, Tananarive	Between 5°S and 30°S and between 60°E and the coast of Africa.	*Not stated in the ALRS*	*Not stated in the ALRS*	When entering and departing the area and daily at 1000 UTC.	To assist SAR operations.	Reports are free of charge and should be addressed to "Cencorsau Tananarive" through the nearest Coast Radio Station in Madagascar.

System name and country (if applicable)	Operating authority	General reporting area description	Voluntary or mandatory participation	Categories of ships entitled to participate	Reporting interval	System purpose/ objective	Where/how to send reports
Peru	The Peruvian Director General of Harbour Masters and the Coast Guard	The north and south maritime borders and a line 200 NM off the coast of Peru.	Mandatory	Mandatory for all Peruvian vessels over 350 GRT and all foreign vessels regardless of tonnage and type.	On entering Peruvian waters or departing a Peruvian port.	*Not stated in the ALRS*	Can be sent free of charge through various Coast Radio Stations (details in ALRS, Volume 1, Part 2) or via satellite. If sent through foreign they are to be addressed to Director General di Guarda Costas.
Singapore SINGREP	*Not stated in the ALRS*	Coverage area encompasses the seas around the Malay Peninsula, most of the Indonesian archipelago, including Borneo and then north to the west coast of the Philipines. Specific details are shown in the ALRS, Volume 1, Part 1.	Voluntary	Vessels of any nationality, tonnage or type are welcome to participate as long as they are within the service area of SINGREP.	Preferably sent daily between 0000 and 0800 UTC.	To aid SAR operations by: – reducing the time between loss of a vessel and start of a search in cases where no distress signals are sent – limiting the size of the SAR area – providing up-to-date information on shipping resources available in the vicinity of the casualty.	Reports should be forwarded through Singapore Radio (9VG) on RTG, RTF, radio telex, or via Inmarsat.

Appendix P

Functional characteristics to consider with computer-based search planning aids

Overview

The computer software, hereinafter referred to as the search planning model, should be designed to accept all inputs that the SAR Co-ordinator can reasonably be expected to use in search planning and present the calculated results to the Co-ordinator as useable information in the form of an optimal search plan, useful statistics and values important to the search planning process. It should not simply produce a mass of data outputs. The desirable functional characteristics of the search planning model should include, but should not be limited to, those in the following list. The model should perform the following functions:

- Accept and integrate various environmental data from multiple sources, together with their estimated error and variability patterns;

- Simulate the effects of the environment on search object status and motion, sensor performance and the survivors;

- Use appropriate sampling techniques for simulating possible search object movements (e.g., drift), and determining the area of containment;

- Have the flexibility to develop updated search plans based on new information or assumptions made by the search planner;

- Have the ability to allow for time uncertainty and/or position uncertainty of the initial distress location;

- Simulate hazards, possible encounters between the missing craft and the hazards, and the probabilities that such encounters would result in a distress incident;

- Have the ability to generate initial probability density distributions using the previous two features together;

- Be capable of simulating post-distress changes (state changes) in the status of distressed persons such as abandoning a vessel into a liferaft;

- Be capable of predicting the survivability of distressed persons based on selectable scenarios and when computing optimal effort allocations;

- Generate valid probability density distributions of possible search object locations based on post-distress search object trajectories using low- to high-resolution[*] environmental data, as available (high-resolution data are always preferred);

- Be capable of handling multiple scenarios simultaneously which includes the ability to compare the scenarios and assign weighting factors to them;

- Produce an operationally feasible search plan that maximizes the probability of finding the distressed persons alive with the available search facilities – i.e., produce an optimal search plan for the situation at hand. Factors to consider are the possible (weighted) scenarios, the dynamic probability density distribution of search object locations, survivor state changes, survival times,

---

[*] High-resolution data are data on a small spatial (e.g., 0.1 × 0.1 degree or 6 NM × 6 NM at the equator) and temporal (e.g., every three hours) grid. Low-resolution data would be on larger grids (e.g., 1 × 1 degree × 24 h or greater).

environmental parameters, search facility characteristics (number, type, location, endurance, sensors, etc.), previous search results, etc. Both tactical (myopic, day-to-day or sortie-to-sortie) and strategic optimisation (when resource availability can be predicted with reasonable certainty) should be available;

- Be able to properly evaluate search results (in the computational sense), including both positive (e.g., debris sightings) and negative (no sightings of search object) aspects. It should perform detailed updates of the dynamic probability density distributions of the possible search object locations based on actual sortie tracks and reports of sensor performance;

- Make proper use of previous search results when computing optimal plans for subsequent searches;

- Correctly simulate the effects of the relative motion between moving search objects and moving search facilities;

- Compute and display estimates of search effectiveness in the form of POS values for sorties and the cumulative POS value for all searching done to date;

- Be capable of processing and re-evaluating new (including late-arriving) information such as update of last known position and/or distress time to produce an updated optimal search plan;

- Consideration should be given to the man–machine interface so that the information generated by the computer-based tool and database would be useful to the search planner. The model should also be capable of displaying large volumes of information in ways that promote rapid assimilation. The model should contain or be integrated with appropriate geographical displays and useful tools for describing search sub-areas, generating search patterns, communicating search plans to search facilities, etc.; and,

- Finally, the software of such a model must be developed using sound software engineering principles to keep life-cycle costs down, maximize reliability, provide for ease of making future improvements, and have it operate with as many hardware platforms and operating systems as possible.

Appendix Q

Sample problem

F/V Sample – alpha search

Alpha search scenario	1	On 25 January 2000 at 2145Z, the *F/V Sample* broadcast a distress radio call. The captain reported the vessel's engines were inoperable and the vessel was taking on water, but the vessel was not in immediate danger of sinking. However, the captain requested assistance. The vessel's reported DR position at 2145Z was given as 37-10N, 065-45W. This DR position was based on a celestial fix at 250100Z JAN 00 in position 38-57N, 068-54W. Communications were lost after this initial call for assistance.
	2	A British Airways flight transiting the area while *en route* to Bermuda at 261100Z JAN 00 failed to sight the *F/V Sample*. Based on enquiries about resource availability, the earliest time at which a search can commence is 261630Z JAN 00. A search is to be planned for this commence search time.
Wind information	3	Observed and forecast wind data

Date	Time	°T/kts	Date	Time	°T/kts
26 JAN	0000Z	175/32	27 JAN	0000Z	200/32
	0600Z	190/30		0600Z	195/30
	1200Z	210/35		1200Z	195/30
	1800Z	205/37		1800Z	200/28

Vessel description	4	The *F/V Sample* is a 75-foot eastern-rigged side trawler, with a black steel hull and a white superstructure.
Search facilities	5	Two four-engine fixed-wing aircraft search facilities are available with GPS navigation systems.

Aircraft Type	Speed	On-Scene Endurance	Crew Fatigue
C-130 Hercules	180 knots	3.00 hours	Normal
P-3 Orion	200 knots	4.00 hours	Normal

Search conditions	6	On-scene weather for 26 January 2000:

Meteorological visibility	5 NM	Ceiling	1500 feet
Winds	210°T/35 knots	Seas	3–5 feet
Sunrise	1100Z	Sunset	2200Z

Datum worksheet for computing drift in the marine environment

Case title ___F/V SAMPLE___ Case number __00-001__ Date __26 JAN 2000__

Planner's name ___SAR SCHOOL___ Datum number __1__ Search plan A B C __A__

Search object __Medium displacement fishing vessel__

A   Starting position for this drift interval

1	Type of position *(Circle one)*	Last known position, Estimated incident position Previous datum	LKP (EIP) PD	
2	Position Date/time		252145 Z	JAN 2000
3	Latitude, longitude of position		37-10 (N)/S	065-45 (W)/E

B   Datum time

1	Commence search date/time	261630 Z	JAN 2000
2	Drift interval		18.75 hours

C   Average surface wind (ASW)

(Attach **Average surface wind (ASW) worksheet**)

1	Average surface wind (*ASW*)	194 °T	31.72 kts
2	Probable error of drift velocity due to probable error of average surface wind ($ASWDV_e$)		0.3 kts

D   Total water current (TWC)

(Attach **Total water current (TWC) worksheet**)

1	Total water current (*TWC*)	057 °T	1.86 kts
2	Probable total water current error (TWC_e)		0.42 kts

E   Leeway (LW)

(Attach **Leeway (LW) worksheet**)

1	Left of downwind	324 °T	1.3 kts
2	Right of downwind	064 °T	1.3 kts
3	Probable leeway error (LW_e)		0.3 kts

F   Total surface drift

Use a manoeuvring board or calculator to add Total water current and Leeway vectors.
(See **figure K-1a**)

		(left of downwind)		(right of downwind)	
1	Drift directions	021	°T	060	°T
2	Drift speeds	2.21	kts	3.15	kts
3	Drift distances (**line F.2** × **line B.2**)	41.49	NM	59.14	NM

4   Total probable drift velocity error (DV_e)

$$(DV_e = \sqrt{ASWDV_e^2 + TWC_e^2 + LW_e^2})$$ 0.60 kts

G   Datum positions and divergence distance

Using a chart, universal plotting sheet or calculator, determine the datum positions and divergence distance (*DD*) (See **figure K-1b**)

1	Latitude, longitude (left of downwind)	37–48.7 (N)/S	065–26.3 (W)/E
2	Latitude, longitude (right of downwind)	37–39.6 (N)/S	064–40.5 (W)/E
3	Divergence distance (*DD*)		37.5 NM

H   Total probable error of position (*E*) and separation ratio (*SR*)

(Attach **Total probable error of position (*E*) worksheet**)

1	Total probable error of position squared (E^2)	1,002.7 NM^2
2	Total probable error of position (*E*)	31.67 NM
3	Separation ratio ($SR = DD/E$)	1.18
4	Go to the **Total available search effort worksheet**.	

Average surface wind (ASW) worksheet

Case title ___F/V SAMPLE___ Case number __00-001__ Date __26 JAN 2000__

Planner's name ___SAR SCHOOL___ Datum number __1__ Search plan A B C __A__

A Average surface wind

1 Surface wind data

Time of observation	Time interval	Number of hours (A)	Wind direction (B)	Wind speed (C)	Wind contribution (A × C)
260000Z	2145 – 0300	5.25	175° T	32 kts	168 NM
260600Z	0300 – 0900	6.00	190° T	30 kts	180 NM
261200Z	0900 – 1500	6.00	210° T	35 kts	210 NM
261800Z	1500 – 1630	1.50	205° T	37 kts	55.5 NM
	–		° T	kts	NM
	–		° T	kts	NM
	–		° T	kts	NM
	–		° T	kts	NM

	Total hours	18.75 (D)	Vector sum of contributions	194 °T (E)	594.76 NM (F)

2 Average surface wind (ASW) [(E)°T (F/D) kts]   __194__ °T __31.72__ kts

B Probable error

1 Probable error of the Average surface wind (ASW_e)   __5.0__ kts

2 Probable error of drift velocity due to probable error of the average surface wind ($ASWDV_e$)   __0.3__ kts

Go to **part C** on the **Datum worksheet**.

Total water current (TWC) worksheet

Case title ___F/V SAMPLE_____ Case number __00-001_ Date __26 JAN 2000__

Planner's name ___SAR SCHOOL_____ Datum number ___1__ Search plan A B C __A___

A   Observed total water current (*TWC*)

1   Source (datum marker buoy (DMB), debris, oil)   _____

2   Observed set/drift   _____ °T   _____ kts

3   Probable error of observation (*TWC*$_e$)   _____ kts

4   Go to **part D** on the **Datum worksheet.**

B   Computed total water current

1   Tidal current (*TC*)

    a   Source (tidal current tables, local knowledge)   _____

    b   Tidal current (*TC*) set/drift
       (attach any tidal current computations)   _____ °T   _____ kts

    c   Probable error of tidal current (*TC*$_e$)   _____ kts

2   Sea current (*SC*)

    a   Source (atlas, pilot chart, etc.)   NOOSP NA6 1400

    b   Sea current (*SC*) set/drift   075 °T   0.8 kts

    c   Probable error of sea current (*SC*$_e$)   0.3 kts

3   Wind current (*WC*)
    (attach **Wind current worksheet**)

    a   Wind current (*WC*) set/drift   044 °T   1.13 kts

    b   Probable error of wind current (*WC*$_e$)   0.3 kts

4   Other water current (*OWC*)

    a   Source (local knowledge, previous incidents, etc.)   _____

    b   Other water current (*OWC*) set/drift   _____ °T   _____ kts

    c   Probable error of other water current (*OWC*$_e$)   _____ kts

5   Computed total water current (*TWC*) set/drift   057 °T   1.86 kts

6   Computed probable total water current error (*TWC*$_e$)
    ($TWC_e = \sqrt{TC_e^2 + SC_e^2 + WC_e^2 + OWC_e^2}$)   0.42 kts

7   Go to **part D** on the **Datum worksheet.**

Wind current (WC) worksheet

Case title ___F/V SAMPLE_____ Case number __00-001__ Date __26 JAN 2000__

Planner's name __SAR SCHOOL_____ Datum number ___1___ Search plan A B C __A__

Wind current (*WC*)

1 Average surface wind (*ASW*)
   (From **Datum worksheet, line C.1**)   _____194__ °T   ____31.72__ kts

2 Downwind direction (*ASW* direction ± 180°)   _____014__ °T

3 Wind current drift
   (from **figure N-1**)   _____1.13__ kts

4 Divergence of wind current
   (from **figure N-1**)   ± _____+30__ °

5 Wind current set
   (Downwind direction ± divergence of wind current)
   (add divergence in northern hemisphere,
   subtract in southern hemisphere)   _____044__ °T

6 Wind current (*WC*) set/drift   _____044__ °T   _____1.13__ kts

7 Probable error of wind current (*WC*_e)   _____0.3__ kts

8 Go to **line B.3** on the **Total water current (TWC) worksheet**.

Leeway (LW) worksheet

Case title ___F/V SAMPLE___ Case number ___00-001___ Date ___26 JAN 2000___

Planner's name ___SAR SCHOOL___ Datum number ___1___ Search plan A B C ___A___

Search object ___Medium displacement fishing vessel___

1	Average surface wind (*ASW*) (from **Datum worksheet, line C.1**)	___194___ °T	___31.72___ kts
2	Downwind direction (*ASW* direction ± 180°)		___014___ °T
3	Leeway speed (from **figure N-2** or **N-3**)		___1.13___ kts
4	Leeway divergence angle (from **figure N-2** or **N-3**)		± ___50___ °
5	Leeway directions		
	a Left of downwind (**line 2 – line 4**)		___324___ °T
	b Right of downwind (**line 2 + line 4**)		___064___ °T
6	Leeway (*LW*)		
	a Left of downwind	___324___ °T	___1.3___ kts
	b Right of downwind	___064___ °T	___1.3___ kts
7	Probable leeway error (*LW*$_e$) (from **figure N-2** or **N-3**)		___0.3___ kts
8	Go to **part E** on the **Datum worksheet**.		

Total probable error of position (E) worksheet
for land and marine environments

Case title ___F/V SAMPLE___ Case number __00-001__ Date __26 JAN 2000__

Planner's name ___SAR SCHOOL___ Datum number __1__ Search plan A B C __A__

A   Probable distress incident/initial position error (X)

(Go to **line 1** to compute probable error of the distress incident position. Go to **line 6** if the starting position for this drift interval is a previous datum.)

1   Navigational fix error
(from **table N-1** or **N-2**)   _2.0_ NM

2   Dead reckoning (DR) error rate
(from **table N-3**)   _15_ %

3   DR distance since last fix   _184_ NM

4   DR navigational error
(**line A.2** × **line A.3**)   _27.6_ NM

5   Glide distance (if aircraft/parachute descent heading
is unknown)   _____ NM

6   Probable initial position error (X)
(X = **line A.1** + **line A.4** + **line A.5**) or
(X = Total probable error of position from **line H.2**
of previous **Datum worksheet**)   _29.6_ NM

B   Total probable drift error (D_e)

1   Drift interval
(from **line B.2** of the **Datum worksheet**)   _18.75_ hours

2   Probable drift velocity error (DV_e)
(from **line F.4** of the **Datum worksheet**)   _0.6_ kts

3   Total probable drift error (D_e)
(D_e = **line B.1** × **line B.2**)   _11.25_ NM

C   Probable search facility position error (Y)

1   Navigational fix error
(from **table N-1** or **N-2**)   _0.1_ NM

2   Dead reckoning (DR) error rate
(from **table N-3**)   _____ %

3   DR distance since last fix   _____ NM

4   DR navigational error
(**line C.2** × **line C.3**)   _____ NM

5   Probable search facility position error (Y)
(Y = **line C.1** + **line C.4**)   _0.1_ NM

D   Total probable error of position (*E*)

1   Sum of squared errors
$(E^2 = X^2 + D_e{}^2 + Y^2)$ _____1002.7_____ NM^2

2   Total probable error of position
$(E = \sqrt{X^2 + D_e{}^2 + Y^2})$ _____31.67_____ NM

Total available search effort (Z_{ta}) worksheet

Case title ____F/V SAMPLE_____ Case number __00-001__ Date __26 JAN 2000__

Planner's name __SAR SCHOOL_____ Datum number ____1____ Search plan A B C ___A___

Datum _____37-48.7 N_____ ____065-26.3 W____ Datum _____37-39.6 N_____ ____064-40.5 W____
(left) _____Latitude_____ ____Longitude____ (right) _____Latitude_____ ____Longitude____

Search object __Medium displacement fishing vessel___ Date/time __261630Z JAN 2000__

Total available effort computations

		1	2	3	4	5
1	Search sub-area designation	A-1	A-2	___	___	___
2	Search facility assigned	C-130	P-3	___	___	___
3	Search facility speed(V)	180	200	___	___	___
4	On-scene endurance	3.0	4.0	___	___	___
5	Daylight hours remaining	7.5	7.5	___	___	___
6	Search endurance (T) (T = 85% of lesser of **line 4** or **5** above)	2.55	3.4	___	___	___
7	Search altitude (metres/feet) *(circle one)*	500	1000	___	___	___
8	Uncorrected sweep width	5.0	5.1	___	___	___
9	Weather, terrain correction factor (f_w, f_t)	0.9	0.9	___	___	___
10	Velocity correction factor (f_v) (aircraft only)	1.0	1.0	___	___	___
11	Fatigue correction factor (f_f)	1.0	1.0	___	___	___
12	Corrected sweep width (W)	4.5	4.6	___	___	___
13	Search effort ($Z = V \times T \times W$)	2,065.5	3,128	___	___	___
14	Total available search effort ($Z_{ta} = Z_{a1} + Z_{a2} + Z_{a3} + ...$)				5,193.5	NM²
15	Separation ratio (SR) (leeway divergence datums only) (from **line H.3** of the **Datum worksheet**)				1.18	

16   If the separation ratio (SR) on **line 15** is greater than four ($SR > 4$), go to the **Widely diverging datums worksheet**. Otherwise, go to the **Effort allocation worksheet**.

Effort allocation worksheet for optimal search of single point, leeway divergence or line datums

Case title ___F/V SAMPLE_____ Case number __00-001_ Date _26 JAN 2000_

Planner's name __SAR SCHOOL_____ Datum number ___1__ Search plan A B C __A___

Datum (left)	_37-48.7 N_	_065-26.3 W_	Datum (right)	_37-39.6 N_	_064-40.5 W_
	Latitude	Longitude		Latitude	Longitude

Search object ___Medium displacement fishing vessel___ Date/time _261630Z JAN 2000_

Effort allocation computations

1   Available search effort (Z_{ta}, $Z_{a(left)}$, or $Z_{a(right)}$)
    (from **line 14** of the **Total available search effort worksheet** or
    line 5.a or **line 5.b** of the **Widely diverging datums worksheet**) ___5,193.5__ NM^2

2   Effort factor (f_Z)

   a   Total probable error of position (E) ___31.66__ NM

   b   Length of datum line (L) _____ NM

   c   Effort factor (f_Z) ($f_{Zp} = E_2$ or $f_{Zl} = E \times L$) ___1002.7__ NM^2

3   Relative effort ($Z_r = Z_a/f_z$) ___5.18___

4   Cumulative relative effort (Z_{rc} = previous Z_{rc} + Z_r) ___5.18___

5   Optimal search factor (f_s) Ideal _____ Normal _X___ (f_s) __1.1___

6   Optimal search radius ($R_o = f_s \times E$) ___34.83__ NM

7   Optimal search area (A_o) ___7,464__ NM^2

   a   Single point datum ($A_o = 4 \times R_o^2$)

   b   Leeway divergence datums [$A_o = (4 \times R_o^2) + 2 \times R_o \times DD)$]

   c   Line datum ($A_o = 2 \times R_o \times L$)

8   Optimal coverage factor ($C_o = Z_a/A_o$) ___0.70___

		1	2	3	4	5
9	Optimal track spacing ($S_o = W/C_o$)	6.45	6.45	___	___	___
10	Nearest assignable track spacing (S) (within limits of search facility navigational capability)	6.5	6.5	___	___	___
11	Adjusted search areas ($A = V \times T \times S$)	2983.5	4420	___	___	___

12   Total adjusted search area ($A_t = A_1 + A_2 + A_3 + ...$) ___7,403.5__ NM^2

13   Adjusted search radius (R) ___34.7__ NM

   a   Single point datum $\quad R = \dfrac{\sqrt{A_t}}{2}$

   b   Leeway divergence datums $\quad R = \dfrac{\sqrt{DD^2 + (4 \times A_t)} - DD}{4}$

   c   Line datum $\quad R = \dfrac{A_t}{2 \times L}$

14   Adjusted search area dimensions

         a   Length   Length   __107__ NM

                i)   Single point datum   *Length $= 2 \times R$*

               ii)   Leeway divergence datums   *Length $= (2 \times R) + DD$*

               iii)   Line datum   *Length of the Base Line (L_b)*   _____ NM

                      a)   No extensions   *Length $= L_b$*

                      b)   One extension   *Length $= R + L_b$*

                      c)   Two extensions   *Length $= (2 \times R) + L_b$*

         b   Width $= 2 \times R$ Width   __69__ NM

15   Plot the adjusted search area on a suitable chart   (Check when done) _____

16   Divide the adjusted search area into search sub-areas
according to the values on **line 11**   (Check when done)_____

17   Go to the **Search action plan worksheet**.

Results of a Monte Carlo simulation using the *F/V Sample* data for the alpha search

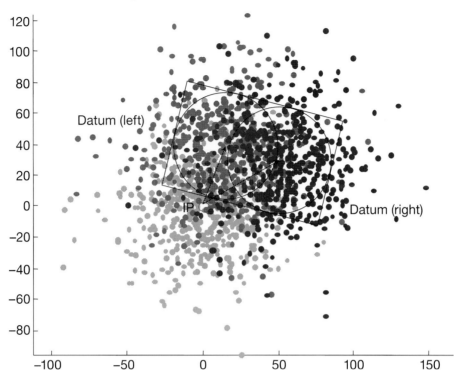

Monte Carlo simulation of *F/V Sample* – alpha search

Area	POC	Coverage	POD	POS
7,343 NM²	70.8%	0.70	50.2%	35.6%

Green/light grey dots represent some of the possible initial search object locations. Blue/black and red/dark grey dots (nearly indistinguishable if printed in black-and-white) represent some of the possible search object locations at the commence search time. There are 500 dots of each colour. Only the blue and red dots inside the search rectangle were counted and used to estimate the probability of the search object being in the search area at the commence search time.

Appendix R

Medical assistance at sea,
TMAS – TMAS Medical Information Exchange Form

Identification of the requiring TMAS

Name: . . . .

Address: . . . .   Tel: . . . .

. . . .   Fax: . . . .

. . . .   Email: . . . .

Confidential medical information

Medical Assistance at Sea
TMAS – TMAS Medical Information Exchange Form

To: TMAS: . . . .

(via MRCC if necessary:) . . . .

Date: . . . . /. . . . . . ./. . . . . .   Time: . . . . h . . . .   Physician: Dr. . . . .

| Patient |

Surname: . . . .   First name: . . . .

Date of birth: . . . . . ./. . . . . . . /. . . . . Age:. . . . .   Sex: M ☐   F ☐

Nationality:. . . . .   Occupation on board: . . . .

| Medical circumstances |

☐ Illness   . . . .

☐ Accident   . . . .

☐ Poisoning   . . . .

Since . . . .

Previous medical history	Ongoing treatments	Care on board before teleconsultation
. . . .	. . . .	. . . .
. . . .	. . . .	. . . .

Medical observation

Pulse: . . . . /min	BP: . . . ./ . . . . mmHg
BR: . . . ./. . . .min	T: . . . . °C
Weight: . . . . Kg	
Height: . . . . m. . . .	

. . . .

. . . .

. . . .

Diagnosis(es) given: . . . .

. . . .

. . . .

. . . .

Identification of the requiring TMAS

Name: . . . .

Address: . . . .   Tel: . . . .

. . . .   Fax: . . . .

. . . .   Email: . . . .

| Medical instructions |

. . . .
. . . .
. . . .

| Medical assistance required |

Medical decision: ☐ Ship diversion to (port): . . . .

☐ Ambulance

Medical team: ☐ Doctor ☐ Nurse ☐ Paramedic

☐ Medical evacuation

MEDEVAC time frame: ☐ Immediate ☐ Daylight hours

MEDEVAC method: ☐ Land on ☐ Winch/stretcher ☐ Winch/strop
. . . .

Medical team: ☐ Doctor ☐ Nurse ☐ Paramedic

☐ Air drop of supplies:
. . . .
. . . .

☐ Quarantine situation
. . . .
. . . .

| Ship |

Ship name: . . . .   Call sign: . . . .

Type: . . . .   Flag: . . . .

Location : . . . .

Port of origin: . . . .   Departure/DTG: . . . .

Destination: . . . .   ETA/DTG: . . . .

Contact: . . . .

Please send back all the available follow-up information to:

TMAS name:. . . . .

Address: . . . .   Tel: . . . .

. . . .   Fax: . . . .

. . . .   Email: . . . .

Appendix S

Search planning for 121.5 MHz distress beacon alerts

1. Searching for beacons is often difficult, and may be impossible without additional information. However, the methods in this appendix should be followed as practicable.

2. Search planning for 121.5 MHz beacon alerts typically result from reports received from commercial aircraft flying at high altitude. The beacon could be located anywhere within a large search area. Reports might also be received via low-flying aircraft and ground stations. The methods that follow will help define and reduce beacon search areas. Maximum detection ranges for beacon signals are assumed to be limited by line of sight.

3. Figure S-1 depicts the geometry when an aircraft receives a beacon signal, and shows labelling used in planning a search for the beacon. *However, potential scenarios discussed in the cautionary notes below may limit the applicability of figure S-1 and should be taken into account when deemed appropriate.*

Cautionary notes

Only a single report and reporting aircraft location might be received. Unless the aircraft can provide additional information, the search area would have to be assumed to include the area within a single circle centred on the reporting aircraft's location.

Reports of *first heard* and *last heard* information may not be accurate. The person monitoring the radio may not immediately hear or recognize the 121.5 MHz distress beacon swept tone, causing the reported time and location to be incorrect.

- The beacon may have started transmitting after the reporting aircraft was already well within the maximum detection range, or the beacon may cease transmitting well before the aircraft is beyond the maximum detection range. Try to determine whether the signal: seemed strong when first acquired and then faded; was getting stronger and then abruptly ceased; or started suddenly, stopped suddenly, and seemed to be about the same strength the whole time it was heard. In such cases, the search planning procedure in this appendix should still work, although the overlapping area where the two circles intersect will be enlarged; the centres of the circles would be closer together than they would be if signal acquisition and loss were solely due to the reporting aircraft coming within and then moving beyond maximum detection range while the beacon was transmitting.

- As a part of the report data gathering process it should also be ascertained that the receiving radio was already on (did not receive the signal when it was first turned on) and that detection of the signal did not occur while squelch was being adjusted. These situations may occur when seeking reports from additional aircraft when they first turn on or adjust their radios to listen. In such cases, the position for the last heard point could be more useful that the position of when the beacon was first heard.

Reports from a single aircraft may occur at different altitudes or courses. Aircraft, particularly those under instrument flight rules, may be ascending, descending and/or changing course according to their flight plan and air route traffic control needs. The first heard and last heard reports could be from different altitudes or on different courses. For a course change, knowing the turn point would allow drawing another range circle to combine with the first heard and last heard generated range circles to more narrowly define the area. When the reports occur at different altitudes, range circles should be drawn for each altitude to identify their intersect points.

The transmitting beacon antenna may have some height above sea level or above its surrounding terrain. The height of the sending antenna should be added to the height of the radio receiver when estimating the detection range.

In areas involving an island, the island should be considered as a possible forced landing site. The first heard and last heard positions may be affected by the forced landing site's altitude and the terrain surrounding the site, which could block the signal in some directions.

The radio horizon range circle may cross land. The altitude of the reporting aircraft should be assumed to be the aircraft altitude above that elevation of the terrain at the lowest land horizon rather than above sea level, as discussed below in this appendix.

The detected beacon may be aboard an in-flight aircraft, and the aircraft, course, speed or altitude could change. The procedures in this appendix do not account for an in-flight beacon scenario, but the search planner should be aware that apparently conflicting data or unexpected search planning outcomes could be caused by this situation.

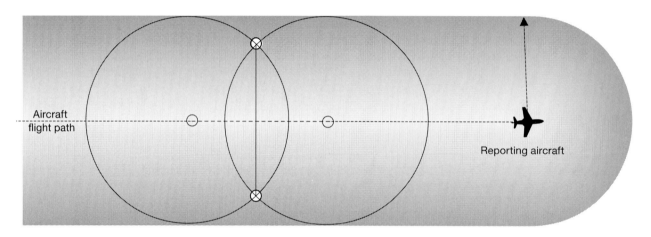

Figure S-1 – *Geometry where reporting aircraft passes within reception range of beacon signal*

Search planning procedure

4. **Record reported data.** Use table S-1 to record data received about a transmitting 121.5 MHz beacon. Of all data collected about the beacon signal, the position and height of the receiving antenna for points first heard (PFH) and last heard (PLH) are most important.

   Note: Obviously, reports from multiple sources can help substantially in narrowing down the search area for a 121.5 MHz beacon. The SAR mission co-ordinator (SMC) should use all reports, and also solicit additional reports from other aircraft in the area, either directly or via the appropriate flight services as appropriate. Aircraft should be asked to report their own altitudes and positions where the signal was first heard, when the maximum signals were heard, and when the signal faded or was lost. Flight services, communications authorities, maritime SAR authorities or others might also be able to obtain fixes or bearings on activated beacons. When receiving multiple reports, consider the possibility that more than one activated 121.5 MHz beacon might be heard. The authorities might also be able to help locate and silence an inadvertently activated beacon.

5. **Plot the reporting aircraft track.** Use a rhumb line or great circle navigation depending on the track being followed by the reporting aircraft, as depicted in figure S-2.

   Note: The geographic area used as an example in figures S-2, S-3, S-4, S-5, S-8 and S-10 is Hawaii and the surrounding area. The illustration shows a Lockheed C-130 search aircraft from Air Station Barbers Point in response to a report from an aircraft at high altitude, but similar plots could be developed for any area and other situations.

Table S-1 – *121.5 MHz beacon alert report data*

Point	Date-time	Position (latitude/longitude)	Aircraft altitude (*h*) (ft)	Course (degrees true)
PFH (first heard)		N/S E/W		
PLH (last heard)		N/S E/W		

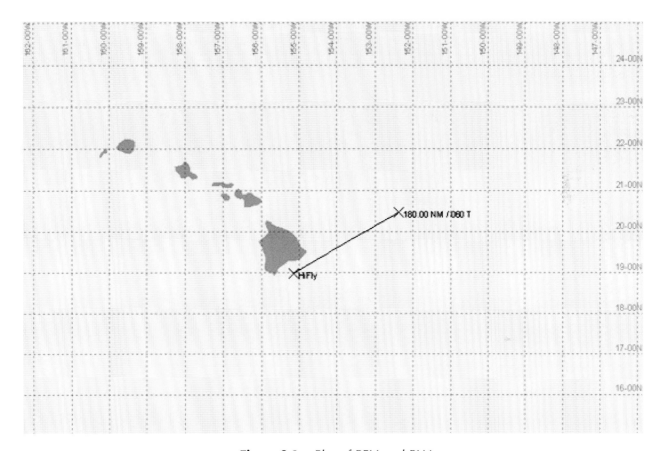

Figure S-2 – *Plot of PFH and PLH*

6. **Plot the radio horizons.** Compute and plot the distance to the radio (VHF/UHF) horizon for the reporting aircraft at PFH and PLH.

   (a) The radio horizon distance is estimated using table S-3 at the end of this appendix or by using the following equation:

   $$d = 1.23 \times \sqrt{h}$$

   where:

   > *h* is the antenna height in feet above the water (e.g., mean sea level) or above ground level (AGL); and

   > *d* is the radio horizon distance (reception range) for the reporting aircraft in nautical miles (NM).

   (b) Use table S-3 and its associated equations to determine the radio range to the horizon from a receiving antenna at various altitudes, where the altitude is measured above mean sea level (MSL) in oceanic environments. If the elevation of the horizon varies in different directions from the aircraft, perfect circles will not accurately represent the potential areas containing the beacon. The conservative approaches are as follows:

- when the horizon is only partly over an oceanic area, plot a circle using altitude above MSL;

- when the horizon is entirely over land, use the above ground level (AGL) altitude, where AGL is the altitude of the reporting aircraft above the elevation of the horizon at its lowest point; and

- be aware that over jungle areas, mountainous terrain, or where similar signal obstructions exist, the radio detection range may be as little as one-tenth of the horizon range (in mountainous terrain or areas covered with dense vegetation, the range of the signal will be reduced considerably compared to the range over water or flat land as discussed in section 5.6 of this Manual).

c. Record the results in table S-2 below.

Table S-2 – *Radio horizon distance*

Point	Aircraft altitude (*h*) (ft)	Radio horizon distance (*d*) (NM)
PFH		
PLH		

d. Draw circles centred on the PFH and PLH with a radius equal to the computed radio horizon distance for each point at the given altitude for each as recorded in table S-2 (shown in figure S-3).

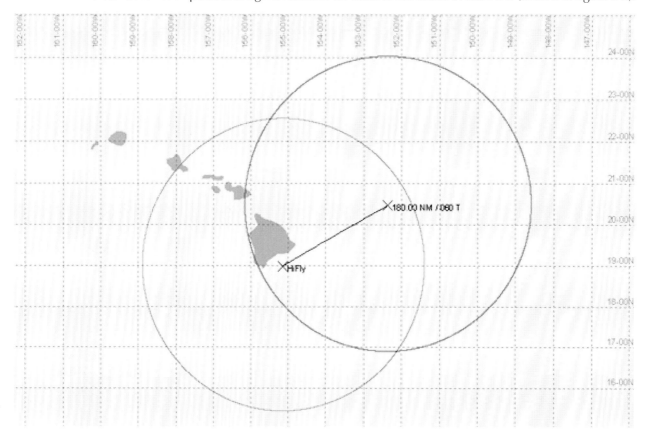

Figure S-3 – *Plot of computed radio horizon distances for PFH and PLH*

7.   **Plot the intersect line.** The circles should intersect in two places. Draw a line between the two points where the circles intersect. This line will bisect the line connecting PFH and PLH positions as indicated in figure S-4.

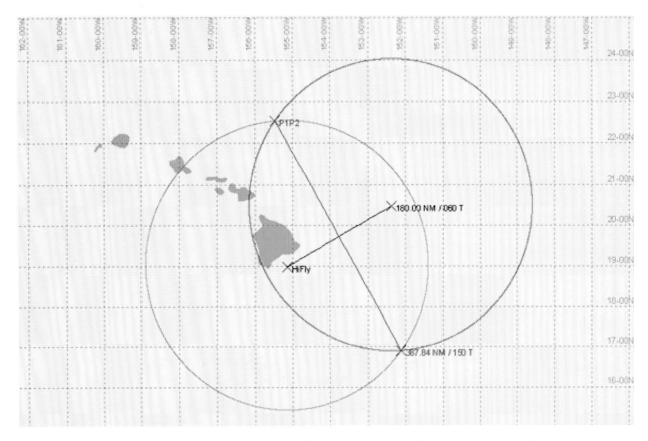

Figure S-4 – *Plot of the intersect line*

8.   **Plan the search.** With only a single report from a high-flying aircraft and the associated long distances, large search areas will result and search options will be limited.

(a)   Generally, with a single report, an electronic search will be needed to attempt to reacquire and home on the beacon signal. An electronic search can often be accomplished reasonably fast with a single aircraft SAR unit (SRU) search track.

(b)   The aircraft SRU should proceed to the nearest point where the two circles intersect and then fly at a high altitude to the other point where the two circles intersect as illustrated in figure S-5. This should allow the beacon signal to be detected so the SRU can home on it.

Note: The other two legs of the triangle are flight from the base to commence search point (CSP) and also return to base from the second intersection point/end of the intersect line.

(c)   The area where the two circles overlap could also be covered with a multi-leg track line pattern. This might be necessary if the maximum altitude of the SRU limits its detection range to less than half the width of the overlapping area of the two circles. A parallel sweep or creeping line search pattern could also be used as discussed in section 5.6 of this volume of the IAMSAR Manual.

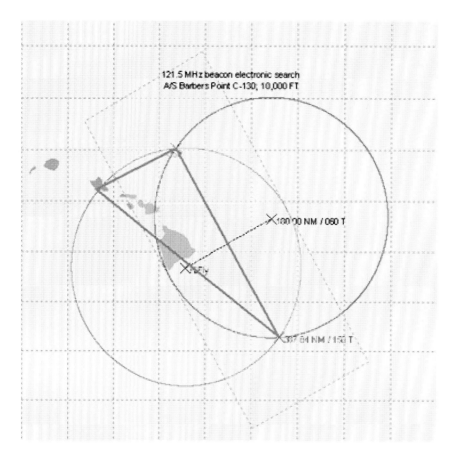

Figure S-5 – *Aircraft SRU search down the intersect line at an altitude of 10,000 ft with a radio horizon range of 123 NM*

9.   **Reporting aircraft position**. When the reporting aircraft passes directly over or nearly over the beacon position as shown in figure S-6, the search aircraft may proceed along the reporting aircraft's trackline. This special case is indicated when the distance over which the beacon was heard is twice (or nearly so) the radio horizon distance (*d*). However, if the reporting aircraft was not near the beacon position and the search aircraft's altitude is substantially lower than the reporting aircraft's altitude, a simple trackline electronic search may provide inadequate coverage to detect the beacon signal.

(a)   As shown in figures S-7 and S-8, with the reporting aircraft at 30,000 ft and the search aircraft at 10,000 ft, two primary locations would be missed by a search along the reporting aircraft's track; even a search at 20,000 ft would not cover the entire area.

(b)   In most situations it would be best to search along the intersect line (figures S-5 and S-9), with the search aircraft at 10,000 ft.

(c)   If searching along and perpendicular to the track does not succeed, a decision will be needed on if conducting a multiple leg track search is warranted based on all available information.

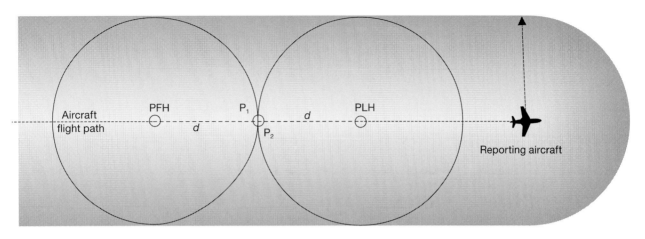

where:

    PFH = point first heard

    PLH = point last heard

    d = horizon distance for radio reception at a given height of antenna (aircraft altitude)

    P_1 = intersect position one

    P_2 = intersect position two

Figure S-6 – *Basic geometry for special case where reporting aircraft passes directly over the beacon position*

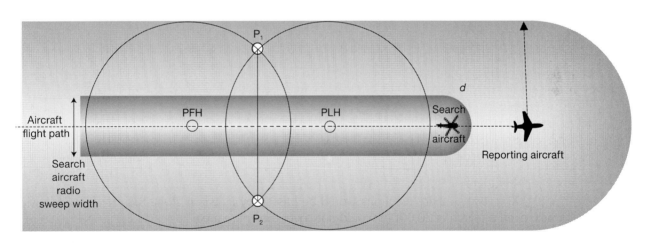

where:

    PFH = point first heard

    PLH = point last heard

    d = horizon distance for radio reception at a given height of antenna (aircraft altitude)

    P_1 = intersect position one

    P_2 = intersect position two

Figure S-7 – *Search aircraft at lower altitude than reporting aircraft – same track; beacon signal not heard*

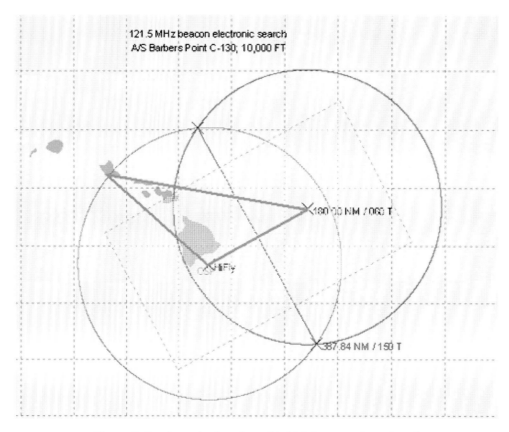

Figure S-8 – *Search aircraft at 10,000 ft, reporting aircraft at 30,000 ft – same track; beacon signal not heard*

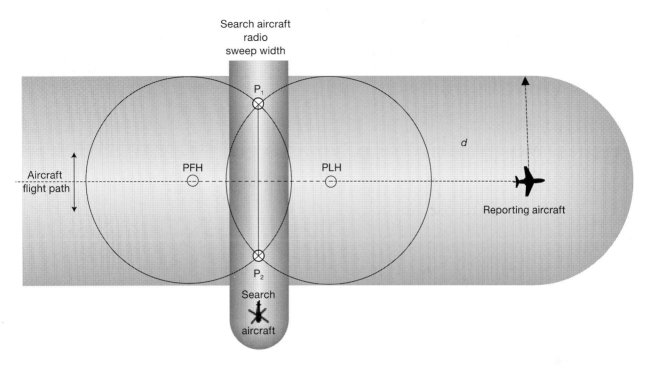

where:

PFH = point first heard

PLH = point last heard

d = horizon distance for radio reception at a given height of antenna (aircraft altitude)

P_1 = intersect position one

P_2 = intersect position two

Figure S-9 – *Searching the intersect line by search aircraft at lower altitude than the reporting aircraft*

10. **Visual search**. If no beacon signal is detected by the search aircraft conducting an electronic search or by other high-flying aircraft, a visual search will usually be impractical based on a single report. A visual search may be practical when the report comes from a low-flying aircraft which results in a smaller search area. If no other information is available besides a single report, the SMC should follow the SAR agency's guidance for responding to uncorrelated reports.

11. **Multiple Reports**. Multiple reports make it easier to reduce the area of the probable location for the distress beacon. (This situation is very similar to uncorrelated distress calls on VHF-FM and the reception by multiple radio towers (without direction finding).)

(a) Plot each report; identify the intersections and areas of overlap of the pairs of radio horizon circles; and, eliminate those areas not covered by the multiple reports.

(b) Figure S-10 shows a plot of reports from two aircraft. The first report is from an aircraft at 30,000 ft on a course of 060 degrees T, and the second report is from a descending aircraft on a course of 242 degrees T from 20,000 ft to 10,000 ft when the signal is last heard. (The smaller search area in this case would reduce the search time needed for an electronic search and could result in a reasonable visual search.)

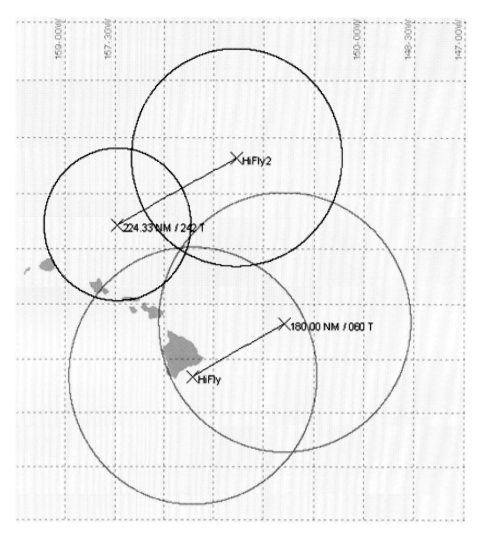

Figure S-10 – *Plot of PFH, PLH and respective radio horizon range circles;*
Hifly at 30,000 ft and course of 060 degrees T; Hifly2 at 20,000 ft
and descending to 10,000 ft and course of 242 degrees T

Table S-3 – *Distance to radio horizon*

Altitude in feet	Radio distance (NM)	Altitude (m)	Radio distance (km)
500	28	152	52
1,000	39	305	72
2,000	55	610	102
3,000	67	914	124
4,000	78	1,219	145
5,000	87	1,524	161
6,000	95	1,829	176
7,000	103	2,134	191
8,000	110	2,438	204
9,000	117	2,743	217
10,000	123	3,048	228
11,000	129	3,353	239
12,000	135	3,658	250
13,000	140	3,962	259
14,000	146	4,267	271
15,000	151	4,572	280
16,000	156	4,877	289
17,000	160	5,182	297
18,000	165	5,486	306
19,000	170	5,791	315
20,000	174	6,100	322
21,000	178	6,400	330
22,000	182	6,706	337
23,000	187	7,010	347
24,000	191	7,315	354
25,000	195	7,620	361
26,000	198	7,925	367
27,000	202	8,230	374
28,000	206	8,534	382
29,000	210	8,839	389
30,000	213	9,150	395
31,000	217	9,450	402
32,000	220	9,754	408
33,000	223	10,058	413
34,000	227	10,363	421
35,000	230	10,668	426
36,000	233	10,973	432
37,000	237	11,278	439
38,000	240	11,582	445
39,000	243	11,887	450
40,000	246	12,192	456

Notes

Notes

Notes

Notes

Notes

Notes